The Cynical Therapeutic

Contemporary Psychoanalytic Studies

VOLUME 34

The titles published in this series are listed at *brill.com/cps*

The Cynical Therapeutic

Self-Concern Gone Awry

By

David Roberts

BRILL

ISSN 1571-4977
ISBN 978-90-04-75813-1
ISBN 978-90-04-75814-8 (PDF)
DOI https://doi.org/10.1163/9789004758148

Library of Congress Control Number: 2026938290

Brill and Koninklijke Brill BV are part of De Gruyter Brill.
www.degruyterbrill.com

Questions about General Product Safety Regulation: productsafety@degruyterbrill.com

Cover illustration: *Exposed* (2024), Lindsey Roberts.

In memory of my mother, Carol Roberts

We are sinful not only because we have eaten of the Tree of Knowledge, but also because we have not yet eaten of the Tree of Life. The state in which we are is sinful, irrespective of guilt.

Franz Kafka, *The Blue Octavo Notebooks*, p. 37

Contents

Preface

We live in a world of mystery, where much of what we encounter is shrouded by our own inability to access its hidden depths. Not simply a hiddenness due to our own ignorance, but a hiddenness that is a ground of "knowing" itself. The various names we choose to give this mystery already says much about how we individually relate to it: the sacred, transcendence, the divine, the unconditional, the irreducible remainder, the unconscious, Being, dark matter and dark energy, etc. These are all ways of getting at what I call the "Excess"—that which *exceeds* our ability to know. The Excess makes some of us mildly nervous, others extremely anxious, and still others excited; however, most are simply indifferent toward it, busy focusing on what can be known and manipulated. How the Excess makes us feel often goes a long way in determining how we will interpret it; the way we interpret it strongly impacts how we will live, not simply in relation to the Excess, but to what we must deal with on a daily basis: the world, others, and ourselves. Being indifferent to the Excess (or even denying it—which only the most closed-minded among us can pull off) does not make it go away, but is merely another way that determines how one will live—there is no neutral ground when it comes to the Excess.

Discussion about the Excess might seem a strange way to preface a book on modern cynicism, but it is appropriate because modern cynicism has become ideological, and all ideologies (along with fundamentalisms, dogmatisms, hegemonies, fetishizations, fascisms, and the like) are particular ways of defending ourselves against what the Excess says about us, and how it makes us feel. What it says about us is that we are not nearly as in control of things as we would like to believe we are; we are not nearly as free and autonomous as we would like to think; we may not be as significant as we would hope—it may ultimately be that nothing we do matters, because we are merely a drop in the cosmic ocean. This insignificance usually does not bother us when things are going our way, or when we are relishing the quantitative excess of an affluent culture, but when we run into problems and begin to suffer (especially those the philosopher Karl Jaspers called "boundary situations"—the immovable problems upon which we feel shipwrecked, such as, addiction, disease, tragedy, and death), we long for the pain we undergo not to be for nothing.[1] Of course, it is just at these times we have run right back into the Excess we are trying to ignore. Ideologies are ways we make sense of our suffering, ways we

1 I have found that people can generally put up with meaningless affluence, but can seldom stomach meaningless pain and suffering.

give meaning to the world in such a way that we can deceive ourselves about our situation—it is the way of maintaining the illusion of control. Modern cynicism is an ideology in this sense: it gives us a sense that we are free, we are in some way significant, and we are self-sufficient.

My interest in cynicism did not begin with these thoughts. Rather, I was led to these thoughts during my research, as I began to make connections that were surprising and unexpected. In an important sense, what I wrote above is more a conclusion or destination we will be moving toward, rather than a starting point. Another surprising connection that became clear to me was the close relationship between modern cynicism and what Philip Rieff called the "triumph of the therapeutic": modern cynicism and the therapeutic are closely connected approaches to life that arose as a response to the ineffectiveness of the traditional ways we seek to deal with the Excess. Our relationship to the Excess has become impoverished, as we begin to *see through* the traditional symbolics (the traditional interpretations and explanations of the Excess). Cynicism and the therapeutic are new ways of relating to the Excess, which in turn promise a new kind of freedom and self-mastery. I will argue that this promise is an illusion, and the cynic is able to hide this illusion through a series of complex mental gymnastics.

My research into cynicism initially arose not as a strictly academic interest, but due to a particular situation I was continually facing: explanations from my students as to why they had turned in their assignments late, why they had missed a quiz, or other such situations in which they had not fulfilled some class requirement or responsibility. The students who talked to me about missing a requirement for class always had a reason or excuse to justify their behavior. There was most often no way for me to know if they were telling the truth—they could rarely provide any evidence. It could be that what they offered as an excuse was legitimate, though it might also have been the case that they were not being honest, but were telling me what they believed would cause me to act in their benefit. I had plenty of evidence that the latter had happened to me in the past (that I had been "conned" or deceived), and the longer I had been a professor, the more the evidence seemed to mount. Eventually, without even realizing it, I got to the point where I was suspicious of every "excuse": whenever students presented a reason for late work, or for not fulfilling some other requirement for class, I simply stopped believing them.

Dick Keyes puts this same issue by asking the questions: "How do you understand the simple request for the sick day? Straight-forwardly, as an ordinary, sincere request to be granted with sympathy and without questions? Or with suspicion, further inquiry and innuendoes that you have seen through to ulterior motives?"[2] I realized I had become suspicious—always suspicious. I had become cynical, in that my first instinct was to think the worst—guilty until they could prove their innocence. This seemed to me to be the wisest way of dealing with these situations. However, while it has the sound of wisdom, and I had all that past evidence to justify my cynical judgments, the fact remained that I did not *actually* know whether a particular student in any given situation was honest or deceptive. There is always an "unknowing" involved within cynicism, an interpretative act about what is *really* going on. The problem of deception always relates to a hidden depths in reality, which are buried under a "seeming to be."

Most of what is hidden from us could hardly be viewed as a case of deception: in reading a book on modern physics, no matter how pedestrian its prose, the world described on its pages sounds very little like the world we inhabit, but we do not generally think of nature as trying to deceive us. On the other hand, when it comes to promises and statements made by others—whether politicians, advertisements, co-workers, friends, and even family—we can never be quite certain if there are in their "hidden depths" motives they do not want us to know, which they hide from us because if we knew their motives we would act and think differently toward them. Cynics suspect that others are usually hiding something, and they refuse to be taken in by it—even if they have no idea what "it" consists of.

The example of my own cynicism above shows several important characteristics of the cynic and cynicism, which will be central aspects in my overall analysis and understanding of why we have become so cynical in our culture.

First, cynicism is a means of protecting ourselves. In many ways, the cynic is more worried about looking like a fool than being a fool. After all, not believing a student when the student is telling the truth is just as foolish as believing a student when the student is not telling the truth (though it is difficult for cynics to see it this way). There is an issue of identity, of what I call throughout the book "mattering." Mattering is about our sense of worth and value, about being taken seriously, respected, making an impact in life—about why we matter. I did not want to be "played" by my students, treated or taken as a fool, perceived by others as a "pushover."

Second, cynics tend to be uncharitable in their judgments and interpretations. They think the worst, expect others to be attempting to "pull one over" on them, and are suspicious of others' "true" motives. They believe that the manifest content (what they see and are told) is always different from the latent content

---

2 Dick Keyes, *Seeing through Cynicism: A Reconsideration of the Power of Suspicion* (Downers Grove: Inter Varsity Press, 2006), 10.

(the true motives and intentions, what is "really going on" beneath the façade). No doubt, there are valid reasons for being suspicious in many situations, but as we will see, cynicism goes beyond mere suspicion. In his book *Critique of Cynical Reason*, Peter Sloterdijk argues that cynics have developed (or been developed by) an "espionage epistemology."[3] As we grasp what he means by this term, and look at how it arose, we will gain a deeper understanding of how cynicism goes beyond mere suspicion or pessimism. While there is no doubt that suspicion and pessimism are necessary for being cynical, they are not sufficient.

Third, cynics believe they are maintaining control in a situation by assuming there is deception (whether it exists or not). This gives cynics a sense of autonomy over situations and the actions of others. Being cynical appears to allow us to maintain control in the face of forces that seek to steal or diminish our freedom and self-sufficiency through deception and manipulation. Cynics believe other people and institutions are trying to make us act in specific ways, ways that appear in our benefit, but are really for their own benefit (and are often to our detriment). To combat this situation, cynics decide to mistrust others: one cannot be conned if one knows one is being conned. Thus, a general suspiciousness allows cynics to feel they are transcending the manipulative situation—staying above, and so outside, it—which allows them to maintain their freedom in relation to it.

Fourth, cynicism creates a disconnect or distance between oneself and others, because one is not sure with whom or what one is dealing. I did not emphasize this in my example above about teaching, but it was clearly at work: cynicism led me into a general alienation from my students and a personal detachment from situations. Cynicism expects the worst, and so defensiveness inevitably creeps into relationships with people. In my situation, I had a clear sense that my relationship with my students had been changing (e.g., I felt more distant from them, tended not to reach out to them, felt more disconnected from them during class, and was generally more defensive as they approached me); however, I had not related it to my growing cynicism, because I was not yet even aware of how cynical I had become—let alone the impact it was having in my relationships. When I became aware of my cynicism, it became clear to me that it had been at the root of my vague feelings of alienation from my students. This is one area we remain blind to in our cynicism, though immense damage takes place in our lives due to it.[4]

---

3 Peter Sloterdijk, *Critique of Cynical Reason*, trans. Michael Eldred (Minneapolis, MN: University of Minnesota Press, 1987), 331–332.

4 At the time, I could not figure out what had changed in my relationship with my students, with whom I had always had a very good rapport. I had received tenure the year before,

All of these points will be addressed in more detail throughout this book as we analyze the impact cynicism has on our lives. My hope is that as we look at these, they will provide a reason to at least reflect on our cynicism, and critically think about it as something we should seek to overcome. Is cynicism the best approach to living in a world that is surrounded by Excess, and is even sometimes willfully deceptive? My answer will be that it is not, and for two overriding reasons.

First, there is a deep element of *self*-deception within modern cynicism. This self-deception is to presume to know something that one does not know, and perhaps even cannot be known. It is a means of keeping the Excess at arm's length. As we will see, it does this in the same manner as other forms of self-deception in relation to the Excess: it narrows and reduces reality to what can be controlled, or can be interpreted in a way that keeps us from feeling anxious or uneasy. Obviously, this is a strong statement, and will be a central issue to be addressed as we analyze the essence of modern cynicism. There is an irony, and even paradox, within modern cynicism, in that the very means we use not to be deceived by others, is how we deceive ourselves. Sloterdijk's definition of modern cynicism points to the paradoxical nature of this approach: he defines modern cynicism as an "enlightened false consciousness." We are enlightened about others' means of deception but remain blind as to how we deceive ourselves. I will argue that what we primarily want to hide from ourselves is our lack of freedom, significance, and self-mastery.

Second, modern cynicism is a surrender to hopelessness and despair. The despair is not conscious or felt *as* despair (indeed, it is the unconsciousness of this despair that is intimately connected to its false consciousness), but it is a narrowing of the perceived and imagined alternatives in life. This reduction of alternatives leads the modern cynic to surrender to the very situations and institutions she has seen through—to give her life to the very things she knows are empty and meaningless.[5]

---

and wondered if perhaps that had somehow changed my relationship with students; or I wondered whether having taken on more administrative and committee work was the cause (some burnout). However, in typical cynical fashion, I mostly blamed the students, who seemed to me apathetic and always seeking the path of least resistance in classes. This, of course, only created further cynicism on my part. I can still remember the day my cynicism "broke" toward my students, as there was an instant change that occurred in the classroom: teaching and relating to students again became relatively effortless—because genuine and non-defensive.

5 Throughout the book I will be using feminine pronouns, except around sections where a quote, or the content from an author I am using in my analysis, uses a masculine pronoun.

My approach to this book is not linear, but instead I lay out concepts and connections in a more "nested" manner. The image I have in my own mind for this approach is much along the lines I experience when watching an artist draw a picture. It often begins with a series of lines that do not give any overall sense of what is being drawn. It takes time for what the artist has in mind to begin to "take shape" into something recognizable. I have chosen this approach because the topic itself appears to me to necessitate it. For various reasons (which will become clear in the book), cynics have been inoculated against critical reflection on their own cynicism. Thus, rather than creating a linear argument, I focus on the various historical and social influences upon modern cynicism, which I hope will lead to personal self-reflection on how these changes have influenced the reader's own life. In other words, I chose not to approach the book as a linear argument because I want the reader to reflect on her relation to the picture I am drawing of the cynical life (that is, what historical problems modern cynicism is addressing, how it is addressing these problems, and what it expects as an outcome). By bringing the picture into view slowly, I hope the reader will personally begin to wrestle with the various nested arguments presented, rather than launching into the defensive and critical maneuvers that try to see through all manifest content.

Basically, I want to keep certain cynical (and I would add, defensive) capacities disengaged while reading this book, capacities that tend to further entrench the cynic in cynicism. When we are cynical, we are outwardly focused, in that we are critical of others (whether the "others" consist of individuals, institutions, businesses, politics, or the media), and have little use for self-reflection. We are too busy trying to see through others' manipulations and "games" to pay attention to the games we ourselves are playing; after all, the cynic thinks, we all have to play games to survive, and so better to focus on others' dissimulations than one's own. The cynic focuses on the deceptiveness of others because she believes she is the only one she can trust, the only one not trying to con her; I hope to show, however, that she *is* conning herself, and it is the most dangerous con she faces.

Acknowledgements

I would like to thank the University of South Carolina Lancaster for the Research and Productive Scholarship Grants provided to me over the course of this project, as well as the University of South Carolina's Palmetto College for the RISE Grant. I deeply appreciate the commitment of these institutions to supporting faculty in their scholarship.

I would also like to express my gratitude to Dr. Peter Seipel, Jacob Roberts, and Susan Lindholm for their feedback on the initial draft of this book. Their insights were helpful in the preparation of the final draft of this book.

Finally, I would like to thank the men I meet with weekly for Friday coffee, Ed Thomas, Brian Jones, Ed Trevillian, and Syd Johnsen, for their wisdom in prompting me to cut the original book in half for publication.

Introduction

We are always in process, restless, never whole. Most people become less than they could be in their attempt to become more than they are. We feel like we have something to prove to others and to ourselves, something about our worth—that it is good that we exist. We hunger for recognition, approval, and affirmation; we bristle when treated as if we do not matter. Our lives, however, are ephemeral and short-lived: in the end we grow old, weaken, and die, feeling as if our time was but a blink of the eye. This reality makes us uncomfortable, so we seek to hide this from ourselves, pretending we are somehow immune from what we know is the truth. Thus, we make death into a mere abstraction we will worry about later. On top of this, our consciousness is fractured between our ideals (who we believe we should be) and our actuality (how we see ourselves). It is this split that causes our restlessness, and out of which a longing for wholeness arises.

We approach this problem through what I, following Norman Brown, will call the *causa sui* project, which is the attempt to be the ground or cause of ourselves. It is most concretely seen in our desire for self-sufficiency, independence, freedom from constraints, and a general drive toward self-mastery. While self-mastery, and so the *causa sui* project, are not possible for us (we are not self-grounding), we seek to create and maintain an illusion that we have achieved these. It is in the midst of this illusion that we attempt to be more than we are, and become less than we could be.

Culture, and its symbolics, have guided and helped us in our attempts to find a sense of wholeness and peace in this situation, and have propped up our illusions of self-mastery. The traditional symbolics (what might be called the traditional therapeutics) began to lose their power over a century ago, and are no longer able to help us justify our existence. So, we have had to turn elsewhere to feel that our lives are not meaningless and insignificant. Social media, for instance, has become one massive scream for recognition, for others to affirm me with their Likes, Karma, Following, and comments. This scream comes with a pretense of happiness and having it all together, but the intensity of the images that project this pretense are so strong, it betrays the emptiness and sense of worthlessness driving it all. It is not surprising that we would begin to question the veracity of those we interact with, and begin to see deception in practically every social exchange. Social interaction no longer seems genuine, but always the fabrication of a fractured soul seeking to prove it is whole. It is not simply individuals we have become cynical toward, but also politics, business, and various traditional

 | HTTPS://DOI.ORG/10.1163/9789004758148-002

cultural institutions. Mistrust has become our default attitude in our social interactions.

Although modern cynicism has grown in the past several decades, I argue that it began with the impoverishment of our traditional symbolics and ways of interpreting the world and our place in it. This impoverishment has often been given the term "nihilism," in that the ways we have justified our existence for millennia have become *nothing* (*nihil*) for us. Nihilism first began to make itself known in sensitive thinkers just prior to the beginning of the Twentieth Century; many different answers were given for its cause, and various recommendations were proposed for how it should be addressed. Some of the more well-known philosophers who addressed nihilism are Nietzsche, Heidegger, Kierkegaard, and perhaps even Marx. It is my contention that Sigmund Freud's answer (psychoanalysis) eventually "won out" as Western Civilization moved into the Twentieth Century. Psychoanalysis, and the various therapeutic trends that followed, have become the new healing arts of our time. Practically every segment of our society and culture are touched by psychological theories, and nearly every problem comes with a psychological interpretation. In the face of the weakening of the symbols of the traditional therapeutics that had soothed human consciousness—but had lost their power to do so any longer—Freud brought a new way of seeing the psyche and the place of humanity in the world. Within a half century, therapists became the new healers of our souls, and we have put our hope for emotional, and even spiritual, well-being in their hands.

Freud's therapeutic process was a response to the nihilistic situation his patients were suffering under, and which were coming out in various neurotic symptoms. The reason I connect his therapeutic process to cynicism, is because Freud's psychoanalytic process is cynical in its conception and approach. When the ideals and morals we put forward as the motives behind our actions become emptied (*nihil*), then moral claims about our actions will become suspect. It all becomes a show, a means of hiding the emptiness and insignificance of what we do, and ultimately of our very lives. And so we find that, for Freud, the patient is never to be trusted: nothing the patient says is to be taken at face value, but must be *seen through*; it is all self-deception and a means of hiding from the nasty truth we are all trying to repress about ourselves (foremost of which, for Freud, is our sexual desires). Every outward manifestation is a game, in which the latent content remains buried, because we know that no one would approve of it.

I have called what has ultimately grown out of this approach the "cynical therapeutic," which I will argue has become ideological, and an unquestioned presupposition of our social interactions. Though the specifics of Freud's psychoanalytic theories have come to be viewed as highly idiosyncratic, and rejected outright in many circles of psychology, his social theories remain highly influential, and continue to impact the way we view morality, relationships, mental health, and the purpose of the social world in general.

1 Part 1: The Back Story—How We Got to Where We Are

The argument given above is a highly complex issue, and I will be spending Part 1 of the book setting up this problem in light of the cynical approach to life. I will start by contrasting ancient cynicism with modern cynicism. In Chapters 1 and 2, I will present the ancient cynical school of thought, specifically in terms of three themes I will be using throughout the book: defacing the currency, exile, and *parrhesia*. Chapter 1 will focus on the general teachings of the ancient cynics, and why their views of life lead to "defacing the currency." Defacing the currency is critically questioning and opposing the cultural ideals, symbolics, norms, and purposes, which the ancient cynics viewed as leading to general unhappiness.

Chapter 2 examines where defacing the currency leads the ancient cynics, specifically in terms of exile and *parrhesia*. Exile is the result of having defaced the currency, as one finds oneself no longer easily able to join into the cultural and social roles that have been set up for us. This does not usually lead to a physical exile, but an alienation from the practices and norms within one's society. Exile is important, in that it opens one up to alternative ways of living. Not that these alternative ways present themselves to one right away, but there is an openness to a transformation in one's life, as one sees the impoverishment of the current social currency. We often fight against this exile, because of the fear and discomfort that come with it. As we will see, there are good reasons for this discomfort, especially from the aspect of mental health. The ancient cynics view it as worth the risk, because there is something better awaiting us.

Parrhesia is a type of speech in which one says what is on one's heart and mind, and so one's communication is without pretense. One can think of it as a type of speech that inspires confidence in others, because of its trustworthiness. I will be using it as a means of thinking about the issue of self-deception. The problem we face in regards to culture is not so much that culture is seeking to deceive us, but that we are using culture in order to maintain our own self-deception. Defacing the currency, exile, and *parrhesia* will be the themes I use throughout the book to analyze and bring to light the self-deception inherent in modern cynicism.

In Chapters 3 and 4, I will take the first, general look at Freud's theories, which I view as important for understanding the ideological form of cynicism. I will not be making the connection between Freud and modern cynicism in these chapters, but connecting Freud to the issues of defacing the currency and exile. As I said, human consciousness is split or fractured, and we will examine this fracture in terms of Freud's theories. He will set up the split as between nature and culture, and we will find that his psychoanalytic process consists of a defacing of the currency of culture. Not that nature is a friend to us, but it is the impoverishment of our cultural values and norms that he viewed as the cause behind his patients' neurotic symptoms.

As noted above, nihilism is the state in which the cultural currency has already been defaced, but in such a way that people are not aware of it consciously. Freud seeks to make us more conscious of the defaced currency, and to empower the ego and reason to stand on its own more securely. Freud provides a different way of thinking about culture, no longer as something that is leading to greater order, progress, and health, but something whose basis is ultimately irrational. With Freud, morality is no longer seen as rational and a means to freedom, but as a means of oppression, which we surrender to because of anxiety; cultural morality and norms are no longer able to lead us to an ordered and healthy soul, but are significant sources of our mental pathology.

Ultimately, culture is the act of sublimation, and sublimation is the desexualization of our sexual aims (which are our deepest aims). With the loss of the authority of the traditional symbolics (the means of sublimation), the ego is left with nothing to lean on as it faces the struggle of its fractured consciousness. In other words, the ego is undergoing an unconscious exile from the ideals of society. From Freud we discover that the exile the ancient cynics viewed as a way to human health and goodness (i.e., freedom and self-sufficiency), is actually the cause of pathological neurosis.

In Chapter 5, I will examine Freud's theories in light of Ernest Becker's critical analysis of Freud, mainly around the issue of what, specifically, humans are repressing. For Freud, we are ultimately repressing the sexual desires we have toward our parents, as we seek to recapture the pleasure and safety we felt as infants. Although Becker agrees we are driven by a desire to repress something that causes us anxiety, he believes it is not ultimately sexual desires, but what he calls "creatureliness": our frailty, vulnerability, weakness, insignificance, and death. The central need and desire driving the human organism is not sexual, but to experience that we matter, which means we must repress the creatureliness that makes us feel that our lives are ultimately insignificant. We have to work out the fracture we sense in our lives, which for Becker consists in the contradiction between our longing for significance and meaning, and the evidence from the world that our lives do not really matter.

My argument will be that cynicism and the therapeutic are the particular ways we seek to work this out in modern American society. While authority was the power that undergirded traditional sublimation, after Freud, cynicism and a "weaponized epistemology" become the powers undergirding our modern sublimation.

In Chapter 6, I examine Becker's analysis of the means by which culture allows us to feel a sense of significance in a meaningless universe. Culture has always been the way of transcending our merely natural selves or creatureliness (in which we sense our lack of significance). It does this through its symbolics, by which it creates a path for us in life that appears meaningful and significant. Becker calls this symbolic action system a "cultural heroic," through which we are provided with self-esteem. As we will see, however, it is all pretense, and so our lives are spent chasing the illusions that help us deny what makes us feel small and insignificant. With the rise of nihilism, however, these illusions are no longer able to convince us, and the growth of neurotic symptoms are the result. This change in the view of the nature of repression has an impact on how we come to view neurosis.

Chapter 7 examines the change in the nature of how the therapeutic is viewed (that is, what would truly be therapeutic for the split within the psyche). We first look at Phillip Rieff's distinction between positive and negative therapeutics. Positive therapeutics were made up of the cultural heroics of the past, whether religious (basically, the Judeo-Christian dogma in the West) or secular (the belief arising out of the Enlightenment of continued human progress). The negative therapeutic offers no heroic to replace those that have been defaced. While the former therapeutic conceived of healing in terms of salvation, the latter thinks in terms of methods that help us cope—that is, cope with having to live unheroically. While Freud writes about learning how to live without new positive therapeutics, we still must find ways to justify our existence or show that we matter, and in negative therapeutics these tend to revolve around various illusions related to freedom and self-sufficiency.

We will see that the negative therapeutic arose due to a mistake Freud made in relation to the nature of our struggle. Freud, viewing sexuality as the basic drive we repress, viewed our struggle to be with a sense of moral guilt put on us by culture and the superego (this can be closely associated with the moral prudery of the Victorian Era in which Freud lived); however, when we view creatureliness as what we are repressing, our struggle is with what I will call "existential guilt" (the struggle to justify our existence, to prove that we matter).

In Chapter 8, I will examine how existential guilt changes our view of neurosis, which I characterize as "self-concern gone awry." It is in this analysis that we first address the *causa sui* project, and the illusion of self-mastery that drives us and leads us to our neurotic symptoms. We will see these symptoms differently than Freud, and I will argue that Freud never deals with the true issue of our repressed desires, and instead even exacerbates it.

This problems will lead us, in Chapter 9, to another thinker, who had an impact on Ernest Becker's reinterpretation of Freud: Soren Kierkegaard. Kierkegaard does not understand our struggle with nihilism in terms of moral guilt, as Freud does, but in terms of existential guilt, which is connected to our illusion of self-mastery, and our drive to be *causa sui*.

Kierkegaard is interested in the task of "self-becoming," which he believes is aborted when we define ourselves in terms of the social masks we wear, and by which we live. We evade the task of self-becoming due to the anxiety associated with it. Rather than face the freedom that accompanies and is necessary for self-becoming, we give ourselves to our culture or the established order, and surrender to the pretenses necessary for social life. Thus, we understand the self in terms of externals—e.g., possessions and social positions. Anxiety exists due to freedom, because there is always something at stake in being or becoming a self. Kierkegaard views anxiety as "educative," which is meant to bring us to a *krisis*. *Krisis*, in Greek, is the decision associated with a stark separation that must be addressed (even not to decide is to have decided).

I will examine the specifically Kierkegaardian view of *krisis* in Chapter 10. Kierkegaard understands why and how we run from a *krisis* (which to us feels like a crisis); it is due to the cost associated with having to decide. We know that with every decision many paths will have to be left behind, and we fear choosing the wrong path. Surrender to the established order protects us from having to face *krises*, because it provides us with one, ready-made path. This analysis of Kierkegaard will be used as a contrast to the cynical therapeutic view of freedom and self-sufficiency, since freedom looks very different when we view our suffering as due to morality, than it does when we view it as due to existential guilt.

Modern cynicism differs from ancient cynicism in an important way: modern cynicism is the result of an enlightened consciousness that is unwilling to move in the direction the enlightened consciousness should move, namely, into exile. This is because it is unwilling to abandon its illusion of self-mastery. While this argument will take several chapters to fully analyze, in Chapter 11 we move into an analysis of two different paths that arose out of the Enlightenment, which react to the defacing of currency in two different ways. The first path we look at is Kierkegaard; the second path is ideology critique, out of which the cynical therapeutic arose, specifically in terms of Freud's ideology critique.[1]

I first look at Kierkegaard's approach to defacing the currency, to see how it leads to exile from the established order. We find that it necessitates a surrender of the project of self-justification, and the drive for self-mastery. In other words, Kierkegaard's defacing of the currency leads to humility in the one who is doing the defacing, and a relinquishing of the weaponized epistemology that grew out of the Enlightenment.

We then turn to ideology critique in order to trace the movement from the Enlightenment to modern cynicism, through ideology critique. In this we will be following Peter Sloterdijk's analysis of this process in his *Critique of Cynical Reason*. The philosophers of the Enlightenment expected people to surrender their ignorance (e.g., superstitious and religious beliefs) on the basis of the more powerful argument of reason. However, it turned out that people were not readily willing to give up their beliefs. Ideology critique arose as an attempt to deconstruct the mechanisms by which people were able to maintain their false consciousness, whether due to economics (Marx), will to power (Nietzsche), or psychological repression (Freud).

As ideology critique was able to see through more and more of these mechanisms, a general mistrust was created, as epistemology was weaponized to show the deceptive and manipulative mechanisms in almost every area of human thought and action. Freud's ideology critique eventually becomes a new therapeutic in line with this cynical epistemology. The insights we take away in this chapter, which will become important in later chapters, are the different results that arise between Kierkegaard's defacing of the currency and ideology critique's defacing. One of the main differences is that, while Kierkegaard believed enlightenment should lead to the end of the pretense of self-mastery, ideology critique sought to strengthen self-mastery in certain important ways. Thus, Kierkegaard believed defacing the currency would humble the person who is defacing the currency, while ideology critique used enlightenment in order to humble others. This means ideology critique was unwilling to let go of its own illusions, and this leads to the insightful definition Sloterdijk gives for modern cynicism: modern cynicism is an enlightened false consciousness. This becomes a central theme throughout the rest of the book.

1 There are three powerful leaders of ideology critique that arose in the mid to late nineteenth century: Marx, Freud, and Nietzsche. As I said, Freud's answer to nihilism became the accepted answer in the Twentieth Century, and is closely aligned with his ideology critique, and the type of cynicism that arose out of it.

In Chapters 12 and 13, I explain the nature of modern cynicism as enlightened false consciousness, and look at how this contradictory approach to life has been justified by modern cynics. We will do this by using the three themes of ancient cynicism: defacing the currency, exile, and *parrhesia*. I look at the defacing of currency and exile in Chapter 12, and *parrhesia* in Chapter 13.

In relation to defacing the currency, a detached ironic stance (enlightened consciousness) allows the cynic to believe she has risen above the manipulation within her culture, and so is in some way superior to it, even though she spends her life possessed by, and immersed within it (false consciousness). Thus, the ironic detachment does not bring freedom from deception, but instead intrenches her more deeply into self-deception. In relation to exile, the contradictory approach of modern cynicism appears reasonable to the cynic because she is continually faced with contradictory and conflicting ideals within her culture, which she feels obligated to fulfill for the sake of the illusion of self-mastery and significance.

In relation to *parrhesia*, the contradictory approach is necessary in order to adapt to the current situation, which is what allows for self-preservation. In other words, the split appears to be healed by allowing the particular situation to guide one's actions, rather than acting according to ideals to which one claims to be committed.

These analyses allow us to see how these three rationalizations narrow life, and lead to abandoning our freedom. This narrowing leads to languishing in life, rather than the flourishing the modern cynic is expecting to experience. We examine this narrowing by looking at Richard Stivers' analysis of a "technological morality," which is the morality of modern cynicism, and is in line with a weaponized epistemology. Technological morality, unlike traditional morality, is a morality of power rather than meaning. The internal essence of the technological morality is power without purpose, or power simply seeking more power. This morality justifies the cynic's new relation to the Excess (which is a lack of relation—a repression of the Excess).

2 Part 2: The Cynical Therapeutic

With this more detailed understanding of modern cynicism, in Chapters 14 and 15 we return to Freud in order to see how his theories had such a strong influence on the direction of modern cynicism, and became what I call the cynical therapeutic. I argue in Chapter 14 that his conception of the psyche is modeled around a cynical consciousness, and in Chapter 15 that

Freud's analytic process is an attempt to lessen our neurotic symptoms by making us better cynics (what I view as moving us from "outsider cynics," who are passive in relation to cynicism, to "master cynics," who are active in their cynical approach to the world).

More specifically, in Chapter 14 I first examine Diderot's *Rameau's Nephew*, a book Freud himself references, in order to show the Enlightenment's influence on Freud's cynical approach, and how the Freudian understanding of "re-education" aligns with the Nephew's. This re-education focuses on an internalization of social norms, not based on authority, but on a strengthening of the ego through mistrust and a weaponized epistemology.

In the next three chapters we analyze Freud's relationship to the three cynical rationalizations. We will see that Freud is much more open and conscious about these rationalizations, as they are each important parts of his therapeutic process. In terms of ironic detachment, Freud's analytic process breaks down resistances, and focuses on the mechanisms of repression (the core of Freud's ideology critique, and his defacing of the cultural currency). In terms of the contradictory ideals the cynic seeks to fulfill, Freud's famous ambivalence toward culture gives a justification for this contradictory relation to culture, which Freud views as due to a lack of alternatives, and the ego's need for cultural support. In other words, exile is not possible, because the ego is too weak to live only by its own power, and so we must, at some level, surrender to culture, even though we have seen through its currency as empty. Thus, adaptation for self-preservation is justified by Freud through a re-education in which we learn to cope in a world and life that is divested of all heroics and ideals. This I relate to *parrhesia* in terms of the analytic approach of "free association." Free association is important for learning to live unheroically, in which the patient abandons the *causa sui* project of a heroism and idealism, for a life of adaptation and coping.

I argue that most people cannot adopt Freud's nihilistic outlook of life. While what Philip Rieff calls the "triumph of the therapeutic" can be directly related to Freud's powerful theories, it became necessary for most people, especially in the U.S., to leave Freud's pessimism behind. Thus, we turn next to an analysis of the triumph of the therapeutic, both looking at Freud's influences upon it, and how it moved away from Freud's darker views of human reality.

In Chapter 15 I will examine how Freud's psychoanalytic therapeutic process is an abandoning of the traditional *causa sui* project (the cultural heroics) in order to create a new *causa sui* project. I argue that Freud views the analytic process as abandoning traditional modes of sublimation (authority) in favor of a cynical sublimation. While this is to aid the patient in becoming more self-sufficient (gain self-mastery), I argue that this is an illusion, because Freud hides the use of authority in the process (namely, in his use of transference), so that authority is not overcome, but changes from backing traditional moral sublimations to backing the cynical sublimation.

In Chapter 16, I examine the famous Freudian ambivalence toward culture. Here we discover Freud's pessimism, and his belief that we cannot heal the fractured psyche, but only help it cope in a better way by strengthening the ego in relation to the id and superego.

In Chapter 17, I examine how Freud moves toward the new cynical sublimation through a re-education of the ego through psychoanalytic therapy. This entails a narrowing of alternatives, and a focus on the needs of any given situation. I argue that Freud's view of health consists of acquiescing to a languishing in life, to what he views as a "common unhappiness."

In Chapter 18, I look at the effects of abandoning Freud's pessimism, which led to three important differences between Freud's therapeutic and those therapies which came after him, especially in the U.S. First, while Freud has a more cautious view of the id and the natural self, the therapeutic generally views nature and openness to the id as essential for freedom and human flourishing. Second, Freud's ambivalence toward culture meant he was much more open to culture (including its morality, which kept the dangerous id in check) than the modern therapeutic. Third, and most importantly in relation to the illusion of self-mastery, the modern therapeutic rejected Freud's view of the ego as weak, and instead views it as powerful and independent. This leads to an even stronger emphasis on the internal aspects of the psyche and its experiences, believing them to be the most trustworthy basis for living a healthy psychological life. And so, external influences, the most detrimental of which are cultural, tend to be seen as the basis for psychological illness and suffering, since it is the basis for all the repression that causes the painful fracturing of the psyche.

In Chapters 19 and 20, I connect the cynical rationalizations, and Freud's concomitant analytic process, to the therapeutic culture and its ideals of freedom, significance, and self-mastery. In terms of freedom, which relates to defacing the currency—which cynicism views in terms of ironic detachment, and Freud views as the ideology critique of defense mechanisms and resistances—the therapeutic embraces abstract possibility in terms of what Rieff has called the "primacy of possibility" and "order-hopping." Basically, freedom becomes "freedom *from*" all constraints, which are viewed as detrimental to our pursuits of personal well-being. In terms of the longing for significance, which is the aspect of exile, and comes out in the conflicting ideals that bring significance, and Freud's ambivalence to culture, the therapeutic turns to a consumerism Philip Cushman likens to a "lifestyle solution." Finally, self-mastery, which relates to *parrhesia*, and we find in cynicism's adaptation for the sake of self-preservation, as well as Freud's analytic attitude, I will analyze by using the Kierkegaardian concept of "estheticism."

Generally, the therapeutic becomes interpreted as the need for personality to be organized around the personal fulfillment of those desires and needs that will bring happiness. The self and its feelings become the only trustworthy guide for life. This creates a new character ideal, which Rieff and others have called "psychological man." Psychological man no longer lives for ideals, but for personal well-being. Much of Chapter 19 is taken up in detailing how this plays itself out in a culture dominated by consumerism, and how it eventually leads to what Philip Cushman calls the "empty self."[2]

The therapeutic, in concert with cynicism, calls all ideals into question, which is simply a playing out of the nihilism that had been gaining momentum for nearly a century. With the loss of ideals that would raise us above our creatureliness, we begin to experience the self, and our lives, as empty. This symbolic emptiness leads to the need to acquire material things and identities. Rather than embracing this impoverished ego (which would lead to seeing self-mastery as an illusion, and an end to the *causa sui* project), we bury the emptiness in distractions and material excess, continuing the attempt to be the master of our own lives. In other words, we move from a qualitative symbolic sense of fulfillment and Excess, to a quantitative compensatory fulfillment of material excesses. As it turns out, this situation fits very well with a capitalistic economic system, which could not ask for a more perfect subject for its continued success.

We come to see that the therapeutic "enlightened" consciousness provides the illusion of freedom and significance, and shows that the supposed enlightened consciousness has led to a deeper false consciousness, due to its unwillingness to abandon the *causa sui* project. This will lead us to the most important of the themes, which is to face the issue of longing for self-mastery. From this, I turn to the three main characteristics at work in psychological man's view of health.

In Chapter 20, I turn to Kierkegaard's dialectical viewpoint, and how it relates to the issue of self-mastery. We examine this by looking at Kierkegaard's view of the esthetic stage of existence. In the examination of the esthetic stage, we come to see that the cynical therapeutic ends in despair, as we recognize its pretense of self-mastery. There is potential for a rise in consciousness within

---

2 Philip Cushman, *Constructing the Self, Constructing America: A Cultural History of Psychotherapy* (Reading: Addison-Wesley, 1995), 245.

the esthetic stage which eventually leads to a *krisis*. Thus, I focus on the rise in consciousness that takes place within the esthetic stage.

The esthetic stage begins at the lowest level of consciousness, which Kierkegaard calls "spiritlessness," and can be thought of as being unconscious about the task of self-becoming. The movement through the esthetic stage goes from spiritlessness, pure immediacy, reflective immediacy, to "despair itself." I look at each of these in terms of how they relate to what consciousness is focused on. It becomes clear that the triumph of the therapeutic described in the preceding chapters is immersed in the esthetic stage. With this realization we are faced with a *krisis*, in which we must, as Kierkegaard puts it, "choose despair" (that is, choose to despair of the *causa sui* project).

Obviously, there are many difficulties that will be confronted in this analysis. The main purpose of the book, however, is to create an openness to an alternative to the cynical therapeutic. No community or society can remain when it is based upon a cynical therapeutic. It will begin to fall apart, and in the midst of this rising chaos, some form of authoritarianism will arise as a means of maintaining order (a false universal). This is not because it is not possible for humans to be free and to be in community, but because a false freedom becomes chaotic and destructive to the whole. The final chapter will be focused on bringing all the threads of my argument together in order to come before a *krisis*.

PART 1

Back Story: How We Got to Where We Are

CHAPTER 1

Ancient Cynicism: Defacing the Currency

The concept of cynicism has a long and varied history. It began as a philosophical school in ancient Greece. The Greek term *kynic* means "dog," which was a derogatory term people used against the cynics, but which they adopted with pride, for reasons we will discover below. The term is ambiguous as to whether it is a good or bad quality to possess. The ambiguity is due not simply to the complexity of its value, but also in terms of how its definition has continually changed throughout history. During conservative periods of history, cynics are viewed as trouble-makers, people who subvert the moral standards, norms, and conventions within society; during periods of change and cultural upheaval, the cynics were often seen as heroic, as they challenged the failing standards, institutions, and hypocrisy within society. What remains constant throughout history, and so points to what the term essentially addresses, is the ability and the drive of the cynic to *see through* hypocrisy, façades, and other aspects of culture that create false pride.

We will begin our study of modern cynicism by examining the general character of ancient cynicism. There are three aspects of ancient cynicism that will be important for helping us understand what drives *modern* cynicism, the problems it is seeking to overcome, and how it fails not only in overcoming these problems, but makes them worse. These characteristics are: defacing the currency, exile, and *parrhesia*. This chapter will deal with defacing the currency and Chapter 2 will look at exile and *parrhesia*. By examining these characteristics in terms of ancient cynicism, we will have a better way of understanding the self-deceptive nature of modern cynicism.

1 Ancient Cynicism: a General Introduction

One of the main problems with presenting and analyzing ancient cynicism is that there are so few original sources from which to draw: most of what we know about the ancient cynics comes from stories handed down and retold, and so are no doubt embellished and altered.[1] However, we will deal with only the most general and widely accepted aspects of ancient cynicism, since they

1 Luis E. Navia, *Classical Cynicism: A Critical Study* (Westport: Greenwood Press, 1996), 91.

HTTPS://DOI.ORG/10.1163/9789004758148-003

are the most critical issues for this book. This allows us to draw a clear picture of the ancient cynics, and enables us to understand their basic teachings. We will approach this understanding by examining what problem troubled the cynics, and how they confronted this problem.

One of the core thoughts of almost all philosophies and religions is that most of us unthinkingly and uncritically follow the structure, values, and paths created by our culture. It is this core thought that drives the ancient cynics. We can see this in what A. A. Long calls the seven grounding propositions that the ancient cynics advocated: (1) happiness is living in agreement with nature; (2) happiness is something available to any person willing to engage in sufficient physical and mental training; (3) the essence of happiness is self-mastery, which is the ability to live happily in adverse circumstances; (4) self-mastery is equivalent to a virtuous character; (5) the happy person is the only person who is truly wise and free; (6) things conventionally deemed necessary for happiness (wealth, fame, political power) have no value in nature; (7) the prime impediments to happiness are false judgments of value, and the emotional disturbances and vicious character that arise from these false judgments.[2] The general focus of the ancient cynics that we can infer from these propositions is that they were concerned with happiness, self-mastery, and that which does not allow for such things ("false judgments of value"). This final point means that our culture has given us false ideas about what thriving, flourishing, and success consist of, and these false judgments or ideas have caused us to miss what is truly important and excellent in life. Further, we do not know that this has happened, and so while we may believe we are flourishing, in reality we are not. We have become content with lives of discontent. The ancient cynics took it upon themselves to make this situation clear to all with whom they came in contact.

The central problem—that which leads to false judgments of value—is that culture not only seeks to transcend natural limits, but also creates artificial constraints on us, adding unnecessary burdens to our lives. A culture creates virtues that are in line with these artificial constraints, and so our conception of what is virtuous, and what good character consists of, is distorted. The ancient cynics conceive of their virtues as being in harmony with nature and its natural limits. Some of the important virtues (which will be explained in more detail below) are self-discipline (*askesis*), self-sufficiency (*autarkeia*), and

2 A. A. Long, "The Socratic Tradition: Diogenes, Crates, and Hellenistic Ethics," in *The Cynics: The Cynical Movement in Antiquity and Its Legacy*, ed. Bracht Branham and Marie-Odile Goulet-Cazé, 28–46 (Berkeley: University of California Press, 1996), 29–30.

shamelessness (*anaideia*).[3] These virtues are necessary for the ancient cynics' fundamental values of freedom and self-mastery—namely, freedom from external cultural control, and the self-sufficiency necessary for being at peace with the limits imposed by nature. The only constraints that one must abide by are those needed in order to live in harmony with nature. It is not merely important to accept there are natural limits that cannot be transgressed, but to recognize that these very limits are necessary for a life of well-being.

Nature, then, is the basis of a good life. The ancient cynics focused on nature in the belief that living in line with it would bring happiness. Not that nature was created for human benefit, or that there is a hidden element in nature that will make life better. Instead, one will find more well-being and contentment by resigning oneself to the way the natural world works, and what we have been given by nature to work within it.[4] The ancient cynics are not saying that we should live like animals, but that we should follow our nature as animals follow theirs. The cynics believed that instead of trying to overcome our nature, we should find satisfaction within it, as an eagle finds satisfaction in flight, a horse in running, or an otter in swimming. Rather than seeing the constraints nature puts on us as something to be overcome, we should embrace these constraints through self-discipline: having wings instead of hands would not feel like a constraint to eagles.

Culture causes us to demean and abandon the natural ways of human life.[5] People have turned away from their nature and begun to focus on social conventions, believing that following these artificial norms and ideals are necessary for happiness. As the sixth grounding proposition of ancient cynicism above points out: "Things conventionally deemed necessary for happiness, such as wealth, fame, and political power, have no value in nature."[6] Culture has convinced us of what success and happiness consist, and so what the focus and pursuit of our lives should be. The ancient cynics believe, however, that this focus leads us away from human happiness, and makes us ashamed of our nature—ashamed of who we truly are. If we are ashamed of who we are, we must live false and artificial lives.

The cynics did not think living like this could ever bring happiness and contentment—indeed, society is built on a general discontent with who we

3 Ian Cutler, *Cynicism from Diogenes to Dilbert* (Jefferson: McFarland & Company, 2005), 30.

4 Marie-Odile Goulet-Cazé, "Religion and the Early Cynics," in *The Cynics: The Cynical Movement in Antiquity and Its Legacy*, ed. Bracht Branham and Marie-Odile Goulet-Cazé, 47–80 (Berkeley: University of California Press, 1996), 67.

5 Cutler, 41.

6 Long, 30.

are, and a demand that we change (though we cannot change our nature). The cynics taught that we must challenge those norms and ideals in society that convince us not to be who we are meant to be. They rejected the shame we often feel in regards to those feelings and actions that arise out of our nature, and they used shamelessness as a weapon to wield against the conventions of society—a means of scandalizing those in society who are wholly given over to conventions.

The cynics take aim at the so-called wise men and women of society, the philosophers and sophists.[7] They believe that philosophers spend their time creating empty ideas, illusions of knowledge and understanding; rhetoricians use language to confuse and manipulate the masses; scientists aim at a conquest of nature, continually altering their truths, as if they were gifts from the gods to humanity, all along disrupting the balance of the natural world; athletes reap financial benefits for their undeserved fame and exalted reputations.[8] Humans are already full of emotional and physical needs, many of which are contradictory, and most of which will never be satisfied. Society increases the intensity of all this, creating new and false "needs" through manipulation. Finding peace or contentment in this situation is impossible. We have been trained to hunger for more things (power, pleasure, wealth, fame, information), believing these things will bring happiness, though in the end, the pursuit of them brings more misery.[9]

Antisthenes is thought to be the first cynic, and was a student of Socrates. He, like his teacher, trusted the sufficiency of reason, but also understood that it could be used for "intellectual obfuscation," as Navia puts it. Indeed, he believed this is exactly what another student of Socrates, Plato, was doing. He saw in Plato's writings the madness that affects the rest of humanity: pride, falseness, pretentiousness, mystification, superstition, and worship of the state. Antisthenes' devotion to reason meant becoming free from the very things Plato held up as ideals.[10]

---

7 John L. Moses, "Cynic Cosmopolitanism," in *The Cynics: The Cynical Movement in Antiquity and Its Legacy*, ed. Bracht Branham and Marie-Odile Goulet-Cazé, 105–120 (Berkeley: University of California Press, 1996), 105.

8 Navia, 30.

9 "People rush as if on a race against time and death, grabbing and grasping anything that comes their way, trampling on one another, giving the impression of being awake, but in reality they are immersed in the stupor of intellectual obfuscation, blindly pursuing transitory pleasures—the illusion of happiness and, at the bottom, they are unhappy with themselves and generate unhappiness for one another. Antisthenes feels entrapped in so abominable world. All around him there is senseless human noise" (Navia, 68).

10 Navia, 58–59.

This is where the virtues of the ancient cynics become important: the virtue of self-sufficiency meant for Antisthenes the process of learning not to need the artificial world of human creation, and being able to dispense with what that world offers (possessions, wealth, honors, positions, pleasures, and even its knowledge).[11] Self-sufficiency is freedom which owes nothing to anyone, needs nothing from anyone, and is under no one's control. It is freedom from the very world that sentenced Antisthenes' beloved teacher to death.[12] Self-sufficiency requires the virtue of self-discipline that is willing to endure the pain and suffering needed to gain strength in character against the world of human creation.[13] For Antisthenes, reason dictates the virtues that are related to nature, not the virtues which helps one live in an artificially created world (e.g., a good work ethic, politeness, manners, and so forth).

Navia says that the "fountain from which Cynicism sprang among the Greeks is then an irresistible urge to say 'no' to the world that human beings have constructed, because in the light of *reason* such a world is built on faulty foundations."[14] This humanly constructed world is seen as a "madhouse," creating a series of circus acts, an uproar for nothing, ultimately leading not to happiness but misery.[15] People spend their entire lives pursuing things like social rank, which are wholly artificial, and whose value is based on the illusion created by social conventions. The focus on the artificial social rank leads to the demeaning of genuine human value.

Due to their optimistic view of human nature, there is a redemptive aspect to the cynics: a redeeming from the cultural prison in which we live. Although the cynics' attempts to awaken others from their madness can seem cruel and vicious, in reality the cynics had a deep concern for others, and sought to warn them not to get caught up in the web of fallacies and illusions.[16] There was a philanthropic aspect to the ancient cynics, and a desire for others to embrace the cynic virtues.[17] As Diogenes, the most famous of the ancient cynics, said, "Other dogs bite their enemies. I bite my friends, for their salvation."[18]

---

11 Navia, 69.
12 Navia, 57.
13 Navia, 69.
14 Navia, 29.
15 Navia, 29.
16 Patrick Vandermeersch, "Reducing Faith to Belief: Religion in a Cynical Culture." From *Longing in a Culture of Cynicism*, Eds. Stephan van Erp and Lea Verstricht, 33–48 (Piscataway: Transaction Publishers [Rutgers University], 2007), 33.
17 Moses, 114–115.
18 Keyes, 20.

This very general picture of the cynics leads to the first of the three aspects of ancient cynicism that I want to focus on, and through which I will differentiate ancient cynicism from modern cynicism. The first of these is "defacing the currency."

2 Defacing the Currency

The idea of defacing the currency comes from a story about Diogenes. As Derek Krueger recounts the story:

> Tradition held that Diogenes had consulted an oracle (either at Delphi or the Delian oracle at Sinope) and was told by Apollo to deface the currency. … Like all oracles, this was open to misinterpretation, and according to one tradition Diogenes was exiled from Sinope for counterfeiting. As time passed, Diogenes understood that he was to deface the political and social currency, the exchange of notions that constituted general opinion. The Cynic critique claimed that the conventions by which the majority led their lives were unnatural and therefore foolish.[19]

Diogenes had initially taken the oracle's command to deface the currency literally, and so defaced the monetary currency in Sinope.[20] Only later, after being exiled, did he realize that the command was metaphorical. The currency to be defaced was not the coins that circulated in the marketplace, but the values and customs of society; "defacing" did not mean chiseling at the coins, but rejecting, challenging, and invalidating the cultural currency.[21] It is with this purpose that Diogenes traveled throughout the Greek city states.

Diogenes' approach to defacing the currency was through violations of the rules of decency and social decorum. If one is to eat in privacy according to society, then Diogenes will eat whenever and wherever he feels hunger; Diogenes was known to masturbate in the marketplace, and when admonished for this, he would say he only wished he could satisfy his hunger by merely rubbing his stomach; he would take care of his bodily functions wherever he

---

19 Derek Krueger, "The Bawdy and Society: The Shamelessness of Diogenes in Roman Imperial Culture," in *The Cynics: The Cynical Movement in Antiquity and Its Legacy*, ed. Bracht Branham and Marie-Odile Goulet-Cazé, 222–239 (Berkeley: University of California Press, 1996), 231–232.

20 Some stories have it that it was Diogenes' father who defaced the currency, which led to the exile of the entire family.

21 Navia, 93.

chanced to feel them, and so defecated in public, just as dogs do.[22] As Krueger points out, Diogenes takes something like passing gas in public as social commentary, using bodily functions as a language of protest against valuing the artificial and unnatural, and shaming the natural.[23] Diogenes mocked social views of decorum, beauty, and the like to expose their hypocrisy.

The hypocrisy of social decorum and beauty reminds me of Jonathan Swift's poem "The Lady's Dressing Room," which starts: "Five hours, (and who can do it less in?) / By haughty Celia spent in dressing / The goddess from her chamber issues / Arrayed in lace, brocades and tissues."[24] It took Celia five hours to make herself presentable according to social norms. As Strephon, who is infatuated with Celia, finds his way into her dressing room, he sees what she hides beneath those five hours of work. Rummaging through her dressing room, he finds the natural and real Celia by what she has left behind in a chest:

> So Strephon lifting up the lid / To view what in the chest was hid / The vapors flew from out the vent / But Strephon cautious never meant / The bottom of the pan to grope / And foul his hands in search of Hope ... / So things, which must not be expressed / When plumped into the reeking chest / Send up an excremental smell / To taint the parts from whence they fell / The petticoats and gown perfume / Which waft a stink around the room / Thus finished with his grand survey / Disgusted Strephon stole away / Repeating in his amorous fits / "Oh! Celia, Celia, Celia shits!"[25]

Strephon was in love with an illusion, five hours in the making. When faced with the reality of the natural Celia he is left empty and disenchanted. What he found was Celia's shame, according to cultural conventions. The ancient cynics, however, saw none of these natural acts as things to be ashamed of, and in embracing nature, they raised shamelessness to a virtue. This virtue became a powerful tool in their attempts to awaken those taken in by the illusion—by scandalizing those very illusions.

Above we noted the "madness" inherent in the norms of culture. The term for this madness used by the cynics was *tuphos*, which points to the illusion inherent in conventional practices. The term carries with it the ideas of "smoke," "mist," and "cloud." It is the idea of raising a "smoke screen," or a "cloud

---

22 Navia, 95–96.

23 Krueger, 233.

24 Jonathan Swift, "The Lady's Dressing Room," accessed May 28, 2019, https://www.poetryfoundation.org/poems/50579/the-ladys-dressing-room.

25 Swift.

of dust," by which one may cloud another's vision (or mind).[26] In Hippocratic medical terminology, *tuphos* was originally used to designate "delirium caused by high fever," and gets applied to a specific disease: typhoid fever.[27] *Tuphos* represents the idea of not being able to think clearly. For the ancient cynic, the person immersed in *tuphos* is a conceited and stupid person, whose mind is clouded, incapable of entertaining a clear thought.[28]

Given this emphasis on *tuphos*, the purpose of the cynics' philosophy was to help people come out of the cloud in which they generally lived, and attain a condition which may be called *atuphos*: clarity of mind. In *atuphos* one breaks free from the conventions and norms that come from blind political and national allegiances, superstitious religion, the pointless pursuit of pleasure and wealth, and the falseness one finds in all forms of social media.[29] It is also a return to living according to nature.

The general view the cynics are arguing against is that nature is to be conceived as chaotic and irrational, and so must be rejected or subdued through reason. Within the *tuphos*, or clouded mind, it is thought that humans are able to transcend the chaos of nature due to the freedom they gain through rational thought. This applies not only to the natural world, but to nature within humans as well. Natural human drives and desires are not rational, but arise as if immersed in anarchy. The ancient cynics seem to be aware of an irrationality within our desires, which is why they hold to the virtue of asceticism. However, asceticism is not primarily about our simple and true natural desires, but the desires that become chaotic and wild when influenced by cultural conventions. Asceticism for the cynic is not about taming the "flesh" or appetites, but living in line within their natural limits as a human being.

Thus, asceticism has several purposes. First, it proves that poverty is not a barrier to achieving health and happiness. Second, it allows one to pursue a bodily life in line with one's nature—our true natural desires—rather than those artificially created or perverted by culture. Third, and most importantly, asceticism brings freedom and self-sufficiency. The ascetic is free by choosing a life of poverty. The ancient cynics possess nothing, and regard the love of money as the source of all evils; they live a life of simplicity that is indifferent toward human customs, arguing that wisdom comes from watching how children and animals live: Diogenes "learned simplicity of life by watching a

26 Navia, 139.
27 Navia, 139.
28 Navia, 140.
29 Navia, ix–x.

mouse running around in the market place, and from children he learned how to drink water from his hand, and so to live without even a cup."[30]

When nothing in culture can control one's choices, and one acts out of one's own nature in line with the simplicity of the natural world, one controls one's destiny. This control of destiny is what the cynics mean by self-mastery, self-sufficiency, and freedom: through asceticism and self-discipline, the cynics free themselves for a minimalistic and austere lifestyle in order to maximize self-direction.[31]

This is not to say that the cynics had a utopian view of nature. They understood that nature is out of human control, and does not exist in order to fulfill human wants. There is a dark side to nature, which may best be understood by the term *tukhe*, or fortune.[32] There is a capriciousness to nature, which makes it unpredictable and at times unpleasant. This points to the tragic view of life in Greek thought.

The schools of ancient philosophy generally set about the task of raising humans above *tukhe*, and hoped to render themselves impervious to its attacks. The conventions of society are one such attempt to overcome *tukhe*, bringing order to one's life in a way that helps one transcend the natural—as if character can make one immune to it, or protect one from it. No doubt, the growth of technology stemming from Aristotelian epistemological approaches to the world has moved Western Civilization in a direction that has, through the introduction of the scientific method, helped us overcome many of the sufferings nature throws at us; however, it has not brought well-being, and seems to come with even more horrible nightmares than those given by nature.

The cynics took a different approach toward *tukhe*: rather than attempting to control it, they treat it with contempt, not even taking it seriously, and interpreting its blows as incitement to greater moral effort. When Diogenes fell into misfortune, he would mock it, and go on his way humming to himself.[33]

3 Conclusion

We can see from this general analysis of defacing the currency, that there is a rational movement of thought in Diogenes' virtuous view of life: nature provides an ethical norm which can be observed in animals; Greek society is at

30 Navia, 95.
31 Cutler, 30.
32 Goulet-Cazé, 55.
33 Goulet-Cazé, 56.

odds with nature, and so its fundamental values are not only false but counter-productive; humans can realize their nature by engaging in rigorous discipline and training of the body, which prepares them for the actual conditions of human life; the goal of this discipline is to promote a happy life, consisting of freedom and self-sufficiency. This movement of thought leads to the second aspect of ancient cynicism: exile.

CHAPTER 2

Exile and *Parrhesia*

Perhaps the most critical difference between ancient and modern cynicism is their reaction to defacing the currency. Both types of cynicism see through the hypocrisy within culture, but they differ in how this impacts their relationship to society and culture. As we will see in this chapter, ancient cynicism's defacing of the currency leads to an "exile" within culture, an alienation from the norms and practices of culture. In modern cynicism, exile does not take place, and this, more than anything else, is the basis of the self-deception within it. Our study of Freud, Becker, and Kierkegaard will be focused on why this exile does not take place, but in this chapter we will see what type of relationship to culture the ancient cynics were led into due to defacing the currency. Their reaction to defacing the currency is consistent with the "enlightened consciousness" that has seen through the *tuphos*.

1 Exile

1.1 The Conflict with Culture

To be in exile is to be displaced from a social context, to be isolated and alone. In exile one is a stranger and alien among others, misunderstood and often victimized due to this misunderstanding. Exile is a groundless life seemingly without roots, and so insecure and ephemeral. While there is an actual physical exile associated with cynicism—as seen in the case of Diogenes—the more important form of exile is one of perspective toward culture. In other words, one can be in exile, alienated from others, even while in the midst of them. The cynics do not, for the most part, physically leave culture and society, but neither do they participate in the cultural activities of others—at least not in the way others do. They remain in society as "meddlers."[1] They are, in many ways, like Socrates, who likened himself to a "gadfly." In Plato's *Apology*, a retelling of Socrates' defense before his accusers, Socrates claims to be a gadfly (a kind of horsefly), and his description is not unlike what we see with the cynics:

1 Navia, 24.

 | HTTPS://DOI.ORG/10.1163/9789004758148-004

> Indeed, gentlemen of the jury, I am far from making a defence now on my own behalf, as might be thought, but on yours, to prevent you from wrongdoing by mistreating a god's gift to you by condemning me; for if you kill me you will not easily find another like me. I was attached to this city by the god … as upon a great and noble horse which was somewhat sluggish because of its size and needed to be stirred up by a kind of gadfly. It is to fulfill some such function that I believe the god has placed me in the city. I never cease to rouse each and every one of you, to persuade and reproach you all day long and everywhere I find myself in your company.[2]

Athens is likened by Socrates to be a great and powerful thoroughbred horse who is now languishing, and requires awakening. He is the gadfly that has come to bite the Athenian steed in order to get it moving.

While Socrates was somewhat alienated within Athens (he is, after all, put on trial and sentenced to death), it is clear from the Platonic dialogues that, unlike the cynics, Socrates had respect for the laws of Athens, and also saw value and beauty in the conventions and institutions within Athens. He seems to be aware, however, that there are those among his students who do not hold this respect. He warns Athens about those to come, whom he has been holding back up until now. Upon hearing from the jury that he has been condemned to death, Socrates says,

> You did this in the belief that you would avoid giving an account of your life, but I maintain that quite the opposite will happen to you. There will be more people to test you, whom I now held back, but you did not notice it. They will be more difficult to deal with as they will be younger and you will resent them more. You are wrong if you believe that by killing people you will prevent anyone from reproaching you for not living in the right way.[3]

I wonder if Socrates has in mind Antisthenes as he makes this statement, whose defacing of the currency left aside all decorum and respect for the laws that had been used to put his teacher to death. And then there is Antisthenes' student, Diogenes, who Plato described as "Socrates gone mad." His "madness," it might be argued, is his state of freedom from the conventions and norms of the culture, a freedom which is the direct result of being an exile in the culture.

---

2 Plato, *The Apology*, in *The Trial and Death of Socrates*, trans. G. M. A. Grube, 21–42 (Indianapolis, IN: Hackett, 1975), 30d-31a.

3 Plato, 39c-d.

Diogenes is free from the cultural currency that had taken over others' lives by becoming the primary source of their motivation. He is perfectly happy living a life of poverty; his poverty is merely an outward manifestation of his internal exile. He has no problem living in a tub. It is a logical manifestation of his indifference to cultural standards of success. He views his success in terms of his willingness to live in poverty, and his ability to find happiness in this poverty.

Exile is basically the indifference the cynics felt toward cultural standards of success. This resulted in seeing things differently from others (the typical "seeing through" that characterizes all cynicism); it defines "mattering" or personal value in a different way than does culture. It flips the very criteria of wisdom, which for most people is connected to the artificial and arbitrary norms of society. Let us look at these issues more closely.

1.2 The Gift of Exile

Diogenes said that his literal exile from Sinope transformed him into a philosopher (a "lover of wisdom"). Although exile was considered to be the greatest evil to befall a person in the ancient world, Diogenes took it as the best possible training for philosophy.[4] When someone reproached Diogenes with his exile, he replied, "Nay, it was through that, you miserable fellow, that I came to be a philosopher."[5] He did not see exile as leading to an impoverished life, but a life that led to the riches of wisdom; it is those who find their life wholly in their culture who are impoverished. When someone reminded Diogenes that the people of Sinope had sentenced him to exile, he would say, "And I them to home-staying,"[6] as if immersion in the culture was the greatest of punishments.[7]

While we noted above that there is a distinction between a physical and an internal exile, it was often the case that external exile led to the cynic's internal

4 David Mazella, *The Making of Modern Cynicism* (Charlottesville, VA: University of Virginia Press, 2007), 35.

5 Mazella, 35.

6 Mazella, 35.

7 This is the lesson modern cynicism has neglected, and it has led to various contradictions and paradoxes, which can be summed up in Peter Sloterdijk's definition of modern cynicism as "enlightened false consciousness." Modern cynicism is enlightened in terms of the deceptive nature of culture, but it remains a false consciousness in terms of its own relationship with culture. We will find in our study of Freud, Becker, and Kierkegaard that there are psychological reasons for this continued false consciousness. However, we will also discover that there is a price to pay for attempting to live in this contradictory form of consciousness.

exile. Externally, the exile of the cynics came through different circumstances: Diogenes was literally exiled, Antisthenes was ostracized by being labeled a "bastard" of a prostitute, and Crates was an outcast to others due to a physical deformity. As each of them internalized their exile, they came to see it as a gift, something that resulted in freedom, self-mastery, clarity of mind, and the happiness that comes from living a vital and flourishing life in line with nature.

In a point that will become important as we move into the analysis of modern cynicism, the ancient cynics' exile *allowed them to see alternative ways to live*, and that there is more to life than what is offered by culture. For those immersed in culture, alternative ways of viewing the world, measuring success, and understanding what human flourishing consists of becomes practically impossible: every other alternative appears to be moving into languishing and failure. This makes sense: when we define health, excellence, and success completely by culture, we define illness and failure as anything not holding to the standards of culture (that is, any other alternative way of life). The cynics believed that aligning oneself with reason and nature will make clear the madness of the world, and one will become free of its influences. This freedom means openness to other alternatives and influences.

Exile, for the cynics, is seeing through the *tuphos* of culture. This was not forced upon them merely because their physical exile, but was also "forced" on them through reason. Reason finds itself in exile when faced with the irrational world of human society. Sloterdijk writes that reason, for Diogenes, becomes,

> homeless in the social world. … Where socialization for the philosopher becomes synonymous with the unreasonable demand to be satisfied with the partial reason and one's own random culture and to join the collective irrationality of one's society, there, the kynic's [the term Sloterdijk uses for ancient cynics, following the Greek spelling] refusal has a utopian significance.[8]

1.3 The Difficulty of Exile

This view of exile is not unlike Albert Camus' description in *The Myth of Sisyphus* of the "stage sets collapsing." Camus writes,

> [I]t happens that the stage sets collapse. Rising, streetcar, four hours in the office or the factory, meal, streetcar, four hours at work, meal sleep, and Monday Tuesday

8 Sloterdijk (1987), 164.

> Wednesday Thursday Friday and Saturday according to the same rhythm—this path is easily followed most of the time. But one day the "why" arises and everything begins in the weariness tinged with amazement. "Begins"—this is important. Weariness comes at the end of the acts of a mechanical life, but at the same time it inaugurates the impulse of consciousness. It awakens consciousness and provokes what follows. What follows is the gradual return to the chain or it is the definitive awakening.[9]

Camus' description offers a contemporary view of exile, but it is worth bringing in here so we can grasp a more contemporary view of this ancient cynical theme, especially in terms of several important points. First, it is a kind of "forced" exile, in that the "why" arises of itself. Second, there is a sense of languishing in Camus' description of the normal life, the weariness of a cyclical rhythm of social life. Finally, it is *seeing through* the façades, where the situations and circumstances appear as stage sets—façades that hide the emptiness behind them. This issue will become critical as we look at modern cynicism, for although modern cynics see through the façade, they still *act* as if there is something meaningful and substantial behind the stage sets. Modern cynicism has chosen what Camus describes as a "gradual return to the chain," though modern cynics remain vaguely aware of its emptiness. This cannot help but have a profound impact on the consciousness of individuals, and how they relate to others, the world, and all they do within it.

Seeing through the illusions and living by this insight takes courage, and a willingness to face the anxiety exile creates. We will see in the coming chapters why this is the case, and so why most people tend to stop short of entirely giving into exile. If we were to see through the illusions fully, we know that things will never be the same for us (indeed, they could not be), and so there comes a critical moment in which we stand before a choice. In the quote above from Camus, the choice is between the "gradual return to the chain" or "the definitive awakening."

This choice or decision is an important theme in relation to modern cynicism: should we move into the exile that has seen through the stage sets, or should we remain invested in the very stage sets (cultural values, ideals, and norms) we have seen through? It is a de-cision. The term "decision" is etymologically made up of *de-* (meaning "off") and *-caedere* (meaning "to cut"). A

9 Albert Camus, *The Myth of Sisyphus and Other Essays*, trans. Justin O'Brien (New York, NY: Random, 1955), 10.

decision is a cutting off, a separation. In Greek, the term *krisis*, from which we get our word "crisis," means decision or judgment, and contains the idea of separation (*krino*). What Camus describes above is an identity crisis, a point of decision that will change my life (or not): will I become an exile, or remain what my culture tells me I am? Another way of asking this, connected to the issue of exile, is: Will I open myself to other alternatives?

The more deeply we move into our analysis of cynicism and the therapeutic, the more critical these issues will become. As modern cynics, I believe one of the most important questions we must face is what we will do after we have *seen through* the illusions and manipulations at work in our society. The modern cynic should ask: What happens when one has seen through it all, and yet chooses to continue to invest one's life in it? To return to the stage set, after having seen through it, creates a split in the psyche, and like all psychical splits, raises the problem of hypocrisy and pretense. We will get to this in due time, but we will now turn to the final theme of ancient cynicism, which addresses the issue of hypocrisy: *parrhesia*.

2 *Parrhesia*

Although *parrhesia* literally has to do with free speech or communication, symbolically it points to a genuineness and confidence in that upon which one bases one's life. Throughout this book, *parrhesia* will carry with it the connotation of authenticity and the overcoming of self-deception. It will have to do with truth that goes beyond the correspondence theory of truth (namely, that what one says matches the state of affairs about which one is speaking), and with what Kierkegaard called "truth as subjectivity," which is the earnestness upon which one stakes one's life upon one's truth. We will see how this plays out within ancient cynicism, in order to contrast it with the failure of *parrhesia* in modern cynicism. As we will see, *parrhesia* results from exile, and so a person who defaces the currency without moving into exile will be incapable of sincerity and genuineness, being in an constant conflict with the world, stemming from a self-conflict (an enlightened false consciousness).

I will be following Michel Foucault's excellent analysis of *parrhesia*, in order to give a concise general understanding of what the term means, and how it relates to ancient cynicism. A *parrhesiastes* (one who uses *parrhesia*) is someone who says everything on his mind: "he does not hide anything, but opens his heart and mind completely to other people through discourse. In *parrhesia*, the speaker is supposed to give a complete and exact account of what he has in mind so that the audience can comprehend exactly what the speaker thinks."[10]

There is both a pejorative meaning to *parrhesia* and a positive meaning. The pejorative meaning has the sense of "chattering." It consists of someone who says anything and everything that comes to his mind. Today we would characterize this by saying that the person "has no filter" when it comes to what he says. Philosophically, however, *parrhesia* has a more positive meaning: it points to a sincerity in what is said, as well as a confidence that what one is saying is true.[11] The person who speaks with *parrhesia* is committed to that about which he speaks, because he is confident about it. In this positive sense of *parrhesia*, it is the determination to have nothing to do with the lies and deceptions that constitute practically every structure that supports human interaction, relationships, and activities.

If cultural conventions are illusions and deceptions, then the communication among those within those conventions (the communication that holds the conventions together in practice) must necessarily deal in lies and deceptions in order to allow the conventions actually to work. For instance, if cultural conventions are an illusion or deception of real happiness and flourishing, then people must say they are happier than they are, that they believe things they do not truly believe, and must say to others what they believe will keep them in good standing in the community (whether they believe what they say or not). The *parrhesiates* determines not to do this.

Parrhesia is not simply the result of overcoming *tuphos*, but as Navia points out, it is an antidote to *tuphos* as well. The overcoming of *tuphos* means the end of having to pretend to be who one is not. One gains a oneness with oneself. The communication that comes from this (*parrhesia*) is a breaking through of truth over self-deception, as light overcomes darkness. According to Navia, *parrhesia* is an antidote to *tuphos* because *tuphos* is created and maintained through the misuse of language (a use of language that clouds our understanding while claiming to be presenting understanding). Language is often used to flatter, threaten, and confuse, and is a powerful tool for maintaining *tuphos*.[12]

10 Michel Foucault, "Discourse and Truth: The Problematization of Parrhesia (Six Lectures given by Michel Foucault at Berkeley, Oct-Nov. 1983)" accessed October 22, 2014, https://www.cscd.osaka-u.ac.jp/user/rosaldo/On_Parrehesia_by_Foucault_1983.pdf, 2.

11 "He says what he knows to be true. ... [T]here is always an exact coincidence between belief and truth." Foucault, 3.

12 Navia, 64–65.

To speak truth in the midst of a community that is trying to maintain an illusion entails risk, since speaking the truth risks bringing that illusion down; thus, those who have a strong interest in maintaining the illusion (not merely those in power, but also those that depend on the illusion to feel empowered—which is most people in a society) will sacrifice the speaker of truth, rather than the illusion. Foucault uses the example of a philosopher addressing a tyrant, who, when telling him "that his tyranny is disturbing and unpleasant because tyranny is incompatible with justice, then the philosopher speaks the truth, believes he is speaking the truth, and, more than that, also takes risks (since the tyrant may become angry, may punish him, may exile him, may kill him)."[13] In more supposedly free societies, the danger is not so much about specific tyrants, as it is about the "tyranny of the majority" (to use a phrase from Alexis de Tocqueville). Foucault writes that the *parrhesiates*,

> risks his privilege to speak freely when he discloses a truth that threatens the majority. For it was a well-known juridical situation when Athenian leaders were exiled only because they proposed something which was opposed to the majority, or even because the assembly thought that the strong influence of certain leaders limited its own freedom.[14]

The issue of risk leads to another important aspect of *parrhesia*: it comes from "below," and is directed at those "above."[15] Someone with authority (e.g., a teacher or parent) who criticizes is not using *parrhesia*, because of the lack of risk. However, when a philosopher or citizen criticizes the majority, or a pupil criticizes the teacher, then the speaker may be using *parrhesia*. *Parrhesia* consists of a person without power criticizing and confronting those with power.

It is the danger and potential cost of *parrhesia* that relates to trusting what the speaker says. The speaker has nothing personally to gain, but plenty to lose. It is a view of truth, then, as that upon which one risks all, that upon which one has put one's own life at stake. One is no longer a social mercenary in one's thinking (that is, "committing" to something only as long as it serves one's personal concrete interests), but one truly believes that about which one speaks. Could the person be mistaken? Yes, but it is, as we would say, an "honest mistake." *Parrhesia*, then, is pointing to a person's motivation, that her implicit and explicit motives and actions coincide.

Risk also points to the aspect of confidence that attaches to the concept of *parrhesia*. This includes both the confidence to speak the truth in the face of

13 Foucault, 4.
14 Foucault, 5.
15 Foucault, 5.

risk, as well as the confidence the listeners have in the speaker's sincerity and honesty. This aspect of confidence helps us understand the relation of *parrhesia* to the ancient cynics, though it is somewhat complex. In a sense, the cynics have nothing to lose, and so it would seem to be a mistake to speak of a risk being attached to their *parrhesia*. Exile means that the cynics had already lost what was at risk in what they said. The source of confidence, then, was that they maintained their possession of the truth, even after having been "punished" for their *parrhesia*; indeed, it was because of the "punishment" that we can trust their sincerity. Diogenes has nothing to lose or gain from the majority, since he has already exiled himself from them. Thus, he can speak the truth and "risk" loss, which means that his listeners can have confidence in his motivation: he is not hiding anything from them, because he has nothing to gain or lose from them by what he says (no hidden or latent motive). As R. Bracht Branham says, "Because he has nothing to lose, he can tell the truth and, therefore, may be worth listening to."[16] To speak the truth in the presence of a risk is to imply that the truth is of more value than what one is putting at risk, or has already lost. This is exactly what is happening with the cynics, though to an extreme degree.

A good example of this is Diogenes' interaction with Alexander the Great. The story, as set forth by the ancient historian Plutarch, is as follows:

> Thereupon many statesmen and philosophers came to Alexander with their congratulations, and he expected that Diogenes of Sinope also, who was tarrying in Corinth, would do likewise. But since the philosopher took not the slightest notion of Alexander, and continued to enjoy his leisure in the suburb of Craneion, Alexander went in person to see him; and he found him lying in the sun. Diogenes raised himself up a little when he saw so many people coming towards him, and fixed his eyes upon Alexander. And when that monarch addressed him with greeting and asked if he wanted anything, "Yes," said Diogenes, "stand a little out of my sun." It is said that Alexander was so struck by this, and admired so much the haughtiness and grandeur of the man who had nothing but scorn for him, that he said to his followers, who were laughing and jesting about the philosopher as they went away, "But truly, if I were not Alexander, I would be Diogenes."[17]

16 R. Bracht Branham, "Defacing the Currency: Diogenes' Rhetoric and the *Invention* of Cynicism", in *The Cynics: The Cynical Movement in Antiquity and Its Legacy*, ed. Bracht Branham and Marie-Odile Goulet-Cazé, 81–104 (Berkeley: University of California Press, 1996), 103.

17 Plutarch, *Life of Alexander*. Trans. Bernadotte Perrin. Chapter 14, 259, accessed February 10, 2022, https://penelope.uchicago.edu/Thayer/E/Roman/Texts/Plutarch/Lives/Alexander*/3.html.

It was a risk to talk to such a tyrant in this way, but such is the way of the *parrhesiates*: Diogenes was honest enough to say what was *truly* on his mind: he wanted Alexander to move out of his light. As Foucault says about this story:

> This encounter, which was often referred to by the Cynics, does not take place in the privacy of Alexander's court but in the street, in the open. The king stands up while Diogenes sits back in his barrel. Diogenes orders Alexander to step out of his light so that he can bask in the sun. Ordering Alexander to step aside so that the sun's light can reach Diogenes is an affirmation of the direct natural relation the philosopher has to the sun in contrast to the mythical genealogy whereby the king, as descended from a god, was supposed to personify the sun.[18]

The person who speaks with *parrhesia* does so with a redemptive mindset, a belief and expectation that the truth will bring about flourishing and thriving in life. Thus, we find that the ancient cynics' approach to interacting with others, whether through words or actions,[19] was one of speaking the truth in order to bring about *atuphos*. Their truth was not an intellectual acquisition and possession, but was their very way of life; they did not *hold to* the truth, but the truth held them, and in it they found the happiness those around them seemed to be searching for in cultural activities.

3 Conclusion

Defacing the currency, exile, and *parrhesia* will be central themes throughout this book. We will find that these themes are important for understanding modern cynicism's enlightened false consciousness, due to the different ways modern cynics relate to these themes—in distinction to what we have seen with the ancient cynics. Modern cynics are exceptional at defacing the currency, but refuse to move into the exile such defacing should naturally lead. Without exile, *parrhesia* becomes practically non-existent among modern cynics, so that they continue to live in the very hypocrisy they have seen through, and of which they often accuse others. This hypocrisy is an essential element of their false consciousness, and what is behind so much of their self-deception. Their refusal to move into exile is due to their anxiety over facing the *krisis* discussed above.

---

18 Foucault, 46–47.

19 Specific actions may be considered *parrhesatic* as well, as they communicate a truth that challenges illusions.

Before moving into the issue of modern cynicism, we will spend several chapters examining the issues of defacing the currency, exile, and *parrhesia* in terms of three thinkers: Sigmund Freud, Ernest Becker, and Soren Kierkegaard. This will help us understand some of the changes in contemporary thinking about morals and social conventions that have taken place in the last century or so. The issue of deception and self-deception will become enriched by these analyses, as we see that the problem is not so much that we are deceived by culture (as it was for the ancient cynics), but that we seek to deceive ourselves, and culture is the "cover" by which we can carry this out. The problem, it turns out, is not deception, but self-deception.

CHAPTER 3

Freud's Defacing of the Currency

1 Cynicism as an Uncharitable Interpretation

Modern cynicism is different from ancient cynicism in many important ways, several of which I have already briefly indicated. One of the most striking differences is that while the ancient cynics focused on defacing the cultural practices they believed clouded others' rational understanding, modern cynics tend to focus on the latent motivations of individuals, institutions, corporations, and communities. The ancient cynics had a general optimism about people's motives, because they had an optimism about human nature. They thought that if the cultural currency could be sufficiently defaced (often through techniques of shock, as if trying to shake a person awake), people would come to their senses and find freedom from the currency. People were seen as foolish or deceived, rather than deceptive.

In contrast to this, the modern cynic has a much more pessimistic view of human nature. The problem is not that we are not sufficiently enlightened about the hypocrisy and deception of the currency of culture, the problem is that people are selfish and manipulative. We are not so much deceived as the deceivers. We are, by nature, self-centered, and so always motivated by self-gain. If a person does not appear to be like this, it is just evidence of his or her shrewdness and deceptive manipulation. Due to our enlightened consciousness, we know the game and how to play it. We know the *tuphos*: we have learned, individually, that we must make our way very carefully through a world where deceptions are erected for the sake of manipulation. We must be extremely careful in whom we put our trust, since we know that in the end, everyone will act for his or her self-interest.

To live in a culture that has become cynical means that we see through everything, finding hidden, self-interested motives in politicians, corporations, institutions, advertisements, media outlets, managers, co-workers, and even family. We are inherently suspicious of most manifest content, believing there is something essential that remains latent or hidden: a self-interest that ultimately motivates all action and speech. We, as humans, have decades, centuries, perhaps millennia of historical knowledge to back up our suspicions, and as individuals we have plenty of personal experience being deceived and manipulated.

The reality, however, is that when it comes to the particular things of which we are cynical, we do not have any direct evidence: modern cynicism is an

 | HTTPS://DOI.ORG/10.1163/9789004758148-005

interpretive act, used to fill in the lack of what is known. I did not know if my students were lying to me (if I did know, I would not be cynical, but would be following my knowledge). I had to make some sort of decision, and lacking the evidence, I assumed that my students were trying to deceive and manipulate me. A cynic is someone who almost always gives an uncharitable interpretation of others' actions, thinking she knows what the latent content is—though she does not.

This is the enlightened aspect of cynicism, and the cynic feels enlightened about the cultural situation with this interpretation; however, there is a false consciousness to this. Sloterdijk's definition of modern cynicism as enlightened false consciousness is profoundly insightful. He describes modern cynicism as,

> that modernized unhappy consciousness, on which enlightenment has labored both successfully and in vain. It has learned the lessons of enlightenment, but it has not, and probably was not able to, put them into practice. Well-off and miserable at the same time, this consciousness no longer feels affected by any critique of ideology; its falseness is already reflexively buffered.[1]

It is this false consciousness, and its reflective buffering to critique, that is our interest in this book, and is the reason we are going to take several chapters to analyze our self-deception and resistance to our false consciousness. False consciousness is a type of repression, a self-deception motivated by an attempt to rid oneself of the anxiety that begins to come to the surface as one comes to understand the true nature of the self. We will be looking at Freud, Becker, and Kierkegaard in order to gain a context by which to understand why the cynic was *not* able to put into practice the lessons learned from enlightenment.

It turns out that we cannot handle the truth. There are things about ourselves that we do not want to admit, and culture serves as a means by which we remain in our deception, hoping to relieve the tension or disturbance. Problems arise, however, when culture no longer functions well for this purpose. When this happens, certain psychological disturbances begin to arise, such as anxiety and depression, and various other disorders. Kierkegaard, living in the mid-nineteenth century, recognized the cracks beginning to take place within culture; Freud saw firsthand in his medical practice the results or consequences upon the human psyche of these cracks, and tried to explain them to mitigate the negative impacts upon humans; Becker rectifies some of Freud's

1 Sloterdijk, 5.

mistaken views about the nature of this self-deception in a way that will help us understand modern cynicism. Rather than follow this chronological order for our analysis, I will start with Freud, then move to Becker, who will act as a transition into Kierkegaard's thoughts on the cultural currency.

In this chapter, I will focus on Freud's essential theories, such as the structure of the psyche, sublimation, his ambivalence toward culture, and neurosis. These themes will become vital as we analyze modern cynicism, and will be picked up again in a later chapter, as I analyze the close connection between Freud and modern cynicism. In the later chapters I will argue that Freud models his view of the psyche after cynicism, and that this becomes the source of a new sublimation of the repressed—that is, our acceptance of Freud's social theories is related closely to modern cynicism becoming ideological, and a means by which we remain in self-deception. We have much work to do before we get to that point, starting with a general analysis of Freud's view of the psyche and its relation to culture.

2 Freud's Theory of the Psyche

Most people have heard of the three parts of the psyche which Freud developed by the end of his work: id, ego, and superego. I will present a general picture of these aspects of the psyche, showing what each aspect is characterized by, how they interact and relate to each other, and how these interactions relate to the currency of culture. Freud's psychoanalytic theory is, in itself, a defacing of the currency of culture: culture and civilization are not some grand creations that stand as a testament to the higher human capacities, but culture is based on irrational, infantile, and self-deceptive workings within the psyche.

2.1 Id

The id (which in German is *es*, and a German would read as "it") is the dark, inaccessible aspect of the psyche, which we think of as the "unconscious." What little we know about "it" was learned, Freud says, through the dream-work, and the construction of neurotic symptoms. Freud characterizes the id as a chaotic cauldron full of seething excitation.[2] It is chaotic in several dif-

2 "We approach the id with analogies: we call it a chaos, a cauldron full of seething excitations. We picture it being open at its end to somatic influences, and as there taking up in itself instinctual needs which find their psychical expression in it. … It is filled with energy reaching it from the instincts, but it has no organization, produces no collective will, but only a

ferent ways. It is, for instance, illogical: its "form" is not structured by what we think of as reason or logic, but is "formed" around the "cauldron" of seething excitations. We feel these excitations (desires) bubbling up throughout the day in random and sometimes disturbing ways. As irrational, the id does not judge these desires, but demands they all be fulfilled. That our desires are often in conflict has no impact on the strength of the id's demands.

The id is also timeless, in the sense that events that happened to us in childhood are as powerful to it as events that happened only moments ago. This is why Freud puts so much emphasis on what we experienced as infants, both in terms of the satisfaction of our desires and their lack of satisfaction.

The id disregards reality, which is to say it takes no notice of the impact that giving into its desires may have on the world, or on itself. It cannot even distinguish between what is external to itself, and what is of its own creation and fantasies. It does not know the difference between "real events" and its own imagined experiences.

Finally, there is an absence of negation in the id, so that it does not comprehend the word "No" in relation to fulfilling its desires. This means that they cannot be "turned off," but must be sublimated (that is, fulfilled in culturally acceptable ways). No matter how much a desire may be buried, if it is not sublimated, the energy of that unsatisfied desire will manifest itself in some way, usually through neurotic symptoms.

The desires within the id are referred to by Freud as "drives" or "instinctual needs" (*Trieb*). The sources of these drives are somatic or bodily, whose demands we feel within our mental lives. They are the ultimate cause of all activity, what drives humans in relation to every aspect of their lives, whether they are conscious of these drives or (more likely) not conscious of them. Freud pictures the drives as a quota of energy pressing in a particular direction: "It is from this pressing that it derives the name '*Trieb*'."[3]

The id's aim or purpose is the removal of the uncomfortable excitation created by this "pressing." To grasp how we feel this instinctual bodily need mentally, think of the "pressing" of an itch you need to scratch (thinking not about the physical itch, but the impact it has upon you mentally); or think about when you hold your breath, and there is a "pressing" upon your mental apparatus to take in air. Addicts of all kinds are familiar with the pressing or *tension* that arises from this excitation of energy, and the need to remove

---

striving to bring about the satisfaction of instinctual needs subject to the observances of the pleasure principle." Sigmund Freud, *New Introductory Lectures of Psychoanalysis*, trans. and ed. James Strachey (New York: Norton, 1964), 65. Henceforth cited as *ILP*.

3 *ILP*, 86.

the excitation. According to Freud, pleasure is the discharge, release, or lowering of the unpleasurable sensations associated with the tension created by instincts. The unpleasurable sensations seek a pathway toward the discharge of this energetic excitation, which when accomplished we experience as pleasure.[4] Thus, pleasure and unpleasure are related to the quantity of the excitation present in the mind.[5]

The striving of the instinctual satisfaction, and so lowering of excitation, is called the *pleasure principle* by Freud. The pleasure principle is a tendency of the system to free the mental apparatus entirely of excitation, or to keep the excitation as low as possible.[6] In other words, the pleasure principle is not the cauldron of desires seeking fulfillment, but the tendency of the organism to keep the tension within it to a minimum, which it accomplishes through the satisfaction of the instincts. In a certain sense, we are seeking to be at peace, to be free of tension—not just tension created by our external circumstances, but more primordially, the tension created internally.

The pleasure principle dominates the id. This is what motivates it: the random, chaotic, seething cauldron of instincts rising for satisfaction, making their impact felt as unpleasure upon the mental apparatus. There is no order to how most of our desires arise, at least no logical or rational order as we understand those terms. No doubt, we are aware that some of these desires arise because the body needs nourishment or liquid, but most of our desires are unrelated to these conscious needs, and so their movement is beyond our rational grasp.

An implication of this is that the id makes no judgments of value: there is no good or evil for the id, no morality or sense of what is important and what is insignificant.[7] It is wholly dominated by an economic or quantitative factor: discharge of energy. This discharge is the only result the id aims at, without consideration of the dangers such a goal may create. As Freud points out, protecting us from danger is the ego's aim:

> The power of the id expresses the true purposes of the individual organism's life. This consists in the satisfaction of its innate needs. No such purpose as that of keeping itself alive or protecting itself from dangers of anxiety can be attributed

4 Sigmund Freud, *The Ego and the Id*, from the Standard Edition of the Complete Psychological Works of Sigmund Freud, Volume XIX (1923–1925), accessed on February 10, 2022, https://www.sigmundfreud.net/the-ego-and-the-id-pdf-ebook.jsp, 8–9 (pagination follows online edition). Henceforth cited as *EI*.

5 Sigmund Freud, *Beyond the Pleasure Principle*, trans. James Strachey (New York: Norton, 1961), 4. Henceforth cited as *PP*.

6 *PP*, 76.

7 *ILP*, 66.

> to the id. That is the business of the ego, which is also concerned with discovering the most favourable and least perilous method of obtaining satisfaction, taking the external world into account.[8]

Here we find in the ego a different aim than the id.

Before getting into our analysis of the ego, I want to emphasize that for Freud it is the id that ultimately determines the real aim or purpose of the organism, and so of human life (including cultural life): "What decides the purpose of life is simply the programme of the pleasure principle. The principle dominates the operation of the mental apparatus from the start."[9] Thus, while the pleasure principle does not consciously govern the self or "ego," the ego necessarily must continually find ways to address the aims of the id or the pleasure principle. The ego is trying to keep a lid on the chaos within ourselves.

2.2 Ego

While the pleasure principle governs the id's activities, the ego's (*ich* or "I" in German) activities are governed by the *reality principle*. Freud says that during the development of the infant, a part of the id undergoes modification because of the child's interaction with the external world; this modification is the ego.[10]

The ego is the seat of intellectual activity, and so is the rational part of the psyche. While the id is exclusively directed to obtaining pleasure, considerations of safety and protection govern the ego: the ego's task is self-preservation of the organism, something which the id completely neglects.[11] Thus, the ego seeks to replace the pleasure principle with the reality principle.[12] Not that the ego seeks to become the enemy of the id; the ego seeks to be a loyal servant of the id, to remain on good terms with it. As we will see below in this chapter,

8 Sigmund Freud, *An Outline of Psycho-Analysis*, trans. James Strachey (London: Hogarth Press, 1959), 55. Henceforth cited as *OP*.

9 Sigmund Freud, *Civilization and Its Discontents*, trans. James Strachey (New York: Norton, 1962), 23. Henceforth cited as *CID*.

10 Joseph Sandler, Alex Holder, et al., *Freud's Models of the Mind: An Introduction* (London: Karnac, 2005), 27. As Freud puts it, "[I]ts constructive function consists in interposing between the demand by an instinct and the action that satisfies it, an intellective activity which, after considering the present state of things and weighing up earlier experiences, endeavours by means of experimental action to calculate the consequences of the proposed line of conduct" (*OP*, 69).

11 *OP*, 69.

12 "In that way it has dethroned the pleasure principle which dominates the course of events in the id without any restrictions and has replaced it by the reality principle, which promises more certainty and greater success" (*ILP*, 67).

and more thoroughly in Chapter 15, the ego recommends itself as an object, so that it can attract the libido (another name for the instinctual drives) to itself, and so control or manipulate the id. Though it seeks to replace the pleasure principle with the reality principle, it is never free from the mechanics that allow this to take place—and so never free of the pleasure principle.

The ego is a kind of "outer skin" of the id, that part of the id that is in contact with the external world. It is the portion of the id adapted for the reception of stimuli, and as a protective shield against perceived unpleasurable stimuli.[13] It controls the voluntary movement through access to the muscles, and is the seat of sensory perception. The id is like the current that moves the vessel (the organism), and the ego is like the captain steering the vessel away from danger.

As stated already, its task is self-preservation, and so an essential aspect of the ego is the ability to assess danger, and make the organism aware of the danger, usually through anxiety. Thus, anxiety is an important aspect of the ego, which Freud sees as an affective (emotive) aspect of the organism which creates displeasure in order to overcome the satisfaction of dangerous pleasures (anxiety creates an unpleasurable experience at the thought of gaining a pleasurable experience, thus keeping the organism from satisfying the dangerous desire).[14] The ego is aware of stimuli from without, and can store up experiences in the memory, so that it can avoid excessive external and internal stimuli through flight (anxiety); in this same way, it can deal with moderate stimuli through adaptation. In terms of internal events or stimuli, the ego can gain control over the demands of the instincts through various methods: it can postpone a discharge, repress an instinct, or sublimate it. Finally, it learns how it can, through its activity, modify the external world for its advantage (e.g., through technological developments, suppression of dangers in the wild, etc.).

Freud's radical new understanding of the psyche is that consciousness is not the essence of the psyche, but a quality within it. In the seventeenth century, Rene Descartes argued that the ego or "I" was the essence of the self, and that it was fully transparent to itself—or at least capable of becoming so. This view of the human self was the reason for the optimism about human progress, especially as intellectual history moved into the Enlightenment period. It was believed that, by becoming more transparently conscious to ourselves, we would be able to overcome the hiddenness and deception of such things as

13 *ILP*, 67.

14 Anxiety is a defensive mechanism, protecting us from perceived dangers. We often understand this as applying only to perceived external dangers; however, Freud views anxiety's more important (and psychologically disruptive) work as an attempt to protect us from internal dangers—to protect us from ourselves.

nature and religion through self-understanding and enlightenment. Through our ego, we could correctly represent the world to ourselves, and this would move humanity in the direction of technological, moral, political, social, and natural progress.

Freud's view of the psyche humiliates this view of the self. Freud destroys this particular idea of individual self-importance and self-mastery. As Copernicus destroyed the view of the human world as the center of the universe, and Darwin showed humanity to be just one more member of the animal kingdom, so Freud believed that he had shown that the human ego is not even master over itself.[15] Powers from within the psyche, over which it has limited control, drive it, and it must continually do the bidding of these powers. The ego is blind to this reality about itself because of its self-deception. It deceives itself through *repression.*

Repression is the ego finding it necessary to lie to itself about itself. As Philip Rieff says, "Repression is the Freudian word for lying to oneself without ever quite knowing it."[16] The ego represses those instincts which, if allowed to obtain satisfaction, would lead to a feeling of shame within the ego, and also those instincts that could lead to the death of the organism. It represses by refusing to admit these desires into consciousness.[17] The unconscious is the repressed contents: if not for the need of repression, the id would be all there is to the human organism.[18] The instincts of the id are never destroyed, and so repression is not destruction, but a keeping from consciousness in order to suppress—to keep from fulfillment and satisfaction. The id is driven to re-experience indestructible desires that were once fulfilled at will, to return to that time (infancy) when desires were freely satisfied, which is why all instinctual desires are infantile at their ground.[19]

There are, then, in the human being, purposes of which one knows nothing, involuntary and unconscious ideas about life, flourishing, and thriving.[20]

15 Norman O. Brown, *Life against Death: The Psychoanalytic Meaning of History* (Second Edition) (Middletown: Wesleyan University Press, 1985), 16.

16 Philip Rieff, *My Life Among the Deathworks: Illustrations of the Aesthetics of Authority* (*Sacred Order/Social Order, Volume 1*), Ed. Kenneth S. Piver (Charlottesville: University of Virginia Press, 2006), 152. Henceforth cited as *DW.*

17 Brown, 8.

18 Brown, 5.

19 "[The] early blossoming of the erotic life must succumb to repression when it finally confronts the reality-principle. But though it is repressed, or rather because it is repressed, this early experience of love stays with us as the immortal dream of love, as an indestructible demand of human nature, as the source of our restless discontent." (Brown, 40).

20 Brown, 4.

These desires are in conflict with the world, which means that every individual is divided, split by cross purposes. From the moment one wakes up in the morning, one is faced with this reality of competing demands and purposes: stay in bed (the pleasure principle) or get up in order to keep one's job (the reality principle). And this is just the beginning of one's day: eat those extra five delicious bites on one's plate even though one is full, or push the plate away; buy those clothes one has neither need nor money for (running up one's credit card), or be satisfied with what one has; binge on Netflix, or do some activity that will be better for one's mind and body. This is a small example of the conflict that is taking place within us every hour of every day we live, with only small windows when the conflict is resolved because the reality principle and pleasure principle just happen to coincide.

Repression is ultimately about refusing to acknowledge and recognize what human nature (oneself) is truly all about. It keeps unconscious those desires that would make one admit some things about oneself one would rather not face—not the innocuous desires I used as examples above, but about the sexual and aggressive desires we have toward our parents. Our true desires are related to the infamous Oedipus complex (which we will get to soon enough), and this, according to Freud, is our true self, our true latent motives behind all our manifest actions. Repression is ultimately about repressing this reality. Thus, we spend our lives trying not to be who we are and will always be, in order to prove to ourselves and others that we are more than we can ever be.

How do we maintain this self-deception? And how could we possibly maintain any satisfaction in life if our true desires were along these lines and in continual conflict? This is where culture comes into play: we are not left to ourselves in repression, for culture is both how we repress our true nature, and the way we find life tolerable—even though we are not fulfilling the most basic aims in life. One of Freud's most profound theories about society is that the need for the psychic organism to deal with the repressed content *is the basis of culture*, the dynamic link between nature and culture. This is the issue around which Freud's social theories and critiques arise, and they have had a powerful impact on American society. This leads us to the third aspect of the psyche: the superego (*überich*, or "over-I").

2.3 Superego

The superego is the source of morality and applies the strictest moral standards to the helpless ego, which is at its mercy. In general, the superego "represents the claims of morality, and we realize all at once that our moral sense of guilt is the expression of the tension between ego and super-ego."[21] The greater part of the superego is unconscious, though aspects of it represent the form of conscious standards and ideals. It is responsible for both the conscious and unconscious sense of guilt, and plays a crucial role in both normal and pathological mental functioning.[22] Through its main function of limiting instinctual satisfaction, it places fresh needs (burdens) upon the psyche.[23]

The superego is the psyche's representative of the parental figures of childhood, arising out of the Oedipus complex—that is, in the resolution of the Oedipus complex.[24] At the beginning of its life, the infant is in what Freud calls primary narcissism: the infant feels omnipotent in the sense of regarding the entire world as a part, or mere extension, of itself. The fulfillment of its desires and instincts are, both literally and as far as it senses them, autoerotic, since there is not yet any differentiation between the self and the world (which first arises with the ego). The differentiation does not immediately take place, because the world meets its needs in a fairly consistent and immediate manner. Eventually, however, the infant begins to perceive that the world is not bending to its desires at its will: the mother does not immediately come when the child is hungry, does not always give the fulfilling "cooing" sounds the infant expects, but sometimes gives harsh and unwanted treatment. At this point, the ego begins to develop from the id, as the infant is forced to deal with reality.

The ego's first objects in the world are those most critical to the satisfaction of its drives and its safety—the parents. In terms of object-choice, the libido follows the path of narcissistic needs, and attaches itself to the objects that ensure their satisfaction. The mother, who satisfies hunger, becomes the first object-choice as a love-object,[25] and is the first to provide a sense of protection against the undefined and threatening dangers of the outer world. Thus, the mother becomes the first protection from anxiety.[26] In the mother, both safety

---

21 *ILP*, 64.

22 Sandler, 170.

23 *OP*, 5.

24 "At a very early age the little boy develops an object-cathexis for his mother, which originally related to the mother's breast and is the prototype of an object choice in the anaclitic model [object cathexis]; the boy deals with his father by identifying himself with him. For a time these two relationships proceed side by side, until the boy's sexual wishes in regard to his mother become more intense and his father is perceived as an obstacle to them; from this the Oedipus complex originates." (*EI*, 14–15).

25 Love is a narcissistic phenomenon for Freud, not a self-surrendering phenomenon.

26 Sigmund Freud, *The Future of an Illusion*, trans. Gregory C. Richter (Blacksburg: Wilder, 2010). Kindle Edition, 401. Henceforth cited as *FI*.

and satisfaction coincide, for the child finds great comfort and satisfaction at the breast of the mother. The child senses its dependence on the mother, and its feelings of helplessness cause the infant to love her. While the mother is the first object of protection, eventually she will be replaced by the stronger father.[27]

Object-choice is not the only way the infant relates to the parents; it also relates through *identification*. Identification is "the assimilation of one ego to another, as a result of which the first ego behaves like the second in certain respects, imitates it and in a sense takes it up into itself."[28] Identification is a vital form of attachment, because it is how the ego is able to give up its object. In other words, and paradoxically, through identification the ego both identifies itself with the object it loves, and is able to be separate from it—namely, by making it a part of itself.[29] The difference between identification and object-choice is that in identification the infant wants to *be like* the object, while in object-choice the infant wants to *have* or *possess* the object.[30]

In these two ways of relating to the parents, parental influence comes to govern the child by giving proofs of love, or by threatening punishment. Punishment is a sign to the child of a loss of love and protection, which becomes a source of anxiety and fear for the helpless and dependent child. This *realistic* anxiety is the precursor to the later *moral* anxiety that comes from the superego. Thus, anxiety is the connection between early childhood development and later adult, socialized behavior: *anxiety is the irrational basis of our surrender to culture and authority*—as well as what keeps us from exile, even after having seen through it.

The child eventually develops an ambivalent relationship toward the father, as the child sees the father as an obstacle to the mother's love and attention, and so the attainment of the child's wishes. The father takes on a hostile quality, so that there arises a wish to get rid of the father, in order that the child can take the place of the father. There is a tension, then, in the relationship with the father (an ambivalence): the father is necessary for protection, and so loved, but is also a danger to the mother's love. This situation, which is the basis of the Oedipus complex (the desire to kill the father, and sleep with the mother), comes to a resolution through castration anxiety: the child comes to fear this punishment from the father to such an extent (the anxiety is so unpleasurable) that he makes "peace" with the father by internalizing the

27 *FI*, 405.
28 *ILP*, 56.
29 *EI*, 13.
30 *ILP*, 56.

father's prohibitions—that is, by identifying himself with the father. This identification with the father leads to a repression of all the desires and wishes revolving around the Oedipus complex. It is a move into the "latency phase" of childhood, which is a desexualized phase, from around age five or six to puberty.

Norman Brown says that castration anxiety is ultimately fear of separation from the mother (fear of losing the instrument for reuniting with a mother-substitute).[31] We will come to see that, for Brown, the Oedipus complex and castration anxiety are not ultimately about sex and the loss of the penis, but about extinction or death. Although we will have to wait for this analysis until Chapters 5 and 6, it is important to understand that what is primarily at stake in the Oedipus complex is not, as Freud had thought, sexual desires: the issue is ultimately about mattering, significance, and meaning, though Freud was unable to recognize this because of his fixation on sexuality.[32]

Freud saw the formation of the superego as a consequence of the child's internal resolution of the Oedipus complex.[33] At first, the child only follows the rules and injunctions of the parents when in their presence—or in the presence of those who represent parental authority. Gradually, the child begins to comply with the parents' rules, even when the parents are not present. This is because the child "internalizes" the parents' prohibitions, and will punish himself or herself through the feelings of guilt and shame when breaking them. It is as if the child is saying, "See, you do not have to punish me for breaking your rules, I will punish myself."[34] The superego arises in this situation because of the intensity of the conflicts and feelings associated with the Oedipus complex: "The child, realizing its longing for the possession of each parent, finds itself in an intolerable conflict of loyalty, love, and hate. This confusion of feelings requires the development of a strong controlling mental agency [the superego], which in effect mutes or brings about repression of the urges towards the parents."[35]

---

31 Brown, 114–115.

32 I bring this up at this point so that the reader is aware that, even though one may disagree with the content of Freud's Oedipus complex (as indeed most people now do), it does not change the social theories that arise from it, and the power of their impact on our society. One is not, then, to throw out the socialized baby with the sexualized nature of the Oedipus complex as conceived by Freud.

33 Sandler, 174–175.

34 Ernest Becker, *The Birth and Denial of Meaning: An Interdisciplinary Perspective on the Problem of Man,* Second Edition (New York: Free Press Paperbacks, 1971), 56. Henceforth cited as *BD*.

35 Sandler, 175.

It is essential to note from this analysis that the superego is formed out of the id as our identification with the parents and the internalization of their prohibitions.[36] The superego is the substitute for the father; it is the ideal father internalized.[37] The internalization of the father extends externally to substitutes for the father, which include social authorities. The desire to be accepted and to fulfill the ideals of society is due to the identification of the father with the various authorities of society, whether institutional or from individuals (e.g., teachers, pastors, managers, etc.).

3 Conclusion

This is a brief and general explanation of the psyche as conceived by Freud. We find within this analysis the basis of what will become his social critique, which has had a profound influence on American culture, and provides the basis for modern cynicism and the triumph of the therapeutic (the combination of which I call the "cynical therapeutic"). We will see that it is in the relationship and interactions of the three parts of the psyche that our human world arises, as we struggle with the painful effects of the internal split and tensions of the psyche.

It is to this analysis we now turn, and in which we will discover the Freudian approach to defacing the currency. His analysis is so powerful that the cynics in society are no longer in an alienated minority, but are the majority within it. I will argue and attempt to show that this cynical consciousness is now the means by which we repress what really scares us about life and ourselves. It is what I will conceive of as a new means of sublimation.

---

36 "A portion of the external world has, at least partially, been given up as an object and instead, by means of identification, taken into the ego—that is, has become an integral part of the internal world. This new mental agency continues to carry on the functions which have hitherto been performed by the corresponding people in the external world; it observes the ego, gives it orders, corrects it and threatens it with punishments, exactly like the parents whose place it has taken. We call this agency the *super-ego* and are aware of it, in its judicial functions, as our *conscience*." (*OP*, 77).

37 *EI*, 18.

CHAPTER 4

Freud's Social Theory

1 The Implication of Freud's Psyche-Structure on Cultural Formation

1.1 The Irrationality of Morality

One of the most powerful aspects of Freud's social critique is that he described social morality as an irrational process. The super ego, and the surrender to cultural authorities, are founded and driven not by the ego or reason, but by the id and the internal workings of the Oedipus complex. This means that all social authority is irrational in its genesis.

Philip Rieff does an excellent job showing how radically different this understanding of morality and character are from the traditional view of morality, by distinguishing the three parts of the soul found in Plato's *Republic*, from those found in Freud.[1] In Plato's psychology, the *epithumios* or appetites is the part of the soul that seeks bodily satisfaction. The rational part of the soul, *nous*, is that which can grasp not only the external world, but the very order or *logos* of the universe, and so align itself with it. This rational part of the soul, then, is the moral part, and takes precedence over all the other aspects. The *thumios* is the spirited part of the soul, which provides passion for action, and can align itself either with the appetites or reason. The good life, in this psychology, is when the rational part of the soul (the part of the soul that can grasp the actual order of the cosmos through reason) rules over the psyche, using the passion or power of the spirited part of the soul in order to keep the appetites in line with the needs of the body. This is Plato's picture of an ordered soul, which leads to an ordered and virtuous life.

For Freud, the rational part of the soul (the ego) is that aspect of the soul that can align itself with either the id or the superego (it plays the part of Plato's spirited part of the soul): it is the mediator that seeks to keep both in harmony. The important insight Rieff demonstrates is that the moral aspect of the soul, the superego, is *not* a rational part of the soul, but is part of the rational—it arises from the id. Thus, morality is irrational for Freud. This

1 Philip Rieff, "Freudian Ethics and the Idea of Reason," *Ethics*, 67, no. 3, Part I (April 1957): 169–183.

 HTTPS://DOI.ORG/10.1163/9789004758148-006

means that morality does *not* guide us in life on a path necessary for maintaining a healthy psyche; on the contrary, according to Freud it is a significant source of mental pathology.

In traditional ethics, the goal is for the rational and moral aspect of the soul to rule over and guide the other aspects (even transform them), in order to create character and integrity in line with the order of the universe (*Logos*, God's will, Providence, and so forth). The person of character, whose psyche and life are in order, is the person who is living a good life, not "good" simply in the sense of "moral," but also in the sense of "pleasing" or "blessed"—that is, a life of flourishing and thriving. The person driven by her appetites, or by the desire to please others, is living a life of languishing, enslaved and oppressed by either the appetites or social pressure. Freud completely deconstructs this view of morality. Moral constraints are now seen as arbitrary and irrational prohibitions, created out of an anxiety stemming from infantile sexual desires, whose acceptance is based on authority rather than reason, and result in suffering and neurosis.

One impact of this change in the basis of morality is that we no longer view conscience as a guide to the good life, but as a cruel taskmaster, who is unable to be pleased, because it knows full well the desires we hold within; it *sees through* our actions to the motivations hidden from view, and ruthlessly punishes the ego with guilt, anxiety, depression, and the fear of punishment. Freud says, "The torments of conscience correspond precisely to a child's dread of losing his parent's love, a dread which has been replaced in him by the moral agency."[2] The conscience keeps us from fulfilling the primary purpose of the organism: the release of psychological tension by the satisfaction of our instinctual drives. As Freud puts it, "There is scarcely anything else in us that we so regularly separate from our ego and so easily set over against it as precisely our conscience. I feel the inclination to do something I think will give me pleasure, but I abandon it on the ground that my conscience does not allow it."[3]

Thus, the *moral* repression and abandonment of one's desires is not due to the reality principle,[4] which is focused externally for the sake of self-*preservation* (survival of the organism), but due to the superego, which is an

---

2 *OP*, 78.

3 *ILP*, 53.

4 For traditional ethics, the order of the universe is the ultimate reality, more real than what our senses experience. This means morality and reality are closely connected, so that the traditional ethics regards evil as abandoning reality for illusion—that is, abandoning the real order of the universe for the irrational order of the appetites or the "flesh".

internal mechanism related to *self*-preservation (preservation of one's sense of significance, meaning, and self-sufficiency).[5]

1.2 Sublimation

While the superego and society are very important for this movement toward repression or self-deception, it is in the concept of sublimation that the true nature of culture and civilization find their source and their justification. Sublimation allows for a modicum of satisfaction of instinctual drives, in that the libido becomes attached to the ego, and the ego can fulfill it in ways that are safely satisfied. Culture is the act of sublimation: "Sublimation of instinct is an especially conspicuous feature of cultural development; it is what makes possible for higher psychical activities, scientific, artistic or ideological, to play such an important part in civilized life."[6]

Sublimation is the binding and limiting of instinctual impulses, replacing the primary processes of the id with cultural activity (what Freud calls secondary processes). Sublimation is not a suspension of pleasure, as repression is in its strictest sense, but a substitution of libido-cathexis on behalf of the pleasure principle. Sublimation means the pleasure principle continues to dominate, even when it comes to culture.[7]

Sublimation is the desexualization of sexual aims. For instance, rather than giving into sexual aims whenever, wherever, and with whatever object one feels at the moment, the libido is taken up by the ego (taken from the object) and combined with other ways of fulfillment: monogamous sexual activity, artistic creations, etc. Culture and its conventions are essentially sublimations or a desexualization of the drives. The pattern of normal adult sexuality is not a natural (biological) necessity, but a cultural phenomenon or creation. Adult sexual organization is made possible by the social organization.[8] The resolution of the Oedipus complex results in the ego finding new directions of satisfaction of the libido—substitute, desexualized satisfactions.

What this means is that much of our highly valued cultural heritage, which we take so much pride in and gives us a sense of significance and mattering, is merely the working out of the Oedipus complex, and is acquired at the cost

5 Throughout this book I will be distinguishing between self-*preservation* and *self*-preservation. As noted, the former is about preserving the organism's existence, while the latter is about preserving its identity, sense of significance, and meaning.

6 *CID*, 44.

7 *PP*, 75–76.

8 Brown, 24.

of raw sexual fulfillment.[9] Therefore, the energy that drives culture is neither teleological nor eschatological (that is, not a continual progress toward "higher" forms of individual and social life, nor a healing and resolution of our problems which were too great for our primitive ancestors to deal with), but is a reformulation of the continual attempt to relive or re-experience the satisfactions felt as an infant at the mother's breast. For Freud, the superego and sublimation means that the so-called "higher" aspects of humans are nothing more than representations of our relation to our parents: "When we were little children we knew these higher natures, we admired them and feared them; and later we took them into ourselves."[10]

1.3 Defacing the Currency

Here we arrive at Freud's explanation of the cultural "currency," of which the ancient cynics were so critical. From Freud, we learn to think of it in terms of its genesis, what is driving or motivating it, and why people find it so difficult to be free from it. Culture is not totally arbitrary, but is bound to our human development, specifically the development of the superego, where the most potent desires for love, significance, and protection are placed within the human psyche. Yet, it is also based on self-deception (repression): all ideals are lies, a way of dealing with a "not having" or a "not being" one tries to overcome. If I cannot have it (possess it as an object), then I will be it (identify with it, and so act and think and be like it).

Culture, which includes all the ways in which human life has raised itself above animal conditions, turns out to be intricately connected to the animal we are.[11] On the one hand, culture includes all the knowledge and power humans have attained in order to master the forces of nature and win resources for the satisfaction of human needs (the ego's drive to self-preservation); on the other hand, it includes all the necessary arrangements whereby human relations with one another, and the distribution of attainable riches, may be regulated (superego ideals).[12]

Freud explains what the cynics felt about culture: our social selves, our relations with one another, and the parts we play in the various institutions of society are not primarily grounded in reality (the reality principle), but in irrationality (the id). Neither the ancient cynics nor Freud view culture

9 *OP*, 72.
10 *EI*, 18.
11 *FI*, 76.
12 *FI*, 77.

as progress, and Freud was able to show why civilization is not a movement toward becoming "better" humans: culture is not the work of reason in line with the supposed "moral" order of the universe, but "a child's super-ego is in fact constructed on the model not of the parents but of the parents' super-ego; the contents which fill it are judgements of value which have propagated themselves in this manner from generation to generation."[13] This means the so-called "higher" aspects of human nature associated with culture, of which the ancient cynics were so critical, are not moving toward anything "higher." It is the blind leading the blind.

Further, as the cynics recognized, the norms, values, and ideals of society do not move toward happiness, but lead to greater suffering. After millennia of trying to tame the repressed instincts, they remain as secure and as unyielding as ever. The unconscious remains faithful to the principle of pleasure, and this calls into question the psychological assumption upon which Western morality has been built—namely, that reason can transform, change, and enlighten the appetites. As Brown says,

> For two thousand years or more man has been subjected to a systematic effort to transform him into an ascetic animal. He remains a pleasure-seeking animal. Parental discipline, religious denunciation of bodily pleasure, and the philosophical exaltation of the life of reason have left man overtly docile, but secretly in his unconscious unconvinced, and therefore neurotic. Man remains unconvinced because in infancy he tasted the fruit of the tree of life, and knows that it is good, and never forgets.[14]

2 The Irredeemable Conflict of the Psyche

And so now, finally, we come to the outcome of Freud's view of the human psyche, and it is neither a pretty nor an optimistic picture that Freud has drawn for us. There is no victory over the conflict within the psyche, no end to its internal struggles. At best (and the best Freud could offer through psychoanalysis) is "coping." What does this situation look like? I will let Freud himself draw the picture:

> [W]e see this same ego as a poor creature owing service to three masters and consequently menaced by three dangers: from the external world, from the libido of the id, and from the severity of the super-ego. Three kinds of anxiety

13 *ILP*, 60.
14 Brown, 31.

> correspond to these three dangers, since anxiety is the expression of a retreat from danger.[15]

Again:

> Thus the ego, driven by the id, confined by the super-ego, repulsed by reality, struggles to master its economic task of bringing about harmony among the forces and influences working in and upon it; and we can understand how it is that so often we cannot repress a cry: "Life is not easy!"[16]

Life is not easy, not merely due to external challenges and burdens, but even more so due to internal struggles; as Freud makes clear in the first quote, the ego experiences its weakness in the pain of anxiety: the "realistic anxiety" of the world, the "moral anxiety" of the superego, and the "neurotic anxiety" of the id.[17]

It is important to note, however, that although Freud put much of the blame for this situation on the superego and culture, he remained ambivalent about culture. On the one hand, Freud believed that psychical pathologies were arising in his time because the traditional forms of sublimation it offered (especially through religion) were no longer working, and had, therefore, become the cause of neurosis. On the other hand, he did not believe that giving into the natural impulses was the answer: giving into the id would result in death and intense suffering for most of humanity. Freud seems to mirror the ambivalence toward culture that we saw in the child's ambivalence toward the father: both a danger and protector. The practice of psychoanalysis is ultimately the struggle to deal with the pain associated with this ambivalence.

I bring up the issue of ambivalence because it is crucial for understanding the nature and inconsistencies we will find in modern cynicism. Freud, like modern cynicism, is unable to see any alternatives from the way things are. Freud has shown the nature of self-deception and its intricate connection to culture (has *seen through* it, as modern cynicism has as well), and yet he does not believe we can give up this self-deception without severe consequences—consequences worse than the "disease" we now possess.

A dark and often neglected conclusion of Freudianism is that there is no rescue, no means for the ego to overcome its anxiety completely. The ego has become weakened due to the ineffectiveness of the traditional means of sublimation (the ego can no longer internalize the values and ideals of culture),

15 *EI*, 32.
16 *ILP*, 69.
17 *ILP*, 69.

and there is no moving back into the unconvincing "metanarratives" that made sublimation convincing. The best we can hope to do is strengthen the ego through the therapeutic process, but even this will leave the essential conflict within the psyche untouched—the analytic process does not heal, but helps one cope better with the inevitable struggles within the psyche, which continually badger the ego.

Freud was aware of what he called typical "palliative measures" the ego uses within its struggles (i.e., ways of dealing with pain without dealing with the cause), and viewed these palliative measures as the epitome of languishing in life, though still necessary and indispensable for carrying on. Freud writes,

> Life, as we find it, is too hard for us; it brings us too many pains, disappointments and impossible tasks. In order to bear it we cannot dispense with palliative measures. ... There are perhaps three such measures: powerful deflections, which cause us to make light of our misery; substitute satisfactions, which diminish it; and intoxicating substances, which make us insensitive to it. Something of the kind is indispensable.[18]

We deal with the difficulties of life by denying its difficulty (that is, through self-deception), and by labeling as "morbid" or pessimistic those who point out how life truly is. We are a culture built on substitute satisfactions, which include all the compensations within our consumer culture, the continual progress in technical products that divert us from reality about our lives, and the multiple ways we have to entertain ourselves. If these measures do not "work," we numb ourselves through various chemical means of intoxication.

It used to be that we could find our happiness in some grand purpose in life, which would give us a sense of personal value and significance, especially in relation to our suffering. Suffering, without some way of redeeming it, or by giving it meaning and significance, becomes unbearable. The internalization of the ideals and values of society through sublimation was, in an important sense, surrendering ourselves to "metanarratives" that felt meaningful, and so gave us a sense that the sacrifices we underwent for our morals and ideals were worth it in the end. It is not nearly as painful to sacrifice desires for something that is more fulfilling.[19] Once these metanarratives are gone, the sacrifice for their ideals becomes painful and difficult.

---

18 *CID*, 22.

19 Examples of this principle are all around us. For instance, it is not difficult to give up the desire to stay in bed when one is waking up to do something fulfilling, though it can be very painful to get up for a job one hates.

Freud abandons a return to this approach to life, thinking that we have grown up too much ever to become children again. He saw the attachment to grand narratives, especially concerning the idea of God, as infantile: an attempt to get back to the feeling of being loved and protected by our parents—God as our Daddy in heaven. Freud thinks metanarratives do not give us a true purpose connected to actual life; rather "what decides the purpose of life is simply the programme of the pleasure principle. This principle dominates the operation of the mental apparatus from the start."[20] But then, with typical Freudian ambivalence, he says that we should not simply give in to this programming: while the purpose of life is no doubt happiness in line with the pleasure principle, it is also clear that the pleasure principle's "programme is at loggerheads with the whole world, with the macrocosm as much as with the microcosm. There is no possibility at all of its being carried through; all regulations of the universe run counter to it."[21]

What a tragic conclusion: the very purpose of human life (pleasure) cannot be carried out, because the universe and our own nature run counter to it. This is a picture of tragic absurdity and despair: human beings seem to be some sort of cosmic screw-up, given desires that, when not satisfied, cause immense suffering, and of which there is no way of gaining any lasting satisfaction. The human being is an organism whose purpose runs at cross-purposes to the universe; this, it seems, is the very picture of languishing. However, it gets worse. Our happiness is not impeded merely by limitations from the visible universe, but also by our very own constitution: the happiness that comes through pleasure "is from its nature only possible as an episodic phenomenon. When any situation that is desired by the pleasure principle is prolonged, it only produces a feeling of mild contentment."[22] In other words, what initially brings pleasure eventually loses the ability to do so.

Culture is the means through which we seek rescue from this tragic situation, but its traditional approaches have lost their ability to rescue us. Culture's failure in this task leads us to the issue of neurosis—the symptoms of its failure. As we will see, Freud believed we are all neurotic,[23] though neurosis becomes pathological when it increases to a point where one can no longer easily and unconsciously take part in the sublimations provided by culture. Although we are all neurotic, neurosis becomes most problematic when an

20 *CID*, 23.

21 *CID*, 23.

22 *CID*, 23.

23 As Brown puts it: "Man the social animal is by the same token the neurotic animal," (Brown, 10).

individual *sees through* the conventions, values, and ideals of society to such an extent that she can no longer unconsciously take part in them.

What this means is that *the exile so crucial to the ancient cynics, which allowed them to be free from the* tuphos *of the cultural currency, is for Freud the very cause of pathological neurosis*. For the ancient cynics, due to their optimistic view of nature, exile was something positive, allowing for the freedom and self-mastery necessary for happiness. With Freud's pessimism, however, exile does not bring healing, but discloses the very neurotic state of human life that always exists. When moderns see through the cultural conventions and ideals, they do not become healed, but diseased.

3 Neurosis

3.1 The Lack of Internalizing Cultural Norms and Morality

Seeing through the conventions, morals, norms, and ideals of society does not, as with the ancient cynics, lead to freedom, self-mastery, and a sense of flourishing for modern denizens, but to constrictions, a contracting of the self, and a sense of languishing. The desire for happiness that humans desperately seek conflicts with the whole world in which they live. Both reality and the superego impose on human beings the necessity of renouncing pleasures; while reality frustrates, the superego punishes. The difficulty in knowing how to deal with the pleasure principle in relation to external reality is relatively easy to see, since the world is often in conflict with our attempts to find pleasure. The more puzzling question to answer is: Why are we not able to overcome the restrictions imposed by the superego once we have seen through the social conventions? Why do they still hold power over us when we have come to see their irrational basis, and the illusions that prop them up? Freud's view of depression or melancholia will allow us to see why this is the case.[24]

The suffering associated with depression and other mental disturbances is, for Freud, related to overly severe attacks of the conscience (the superego), as it abuses the weak ego, humiliates it, and threatens it with the most severe punishments. The reason the superego can do this is due to its attachment to the parents, whose love gave the ego a sense of esteem, worth, and protection. The superego draws upon these most central of human needs in order to threaten the ego into conformity with its ideals. The ego of a child fears the

24 *EI*, 27–30.

loss of love and acceptance from the parents, and as the need for love and acceptance turns inward as the superego, the child becomes her own punisher. Identification with the parents means that the child internalizes not only the parents' ideals, but also their threats. Thus, it is no longer necessary for others to tell us we are losers, worthless, and insignificant, because we will convince ourselves of this (through the superego). What is at the heart of depression, for Freud, is the superego's punishment: one is under a continual dark cloud of failure, which affects one's sense of personal worth; one feels like a loser, and that all one does is without meaning and significance. All of life's activities appear empty, meaningless, and a waste of effort.

This means that the psychological conflict that afflicts humans is not due to intellectual or rational issues, as it was for the ancient cynics (it is not a matter of rationally seeing through the mechanisms of *tuphos*), but to desires, wishes, and differing purposes in life, the unfulfillment of which is felt deeply within the psyche, decimating an individual's identity and sense of being "somebody." In other words, when addressing the superego, we are not merely dealing with an intellectual puzzle or riddle (though Freud partly saw it this way in terms of psychoanalytic therapy), but with dark longings that are a crucial aspect of human nature, and cannot be tamed or annihilated. All our attempts at harmony within the ego, a singleness of purpose and character that brings fulfillment, will ultimately fail. Even if we could act in line with cultural ideals, the superego is aware of the desires we repress, and so even our attempts to be better will be seen through as hypocrisy. Freud says that the drive to self-mastery through ethics,

> assumes that man's ego is psychologically capable of anything that is required of it, that his ego has unlimited mastery over his id. This is a mistake; and even in what are known as normal people the id cannot be controlled beyond certain limits. If more is demanded of man, a revolt will be produced in him or a neurosis, or he will be made unhappy.[25]

This all came to a head in Freud's time because cultural sublimation was no longer convincing, and so no longer worked as a sublimation of desires. Although the morality maintained a relative authority with the superego, the moral authority was less able to be internalized. This means the ego no longer had the help of culture, but was on its own to live up to the impossible demands.[26]

---

25 *CID*, 90.

26 The impact of this will become important as we look at the contradictions within the modern cynic.

3.2 "Normal" and "Abnormal" Neurosis

This can be more clearly understood when we realize that what we call neurosis or neurotic is not qualitatively different from the psychological conditions under which we all live. As we saw above, we are all neurotic. What makes someone pathologically neurotic is the *degree to which* her neurosis is individualized—that is, how much she is on her own. There is, then, "normal" neurosis and "abnormal" neurosis, so that to be "healthy" does not mean to be free from neurosis (that is, free from living a life of pretense based on self-deception and repression), but to have a socially acceptable and usable form of neurosis. Neurosis becomes pathological when the ego is no longer able to fulfill the tasks set for it by the external world and culture. A healthy neurotic can use the support and reinforcement of those around her to internalize the culture and sublimate the id's libido. Once one has seen through the support, however, one becomes alienated, exiled, and is left to carry the entire load by oneself (the entire conflict and struggle described above). Under this kind of pressure, the ego succumbs to pathological means of dealing with the inability to fulfill the pleasure principle.

For example, religion has been a cultural support for individuals. Freud argues that, while it may have helped in centuries past, it no longer convinces since so many people now see religion as an illusion. When this happened, religion became a hindrance rather than a help to mental health, as Freud saw over and over again in his psychoanalytic practice. Here is how Freud describes the social or normal neurosis of religion:

> Religion restricts this play of choice and adaptation, since it imposes equally on everyone its own path to the acquisition of happiness and protection from suffering. Its technique consists of depressing the value of life and distorting the picture of the real world in a delusional manner—which presupposes an intimidation of the intelligence. At this price, by forcibly fixing them in a state of psychical infantilism and by drawing them into a mass delusion, *religion succeeds in* sparing many people of individual neurosis.[27]

There are several things to take notice of in this quote.

First, Freud's description of social neurosis (the neurosis considered to be healthy) is a constriction of life that brings to a halt the individual's ability to flourish: there is an imposition from religion, a "depression" of the value of life,

---

27 *CID*, 31–32. (emphasis added).

and an intimidation that fixes people into a state of infantilism. It is important to understand that neurosis is, whether normal or abnormal, a limiting or constricting of life which closes off avenues for flourishing and thriving, and leads to languishing.

Second, as noted above, neurosis can be carried or handled when one has the support of those around one; the larger the support, the greater one's ability to manage in life with relatively few psychological symptoms. In other words, the greater the social support, the less the individual's psychological difficulties become manifest. It is when we see through the support and are exiled that neurosis becomes unworkable.

Thus, third, abnormal neurosis is "individual neurosis." Religion, for Freud, is a social obsessional ritual (which is neurotic), while abnormal neurosis is a private obsessional ritual. The religious person bows and kneels over and over during a service, prays the rosary dozens of times, falls over at the touch of a faith healer, and so forth; the neurotic washes her hands until they bleed, checks dozens of times to make sure the door is locked, and displays physical symptoms to fixate on.

As Rieff puts it, the pathological neurotics are rebels out of weakness rather than strength: they witness the inadequacies of cultural restraint, but are unsuccessful in their rebellion against this insight. They are defined as "unsuccessful," not because others are successful at living lives of flourishing, but because neurotics pay too high a price for their revolt: they turn their rebellion (exile), not against culture (as the ancient cynics did), but against themselves (self-alienation).

Neurosis is, Rieff says, the price one pays for the failure of normative authority. He says that Freud thought the extraordinary increase in neuroses "could only be understood … as the accompaniment to the failure of normative authority; it was the inevitable price mankind pays during the transition between waning moralities and the healthy indifference of science, as such, to all moralities."[28] The old supports are no longer supportive, and we have not yet created any new meaningful moral supports. In this time between, the ego is on its own, and it does not have the strength to support the pressure and conflict by its feeble power.

The pathologically neurotic are creating substitute compensations through abnormal ways of displacing the energy of repressed instincts. They are not viewed as unhealthy merely because they are destructive, but because they are

28 Philip Rieff, *Freud: The Mind of the Moralist* (New York: Viking Press, 1959), 305. Henceforth cited as *MM*.

too particular or individual.[29] One is deemed "normal" if one fixates on one's lawn, washes one's car on a daily basis, becomes anxious if not working sixty hours a week, shops for clothes to the point of maxing out one's credit cards, spends hours on social media, and follows every tweet and story about a celebrity. These fixations are viewed as normal (not unhealthy) only because so many others are doing the same, and value the same fixations. However, these are merely substitute gratifications, much like those of the unhealthy neurotic.

The sublimations, whether social or individual, are all in the service of self-deception, which hide the true problem lying irreconcilably within. For Freud, neurosis, and all mental illness, is about self-deception, which means that one can become healthier by overcoming these deceptions. If therapy can overcome the deceptions (a practice in which *parrhesia* becomes important, in the sense of the "free association" of the patient), then the pathological neurosis will be lightened: "When the riddle they hold is solved and the solution accepted by the sufferers these diseases will no longer be able to exist."[30] This leads to the issue of Freud's "cure."

3.3 The Therapeutic Process

The psychoanalytic therapeutic process will be examined in more detail in Chapters 15 and 16, though a general understanding of Freudian psychoanalysis, and its relation to *parrhesia*, will be given here. In terms of the analytic process itself, *parrhesia* is related to "free association," in which the patient is to let the mind wander at will and tell the analyst whatever comes to mind. While this view of *parrhesia* is more in line with the derogatory meaning given by Foucault, this free association of speech was thought eventually to lead to *parrhesia* in terms of freedom from dissimulation and deception in speech (that is, freedom from the need to deceive in speech).

Obviously, honesty is very important for *parrhesia*, as it is with psychoanalytic therapy. To speak of honesty for Freud is to be unrepressed, honest not only with others, but also with oneself (for one's dishonesty with others stems from one's dishonesty with oneself). The cost of abnormal neurosis is high, and the way to diminish it is to own up to who one is (the very thing the neurotic is so resistant to doing). This means owning up to one's instincts and

---

29 M. A. Casey, *Meaninglessness: The Solutions of Nietzsche, Freud, and Rorty* (Lanham: Lexington Books, 2002), 47–48.

30 Sigmund Freud, "The Future Prospect of Psychoanalytic Therapy," in *Collected Papers, Volume 2*, trans. Joan Riviere, 285–296 (New York: Basic Books, 1959), 292. Henceforth cited as *FP*.

desires: neurotics must "be honest, own up to the instincts that are at work in them, face the conflict, fight for what they want to go without, and the tolerance from the community, which is bound to ensue as a result of psychoanalytic knowledge, would help them in their task."[31]

The point of honesty, then, is about gaining self-knowledge. By self-knowledge, Freud means an increase in the ego's control over the libido. There is a lack of self-knowledge in repression, as the ego surrenders power and influence to the id and superego; this means it is constricted and hampered by the demands of unconscious desires (id) and guilt (superego).[32] As Freud says, psychoanalysis is "to strengthen the ego, to make it more independent of the super-ego, to widen its field of perception and enlarge its organization, so that it can appropriate fresh portions of the id. Where id was, there ego shall be."[33] Alternatively, as he says elsewhere, "Psycho-analysis is an instrument to enable the ego to achieve a progressive conquest of the id."[34] To overcome the repressed is to strengthen the ego, to allow the ego to gain more control over the id (over its repressed contents), and so allow for the release of the drives in a "healthy" manner. The ego is to have control over more and more of the psyche, rather than being unconsciously badgered by the repressed contents.

Freud gives an allegory of what freeing up of repressed contents can mean, both for the person and for society as a whole. He writes,

> Suppose that a number of ladies and gentlemen in good society had planned a picnic in an inn in the forest one day. The ladies make up their minds that if one of them wants to relieve a natural need she will say aloud that she is going to pick flowers; but a wicked fellow hears this secret and has printed on the programme which is sent around to the whole party—"If the ladies wish to retire they are requested to say that they are going to pick flowers." Of course after this no lady will think of availing herself of this flowery pretext, and other freshly devised formulas of the same kind will be seriously compromised by it. What will be the result? The ladies will own up to the natural needs without shame and none of the men will take exception of it.[35]

Not coincidentally, the "wicked fellow" in the allegory sounds a bit like Diogenes, creating a means of defacing the currency, and forcing people to live

---

31 *FP*, 294.
32 *OP*, 42.
33 *ILP*, 71.
34 *EI*, 32.
35 *FP*, 294.

without dissimulation or pretext. In the allegory, people are forced to be who they are, with all their natural needs and desires, which society has deemed unseemly. Once we destroy the deception that these natural needs are unseemly, the individual is free to partake in them without shame. This freedom is what Freud believes can happen in the psychoanalytic process with the patient, and, if psychoanalysis were accepted enough by society, within society as a whole.

There are, however, resistances set up to this by the ego, because it lacks the courage to face itself as it is. In Chapter 15 we will examine in more detail how these resistances can be overcome, but it is important at this point to understand the most general way they are overcome in psychoanalytic treatment, since it shows what it means for the ego to gain control of the repressed contents.

The resistances are overcome in the therapeutic process through *transference*. In transference, the patient transfers the authority of her superego to that of the analyst.[36] In this transfer of authority, the analyst takes on the function of the parental authority from the patient's past, and so substitutes both for the initial relationship with the parents (out of which the superego gained authority), and the social authorities in the patient's life—such as, teachers, pastors, bosses, and so forth.

There are two things that happen in transference. First, the analyst becomes a support for the weakened ego as it seeks to face what it has been anxious about for most of its life. Remember, the neurotic is a person who has lost support, and is trying to deal with the repressed contents on her own. In therapy, the analyst becomes this authority, not in order to maintain control over the patient, but in order to release the patient from the irrational psychical phenomena that led to this need for authority figures in life (the need to be loved, accepted, and protected).

This leads to the second thing that happens: by working through the irrational relation of transference toward the analyst, the patient can use the rational part of the psyche (the ego) to rework its way through the Oedipus complex (Freud sometimes calls this the process of "re-education"). The vulnerable child did not have the analytical tools to think through a resolution of the Oedipus complex, but resolved it through the irrational anxiety of castration. As an adult, the patient can work through the same feelings he once had for his parents, but with his analyst, to whom he has transferred the same feelings and desires. In this way, the repressed content is allowed to be admitted (the

36 *OP*, 47.

irrational contents of the Oedipus complex are faced and acknowledged, as is the general sexual nature of all one's actions), and can be dealt with by a strengthened ego.

This is ultimately to deface the currency, not only of culture but of the superego as well (though there is hardly a distinction between the two). There is a partial exile, but this time in terms of more freedom for the ego to become master of its desires, and satisfy them rationally and in a healthy manner. The result is authenticity and self-honesty, which falls in line with *parrhesia*. However, we must remember that, unlike the optimism of the ancient cynics, or the hope within religion, there is no full healing for the patient (or any human). What psychoanalytic therapy accomplishes, is giving the patient more power to deal with the continual and irredeemable struggle of being human. Freud does not provide a way of resolving the neurosis, but of dealing with it in the healthiest manner possible.

4 Conclusion

Freud's social theories, which grow from his analyses of his patients' failures to internalize their cultural ideals and morality (a failure of sublimation), show that the movement from defacing the currency to exile is not as smooth for modern individuals as it was for the ancient cynics. The stress and tension of carrying the conflict within the psyche had become too much for Freud's patients. His patients were thrust back upon their own resources, without recourse to any newly formulated ideals, such as the optimistic view of nature upon which the ancient cynics drew. The exile was partial, a rebellion out of weakness rather than strength, as Rieff put it.

In the next chapter, we will discover that Freud's fixation on sexual repression misses the true nature of this rebellion, and the impact it has on the weakening of the ego. While Freud is able to show the connection between repression and culture, he is mistaken about the true content of the repressed. In other words, Freud is mistaken about what it is that culture is helping us deny. He is correct in seeing that the conflict is between nature and culture, but narrows "nature" down to "sexual," and so misses what it is about being animals that really makes us anxious. It is to this more accurate content of the repressed that we now turn.

CHAPTER 5

Ernest Becker: Rethinking Freud

1 The Peculiar Human Bind

Humans are caught in a peculiar bind. On the one hand, they are aware of their uniqueness as individuals, which is accompanied by a sense that their lives matter and have meaning. They have the potential to bring something to the world that has never existed. Each person, in himself or herself, is a "one and only," something that has never existed, and will never exist again. On the other hand, reality (evidence and facts) appears to show the ultimate insignificance of human life and its meaninglessness.[1] For instance, death not only brings our lives to an end, but time takes away all we have done: the ripples of our lives—its impacts and effects—eventually go flat. As Arthur Schopenhauer has said, "That which *has been* exists no more; it exists as little as that which has *never been*."[2] No doubt, there is a small percentage of humans whose ripples outlast their lives, but for the vast majority of us, we die in obscurity, and the earth is no different for us having been on it. Perhaps we have had children, and we will turn up on some future Ancestory.com account, but eventually the ripples of humanity itself will go flat, a mere blip on the cosmic radar.

The unique problem for humans, of course, is not that they are caught in this bind (all organisms are caught in this bind), but that they can become aware of this: we can consciously recognize, while in the midst of doing something costly and sacrificial (is not forty hours a week of one's life a sacrifice), that all the sacrifice is ultimately for nothing, and will come to nothing—will disappear as if it had never been done.[3] We are living the Myth of Sisyphus. Sisyphus, after death, was given a task by the gods. He was to roll a rock up a mountain, and just as he reached the top, the rock would become unsteady and roll back down the mountain. He was to go back down, and roll his rock back up the mountain, which would again become unsteady and roll back down. This is what Sisyphus is to do for all eternity. Was Sisyphus being rewarded or punished for his life on earth? The obvious answer is that this was his punishment: all that sacrifice and toil comes to nothing. Our lives are not

1 *BD*, 141.

2 Arthur Schopenhauer, *The Works of Arthur Schopenhauer: The Wisdom of Life and Other Essays* (Roslyn: Walter J. Black, 1932), 231.

3 *BD*, 141.

 | HTTPS://DOI.ORG/10.1163/9789004758148-007

unlike this myth, as they all end in bankruptcy, where all our investments and sacrifices come out to zero on the ledger of life. This awareness makes life feel meaningless.

What does it mean to say that life *feels* meaningless? Think about a movie you have watched that turned out to make no sense. As you were watching the movie, it was chaotic and random, though you hoped that all the random parts would make sense (be meaningful) in the end. But they did not. There is nothing that connected each individual scene to the others. The scenes were aimless and chaotic, merely random incidents, rising up from out of nowhere, and then disappearing back into the void. What does it feel like as you walk out of the theater? That you wasted your money and your time? You may have felt unsettled in some way. If that is what meaninglessness feels like in terms of something as unimportant as a movie, imagine when that "movie" is one's own life: the feeling of "waste," and the unsettledness, is magnified. It is no wonder we do not want to think deeply about whether our lives are ultimately meaningless.

It is this feeling, and the self-contradiction it creates, that drives humans—with varying degrees of consciousness.[4] We are driven in life, most often unconsciously, to find ways not to despair and become hopeless. How we deal with this drive determines whether we will flourish or languish in life, whether we will be healthy or ill. We have already seen this contradiction at work in Freud's theories, and have seen how it relates to his understanding of mental health. The self-contradiction arises, for Freud, in terms of the intrapsychic conflict between the pleasure principle (id), the constraints of conscience (superego), and the demands of the reality principle. For Freud, as we have already seen, the conflict is ultimately between what we might call "nature" and "culture." What determines the mental health of the individual is how the ego goes about finding something to lean on, which provides a sense of balance amid these conflicting demands. When what we repress in terms of our nature cannot be efficiently sublimated by culture, we begin to languish, and our neurosis become pathological or abnormal.

The anthropologist Ernest Becker accepts Freud's view that we live in self-deception, and that the nature of repression stems from our need (felt as anxiety) to repress what makes us uncomfortable; however, Becker disagrees with Freud about what it is we are generally repressing. For Freud, the focus is on the sexual desires connected to our parents (the pleasure principle); for Becker, the main issue we are repressing is our "creatureliness": our frailty,

---

4 *BD*, 141–142.

vulnerability, powerlessness, helplessness, insignificance, and the fact that all our lives end in death. The title of his most famous work gets to the core of this repression: *The Denial of Death*.

What is most important to humans is that we matter in some way. Freud recognized this desire as well, though he believed it was a secondary process, stemming from our relationship with our parents, without whose approval we would be thrust out into danger and ultimately death. For Freud, our desire to matter (to be of value, have significance) stems from this early need for acceptance from our parents. Becker agrees that the relationship with our parents is an important aspect of this issue, but he thought Freud's fixation on the sexual element as the core of the primary process kept Freud from recognizing the importance of his analysis. The central need driving the human organism is not sexual, but the need to experience the acceptance, safety, and ultimately the sense of control that comes with these early parental relationships. We will see that this gives a very different focus when it comes to the cynical issues of defacing the currency, exile, and *parrhesia*.

An important thesis I am presenting in this book is that modern cynicism is not simply (or even primarily) an intellectual and rational critique of society (a *seeing through* the hypocrisy and *tuphos*), but is a particular manner of seeking to resolve the conflict between nature and culture, though one which only makes the situation worse. As we have already seen, Sloterdijk has defined modern cynicism with the paradoxical phrase "enlightened false consciousness." What is so fascinating about modern cynicism is that its false consciousness or self-deception is intimately connected to its enlightened consciousness—with its having seen through the deceptions of others, the deceptions of institutions, and traditional views of the world. Seeing through these deceptions has not freed the cynic from her self-deception, but only made it more entrenched. By examining Becker's analysis of this conflict between nature and culture, we will gain a better grasp of what is at work within modern cynicism as enlightened false consciousness, a consciousness which remains in conflict with itself.

Modern cynicism, together with the triumph of the therapeutic, are particular ways people seek to work out the contradiction of trying to matter in a universe where human life ultimately appears to be insignificant. They are a particular means of self-deception, and the attempt to keep the anxiety associated with this contradiction from arising. Given the growth of anxiety in America, it is worth examining whether these two approaches to life are not merely failing us, but making matters worse. Examining Becker's analysis of this general bind, and the part culture plays in it, will give us a better perspective of how cynicism is failing us.

2 Nature

2.1 The Repression of Creatureliness

We are not primarily repressing and deceiving ourselves about our sexual wishes for our mothers and hatred of our fathers; rather, we are repressing the reality of what it means to be an animal organism on this planet. Becker writes,

> Man is reluctant to move out into the overwhelmingness of this world, the real dangers of it; he shrinks back from losing himself in the all-consuming appetites of others, from spinning out of control in the clutching and clawing of men, beasts, and machines. As an animal organism man senses the kind of planet he has been put down on, the nightmarish, demonic frenzy in which nature has unleashed billions of individual organismic appetites of all kinds—not to mention earthquakes, meteors, and hurricanes, which seem to have their own hellish appetites. Each thing, in order to deliciously expand, is forever gobbling up others.[5]

What we deny is what Becker calls our *creatureliness*. We break, burn, and tear easily, and so our time on this planet is short and fraught with dangers. Although our society has moved far beyond the repression of sexuality that Freud witnessed toward the end of the Victorian Era, this freedom from sexual repression has not freed us from anxiety, nor has it strengthened our ego to cope better with life. This is because sexuality was never the main drive we were repressing. What we are afraid to look closely at is our creatureliness.[6]

In reflecting on the pages to come in this chapter, I am well aware that many people will view this analysis as unnecessarily morbid. However, the picture Becker draws of the human animal is not a creation of his imagination, but something we are all familiar with from reading newspapers and watching the news on television, which serve as daily reminders of our creatureliness.[7] Creatureliness is about our helplessness against the fundamental problems we face in life. We may be able to prolong life a couple of decades, but we cannot

5 Ernest Becker, *The Denial of Death* (New York: Free Press Paperback, 1973), 53–54. Henceforth cited as *DD*.

6 "*Consciousness of death* is the primary repression, not sexuality" (*DD*, 96).

7 As Blaise Pascal puts it, "Imagine a number of men in chains, all under sentence of death, some of whom are each day butchered in the sight of others; those remaining see their own condition in that of their fellows, and looking at each other with grief and despair await their turn. This is an image of the human condition." Blaise Pascal, *Pensées*, trans. A. J. Krailsheimer (Baltimore: Penguin Books, 1966), 165.

overcome death itself. The very fact that we seek to extend life shows that we do not want to die, and yet we seem to hide this terror from ourselves. We think of death in theoretical terms, as something we admit happens, but happens to others. We tend to believe that it is a waste of time, and that it is useless to think about our own deaths. If it is inevitable, so the thinking goes, what good can come from reflecting on it? However, when creatureliness becomes real (especially in relation to death), we see through all these rationalizations.

In the short documentary *Being 97*, the philosopher Herbert Figarette, author of several books, one of which is *Death: Philosophical Soundings*, reflects on what he argued in this book, and how his view has changed in the intervening twenty years, now that he is ninety-seven years old. He says,

> In the book about death, what I said in a nutshell: there's no reason to be afraid or concerned of anything about death, because when you die, there's nothing. You're not gonna suffer, you're not gonna be unhappy, you're not going to … well, you just, you, you are not going to be. I mean at a certain point, there's nothing. So it's not rational to be afraid of death.
>
> I now think that is not a good statement. Because, I think it's important to figure out why it is, then, that people are afraid of death. Why am I concerned about it? My argument was, there's no good reason for it. My sense of realism tells me, "Well, no good reason or not, it's something that haunts me … the idea of dying soon."
>
> I often walk around the house, and I ask myself—often out loud: What is the point of it all? There must be something I'm missing in this argument. I wish I knew.[8]

Yes, there must be something we are missing, something we cannot grasp, something we cannot wrap our minds around, something our rationality cannot fathom. This is unsettling to us, because it is a sign of our lack of self-grounding and self-sufficiency. Because this reality is so uncomfortable, we do not think about it; or if we do, we think about it in a way that moves away from true self-knowledge into an abstract and objective thinking that keeps our actual lives (that we will die) at arm's length. However, Figarette's "sense of realism" made him face the haunting and uncanny reality of death—his death.

Life (every single day) takes on a different hue and significance when we truly understand our days are limited. Reflection on our creatureliness, of which death is but one aspect, changes our focus, bringing clarity to the *real*

8 Andrew Hasse, *Being 97*. *Vimeo*. 275760948. June 19, 2018, https://vimeo.com/275760948.

problems we are facing. We spend our lives hiding those haunting problems, focusing on pet projects that are illusions of significance and importance. No matter how hard we work on the surface problems of our lives, we are not addressing the problem of our essential nature; when this essential problem is not addressed, we keep coming back around to the same issues: poverty, war, hunger, injustice, cruelty, brutality, oppression—all the ways we bring suffering upon others. Sometimes the *tuphos* lifts, and we awaken from the plodding and automatic way we wander through life; it is then we discover that thinking about death and our creatureliness is not useless, because the question is not whether we can change death (we cannot), but how reflecting on death can change us.

2.2 The Ancient Cynics, Freud and Becker on Nature

Reflecting on our creatureliness is ultimately thinking about our place in nature and the cosmos. Here we run into a disagreement with the ancient cynics, who held nature up as the measure for a happy and good life. Nature in general, as well as human nature in particular, were viewed by the ancient cynics as the grounds for a good life; it consists of a simple and uncomplicated approach to life, not requiring self-consciousness because it is not artificial (humans become self-conscious when they need to think about how to be "artificial"—that is, how to pretend to be someone and something other than they are). While they did not shy away from the *tukhe* or "fortune" associated with nature, they viewed it as less problematic than trying to live according to the arbitrary demands associated with culture.

The cynics, Freud, and Becker differ in their views of nature, and what it means for humans to be animals. These differences impact how each interprets the significance and meaning of culture. In order to examine their different views on human nature, we can look at something as necessary and natural as the bowel movement.

Diogenes relieved himself physically at will: he would defecate whenever and wherever he felt the need. This was a kind of *parrhesiastic* action, a sign or "communication" that he was not ashamed of what is natural; he was defacing the cultural currency around this most basic of human actions. He wanted to show how strange it is to be ashamed of an act that every human being must do. As we saw with Swift in regards to bowel movements, the cry "O Celia, Celia, Celia shits," is a lament over having seen through the illusion of who Celia truly is: a creature out of whom comes foul and disgusting excretions. According to the ancient cynics, this is nothing to be ashamed of, because it is a natural and ordinary part of life, something each of us regularly does. When one reflects on it, it seems a strange thing to be ashamed of and seek to hide from others. We feel shame, however, because of the illusion created by culture—an illusion that took Celia five hours to create.

Freud discusses bowel movements in terms of the anal stage of development. This stage takes place during the toddler years, when the child is toilet trained—which is a cultural activity, not something nature necessitates. During this phase, in keeping with Freud's fixation on sexuality, the anus becomes the primary focus of the libido or pleasure. The child gains pleasure from both giving into the bowel movement and controlling it. This is a time of socialization, when the child is controlling what is "natural" for the sake of acceptance and love from the parents. Thus, like it is for the ancient cynics, the process of socialization around bowel movements is an artificial process, something whose basis does not arise from nature, but the arbitrary ideas of human value.

Freud used this theme in his allegory for the process of psychoanalytic treatment, as we saw in the last chapter. Freud believed that by seeing through the artificial to the natural (that is, by making the deception "I'm going to pick flowers" useless), we would gain more control for the ego, and so become more psychologically healthy. We also saw, however, that Freud remained ambivalent toward giving into nature: while bowel movements are nothing of which to be ashamed, they also are not anything of which to be proud. The natural, in other words, is not to be raised up as an ideal for humans, as is the case with the ancient cynics. Freud recognized plenty of dangers associated with the natural human desires within us, as well as the natural world outside of us.

For Becker, anality takes on a very different sense, because of what bowel movements say about human beings: we cannot transcend our strange and fallible bodies, which come with demands beyond our ability ultimately to control.[9] For Freud the anal phase represents a particular focus for the libido; for Becker it points to an ontological neediness we would like to cover up and hide. It represents the fact that each individual is nothing *but* body, so far as nature is concerned: "Once admit that you are a defecating creature and you invite the primeval ocean of creature anxiety to flood over you."[10] The anal phase is not about sexual libido, but about control over nature, about not being ruled by nature, something to which the cynics acquiesced. To admit that we are nothing *but* nature is to admit that we are nothing, nobodies—just one among billions of other human organisms on a planet with countless other organisms, rising up for a while, and then sinking back down into oblivion. Ultimately, the

9 *DD*, 30–31.
10 *DD*, 87.

anal phase represents the illusion of our purity, value, and importance. Becker points this out, quoting Montaigne:

> As Montaigne put it, on the highest throne in the world man sits on his arse. Usually this epigram makes people laugh because it seems to reclaim the world from artificial pride and snobbery and to bring things back to egalitarian values. But if we push the observation even further and say men sit not only on their arse, but over a warm and fuming pile of their own excrement—the joke is no longer funny. The tragedy of man's dualism, his ludicrous situation, becomes too real. The anus and its incomprehensible, repulsive product represents not only physical determinism and boundness, but the fate as well of all that is physical: decay and death.[11]

The anal phase, and culture in general, is about control over nature, about rising above and transcending the merely natural, and hiding the things that would make us face our creatureliness. To give into nature is not, as the ancient cynics had believed, a victory. The ancient cynics were not moving toward authenticity in their "natural" lifestyles. If they were totally honest, they would have to admit that their "giving into nature" was only possible because of the *tuphos* all around them, which allowed them the "freedom" to follow the "natural" life. They were able to live "naturally" only because other people were living culturally organized lives, and in this way carrying many of the ways nature must be tamed and domesticated in order for human life to flourish. Without culture they would not have had easy access to the food for which they begged, and would be in continual danger for their lives: they would not freely be defecating in the marketplace, but would need continually to be watching their backs while in that vulnerable position.

To be anal is, for Becker, trying extra-hard to protect oneself against the accidents of life, and the dangers of death.[12] This gets at the heart of the ambivalence Freud felt concerning culture: as much as Freud viewed civilization as contrived and full of illusions, built not from the ground of rationality but out of the irrational desires of the id, he also recognized that individual human lives would not last long without it, and their lives would be filled with anxiety, suffering, and the ever-present burden of merely staying alive. This ambivalence is a statement about human life in relation to the world, and the sheer nonsense of creation: "to fashion the sublime miracle of the human race," the

---

11 *DD*, 31.

12 *DD*, 32–33.

beauty and wonder of women and men, "and to combine it with an anus that shits! It is too much."[13]

Anality is but one example of the underlying creature anxiety, which comes from the ludicrous nature of what it means to be a self-conscious animal: "It means to know that one is food for worms. This is the terror: to have emerged from nothing to have a name, consciousness of self, deep inner feelings, an excruciating inner yearning for life and self-expression—and with all this to die. It seems like a hoax."[14] For Becker, it discloses the emptiness and meaninglessness of all we do. We rise up for a while, spend decades gaining some sort of organization for our lives, only to become a form of organic waste on this planet. This is what we repress, and against which we build our defenses. If we genuinely faced this reality, we would find it impossible to function.

Several years ago, I was discussing defense mechanisms with a psychology instructor where I teach. At one point she said that what used to be called a "nervous breakdown" (that point at which it becomes impossible for a person to function) is when a person's defense mechanisms no longer work for them. I was astonished by the reality of this statement: when humans begin to see life without self-deception, the terror of the reality in which they live becomes overwhelming for them. We cannot function without an ability to deceive ourselves about life. For Becker, culture is the means by which we are able to deceive ourselves.

2.3 Anxiety and Culture

Culture is our defense against who we are, and addresses a central issue in life: our inability to accept our creatureliness. Our basic creatureliness creates anxiety, not merely because of the dangers associated with our helplessness, but also because it brings into question our sense of value and worth.

Anxiety is the feeling one has when thinking about or dwelling on an ambiguous danger. Kierkegaard, in his insightful and influential book, *The Concept of Anxiety*, differentiates fear from anxiety or dread (*Angst*): fear has an object, while anxiety does not. As a teacher, if someone were to walk into my classroom brandishing a gun, I would feel fear; however, if every day I worried about someone possibly walking into my classroom with a gun, I would feel anxiety. Fear has an actual concrete object, and so one has an object to fight against (or run from). There is no real object with anxiety, but it is a dread of what is possible, of what could be "on its way": we are anxious about the unknown.

---

13 *DD*, 33–34.
14 *DD*, 87.

Fear, then, arises due to something separate from us (something that is not a part of our own consciousness); anxiety, however, arises due to our own self-consciousness or thoughts. This means that in fear we struggle with something else, while in anxiety we struggle with ourselves. Anxiety is often much more difficult for humans to bear than fear. One sees this in instances where a person stays within an abusive relationship: the fear of the abusive person is often accepted over the anxiety of the unknown if one walks away from the relationship. Or, the sense of relief that can come with even a difficult diagnosis for symptoms one had been suffering with for months or years—at least now one has something one can fight against.

The primary function of the ego, according to Freud, is to help the organism avoid creature anxiety, and Becker holds to this view as well.[15] Freud's analysis of early childhood development is concerned with the child's attempts to deny the anxiety of the child's emergence: the child's anxiety over losing support, of having to stand alone, helpless, and afraid.[16] The danger anxiety is concerned about is object-loss: the loss of those objects the child depends on for protection and acceptance.[17] Object-loss is related to the feeling of helplessness and vulnerability in a world that is full of dangers, strange modes of behavior, and the ever-present knowledge that one can make those on whom one depends unhappy. The child deals with this uncontrollable anxiety by placing it in the ego: it takes the anxiety that is due to possibilities in the world and places it upon the ego to deal with, thereby gaining control over it. Freud's theory of neurosis is the study of how the child comes to control anxiety.[18]

Anxiety is controlled by the child's conduct, which is the ego's responsibility in the psyche. It can control the potential dangers it faces and imagines, not only by how it adjusts to situations, but also by how it *perceives* the world, others, and itself. The ego's task is to navigate the world without anxiety, and it does this by choosing the actions that are satisfying to it, in terms of bringing praise rather than blame from its parents.[19] Further, it handles anxiety by narrowing the world through restrictions. Becker writes,

> The historic value of Freud's work is that it came to grips with the peculiar animal that man was, the animal that was not programmed by instincts to close off perception and assure automatic equanimity and forceful action. Man had to

15 *BD*, 17.
16 *BD*, 66.
17 *BD*, 43.
18 *BD*, 43. I did not make this point explicitly earlier, but a weakened ego is an anxious ego.
19 *BD*, 78–79.

> invent and create out of himself the *limitation of* perception and equanimity to live on this planet.[20]

In other words, we do not have instincts that narrow down what we need to pay attention to in this world, but must, in a sense, create our own world—that is, define what is of value, and so worth paying attention to. A child does this in two main ways: by learning and adapting to expectations from the parents, and building defense mechanisms that protect it by restricting the world.

First, it learns and adapts to the expectations of the parents. It learns the rules for safety that are established through interaction with parents.[21] Socialization means that the child's natural urges are blocked, urges that are related to the feelings and actions of flourishing. No doubt, sometimes this blockage is for the child's own good (safety from actual dangers, learning self-control and discipline); however, more often the interference takes place because of the parents' anxieties, irritabilities, and tempers. The child must wash her hands because the *parents* fear germs; the parents prevent her from stepping into the garden because the *parents* like flowers; the parents prevent her from jumping on the bed because of *their* anxieties.[22]

The child is learning to earn support by renouncing action and satisfaction: the child is not making her own closure, or narrowing the world by her own passions, but the parents are putting it upon her. She gives into these renunciations for the sake of keeping anxiety from arising.[23] Since this capitulation is against the child's will, and is for reasons the child does not understand, the capitulation can be accomplished only by repression.[24]

Second, the child builds defense mechanisms to protect it by restricting the world. In other words, the child's ego develops by skewing perceptions of the world.[25] The most general of these are *denial* ("That's not happening to me. I don't want that"), *projection* ("That person is thinking these vulgar thoughts, not me") and *repression* ("That did not occur").[26]

As we noted above, all these restrictions are a way of narrowing experiences for humans. Animals have instincts that narrow their perception and interaction with the world; humans do not have these instincts, and so the world is narrowed for them through socialization. Without this narrowing, the world

---

20 *DD*, 51. (emphasis added).
21 *BD*, 47–48.
22 *BD*, 58.
23 *BD*, 58.
24 Brown, 25.
25 *BD*, 55.
26 *BD*, 55.

would be too much for the human animal to handle, and it would live in continual and intense anxiety from all the dangers it can perceive, remember, and imagine. The child must, as Becker says, learn to take little bites.[27] Becker likens the child to a "prodigy in limbo," who buys freedom from anxiety with a price:

> In both halves of his experience [nature and culture] he is dispossessed, yet impressions keep pouring in on him and sensations keep welling up within him, flooding his body. He has to make some kind of sense out of them, establish some kind of ascendancy over them. Will it be thoughts over body, or body over thoughts? Not so easy. There can be no clearcut victory or straightforward solution of the existential dilemma he is.[28]

Thoughts will attempt to win out over body in this struggle, because the need for value and significance is the strongest and most basic need for humans. The child attempts to surrender the needs of the body in order to gain the acceptance of the parents. This dynamic does not end with childhood, however, but is at work in adults as well.

3 Conclusion

We see that the peculiar bind humans face as self-conscious animals is connected to the judgments they continually make about the meaning and worth of all they do, and their lives as a whole. Although it is a central concern for all of us, few of us ever consciously think about this issue, which should strike us as strange. The reason for our unwillingness to confront this issue is that we are worried about the answer we will come to. The evidence all around us is that our lives are fragile and vulnerable, and that we are all ultimately insignificant. We cannot face this reality. Indeed, those who do face it will often not even bother to get out of bed, because nothing they will need to do that day is worth the sacrifice.

I will now turn to examine this need for meaning more deeply. It is a strange phenomenon when one begins to think through it. It most likely arises from our ability to assess and judge what is of value in life. Eating of the tree of the knowledge of good and evil truly may be a curse for humans, as we judge whether anything we do is worth the trouble. We will find that culture saves us from the anxiety we feel when having to think about such things.

---

27 *DD*, 23.

28 *DD*, 28.

CHAPTER 6

The Human Need for Meaning

1 Significance and the Cultural Heroics

1.1 Our Need for Meaning

From our animal nature we have a sense of wanting our lives to continue perpetually. In our attunement toward the world, we have a restlessness for more, a sense of being individual and set apart from the objects in the world for something unique and significant, a desire for fulfillment and joy. We are also conscious of our self in this entire process: we are able to evaluate and measure what we do (seeing some things as more significant and meaningful than other things), to expand our desire into the future through hope, and to relate to all of this symbolically. We want to be something rather than nothing, to matter rather than be disposable—a mere replaceable organism. We feel this most powerfully in those times when others have disrespected us, treated us unjustly, or when others simply ignore us.

This primordial desire for meaning and significance causes us to feel vulnerable, not only in terms of our physical safety and security, but also in terms of the security of our identities (our self-esteem). Our "natural" identity is simply as one of the innumerable organisms on this planet, living out our lives in general obscurity and insignificance; in contradistinction to this, there is our sense of significance and meaning, which finds fulfillment in culture. The narrowing or self-contraction of socialization plays itself out in this dualism of nature and culture. The physical and psychical protection we first gain from our parents we later acquire from culture.

Freud correctly understood that there is an energy or force at the root of the human psyche, and that it is the basis of all human activity—and is the ground of culture—often driving us unconsciously. He mistakenly thought the energy or force was sexual in nature, connected to the libido. Instead, the energy is the need for self-esteem, to matter, that one's life is meaningful, and that this significance is durable and lasting (that is, it outlasts even our own natural lives). This is the energy that is responsible for human culture: our desire to be objects of value in the universe.[1]

1 *BD.*

 | HTTPS://DOI.ORG/10.1163/9789004758148-008

Culture does this by producing what Becker calls a "symbolic hero system." Our creatureliness is repressed and sublimated into a cultural heroic. In other words, the anxiety we feel due to our creatureliness does not have to be felt when we throw ourselves into a cultural heroic—something that makes us feel significant and in control.

In this view, sublimation is about identifying ourselves with a cosmic process, a "metanarrative," something that takes our obscure individual lives, and makes them significant by being a unique part of something larger and lasting. Brown calls this an "objective dependence," and it stems from the child's anxiety over separation from the mother, and the need to be loved.[2] Freud viewed this desire as a form of narcissism, and our significance as an illusion—which is why he looked past it to the seemingly more natural sexual instincts. Freud viewed himself as part of a movement of thought that is to bring an end to this *hubris* of significance: in Copernicus we discover that we are not the center of the universe; with Darwin, that we are not the highest point of life on earth; with Freud, we are not even masters of our own psyches.

1.2 Our Lack of Meaning: Nihilism

The motive for being a part of a cosmic process comes from the individual's horror of isolation, of being thrust back upon her feeble energies, of not being in control of her own safety and esteem. We desire to be a part of something larger than our own little, insignificant self; we long for the ripples of our lives to continue, for the rocks we roll up the mountain to stay and be a permanent memorial of our lives. What struck me most forcefully when my father died, however, was how the world just went on as if nothing had happened, not even registering the loss. I have had this same sensation at the death of colleagues and friends. If the world can continue as if nothing happened when one has died, is not Freud right about our sense of importance—that it is merely a narcissistic illusion?

This issue is much more complex and dialectical than Freud saw. There is, of course, a way of looking at this need for self-esteem as a narcissistic tendency, as a *hubris* that we should overcome. However, this does not mean that there is nothing significant in human life. There may indeed be dignity to human life, something sacred and important about each person. But it is also clear that this need for self-esteem can become not only questionable, but pointed to as the basis for many problems that have stricken humanity throughout its

2 Brown, 2.

history. At this point in the analysis, however, we will stick with what is the case: this need is our deepest passion, and culture has grown out of our need for esteem and worth. There is no doubt that this need comes with dangers: the very subtitle of this work, *Self-Concern Gone Awry*, speaks to these dangers, and to whether, or in what ways, this need should be overcome, or reckoned with in a healthier manner.[3]

The Freudian perspective is a type of nihilism, where human life is without meaning, and the world without value—at least not the type of value constructed by humans. Indeed, in *Beyond the Pleasure Principle* Freud puts it in italics: "*the aim of all life is death*."[4] There is not much more of a nihilistic view of human life than this: that what we really want, and is one of our basic instincts (Thanatos), is the desire to die.

We will not get into a deep analysis of nihilism—at least not at this point—but it is important to understand that what Freudian psychoanalysis was addressing (whether Freud was aware of this or not) was the growing nihilism of Western culture. What this growing nihilism points to is the end of traditional metanarratives (mainly, the Christian-Judeo metanarrative), and the loss of morality, meaning, and human significance that results. It is my argument that out of the many answers provided to nihilism (Nietzsche, Marx, Kierkegaard, and those who desired to return to traditional metanarratives), Freud's approach to nihilism "won," and has been the approach used for the past century, at least in America. My argument goes beyond this, however, to a critical assessment: following Freud's answer was a mistake, in that it has led to the general sense of languishing and malaise we are now experiencing due to a cynical therapeutic.

2 Our Approach to Meaning: Cultural Symbolics

We desire to merge with something bigger and more lasting than our natural lives. This desire to merge is what psychologists call "identification," of which childhood identification with the parents is merely a special case. Whether it is a child merging with the self-transcending parents, or the adult with her social group, both are trying to live in some larger expansiveness of meaning, while

3 For more on my understanding of this difficult and complex issue, see my "In Defense of Defenselessness: Kierkegaard and an Accepted Narcissism" (*The Heythrop Journal*, 55, no. 5 [September 2014]: 827–844).

4 *PP*, 46.

at the same time playing some unique and valuable part in the whole.[5] This merging is what Becker means by our need for heroic self-identity.[6]

In order to be heroic, there must be a heroic action-system through which we can realize our heroism. This action system is symbolic, and this symbolic action system is what we mean by "culture."[7] A crucial function of culture is to make continued self-esteem possible. Its task is to provide the individual with the conviction that she is an object of primary value in the world of meaningful action.[8] Culture, then, reflects a particular style that a society adopts to deny the despair and anxiety of being merely a human animal (nature); culture reflects the particular ways we lie to ourselves about the nature of reality;[9] culture is a set of rules, customs, and ideas that serve as a vehicle for a groundless and arbitrary heroism.

It is not merely the rules and customs of culture that are important for a sense of human significance, but also the artifacts of culture, which become the monuments to human meaning and greatness:

> The skyscraper building, the cloverleaf freeways, the houses with their imposing facades and immaculate lawns—what are these if not the modern equivalent of pyramids: a fact to the world that announces: "I am not ephemeral, look at what went into me, what represents me, what justifies me." The hushed hope is that someone who can do this will not die.[10]

These are testaments to our durability and immortality, and as such, serve as a denial of death, and what death means for our individual lives.[11] These provide "symbolic extensions" by which one can project oneself out of the body, and symbolically be located wherever one feels a part of what really matters.[12]

A car, for instance, is not simply a means of transportation, but it gains a new meaning symbolically: it is a symbol of status and importance, a sign of one's

5 *DD*, 152.

6 "Once you took the general instinct of self-preservation of the lower animals, the basic irritability of protoplasm, the self-identity of the physio-chemistry, the vague pulsation of the warmth of the animal's inner process, the nameless feeling of power and satisfaction in carrying out his instinctual behavior—once you took all this and gave it a directive of self-control via the ego, and a precise, symbolic designation in a world of symbols, then you resulted in nothing less than the need for heroic self-identity" (*BD*, 77).

7 *BD*, 78.

8 *BD*, 79.

9 *BD*, 148–149.

10 *BD*, 149–150.

11 *BD*, 33.

12 *BD*, 32–33.

ordered life, and that one has “it” together. This is why a tiny dent or scratch on one’s car can become a major source of anger, anxiety, and unhappiness—it isn’t just the car that was lessened by the scratch, but because of its symbolic “value,” the pristine status that reflects one’s identity has been marred. In the same way, a purse or handbag is not simply a purse: the logo stitched into or stamped upon it serves as a symbol and message to others (and so to oneself) that one is important, better and more durable than others. One is willing to pay four times more for this purse than another comparable purse (in terms of quality and craftsmanship) in order to send this message; indeed, it is the very price tag that gives the symbolics grounding and basis, as monetary value points to personal value. A lawn is not to be natural, but groomed; if one happens to live in a place where grass does not grow easily, or where weeds are a persistent problem, one will pay exorbitantly to maintain the artificial “nature” of one’s lawn.

Culture protects us physically and psychically, providing safety both for our bodies and our egos, and in this way protects us from the anxiety always just beneath the surface. As Becker says, the individual

> [D]oesn’t have to have fears when his feet are solidly mired and his life mapped out in a ready-made maze. All he has to do is plunge ahead in a compulsive style of drivenness in the “ways of the world” that the child learns and in which he lives later as a kind of grim equanimity.[13]

We do not have to think about our lives (its meaning, whether it is with or without purpose, its real dangers), because culture does the thinking for us. We need only mindlessly surrender to the maze, which provides a heroic system of symbolic meaning. This surrender means that we relate to the world and our lives, not through nature, but through symbolics: the cultural heroics is a symbolic creation of an ego-controlled animal that permits action in a psychological world rather than a biological one.[14] It was just this psychological world that the ancient cynics called *tuphos*, and from which they felt exiled (and so sought to return to the biological world). It is a false world, full of deception, and a world they believed it was their job to deface.

This truly is madness, *tuphos*, a crazy way to spend one’s life. One’s symbolics do not, however, seem crazy to oneself, because one so closely associates one’s identity and sense of meaning with them. While we have difficulty seeing our own insanity, we rarely have problems seeing the insanity of what other people find their identities in; indeed, this ability to *see through* others’

13 *DD*, 23.
14 *BD*, 139.

symbolics (and our inability to see through our own), has become a central aspect of modern cynicism as enlightened false consciousness: we are very capable of seeing through the traditional symbolics, but remain entranced by the *tuphos* of our present culture. Becker says, however, that it does not matter whether the hero-system is magical, religious, primitive, secular, or scientific (that is, whether traditional or contemporary), it is "still a mythical hero-system in which people serve in order to earn a feeling of primary value, a cosmic specialness, of ultimate usefulness to creation, an unshakable meaning."[15]

One finds an example of this in Carl Sagan's book *The Pale Blue Dot*. He writes about the Voyager Satellite's photo of our solar system, in which the earth is but a blue pixel in a sea of empty darkness. He says in relation to this photo, that,

> Our posturings, our imagined self-importance, the delusion that we have some privileged position in the Universe, are challenged by this point of pale light. Our planet is a lonely speck in the great enveloping cosmic dark. In our obscurity, in all this vastness, there is no hint that help will come from elsewhere to save us from ourselves.[16]

He continues, sounding somewhat like Freud in reference to the traditional heroics:

> The significance of our lives and our fragile planet is then determined only by our own wisdom and courage. *We* are the custodians of life's meaning. We long for a Parent to care for us, to forgive us our errors, to save us from our childish mistakes. But knowledge is preferable to ignorance. Better by far to embrace the hard truth than a reassuring fable.
>
> If we crave some cosmic purpose, then let us find ourselves a worthy goal.[17]

Dr. Sagan has no problem seeing through the traditional symbolics and their emptiness—the illusion of meaning and significance they claim to provide for our lives. At the same time, he has difficulty separating himself from the illusion of the importance of those things that give him an identity and a sense of doing something (being someone) significant:

> Planetary exploration satisfies our inclination for great enterprises and wanderings and quests that has been with us since our days as hunters and gatherers

---

15 *DD*, 5.

16 Carl Sagan, *Pale Blue Dot: A Vision of the Human Future In Space* (New York: Random House, 1994), p. 9.

17 Sagan, 57.

> on the East African savannahs a million years ago. By chance—it is possible, I say, to imagine many skeins of historical causality in which this would not have transpired—in our age we are able to begin again.[18]

Other (that is, traditional) heroics, for Dr. Sagan, are clearly ignorant posturing and imagined self-importance; however, planetary exploration and scientific discoveries, now that is something truly important and significant! Or so it seems to Dr. Sagan, who has poured his life into such activities.

Brown has argued that Western society since Newton, no matter how scientific or secular it claims to be, is still as "religious" as any other.[19] This is because "civilized" society is a hopeful belief and protest that science, money, and goods *make humans count* for more than any other animal. It is in this sense that everything humans do that are related to some "heroics" are ultimately religious in nature: we believe that what we do is in some way hallowed, sacred, and worthy of adulation or worship.

While it may be the case that we no longer worship divinities at religious altars, for which we are willing to sacrifice our time and even our lives, we now worship our bank accounts, and our places of worship are malls, discount stores, car dealerships, sporting events, and the multiple social media accounts through which we try to show that we are a "somebody," and make what we do seem to matter. Since we all begin to feel anxious when we become aware of the meaninglessness and insignificance of our individual selves, we worship (spend our lives pursuing, praising, and glorifying in) what *makes us count* symbolically.

Our culture provides our heroics, and we must play our parts in them correctly—that is, play the role our culture puts us into. Our cynical culture has thoroughly seen through the old traditional ideas of right and wrong, good and bad, and what "heroic" means in relation to these notions; however, this does not mean that we are free from our culture's pressure to live in a "right" way. Indeed, as we will see in Chapter 13, it is this very phenomenon over which modern cynicism has become confused, and around which its self-deception revolves.

In seeing through the old, we believe we have become free and independent selves, following our personal destinies. Combined with the triumph of the therapeutic, we spend our lives seeking to actualize ourselves in an attempt at personal well-being. In both of these approaches, we remain blind to, or unconscious of, the arbitrariness of the cultural heroics that is so much a part of our own identities. As Becker says, there is nothing routine about social life, because of the stakes: the need for positive self-evaluation through continual

18 Sagan, 282.

19 Brown, 240.

exposure to public scrutiny, which can at any moment intolerably undermine one's sense of meaning and value. Every social encounter, Becker says, is a "hallowed event."[20] And yet, as both the ancient cynics and Freud recognized, it is full of deception from without, and self-deception from within.

3 Transference: the Need to Lean on Others

Becker says that various thinkers such as Augustine, Kierkegaard, Scheler, and Tillich have seen that we can strut and boast all we want about our self-sufficiency, but we all draw our "courage to be" from a god, a string of sexual conquests, from Big Brother, a flag, our social class, the number of "followers" on our social media accounts, or the fetish of money.[21] This is the basis of the cult of personality. Why do we burn with such an all-consuming passion for some people, when we are all more or less alike?[22] Why are the Kardashians a thing? Why do we latch onto specific politicians? Is it because of their ideas, or because of an aura we find attached to them that draws us with a kind of fanaticism beyond the ideas they express (which, after all, others express, though we do not embrace them in the same way)? Why do we suddenly act like children—shyly seeking to be noticed, nervous, have trouble speaking, etc.—when in the presence of a famous actor, musician, or politician? The answer, in Freudian terminology, is "transference." As we already saw, Freud observed in the analytic situation the phenomenon of the patient transferring the feelings she had toward her parents as a child, onto the analyst. In this, she blows the analyst up to larger than life, just as the child does with her parents (they can do no wrong, one must have their approval and acceptance, one fears their disapproval, and one needs them to recognize one's existence and value).[23] In transference we see that grown-up adults are children at heart. Just as a child distorts the world in order to relieve the sense of helplessness and fear it creates, adults narrow and skew the world to affirm a sense of their significance and value.[24]

The child comes to see things the way she wishes for the sake of her safety. With this, she uncritically and automatically accepts what the transference object says and does. The same thing happens with adults. Freud

---

20 *BD*, 88.

21 *DD*, 55–56.

22 *DD*, 128.

23 *DD*, 188.

24 *DD*, 129.

wrote about the uncanny aspect of transference, in that the individual feels as if the transference object truly has greater control and understanding than a normal individual—almost as if possessing a supernatural power.[25] Freud viewed transference in terms of suggestibility, and so in line with hypnosis.[26] Hypnosis is also uncanny, the power of which is based on "the big lie upon which their whole conscious lives are based: the lie of self-sufficiency, of self-determination, of independent judgment and choice."[27] The "big lie" is that the patient is self-sufficient, making choices independently, when in reality she has been leaning upon various parental figures her entire life. Once this big lie is exposed, the power of transference (its *tuphos*) becomes apparent.

Again, this is all driven by anxiety. Freud believed that the child seeks to merge with the parental omnipotence not out of desire (love), but out of cowardice. The only way a child, and we adults, dare to emerge into the terrifying world with confidence, is through some form of transference—by leaning on a power other than ourselves.[28] The motivation for transference is the taming of terror.

The universe contains overwhelming powers, and we sense beyond ourselves chaos and danger over which we have no control. Since we cannot do much about these untameable powers, we endow certain persons with power and put our trust in them. The child takes all the natural awe and terror she feels, and puts it on the individual beings who keep her warm and fed. They become the focus of her awe and terror, rather than having to disperse it throughout the entire universe.[29] One can often see this reality when a toddler is separated from her parents: at that moment one sees in her face and hears in her cries the terror of being separated from her source of protection and safety.[30] Transference, for both children and adults, reflects the attempt to create and sustain an environment that will give safety and satisfaction.[31]

Becker sees transference as a form of fetishism—a form that narrows control, and anchors all our problems to a single object.[32] A politician (whether Obama or Trump) becomes the answer to our problems, one who calms our

25 *DD*, 129.
26 *DD*, 129.
27 *DD*, 129.
28 *DD*, 145.
29 *DD*, 145.
30 One sees this in adults when their transference object is critiqued or attacked (an attempt to take it away), though rather than seeing terror in their faces and hearing cries, one often sees hatred in their faces and hears it in their yelling.
31 *DD*, 142.
32 *DD*, 143.

fears, which is why their supporters hold onto them uncritically and with such tenacity. This fetishism, however, does not have to be a person, we can also focus a sense of safety on a bank account, an automobile, sexual conquests, promotions or positions, and the like. Both Freud and Becker see all fetishism as a form of neurosis, (what was called "idolatry" in religious traditions), because of its narrowing and reductionism.

Transference is not entirely negative for Becker, since it gives humans what they need: "a certain degree of sharply defined individuality, a definite point of reference for the practice of goodness, and all within a certain level of safety and control."[33] What makes transference problematic is that the process is unconscious and passive: it is not under one's control, not a real choice, and so an illusion of where one's strength is truly residing. It is a means of ignoring the slavishness of our souls, enabling us to believe that we are thinking and acting and speaking independently, living lives of self-sufficiency.[34] One's whole life is an attempt to "be cool" about one's lie, as we try to appear not only like we have it "together," but that what we are doing and chasing makes good, logical sense.[35] We must at all times pretend to be something we are not, pretend that we are in control and following our own course, rather than the course of our cultural and individual transference objects.

We pay a price for this self-deception, as life becomes narrowed, and a completely passive and defensive maneuver—reactive rather than active. We spend our days defending and protecting the delicate, fragile constitution of our fiction, while also denying its artificiality.[36] Our fragility, vulnerability, and helplessness is our true repression, the urgent lie we tell about the nature of reality and ourselves.[37] As Becker says, "The real world is simply too terrible to admit: it tells man that he is a small, trembling animal who will decay and die. Illusion changes all this, makes man seem important, vital to the universe, immortal in some way."[38]

Although we will languish in our lives if we continue to live this lie, this is not the true tragedy for Becker: the real tragedy is that we may develop even worse problems if we face the reality of the situation. We are damned if we do, and damned if we don't. This is the actual basis for neurosis, the tragedy we face and live as self-contradictions. Becker recognizes that our fictions

33 *DD*, 156.
34 *DD*, 129.
35 *BD*, 148.
36 *BD*, 139.
37 *BD*, 148.
38 *DD*, 133.

and deceptions are not superfluous creations we can simply put aside, as the ancient cynics believed; they are not fictions which, once overcome, allow us to deal with the more serious business of life. There is no "serious business" in life. We no longer live in a time when we can simply put aside our illusions for something "better," or move back to nature as the ancient cynics did. There is nothing serious under the fiction. Camus' image of the "stage sets" fits well: behind the façade of cultural life, and our illusions about ourselves, is nothing (which is why Camus describes life as "absurd").

This is a point that will be very important for understanding modern cynicism, for although modern cynics have seen through it all (defaced the currency) they leave themselves with no alternative than to give into the illusion: they must invest themselves in the very activities they know to be empty, manipulative, and deceptive. The only way to do this is to create a new level of self-deception, ways of rationalizing the contradictions we have become—that is, a new form of illusion of self-sufficiency, freedom, and significance. Already our fictions have changed in important ways: people no longer derive their power from the invisible dimension, from the "sacred" or divine dimensions of reality, because these have been dis-enchanted (our world, and we, have become disenchanted); now we find our power through the manipulation of the visible dimension.[39] We attach our identity to a corporation, a branch of science, a political party, a nation, or a cause (one is an environmentalist, a vegan, fundamentalist, Trumpist, social justice warrior, etc.). Of course, these visible heroics are as fragile as the traditional heroics; as we will see, they are easily seen through into the self-interest that motivates them.

Becker has described the modern approach of trying to maintain a false consciousness in an enlightened age. He points to the palliative ways, as Freud put it, we use to ignore the entire situation:

> Modern man is drinking and drugging himself out of awareness or he spends his time shopping, which is the same thing. As awareness calls for types of heroic dedication that his culture no longer provides him, society strives to help him forget. Or, alternatively, he buries himself in psychology in the belief that awareness all by itself will be some kind of magical cure for his problems. But psychology was born with the breakdown of shared social heroisms; it can only be gone beyond with the creation of new heroisms that are basically matters of belief and will, dedication and vision.[40]

---

39 *BD*, 125.
40 *DD*, 284.

Psychoanalysis arose because we were already seeing through the illusions. To Freud's credit, he understood that analysis was not offering a new solution or answer by which to overcome this dilemma; at best, he hoped to help us cope. While it is true that post-Freudian therapeutic movements hope for healing, they offer only inconsistent messages of jumping into what one knows is meaningless, but in one's unique style, as if this will give the whole process more significance.

4 Conclusion

Becker's analysis or picture of the human situation is as pessimistic as Freud's, and in certain respects, even more so. But he has a better grasp than Freud on the true nature of what it is we are running and hiding from. Due to Freud's influence, Western Civilization, especially in America, focused on bringing our sexual instincts into the light, and giving them free rein for the sake of emotional health. We have been succeeding at this, but we are not seeing the results we expected. This is because we have been focusing on the wrong issue, and so have come to understand freedom in the wrong way.

We will now turn to the issue of neurosis from this different perspective, and see what the implications this change in focus from sexuality to significance and meaning will be. The main difference in perspective that I have oulined is that, while Freud grounds the psyche, and so neurosis, in the body, Becker grounds it in the psyche's meaning and significance—that is, *in the symbolics*.

Is there more to humans than body? What would this "more" be? As has been implied throughout this chapter, our relationship with this "more" is our relationship with the unknown, the Excess. It is our relationship to the Excess that we are anxious about, and before which we feel helpless and meaningless, and so is at the heart of neurosis. We are suffering emotionally and psychically due to the loss of traditional interpretations (symbolics) of the Excess, and we struggle to find new ways of overcoming the anxiety associated with it. We are lost in the Excess, no longer anchored within it, but adrift within a storm of an unknown. This is the basis of our neurosis; if only it were all about sex and the libido. Even Freud had to admit in the end that the conflict was not *all* about sex, and that there was something else at work, another instinct. He gave a name to this "something else": Thanatos, or the death instinct. This, in my view, was a deepening of Freud's view of the Excess as the unconscious desire for the void of the Excess, but also a way of maintaining some control over it.[41]

---

41 An entire analysis could be given on the relationship between the Excess and Freud's death instinct, but we do not have the space for such an analysis in this work.

We turn to the issue of neurosis in the next chapter in order to analyze what I believe should be our new focus in relation to it. We will see that the difficulty we face in dealing with neurosis is a much harder pill to swallow than Freud thought. Does a problem like repressed sexuality really sound like something we cannot overcome, or that we would shy away from? Who doesn't want more sex?[42] It is little wonder that, as pessimistic as his overall picture was, Freud's answer to nihilism won out. He knew the importance of his views on sexuality for the success (that is, acceptance) of his theories, and held onto them tenaciously.[43] But what if the problem is that we need to give up what we most passionately and grimly (I dare say ferociously) hold onto—our false sense of freedom, significance, and self-mastery? It is to this question we now turn.

---

42 I am, of course, being hyperbolic here, but for all Freud's pessimism toward the id, and the impossibility of full healing, his critique of culture seems to me pretty much what most people would want to hear. He is asking us to give up what we want to give up, and give into what we want to give into. He does an ingenious job explaining how we got into this situation, but once the explanation is given (the riddle is solved), it would seem just a matter of time before we could quiet the superego, and wisely give into what we have been repressing.

43 *DD*, 94–95.

CHAPTER 7

A New Understanding for Neurosis

1 The Failure of Tradition

The analyses in the past couple chapters sets up a new way of understanding neurosis. As we saw in both Freud Becker, neurotic symptoms are the result of being in "exile" from culture. As Becker puts it, neurosis is "the miscarriage of clumsy lies about reality."[1] Neurosis is a complicated technique of avoiding the unavoidable: the misery associated with living.[2] While neurosis is normal, something we share as social beings, it becomes problematic when the lies we tell ourselves are no longer fully able to convince.[3] This is what Freud saw in his patients. Sexual issues seemed more significant to him than they actually were, mainly due to the Victorian sexual norms of his time. However, they were only one aspect of the creatureliness that culture was no longer able to keep under covers. Freud may have fixated on the sexual drives because they were the tip of the spear, so to speak, but the sexual struggles of Freud's patients were not the true source of their neuroses. The real source was that culture was no longer able to help individuals accept the lies they needed in order to feel safe and significant; the traditional cultural heroic was seen through, and it was failing them.

Becker says that this failure characterizes our historical era. He has argued that neurosis or mental illness is a widespread problem today because of the disappearance of a convincing heroic drama within which we can play a part, and so find our value, meaning, and security. The illusion of our independence and self-sufficiency is becoming more difficult to maintain: we have been *exiled*, and it is making us sick.

1.1 Positive and Negative Therapeutic Communities

Philip Rieff speaks of this situation as the end of "positive therapeutic communities," and the rise of only "negative communities." Positive communities guarantee some sort of salvation, some way of bringing healing and peace to

1 *DD*, 178.
2 *DD*, 63.
3 *DD*, 178–179.

HTTPS://DOI.ORG/10.1163/9789004758148-009

the inner conflict, and the sense of guilt we carry.[4] These communities are held together by a common purpose into which each individual fits, and through which she performs her heroic and salvific actions. Hence, our relationships are connected to this common purpose, so that we subordinate our strictly personal desires to the goals necessary for fulfilling the agreed upon public purpose.

These positive communities are held together by values, ideals, rituals, etc., which are all connected to the communal purpose or aim that leads to some sort of salvation. Because of this, the positive community can explain why life is worth living, and why one's individual life has worth. These communities provide the heroics and the paths necessary for attaining meaning, value, and security in the universe. They also define and uphold the value of the cultural currency. It is through participation in these communities that pre-modern people internalized their symbolic representations of salvation, that formed the basis of both social and personal integration (stability).[5] For most of Western history, the main heroics were religious—e.g., Judeo-Christian and Islamic.

Negative therapeutic communities, of which psychoanalysis is a prime example, do not offer salvation, but a methodology—a "self-sustaining technology," as Rieff puts it.[6] Whereas the therapeutic experience of positive communities view knowledge as *transformative* for the individual, negative communities view knowledge as *informative*. As transformative, knowledge is the basis of learning actions and ways of life that lead to salvation. Thus, salvation consists of a transformation of the inner self (a transformation of one's desires, in that one comes to desire what is valuable, rather than merely pleasurable) in such a way that the inner conflict is progressively overcome. The end of the inner conflict is the basis of healing for a positive community.

As informative, knowledge is a power one gains, not in order to resolve the inner conflict, but to strengthen the ego-control over the conflict.[7] Informative knowledge is insight that sees through the deceptions of manifest content into the hidden mechanisms at work. Once one understands these mechanisms, one is better able to cope with the situation.

---

4 Philip Rieff, *The Triumph of the Therapeutic: Uses of Faith After Freud* (Wilmington: ISI Books, 2006), 61. Henceforth cited as *TT*.

5 Antonius A. W. Zondervan, *Sociology and the Sacred: An Introduction to Philip Rieff's Theory of Culture* (Toronto: University of Toronto Press, 2005), 74–75.

6 *TT*, 61.

7 *TT*, 61–62.

As we have already noted, according to Freud we cannot transform our desires; thus, communal desires are not a reality to which our personal desires are to become subordinated, and to expect such is to cause the latter to become repressed, and necessitate that the individual act in a split and hypocritical manner. Our personal desires are our reality, our nature, and the primary aim we have; knowledge is used to inform us about these inner workings of the psyche, and provide ways of strengthening the ego. The information does not transform the person, but helps her to cope or adapt to how life is in a more healthy (rational) manner. The ideal patient for negative communities is the one who has been so strengthened that she can tolerate and return to nothing more compelling than an environment in which the ego is in control, rather than a community to which the ego is to be sacrificed for something "higher," more heroic.[8]

One of Freud's great insights was that positive communities had become dysfunctional, and were no longer able to provide a clear path for sublimation. Without sublimation, the energy of repressed desires needs another way out, or means of satisfaction: neurotic symptoms.[9] Positive communities had become suffocating and oppressive (because they had become manipulative), crushing the ego under both cultural demands and those of the superego. The growing general historical characteristic of Freud's time was that there was no longer any effective, traditional sense to ground a surrender to the community, nothing for which one would need to subordinate the inner self-will. Therefore, the constraints of conscience do not allow for the satisfaction of libidinal energy, and the trapped energy comes out in neurotic symptoms.

Psychoanalysis was Freud's attempt to provide a new way of managing the ensuing malaise of our exile. His solution to the encroaching nihilism (the loss of positive communities is an important aspect of nihilism) was to use psychoanalytic therapy to strengthen the ego; as I have mentioned before, this approach has won the battle for how we have come to deal with nihilism.[10] Psychoanalysis supplies the individual with a secular substitute for the ineffective positive religious community.[11] Since the self's grounding motives cannot be transformed, knowledge is no longer in service of a communal narrative,

8 Philip Rieff, "The Analytic Attitude," *Encounter,* 17, no. 6 (June 1962): 22–27, 22.

9 Rieff, "The Analytic Attitude," 23.

10 Philip Manning, "Philip Rieff's Moral Vision of Sociology: From Positive to Negative Communities—and Back?" *Journal of Classical Sociology*, 3, no. 3, (2003): 235–246, 240. Jcs.sagepub.com at University of South Carolina.

11 Rieff, "The Analytic Attitude," 23.

but is necessary for the therapeutic tasks of negative communities: to become a genius about oneself.[12]

Rieff calls this approach a "*negative* community" because, once having seen through the positive communities, they offer no new basis for creating a new positive community, nothing greater or more significant for which to sacrifice oneself; there is merely the individual, making her way through life by the power of her own might, and with no new heroics or transference object to lean upon. Thus, there is now, in varying degrees of awareness, and among the vast majority of people, a sense that their activities and aspirations are essentially meaningless. At best, we can find a private meaning, which of course, is as arbitrary and groundless as those we have already rejected. Alienation is a regular, understandable, and expected risk in life.

We are living in a strange kind of exile, one within which we have come to feel both alienated and at home. We are cynics because we have all *seen through* and defaced the cultural currency of the past; we are *modern* cynics because this enlightened consciousness has led us to a new form of false consciousness, one which makes *parrhesia* impossible. We are alert to discover fraud everywhere, and indeed, it is a characteristic of modern cynicism to see fraud even where it is not. And yet, we also try to hide our own fraud, as we continue to participate and invest our lives in the very institutions, practices, and cultural *scripts* we have seen through.[13]

We must maintain our false consciousness so the terror of creatureliness, and the anxiety it creates, will not rise to consciousness. It turns out that it is the most unconscious and least honest about themselves who appear to be the "healthiest" in society (the normal neurotics), while those who are most honest about the truth of their lives are in dire mental and emotional straits. As Becker, quoting Otto Rank, says of the pathological neurotic, he

> perceives himself as unreal and reality as unbearable, because with him the mechanisms of illusion are known and destroyed by self-consciousness. He can no longer deceive himself about himself, and disillusions even his ideal of personality. He perceives himself as bad, guilt-laden, inferior, as a small, weak, helpless creature, which is the truth about mankind, as Oedipus also discovered in

12 *TT*, 25–26.

13 While we still lean on culture for our sense of significance, the words "heroic" or "heroism" are too strong, since they imply a sacrifice for the greater good. "Script" is a better term, for our lives become scripted by our culture in accordance with advertising, media, and the ever-changing established order. This issue will be analyzed in more detail in Chapters 18 and 19.

> the crash of his heroic fate. All other is illusion, deception, but necessary deception in order to bear one's self and thereby life.[14]

Becker believes the only reason humans can get away with these illusions is that the earth has been so bounteous.[15] We cope with the meaninglessness of our lives through consumerism and busyness, and our world and culture can provide seemingly limitless compensation and things to do. As noted above, we can run from this consciousness by drinking, drugging, shopping, electronics, binging Netflix, social media, etc. Humans have been allowed to live in a world of playful fantasy—in the past due to a natural bounty, and now due to an artificial one.[16] We can maintain the illusion of self-sufficiency because of this artificial and technological bounty; however, take away people's smartphone for a few days, and the anxiety lying just beneath will begin to surface. Our constant busyness is nothing more than a defense mechanism against the awareness of the fictions of our cultural scripts, and the attending anxiety.

1.2 The Illusion of Self-Sufficiency

Otto Rank recognized that our hyper-self-consciousness, and all our ideology critiques, have left us to our own resources. Hence, he called us, as did Rieff, "psychological man." We have become isolated from the ideologies of the positive communities that protected us psychologically. As "psychological man" (that is, within the therapeutic culture), we must now find ways to justify ourselves from within ourselves, and not based on a communal heroic; however, this raises more problems than it solves. As Becker says, "Freud summed it up beautifully when he somewhere remarked that psychoanalysis cured the neurotic misery in order to introduce the patient to the common misery of life."[17]

---

14 *DD*, 188.

15 *BD*, 128.

16 Every generation lives off the sacrifice and labor of preceding generations. This does not release it from sacrifice, because it must labor for the generations to come. Our current American generations, however, must opt out of this sacrifice, by living not simply off the labor of past generations, but also future generations: we live on credit, whose bill will come due upon the backs of those who come after us. Our affluence and self-sufficiency are based on the illusion created by credit, and by a governmental debt which grows greater every year. We are a pathetic (pathological) generation, ungrateful for the labor of past generations that have brought us to our current standard of living, and stealing from future generations in order to live a life without sacrifice. Sacrifice is too much for us, because there is no longer anything viewed as truly worthy of personal sacrifice.

17 *DD*, 57. I believe Becker is referring to a statement made in *Studies on Hysteria*, in which Freud says, "much will be gained if we succeed in transforming your hysterical misery into

Freudian psychoanalysis leaves the self isolated in this condition, with very little in the way of cultural supports.[18] If you narrow the idea of a sacred soul to the self, and the self to early childhood conditioning, all you have left is the individual stuck with multiple levels of self-deception (repressions) to see through, and the various techniques in self-analysis.[19]

We will come to see that the focus of the psychoanalytic and more contemporary therapeutic approaches are missing the mark. The problem Freud failed to comprehend is that we are not struggling with moral guilt, but ontological or existential guilt. Freud correctly saw the devastating effect of the brutal nature of the superego, which punishes the ego mercilessly with the various ways it attributes failure to the ego—a sense of moral guilt and shame, a dark cloud over one's sense of self. Psychoanalysis attempts to lift the excruciating burden of this moral guilt, but leaves the existential guilt (the attempts at self-sufficiency and self-justification) untouched; indeed, psychoanalysis and the therapeutic intensify it.

2 Existential Guilt

Freud was correct in seeing that cultural conditioning and the superego do not lead to human thriving, but to painful despair, human narrowing, and languishing. We have abandoned ourselves in such a way that we relate to society out of weakness, oppressed by demands that are often alien to our deepest passions and inclinations. Neurosis is a universal blindness to the slavery by which we deceive ourselves. We believe we are learning to stand on our own when we identify with our parents, but the reality is that we are surrendering ourselves thoroughly to their authority—and later to the cultural authorities. Becker says that the whole psychoanalytic theory of repression and the internalization of parental ideals (the core of sublimation) is summed up in one thought:

> "You no longer have to punish me, Father; I will punish myself now." In other words, "You can approve of me as you see how well I do as you would wish me to."

---

common unhappiness." *Studies in Hysteria*, in *Freud – Complete Works*, trans. Ivan Smith, 2010: 1–269, 269, https://www.valas.fr/IMG/pdf/Freud_Complete_Works.pdf. Henceforth cited as *SH*.

18 The analytic community between patient and analyst is often the sole support for the patient, but this is a wholly artificial relation: it is one-sided in terms of sharing, it entails payment, and with Freud was rarely face-to-face.

19 *DD*, 192.

> Or, more fatefully, in words the child would not admit to himself: "I am a social person *because* I am no longer mine; *because* I am yours."[20]

The humanization process (going from natural and biological aims to symbolic aims) itself is, when it is surrendered to unconsciously or with a false consciousness, the neurosis: it is the limiting of experience, the fragmentation of perception, the dispossession of genuine inner control for the sake of the illusion of external control, and the attempt to conceal from ourselves who we really are.[21] It is little wonder, then, that Freud would turn from this to self-mastery and self-sufficiency, just as the ancient cynics did. No doubt, he viewed a much less stringent and more conservative type of self-mastery, but this only intensifies the malaise and languishing, as one pursues a "common unhappiness."

When the child says, "I will punish myself now," she is not merely affirming a kind of slavery, but also affirming that she has control over anxiety—the anxiety of being a helpless, fragile organism moving toward death.[22] In a strange mental gymnastics, she abandons herself through the internalizations of others' ideals, and because they are internalized, she believes she has become self-sufficient—she believes that they are her own ideals. Freud was aware that conscience or socialization is not real control but an illusion of control; it is not rational, but irrational, based on the need for authority and transference arising out of the Oedipus complex. Our most cherished human traits (our sense of right and wrong, the higher capacities by which we determine values in life, our sense of wanting to be good and acceptable, and fulfilling this task) are nothing more than arbitrary social norms, our cultural currency, which are accidents of the time and place of our births.[23]

Freud sought to deface the currency because he realized that the child's urge to move freely forward, to manipulate, experiment, and exercise her powers, are continually being blocked, and this is what makes her a neurotic organism.[24] There is no doubt that sometimes this blockage is for the child's safety, as well as in order to learn the vital discipline of putting off momentary pleasure for the sake of greater fulfillment down the road, but much of the time this blockage consists only of the parents' own fears and superego.[25]

---

20 *BD*, 56.
21 *BD*, 56.
22 *BD*, 57.
23 *BD*, 58.
24 *BD*, 58.
25 *BD*, 58.

Freud's mistake of focusing on the sexual instincts caused him to miss the true nature of this guilt—that is, what we are repressing, the basis of this repression, and so ultimately the true nature of neurosis. His focus on the sexual instincts and the moral demands for sacrifice in relation to them, caused him to miss the deeper level of our guilt. This all stems from a misinterpretation of the Oedipus complex as the child's desire to kill the father in order to sleep with the mother. The desire to kill the father is not in order to sleep with the mother, but in order to become father to ourselves (for the sake of self-grounding and so self-sufficiency).

Becker, following Rank and Brown, reinterprets the Freudian phases of psychological development (e.g., oral, anal, and especially the Oedipal phase). Becker believes that all the talk about blood and excrement, sex and guilt, are not really about the urge for the child to sleep with his mother and kill his father, nor is there a fixation on physical castration. These are mere reflections and placeholders for the real issues or causes of anxiety and guilt: they reflect the horror of our basic animal condition, a condition we cannot understand, accept, or overcome.[26]

Brown points out in his book on Freud, that the Oedipus complex is not a narrowly sexual problem of lust and competitiveness; rather, the *complex* is a *project*, which sums up the fundamental problems of the child's life: whether to be a passive object of fate, an appendage of others, a plaything of the world, or to be an active center within oneself.[27] The child's primary task is a flight from a sense of helplessness, of becoming an insignificant object in the movement of fate; sexual matters are secondary and derivative. The Oedipus *project* is a flight from passivity, from annihilation, contingency, and insignificance.[28] Due to anxiety, the child wants to conquer death by taking the father's place—that is by becoming *father of himself*, creator and sustainer of his own life.

Seeking to take his father's place is the *causa sui* project ("cause of itself"), and it is closely connected to the desire for self-sufficiency—to get the ground of one's existence under oneself, or as it is often put, to be able to pull oneself up by one's bootstraps. The *causa sui* project is a pretense that one is invulnerable and self-sufficient; it is an illusion built on, and protected by, the power of others and culture. It is also the belief that one is important in nature, and can do something to show one's significance. Indeed, as humans, we are

26 *DD*, 35.
27 Brown, 127–129.
28 *DD*, 36.

continually working on our "resumes" and touting our accomplishments, in order to maintain this illusion.[29]

A very important point to grasp is that Freud's attempt to overcome the Oedipus *complex* merely falls into and intensifies the Oedipus *project*. Psychoanalytic therapy weakens the complex, so that one gains satisfaction by controlling oneself with cultural symbols and various forms of self-mastery (as Freud put it, by placing the creature anxiety onto the ego).[30] What Freud misses is that both the complex and project are essential in the creation of the superego, which is the internalization of the parents' values, and become the basis of not only the child's conduct, but also his or her character.[31] By intensifying the *project* in order to overcome the *complex*, Freud overcomes moral guilt, but he does so at the cost of intensifying existential guilt.

Freud overcomes the fantasy of self-sufficiency in the complex, by intensifying the fantasy of self-sufficiency in the project.[32] This covers over what Becker calls a person's "*hopeless lack of genuine centering on his own energies to assure the victory of his life*. No creature can assure this, and man can only attempt to do so in his *fantasy*."[33] Freud's mistake is that, after showing the lack of self-mastery in relation to the traditional heroics and authorities, he then turns to a new, rational form of self-mastery, rather than surrendering it completely. Ultimately, Becker says, the *causa sui* project is doomed to failure, because humans cannot simply justify themselves with their own heroism or rationality. As Becker puts it, the individual's yielding to creatureliness (the surrender of self-mastery),

> [R]epresents nothing less than the abandonment of the *causa-sui* project, the deepest, completest, total emotional admission that there is no strength within oneself, no power to bear the superfluity of experience. To yield is to admit that support has to come from outside oneself and that justification for one's life has to come *totally* from some self-transcending web in which one consents to be suspended—as a child in its hammock-cradle, glazed-eyed in helpless, dependent admiration of the cooing mother.[34]

Trying to be sufficient within ourselves is the existential guilt with which we must all contend: we never measure up to the value we feel we should have—because such measures are impossible, given the situation into which we were born.

---

29 *DD*, 187.
30 *BD*, 46.
31 *BD*, 46.
32 *DD*, 107.
33 *DD*, 107.
34 *DD*, 107.

3 Conclusion

This new understanding of guilt changes our understanding of human evil, because evil is no longer seen primarily as a moral issue, but an ontological issue. One of the results of a true exile from the cultural currency is the freedom from notions of good and evil that have been created for the sake of control and oppressing others. We will see that traditional morality is not always good and moral, because it can be used for the *causa sui* project. In other words, morality can, and often is, used in order to maintain the illusions of significance and self-mastery. Thus, morality is often used in the service of maintaining existential guilt.

At the same time, a cynical defacing of the moral currency does not necessarily free one from existential guilt. While such defacing is necessary for addressing existential guilt, it is not sufficient. This is because the defacing of one currency may be nothing more than an attempt to maintain another currency. It is my argument that this is exactly what modern cynicism does: it defaces the traditional currency, not in order to overcome the *causa sui* project (existential guilt), but to maintain it. It is to this argument I now turn.

CHAPTER 8

Evil, Neurosis and Immortality Striving

1 Sin and Neurosis: Traditional Views of Evil

The typical or cultural view of evil—a view Freud also holds—is that evil is a breaking of social rules, a lack of self-control, summed up in the venial sins of the flesh, about which the superego berates the ego, and of which the id demands satisfaction. These rules are the norms, laws, ideals, divine commands, etc., whose essence is to control the "animal" within (our lusts, sexuality, and aggressiveness). Freud is correct that this type of moral currency can be used to manipulate and oppress, and history has also shown that much destruction and pain have been wrought in the name of cultural religion, morality, and our ideologies. It is because Freud viewed evil moralistically that he viewed the *idea* of evil and sin (moral guilt) as the very cause of neurosis. Morality demands of us more than we can give, ideals to which we cannot attain; rather than admit this, we fall into pretense.

With the existential understanding of guilt, we can come to see that the root of the *spiritual* concept of sin (missing the mark—*harmatria* in Greek) is not so different from the root of the current concept of neurosis: at their *roots*, sin and neurosis are the same, not at odds with one another. At the root of both is the *causa sui* project.[1] We are not to think of "sin" here in strictly traditional moral terms (which almost always come with some form of blame and condemnation), but as something from which we need to be rescued or saved; its essence does not consist in breaking some law, command, or prohibition, but that it leads to death rather than to life, and that it is a lie about who we are and our true situation. We will see that this is in direct distinction to the moral judgments we commonly think of when we hear the term "sin."

---

1 This identity of the *root* of sin and neurosis is not an argument that mental illness and sin are the same. Both grow out of the *causa sui* project, which is the root of the brokenness in the human *psyche*. Something has gone awry within the *psyche*, and it is the root of this "having gone awry" that is the focus of this analysis. This is a complex issue, in that it changes the very way we approach the issue of evil. Basically, both the traditional positive communities and the current negative communities are immersed in, and see as "good," what can in reality be evil. In other words, our "moral goodness" can be, and often is, an aspect of our existential guilt—our brokenness, self-deception, and the spreading of our personal pain and suffering onto others.

HTTPS://DOI.ORG/10.1163/9789004758148-010

Becker explains the connection between sin and neurosis by pointing out that they are both

> [T]he *complete isolation of the individual*, his disharmony with the rest of nature, his hyperindividualism, his attempt to create his own world from within himself. Both sin and neurosis represent the individual *blowing himself up to larger than true size*, his refusal to recognize his cosmic *dependence*. Neurosis, like sin, is an attempt to force nature, to pretend that the *causa-sui* project suffices. In sin and neurosis, man fetishizes himself on something narrow at hand and pretends that the whole meaning and miraculousness of creation is limited to that, that he can get his beatification from that.[2]

This is self-concern gone awry: it is fetishizing objects as illusions of control, a narrowing which is the essence of both neurosis and what is called "idolatry" within spiritual traditions. There is, however, one important difference between the classic sinner and the modern neurotic in relation to existential guilt, though the difference is not so much one of essence, as it is the historical situatedness between the two: "both of them experience the naturalness of human insufficiency, only today the neurotic is stripped of the symbolic worldview, the God-ideology that would make sense out of his unworthiness and would translate it into heroism."[3] As Rank says, "The neurotic type suffers from a consciousness of sin just as much as did his religious ancestor, without believing in the conception of sin. This is precisely what makes him 'neurotic'; he feels a sinner without the religious belief in sin for which he therefore needs a new rational explanation."[4]

Something is wrong within the human psyche, and it is so wrong that it can cause deep emotional pain and brokenness within the individual. This pain, and the anxious recoil of having to experience it, often flows out of individuals onto others, in what can be cruel and unjust acts. These external manifestations of internal pain, which results in bringing pain to others, is where moral and existential guilt often coincide. The problem arises when someone uses moral guilt (morality) as a means of spreading the pain.

The healers of traditional therapies turned to metanarratives and ideologies to heal and overcome this brokenness. This, of course, came with all sorts of explanations of the genesis of the brokenness—its cause, what intensifies it, and how to be on the path of healing. It is just these complex ideologies that

---

2 *DD*, 196. (emphasis added).

3 *DD*, 197.

4 Otto Rank, *Beyond Psychology* (New York: Dover, 1941), 193.

have been defaced and rejected, perhaps in large part because of the evil and hypocrisy that was perpetrated in the name of "healing." However, the fractured psyche still existed, and so needed a new way of being understood. Freudian psychoanalysis is what won out among the various other explanations. Even though many of his individual theories have been rejected, his general explanation of the cause and "cure" of suffering has been maintained.

I will show that this has led to modern cynicism as a new means of sublimation, due to the ultimately cynical nature of Freudian psychoanalysis. I will get to this argument in a couple chapters, but I want to first examine why psychoanalysis is not addressing the core problem we face within ourselves: namely, that the existential guilt remains even after the moral guilt has disappeared. When Becker and Rank argue that the neurotic feels a sinner without the religious belief in sin, this means, in the context of modern cynicism, that the existential guilt remains even after the moral guilt has disappeared. The modern therapeutic is the ideological means by which we repress our existential guilt in the name of overcoming the illusions and constraints of moral guilt.

2 Immortality Striving and the Nature of Evil

In Becker's final book, published after his death, he specifically connects the *causa sui* project to the concept of evil, and to the actual evil manifested throughout history. The *causa sui* project is related to the overall creatureliness of humans, which the reality of death epitomizes (what we deny the most); it is for this reason that Becker connects the *causa sui* project to what he calls "immortality striving." We will look at his analysis to gain a better understanding of how the concepts of sin and neurosis can be linked to the *causa sui* project, and so show that *Freud and the therapeutic culture are mistaken when they believe the idea of sin and sinfulness are the cause of neurosis, instead of sharing a common root with it.* With his focus on the repressed sexuality of the Victorian Era, Freud was not able to recognize that his patients were ultimately suffering due to their *causa sui* project—that is, their attempt to maintain the illusion of the project without the cultural supports that maintained the illusions.

Humans have sought to transcend death through culture by finding meaning in life through some larger scheme, a metanarrative through which our Sisyphean rocks can stay and hold at the top of the mountain.[5] Such durability is how one assures oneself of the expansive meaning of one's life (flourishing)

5 Ernest Becker, *Escape from Evil* (New York: Free Press, 1975), 3. Henceforth cited as *EE*.

in the face of real limitations. We are all driven by a burning desire to count or matter, to make a difference and an impact on this planet. As noted, it is symbolics that provide for this artificial self-transcendence. Everything cultural is fabricated and given meaning by the mind—a meaning not given in nature. This fabrication of symbols for the purpose of meaning is what Brown means when he says culture is "supernatural" or religious.[6] These symbols are the basis for one's sense of durability (immortality) and meaning.[7]

2.1 Cultural Support and Symbolic Durability

Society provides two general ways of creating significance for humans: support and competition.[8] Support means providing symbols that support and protect tender human feelings, keeping one from feeling diminutive or impoverished.[9] This means that our fears are attached to more than the natural powers that threaten us physically, but we also fear the durability of our symbols.[10] Our physical natures not only need to be protected (self-*preservation*), but our symbols by which we gain esteem also need to be protected (*self*-preservation).

It is this need for support that is the basis of repression, as we attempt to deceive ourselves about our creatureliness. Rank and Brown have both argued that humans repressed themselves (tamed themselves) in a barter for greater power and durability, by surrendering to the group or culture, *in the strange illusion that this surrender is actually self-sufficiency*. Rank argued that taboos, morals, customs, and laws represent a self-limitation so that one can transcend one's natural condition, and thereby get more life in the long run—denying life in the present for enduring life in the future. Preserving durability and immortality is more important than preserving the transience of physical life.[11]

This is a very different view from Freud, in terms of the ground of repression: Freud saw repression as primarily connected to the pleasure principle, and the gratification of erotic drives. Freud believed that we gave up these drives grudgingly, sacrificing them to superior authorities and powers for the sake of security.[12] Rank, however, said sexual restrictions were from the first voluntary, spontaneous acts, not the result of external authority. Humans are willing to barter the body for the higher spiritual values which promised more

6 *EE*, 4.
7 *EE*, 5.
8 *EE*, 14.
9 *EE*, 14.
10 *EE*, 5.
11 *EE*, 65.
12 *EE*, 65.

life. We are, for Rank, trying to overcome existential guilt, not moral guilt. This changes the focus of flourishing, and so the focus of repression.[13] The higher spiritual ideals, for which we sacrifice our individual drives, are a quest for energy and power, a desire for durability and meaning.[14]

Although there is a willingness to sacrifice for a future life, there still needs to be proof of the power of one's symbols in the present life, which we find through a kind of social prestige, which is the smile of fate upon our lives and decisions—upon who we are. This requires inequality in life, as proof that one's symbols are the real symbols of power, the power for durability.

Society is, from the very beginning, a struggle by individuals and groups for special privileges (who would get the best meat, easiest access to sexual partners, some leisure and security). The elders and shamans always attempted to arrange these things for their own benefit, much like corporate CEOs and politicians, religious leaders and celebrities, do today. There is no "trickle-down" economics when it comes to immortality striving. This need for inequality to prove one's worth leads to the second way culture provides for significance: competition.

2.2 Competition

Competition is driven by our need to compare our achievements and virtues to others, so that we can outshine our rivals.[15] Every organism, in a struggle for more life, tries to expand and aggrandize itself as much as possible, (what Nietzsche appropriately called "will to power"), which has destructive consequences for the world. Humans are not simply biological organisms, but also symbolic, and so they do not only need more space, food, and water, but they also have something they need to prove. Humans can expand their feelings of worth through many symbolic triumphs and demonstrations of excellence: games, sports, puzzles, riddles, mental tricks, or by boasting about achievements, taunting and humiliating adversaries, or torturing and killing them.[16] Society is set up to provide for these competitions and for codes of self-aggrandizement;[17] society provides the ability to boast, to humiliate, and outshine others in quiet and culturally acceptable ways—that is, culturally

13 *EE*, 65.
14 *EE*, 22.
15 *EE*, 14.
16 *EE*, 11.
17 *EE*, 13.

acceptable sublimations of our immorality striving.[18] Anything that reduces other organisms and adds to one's size is a way of gaining "self-feeling" (esteem, worth, a sense of importance).[19]

People are in a continual struggle not to feel *diminished* or *impoverished* in their organismic importance.[20] Since this importance is wholly symbolic, this struggle must be carried out on the most minute levels of symbolic complexity, as one seeks to prove that one possesses some extraordinary excellence that makes one immune to diminution and death.[21] One needs to show not merely that one has the right symbolics (for each culture has its own symbolics), but that one is attaining to the symbolics—is pure, righteous, virtuous, just, etc. One can prove this by comparing oneself to others, by which one can judge if one has extra claim to importance.[22]

It should be noted, again, that there is no essential difference between a "sacred" or "profane" symbolics.[23] They both have the same goal in the end: to raise humans above nature, to assure individuals that they count in the universe, and that they are acceptable for durability and immortality. Bank accounts are often such a symbolic that is assumed to assure durability, as is having one's name on a building, or proclamations of a thousand-year Reich. All power, according to Brown, is sacred power: a hunger for immortality.[24] Beliefs and rituals vary, ideologies are all different and change, but what is fixed is the principle of a "dominant immortality ideology."[25] We have staked our esteem and significance on these artificial ideologies and symbolics, and so we will rage over fine points in our beliefs.[26] If your adversary (your "Great Satan") wins the argument about truth, *you die*—your immortality system is shown to be fallible, and so your life becomes fallible (the illusion is up, and your existential guilt becomes manifest).

This is when things get ugly, and when we come to understand the true nature of evil: it is not the venial acts of giving into our animal nature (over

18 *EE*, 13. I believe Freud was beginning to struggle with this issue in *Civilization and Its Discontents*, in which he thought about it in terms of the instinct of aggression—the Death Instinct. Due to the World Wars and growing antisemitism he was witnessing, and the inability to make sense of it based solely on the Erotic Instinct, he was becoming open to another primary process at work in the human psyche.

19 *EE*, 11.

20 *EE*, 11.

21 *EE*, 12.

22 *EE*, 12–14.

23 *EE*, 4.

24 *EE*, 49.

25 *EE*, 64.

26 *EE*, 64.

which the superego and our consciences continually badger us) that is at the basis of both evil and neurosis; instead, it is our ideologies and ideals, our sense of right and wrong, our immortality striving and *causa sui* project. Evil is not due to irrationality, as the Enlightenment period thought, but it is connected to a distorted desire to flourish, one that is self-grounding in this task.[27] As Paul Ricoeur says,

> Evil, in moral consciousness is essentially transgression, that is, subversion of a law; it is in this way that the majority of pious men continue to consider sin. And yet, situated before God, evil is qualitatively changed; it consists less in a transgression of a law than in a *pretension of man to be master of his own life. The will to live according to the law is, therefore, an expression of evil—and even the most deadly, because the most dissimulated*: worse than injustice is one's own justice. Ethical consciousness does not know this, but religious consciousness does.[28]

There is plenty of evidence in the past couple hundred years or so to show that the spread of reason, and the renunciation of irrationality and superstition, did not lead to human moral progress or goodness.[29] The anxiety associated with our sense of insignificance and fear of diminution spills over into the affairs of humans as much today as it ever did, for in the defense of our symbols (whether religious, moral, and sacred, or secular, economic, nationalistic, and militaristic), and the need to assure ourselves that they are real (that they will come out on top), we have brought more pain and suffering into the world than non-symbolizing organisms. *Evil is not connected to our natural needs, but our symbolic needs*—to our very "knowledge of good and evil."

The irony is that some of the most intense forms of evil are done in the very attempt to avoid and fight "evil!"[30] As Pascal has said, "Men never do evil so fully and cheerfully as when they do it out of conscience."[31] This is because we feel justified in what we do to others, for "the others'" symbolic heroism is viewed as evil; one believes it is one's moral and immortal duty to stand for what is good, and so condemn and destroy what is evil. Think of the Twin Towers, the Crusades, the Inquisition, the Holocaust, Stalinism, Hiroshima and

27 *EE*, 160.

28 Paul Ricoeur "Guilt, Ethics, and Religion," in *Conflict of Interpretations*, ed. Don Ihde (Evanston: Northwestern UP, 1974): 425–439, 438. (emphasis added).

29 *EE*, 160.

30 *EE*, 5.

31 Pascal, 272.

Nagasaki.[32] Every one of these events is connected to a symbolic, an ideology of immortality striving and power.

When it comes to existential guilt, it is *not* our enemy who is evil, but evil is our need to see the "enemy" as evil, and the means by which we seek to destroy (or cancel) him or her. What if overcoming evil and neurosis truly is about taking the log out of our own eye (focusing and working on overcoming our false consciousness—our own self-deception of the *causa sui* project), before trying to remove the speck of dust from another's?

Our self-righteousness is our great self-deception, and is something that should make us pause and reflect upon our own character. We should carefully and critically reflect upon our *causa sui* project, our attempt to be more than we are. As Becker says, evil is not to be understood as a person's animal heredity, but is "the *toll that his pretense of sanity takes,* as he tries to deny his true condition."[33]

Neurosis and sin are systemic, and institutional religion and morality have often been built up, not to rid us of this situation and heal us, but to hide it from ourselves. The pathologically neurotic are those who have come to see this, but no longer have the symbolic means of hiding the existential guilt. Recognition of existential guilt, unlike moral guilt, does not create in sensitive individuals the drive toward judgment and condemnation, but leads to compassion, an understanding and empathy for the pain and anxiety we are all struggling with and facing due to existential guilt.

3 The Lie of Character

The ancient cynics were correct that in abandoning a natural, animal sense of life, we opt instead for a contrived, symbolic illusion that clouds our minds. Our character is not natural, but social, not bound to any truth about who we really are, but the construction of a symbolic mask we wear for others (and ourselves). We no longer belong to ourselves, though we continually put forward an image of independence and self-sufficiency. This character is social, and the basic process of character formation is to become *somebody* in the symbolic world.[34]

Nature, having created a self-conscious organism, has put us into this impossible bind: in the face of the evidence of our existential guilt, and with

32 *EE*, 5.
33 *DD*, 30.
34 *EE*, 75.

the anxieties of our own life and experience, we accommodate to the superior powers of our trainers, hoping to salvage a sense of superiority and confidence for ourselves.[35] We spend our lives in a symbolic action system (whether heroic or scripted) seeking to gain feelings of self-worth and superiority in terms of beauty, intelligence, athletic acumen, generosity, charity, humility, wealth, positions, etc.[36]

Character, then, is what is built up to deny our despair, anxiety, and existential guilt, the denial of the annihilation that turns our lives back into nothing. The process starts with childhood development, for the child knows the anxiety of being small, helpless, and dependent, and the fear of being abandoned by those who keep her warm, fed, and alive.[37] The child does not want to remain small and helpless, because this keeps anxiety much too close to consciousness to be carried. Taking anxiety into the ego, the child attempts to create a symbolic self of mastery and control that will change the situation from weakness to strength; this *causa sui* project is the basis for the development of character, the face we put to the world and ourselves.[38]

The child's character is his style of life, his way of using the powers of others, the support of things and the ideas of his culture to banish the awareness of his actual natural impotence.[39] The development of character is the creation of defenses that allow a person to feel some basic sense of self-worth, a sense of power and self-mastery. It allows one to feel in control, to be unique, and a self-created and self-actualized individual—to be *somebody*.[40] It is the child's (and later, the adult's) attempt to relieve the tension of the paradox of his nature as a self-contradiction.[41] As Becker says,

> The child emerges with a name, family, a play-world in a neighborhood, all clearly cut out for him. But his insides are full of nightmarish memories of impossible battles, terrifying anxieties of blood, pain, aloneness, darkness; mixed with limitless desires, sensations of unspeakable beauty and majesty, awe, mystery; and fantasies of hallucinations of mixtures between the two, the impossible attempt to compromise between bodies and symbols.[42]

35 *EE*, 75.
36 *EE*, 75.
37 *EE*, 119.
38 *EE*, 119.
39 *DD*, 54.
40 *DD*, 55.
41 *BD*, 144–145.
42 *DD*, 29.

While character is the face one sets to the world, Becker says it hides the inner defeat. It is a series of techniques and styles of living aimed at two things: (1) to secure one's physical survival and safety (self-*preservation*), and (2) to deny the fact that one has little control in life, and that all one does, sacrifices, and suffers is ultimately irrelevant (*self*-preservation). Becker calls character the "vital lie": "it is a *necessary* and basic dishonesty about oneself and one's whole situation."[43] It is a source of self-deception, the mask that looks to have it all together.

Yet, if we really felt we had it together, why would we have so much to prove? Why pay hundreds of dollars more for a handbag or clothes, simply because of a logo that is on it? Why pay tens of thousands of dollars for physical augmentations that make us stand out? Just look around, and you will have no difficulty seeing numerous people quietly screaming out, "Look at me! I matter! I am worthy of being recognized! I am not irrelevant!" Watch yourself for a week or two, asking yourself why you felt the need to boast, or to diminish another person, to tell a better story than the person before, to spend more time thinking about what you will say next rather than listening to the person in front of you, fantasizing about having stood out in some past experience. Our character is the face of lostness within the world and our culture, the face of a domesticated animal, the face that takes Celia, the shitting organism, five hours to put on. This lostness is our neurosis, our sin, our despair, and languishing, in which we

> follow out the styles of automatic and uncritical living in which [we] were conditioned as children. [We] are "inauthentic" in that [we] do not belong to [ourselves], and are not "[our] own" person, do not act from [our] own center, do not see reality on its terms; [we] are one-dimensional men totally immersed in the fictional games being played in [our] society, unable to transcend [our] social conditioning.[44]

4 Conclusion

The failure of traditional positive communities have allowed for our focus on moral guilt to give way to a focus on existential guilt. It allows us to see the deeper motives of our self-deception, due to a deeper recognition of what it is we are repressing, or trying to hide from ourselves. This provides us with a

43 *DD*, 55.
44 *DD*, 73.

new understanding of neurosis, the painful and broken ways we attempt to feel whole in the midst of our *causa sui* project. The analyses on cultural heroics, transference, immortality striving, the character lie, and fetishes all point to an attempt to narrow the world in such a way that we can maintain the illusion of control and self-sufficiency.

I am editing my manuscript at the beginning of the pandemic, and am struck by the fixation of hoarding toilet paper. It is neurotic. The anxiety at the beginning of the pandemic, in relation to what the coronavirus will mean for our lives and the powerlessness over it, must be sublimated. It is as if the neurotic is saying, "If I can just get the toilet paper issue solved or under my control, everything will be okay, and I'll come out on top." It is also no surprise, given the fetishization and transference within politics prior to the coronavirus, that the pandemic would appear to many to be more of a political, than a health, issue. Symbolics become more important than nature or the natural, because these allow us *not* to have to face the anxiety of our powerlessness and vulnerability. An entire book could be written on the relation between the various reactions to the pandemic in America, and the analyses of the past several chapters.

But this is a book on the general aspects of modern cynicism, and so the next task is to turn the corner from the analyses of Freud and Becker, to an analysis of modern cynicism. We will turn this corner by looking at Soren Kierkegaard's view of the self, and the task of becoming a self. Kierkegaard will help us lay the groundwork for understanding the paradox of modern cynicism as both enlightened consciousness and false consciousness. Kierkegaard aides us in this because of the complex and insightful ways he understands what is going on as we live in, and maintain, our self-deception. While some of his analyses on self-deception intersect with Freud's theories, there are also important differences, the main ones being that we should abandon the *causa sui* project and move into exile.

CHAPTER 9

Kierkegaard and the Task of Self-Becoming

1 The Repression of the Self

This issue of the character lie brings us to another important thinker for the development of our picture: the Danish philosopher and theologian Soren Kierkegaard. Becker says of Kierkegaard, that he "wanted to show the many ways in which life bogs down and fails when man closes himself off against the reality of his condition. Or, at best what an undignified and pathetic creature man can be when he imagines that by living unto himself alone he is fulfilling his nature."[1] Kierkegaard's entire authorship was the attempt to awaken us to the fact that we are living in despair, languishing under a spiritlessness that has the capacity to close us off from our depths and true selves, making us into superficial automatons of the "established order."

Kierkegaard is interested in what he called the "task of becoming a self," which sounds like a strange task, since it would seem that we are a self as a matter of course. There is a difference, however, between the masks we wear and live by, and taking responsibility for the self (its past and future); there is a difference between the lie of our character that runs our lives, and deciding how we are going to be ourselves in the face of the contradiction and struggles described thus far.

Like Freud and Becker, Kierkegaard believes our neurosis or despair (as he calls it) is that we repress who we truly are. However, unlike Freud, for whom we repress our instincts, and unlike Becker, for whom we repress our creatureliness, for Kierkegaard we repress our "infinite passion" and relation to the Excess, because it would be too risky and too strenuous to actualize. It is an understanding of this repression that we will be focusing on in this chapter.

2 The Self

For Kierkegaard, a human being is made up of a synthesis of contradictory poles, along the lines of the Freudian nature-culture duality, and Becker's creaturely-symbolic contradiction. Kierkegaard thinks of the poles of the

1 *DD*, 85–86.

 | HTTPS://DOI.ORG/10.1163/9789004758148-011

synthesis in terms of the general categories of *limiting* and *expanding*. The limiting pole contracts, like a centripetal force pressing inwardly; the expanding pole is a centrifugal force pushing outward into new areas. Kierkegaard describes these poles through various dualities or potential syntheses: somatic-psychic, finite-infinite, actual-ideal, necessity-possibility, external-internal, and temporal-eternal.

The synthesis by itself does not make a human being a self; instead, it is our ability to relate to these poles (in the struggle to bring them together) that makes a human being a self. We are not merely made up of contradictory forces or poles, but are a self-contradiction. As Kierkegaard says,

> His soul is a self-contradiction between the external and the internal, the temporal and the eternal. It is a self-contradiction, because wanting to express the contradiction within itself is precisely what makes it what it is. Therefore, his soul is a contradiction and a self-contradiction. If it were not a contradiction, it would be lost in the life of the world [like animals]; if it were not a self-contradiction, movement would be impossible [self-becoming could not happen].[2]

The practical implication of the way the self is structured is that we cannot be indecisive in life: our lives are always a concern for us—we are never indifferent to ourselves, to a desire for well-being, and to living a meaningful life. There is no neutral ground for humans to stand on, and so there is a restlessness within us, driving us toward something to bring us peace, to bring the two poles together. We cannot simply "chase our tails," or feel like we are on a treadmill going nowhere; we cannot merely roll rocks up mountains, and watch them go back down again.

This impact of being a self-contradiction is that the task of becoming oneself has been given to each person—that is, we must relate to the synthesis. Kierkegaard might say that the human self is not finished, but is a structure in which becoming oneself is a task, and so not something already worked out or accomplished—the essence of the self is this self-becoming.

Another way to think about this is that we always have an image of ourselves, a self-perception that gives us comfort, an identity that gives us a sense of worth, and which we want to defend. Most of the time this self-perception is a lie, the character lie that Becker describes. If we have the task to relate to the synthesis in such a way as to bring the two poles together, it is possible as well to misrelate to the synthesis, and, for Kierkegaard, most people do the latter.

---

2 Soren Kierkegaard, *Eighteen Upbuilding Discourses*, trans. and ed. Howard V. and Edna H. Hong (Princeton: Princeton UP, 1990), 166. Henceforth cited as *EUD*.

This is because we are looking for easy ways to find peace, and to suppress the anxiety of this task. The way we do this is by relating to only one pole of the synthesis at a time, to the exclusion of the other pole. Two examples (love and freedom) will clarify this.

Let us say a person has as her self-perception the image of being a loving and compassionate person. This is her infinite passion, that about which she claims to be earnest, and around which her concerns in life revolve. This image of herself gives her comfort, makes her feel like she is living a good life, as well as giving an important sense of personal worth and significance. But loving others is difficult and costly, and one will fail at it over and over again, which will bring anxiety and a sense of weakness—the cracks of the mask will begin to show, not just to others, but also to oneself. She does not have it in herself always to be a loving person: she cannot merely will it as if the *causa sui* project were a reality. Attaining to such an identity entails a long and sacrificial process. In the face of this existential guilt, she seeks to maintain the lie in self-deception. One way she can maintain the lie is by loving "humanity." To do this is to *expand* her love completely into the infinite pole and reside there. She can appease her guilt with the thought of her love of humanity, perhaps weep upon hearing about the suffering in other countries, or the suffering she sees in the media. The problem is that "humanity" is an abstraction, a "no one" in particular. It is easy to love humanity, the difficulty is in loving the person who just cut in front of her in line at the grocery store, or the person who smells, or disagrees with her politically, or has taken from her what she desperately wanted. By loving humanity, she dodges the cost that makes love what it is; in dodging the cost, she is dodging love. Through relating only to the infinite pole, and ignoring the finite or concrete pole, she can maintain the image of being a loving person, without actually having to love anyone, or pay the inevitable "cost" of love.

Another example is that of freedom, and our desire to feel individualistic and independent. As independent, we say we value freedom and carving out our own path. It makes us feel like we matter, like we are in control of our own existence, and so it keeps the anxiety of reality suppressed. What we often mean by "freedom" in America is something along the lines of rights, such as the right to choose between two alternatives. Real freedom, however, is the ability to walk outside the paths created for one, to be self-determined rather than externally determined.

When I taught English, at the beginning of the semester, I would ask the students to read the Robert Frost poem "The Road Not Taken." In this poem the traveler comes to a fork in the road; one direction is a path well-worn and well-traveled, while the other is a path that looks barely taken. I would ask my students which path they would take in this metaphor of life. They are going to base their choice on their self-perception, who they imagine themselves to be—that is, who they want themselves to be. Almost all the students would choose the latter path, because they saw themselves not as followers, but as unique and independent. I would then spend some time in class having them think through this in various ways, reflecting on how they had been making decisions in life, how they had gotten to be where they were (how it was that they were sitting in that seat in English class at that particular moment, when they could be almost anywhere in the world—given what they were paying for school). After a few weeks, we would reread Frost's poem, and I would again ask them to write about which path they would take, and why. Most would admit that they would take the well-tread path, because they recognized that is what they had been doing up to this point in their lives.

Kierkegaard analyzed what is going on here. The paths represented alternative directions in the future—they represented possibility. The future is, for humans, inherently risky, because we cannot control all that will happen on the path we take. This unknown makes us anxious because we feel our helplessness before the future and its unknown actualities. And so, we take the path we have seen others taking (the path provided to us by society), because it gives a sense of safety. As Kierkegaard says, "anxiety is the dizziness of freedom, which emerges when the spirit wants to posit the synthesis and freedom looks into its own possibility, laying hold of finiteness to support itself. Freedom succumbs in this dizziness."[3] The "laying hold of finiteness to support itself" is what Becker describes as "transference," and is the path most people take. In true freedom we tend to feel that we are in over our heads; we do not have enough information to secure the future for ourselves, and so are anxious over the decision.

Thus, rather than deciding for ourselves, we allow our culture to do it for us, following the necessary, general path it provides. This, however, offends our sense of self, and so we must deceive ourselves through relating only to one pole of the synthesis, believing we are relating to both. In terms of the example of freedom, we have opted for necessity over the freedom of possibility, though we have deceived ourselves about this, by thinking the "choices" we make on this path are actually our choices. If we are honest with ourselves, we will admit that these are not really our choices, but we are simply following the established order or crowd. We will take a closer look at this, because Kierkegaard believed that the main place we hide from ourselves is within the

3 Soren Kierkegaard, *The Concept of Anxiety*, trans. Reidar Thomte and Albert B. Anderson (Princeton: Princeton UP, 1980), 62. Henceforth cited as *CA*.

crowd. Further, as we have already seen in relation to Freud and Becker, hiding in the crowd is an important element for understanding modern cynicism and its therapeutic.

3 The Crowd and Established Order

If we have the task of becoming ourselves, and so are not yet ourselves, who, then, are we? We are the "crowd."[4] Kierkegaard writes, "One becomes a human being by aping others. One does not know by himself that he is a human being but through an inference: he is like the others—therefore he is a human being. Only God knows whether any of us is that!"[5] The song "The First of Me" by the band Hoobastank presents a good concrete picture of what Kierkegaard is getting at:

> I must make a choice / A tough decision / Listen to my voice / Should I give in / To temptation, admiration / One leads to myself / The other to someone else / Just an empty shell / Just an empty shell. …
>
> I hear a voice inside / It's grown into a scream / I'm not the next of them / I am the first of me / 'Cause I can't live the lie / I am just what you see / I'm not the next of them / I am the first of me.

This song speaks of a decision the band must make regarding who they are, and which path they will follow. The one direction is known, a path that follows the cultural heroics and what the crowd wants; the other path leads somewhere else, which they know will define them, though they are unsure of how it will define them (i.e., they could fail, and so be defined as "losers"). At this point in their decision, they realize that if they choose to be the "next of them" they will no longer be choosing for themselves—they will no longer be free. No doubt, if they make the choice to be the "next of them," they will—in order to save their sense of worth, and rescue their self-perception—need again to believe they are free in all the little choices they are making. At this point, however, they see the choice clearly, without self-deception. The question Kierkegaard is asking is whether one will be the next of them, or the first of me.

---

4 This is in line with Heidegger's analysis of *das Man* in *Being and Time*. See Martin Heidegger, *Being and Time*, which is an echo of Kierkegaard's views. Trans. John Macquarrie & Edward Robinson. (New York: Harper and Row 1962), pp. 149–168.

5 Soren Kierkegaard, *Soren Kierkegaard's Journals and Papers, Volume III*, trans, and ed. Howard V. and Edna H. Hong (Bloomington: Indiana UP, 1975), #3559. Henceforth cited as *JRNL III*.

What is the next of them? The "them" is not anyone in particular, but an abstraction, the "crowd," the ground out of which arises our character lie. Kierkegaard writes, "From the 'others' a person of course actually finds out only what others are—it is in this way that the world wants to deceive a person out of becoming himself. 'The others' in turn do not know what they themselves are either but continually know only what 'the others' are."[6] It is like Freud's and Becker's argument that our superego is not so much internalizing our parents, as internalizing their superego. It is the blind leading the blind, going down paths for no other reason than that is the path everyone else is going down. No one knows if it leads to anywhere less risky than the path that is untrod, but there is safety in numbers, as we say.

What we do not think about is the cost to ourselves of this movement, what it is we abandon when we surrender ourselves to the crowd: we exchange our true passions for what the crowd is pursuing; we become empty shells, passive, and ultimately surrender our very lives and selves to the crowd. To fulfill our true passions is to experience a sense of fulfillment; to fulfill the "crowd's" expectations is to leave oneself (one's self) unfulfilled. This unfulfillment is an empty feeling we seek to fill by palliate measures. We live lives of languishing in an aimless and chaotic journey, taking paths of least resistance, because nothing is worthy of any sort of cost—no path is valuable enough for any kind of personal sacrifice. As Brown puts it, we become the very thing we feared becoming amid the struggle of the Oedipus project: "a passive object of fate, an appendage of others, a plaything of the world." Like Oedipus, in the very attempt to run from our fate, we succumb to it.

Kierkegaard believes there is a way out of this fate, a way "to be an active center within ourselves," and this way begins with seeing through our self-deceptions. Becker quotes Kierkegaard, in an excellent description of how the self loses itself to the crowd:

> the *immediate* man ... his self or he himself is something included along with 'the other' in the compass of the temporal and the worldly. ... Thus the self coheres immediately with 'the other,' wishing, desiring, enjoying, etc., but passively; ... he manages to imitate other men, noting how they manage to live, and so he too lives after a sort. In Christendom he too is a Christian, goes to church every Sunday, hears and understands the parson, yea, they understand one another; he dies, the parson introduces him to eternity for the price of $10—but a self he was not, and a self he did not become. ... For the immediate man does not recognize

6 Soren Kierkegaard, *Christian Discourses/The Crisis and a Crisis in the Life of an Actress*, trans. Howard V. and Edna H. Hong (Princeton: Princeton UP, 1997), 40. Henceforth cited as *CD*.

> this self, he recognizes himself only by his dress, … he recognizes that he has a self only by externals.[7]

This is what self-deception consists of in the limiting pole for Kierkegaard: to define oneself by externals, to change ourselves as one changes clothes.[8] This is what it means to be in the *tuphos* of the cultural currency.

One of the things that makes this self-deception so tricky to recognize, let alone overcome, is that it "works." One can live comfortably and secure in this self-deception, relatively free from anxiety, as long as things continue to go according to the cultural plan. One is languishing and in despair, without a deep sense of fulfillment in life; however, as long as life obliges in preserving the chosen image, and the cultural heroic or script can be internalized, one can remain unconscious of, and repress this despair. Kierkegaard writes,

> Just by losing himself in this way, such a man has gained an increasing capacity for going along superbly in business and social life, indeed, for making a great success in the world. … He is so far from being regarded as a person in despair that he is just what a human being is supposed to be.[9]

We noted above that the "healthy" neurotic is the one who does not feel his neurosis, whose neurotic symptoms are working to hide his self-deception. It is the one who has seen through the deception (or come close to seeing through it) whose neurosis becomes problematic, since he cannot quite give himself to the lies and illusions any longer, and so in his exile senses the despair. Becker has pointed out that Kierkegaard "is attempting to ferret people out of the lie of their lives whose lives do not look like a lie, who seem to succeed in being true, complete and authentic human beings."[10] In other words, Kierkegaard is trying to make one neurotic (or better, aware of one's neurosis), to feel the despair and anxiety that is always there, held beneath consciousness; he is hoping we will see that we are poor in spirit, and in need of healing.

For Kierkegaard, our deepest problem is not that we are lost, but that we do not realize our lostness, or do not care about it. Kierkegaard thought that our only hope for healing was to recognize our lostness and the failed attempts at

---

7 *DD*, 77–78.

8 This will become more connected to our present culture when I analyze the relation between the therapeutic and consumerism in Chapter 19.

9 Soren Kierkegaard, *The Sickness Unto Death*, trans. Howard V. and Edna H. Hong (Princeton: Princeton UP, 1980), 34. Henceforth cited as *SUD*.

10 *DD*, 82.

being *causa sui*; this is what the bulk of his authorship was attempting to do. But he knew that we are unwilling to recognize it because of the anxiety it creates, which causes us to set up various types of resistances to this knowledge. The greatest resistance is what he called "hiding in the crowd," and so living by the established order (the cultural heroics).

Our despair is neurosis, the price we pay for hiding from our creatureliness, and our own inner depths (out of which our infinite passions arise, passions that would allow us to flourish). We end up living trivial and insignificant lives in this *causa sui* project, and so our very self becomes trivial and insignificant—all in the process of believing that we are becoming significant. We are like Ivan Ilych in Leo Tolstoy's story *The Death of Ivan Ilych*. This short story is about the last days of a successful judge named Ivan Ilych. Ivan knows he is dying, and in the light of this knowledge he looks back at his life, and reflects:

> Then all became confused [for Ivan] and there was still less of what was good [about his early life]; later on again there was still less that was good, and the further he went the less there was. His marriage, a mere accident, then the disenchantment that followed it, his wife's bad breath and the sensuality and hypocrisy; then the deadly official life and those preoccupations about money, a year of it, and two, and ten, and twenty, and always the same thing. And the longer it lasted the more deadly it become. [Ivan reflects], "*It is as if I had been going downhill while I imagined I was going up. And that is really what it was. I was going up in public opinion, but to the same extent life was ebbing away from me.* And now it is all done, and there is only death."[11]

The despair was always with Ivan, but life functioned for him; he seemed to be able to control life, and so he never reflected on how much of it was languishing. He thought he was going uphill, becoming a successful person, when in reality his life was ebbing away. It is Camus' stage set, the bitter routine of life. Every day he was getting up to roll another rock up a mountain, a year of it, and two, and ten, and twenty, and always the same thing.

Like Freud, Kierkegaard believed that such a life is immature, a running from the task of growing up and becoming a self, of having to make the unconditional choice on which one will stake one's life:

> One can be thirty years old and more, forty years old, and still be just a child—yes, one can die as an aged child. But to be a child is so delightful! So one snuggles

---

11 Leo Tolstoy, *The Death of Ivan Ilych and Other Stories*, trans. Aylmer Maude (New York: Signet, 1960), 148. (emphasis added).

> at the breast of temporality in the cradle of finitude, and probability sits by the cradle and sings to the child. If the wish is not fulfilled and the child becomes restless, then probability calms him and says: Just lie still and sleep, and I shall go out and buy something for you.[12]

4 Conclusion

We protect children from the dangers of the world, from the risks inherent in living in a world we do not control. We coddle them in their helplessness, as we should. The problem is that we remain these children into adulthood, running from the risks inherent in life, and the decisions that would lead us into more fulfilling and significant lives. We do this because of anxiety, but there comes a time that we must face this anxiety, and make a choice concerning it.

It is important to note that the anxiety exists because there is something at stake. If there were nothing significant at stake, we would feel no anxiety—which is precisely why Kierkegaard says the "spiritless" are incapable of experiencing anxiety. Kierkegaard hoped his readers would face this anxiety, and that it would bring about an identity crisis—an awakening to the task of self-becoming.

Since it is anxiety that causes us to run from ourselves, it is anxiety we must face. It is faced in the *krisis* I mentioned above, which Kierkegaard conceived as an identity-*krisis*. We must come before this *krisis* or decision about who we are. Kierkegaard hoped this *krisis* would eventually lead us to abandon the desperate *causa sui* project.

12 *EUD*, 316.

CHAPTER 10

Identity-*Krisis*

1 The Decision

1.1 *Krisis*

As mentioned earlier, our English word "crisis" is derived from the Greek term *krisis*. *Krisis* means decision or judgment that needs to take place before a fracture or separation. It is like the separation on the path in Frost's poem, which, if one is to continue moving forward, requires one makes a choice. I point to the idea of a fracture, because we can think of a crisis as a time in life when things no longer work, and we are faced with a difficult decision. It is a crisis because the means of automatic living are no longer working, or are leaving us empty, perhaps depressed. It is this *krisis* that Kierkegaard believes will cause us to grow up, to take responsibility for our lives, and to become a self. He wants us to stop lying to ourselves so that we face the despair of our creatureliness. It is in that moment, which Kierkegaard views as an "atom of eternity," that we will decide on who we will be. It is a moment when one gathers one's past and future, bringing meaning to one's life as a whole through an infinite passion. It redeems the past by drawing it up into the future, giving the future meaning through the expectancy of the passion. Frederick Buechner describes this when he writes,

> As humans we know time as a passing of unrepeatable events in the course of which everything passes away including ourselves. As human beings, we also know occasions when we stand outside the passing of events and glimpse their meaning. Sometimes an event occurs in our lives (a birth, a death, a marriage—or some event of unusual beauty, pain, joy) through which we catch a glimpse of what our lives are all about and maybe even what life itself is all about, and this glimpse of what "it's all about" involves not just the present but the past and future too.
>
> Inhabitants of time that we are, we stand on such occasions with one foot in eternity.[1]

1 Frederick Buechner, *Listening to Your Life*, ed. George Connor (San Francisco: Harper-Collins, 1992), 267.

 | HTTPS://DOI.ORG/10.1163/9789004758148-012

This "meaning" is the infinite passion, a decision one makes in *krisis*, not a decision passively undergone; it is a truly free choice. We find a good example of this in one of Kierkegaard's journal entries:

> What I really need is to become clear in my own mind *what I must do*, not what I must know—except in so far as knowing must preceded every action. The important thing is to understand what I am destined for, to perceive what the Deity wants *me* to do; the point is to find the truth which is truth *for me*, to find *that idea for which I am ready to live and die*. ... It was this that I lacked, the experience of living a *complete human life* and not merely a life of understanding, so that with this I would not be basing the development of my thought—well, upon something that is called objective, something which at all events is not my own, but I should be basing it upon something connected with the deepest roots of my soul, through which, so to speak, I have grown into the divine nature and cling fast to it even though the whole world collapses. This is what I *lack*, and *towards it I am striving*.[2]

1.2 The Cost

Kierkegaard is thinking about a decision that he will stake his life and death upon, which means it is a decision in which he understands that there will be loss in the choice. It is in this understanding of what one sacrifices for this choice that anxiety arises. When people are anxious before getting married, it is usually not because they are going to say "Yes" to the person they love, but the anxiety is due to all they are saying "No" to in that choice—the way the choice will limit and define them, and close other opportunities. It is the cost, the sacrifice, and determinative nature of such a choice over which we are most anxious.

This is why following the crowd relieves us of anxiety: when we spiritlessly follow the crowd, we never really feel like we are saying "No" to anything, because we are not committed to anything, except the crowd; every choice is made in moderation, "to a certain degree."[3] This lack of commitment reminds me of a conversation I had with a friend on the night before his wedding. I asked him if he was nervous. He said, without a bit of

2 Quoted in Walter Lowrie, *A Short Life of Kierkegaard* (Princeton: Princeton UP, 1970), 82–83.

3 "All human wisdom consists in this glorious and golden principle: to a certain degree, there is a limit." Soren Kierkegaard, *Judge for Yourself!*, in *For Self-Examination/Judge for Yourself!*, trans. and ed. Howard V. and Edna H. Hong, 89–215 (Princeton: Princeton UP, 1990), 154. Henceforth cited as *JFY*.

reflection: "No, I can always get a divorce if it doesn't work out." The next day, as I watched him say his vows, and make his commitment and promises to his bride, I had a sick feeling of being a part of a charade, a child's pretend game of dress up. Nothing special was taking place, nothing worthy of the money or emotions or time being put into it. It was never going to last, because there would come a time when it would be difficult, and he had already decided, for the sake of freedom from anxiety, that when it got difficult, or "better" opportunities presented themselves, it would be over—and it eventually ended.

It is what is at stake that gives life significance. It is what one gives up in order to gain something, the choice to pursue something at all costs, that gives value to what is pursued. When things are given to the children of the wealthy, they seldom understand the value of it, because there was no cost to them. It is the same when culture gives us our values and significance, which can be changed and altered as soon as it becomes something requiring sacrifice. We do not realize that it is the cost and sacrifice in the decision that makes the decision a matter of earnestness.

1.3 Does the Decision *Really* Matter?

After analyzing Freud's and Becker's views on human significance, the question may arise: Does the decision *really* matter? Have we not already seen, in our analysis of Becker, that this very earnestness that Kierkegaard points to is an illusion, and the sacrifice (whichever one chooses) will come to nothing—the rock will roll down the mountain? This is where Kierkegaard parts ways with Becker.[4] Becker and Kierkegaard agree that coming to the point of the despair of creatureliness is coming to the point of understanding something essential about being human: in our helplessness, we have to (we will) surrender to something, since we do not have the strength within ourselves to make it on our own. Both Becker and Kierkegaard understand that self-sufficiency is a lie and that we have to lean on something. Further, they both recognize that deceiving ourselves around this is the very nature of our neurosis, sin, and despair.

What they disagree about is the nature of this "leaning" on something. For both it is to be a conscious choice, but for Kierkegaard the decision (*krisis*) is to be made in all earnestness and inwardness (in a faithfulness that is genuinely committed), whereas for Becker the decision seems to come with a kind of

4 Something Becker is well aware of, and analyzes in *DD*, 258–260.

irony or jest that has a connection to modern cynicism's ironic detachment (one knows it is a lie, but at least one has chosen it self-consciously). This is a subtle, yet important, distinction, because even though it appears a decision is being made, without earnestness it lacks what we could call the *parrhesiastic* element. This can be clarified by looking at Kierkegaard's distinction between the "what" and the "how" of *krisis*.

1.4 The Emphasis on the "How"

Kierkegaard believes *what* we choose to surrender to is very important (indeed, eternally significant), but given our current cultural (nihilistic) situation, it is the *how* of the choice on which we should focus. Focusing on the *what* is putting the cart before the horse. One will most assuredly not get the right *what* (or get it in the right way—which is the same thing as not getting it at all) if one does not get the right *how*. To put the *what* before the *how* is to "evade some of the pain and *crisis* of decision."[5] In an important sense, Kierkegaard views the *what* as important for the potential for deception, and views the *how* as important for the potential for self-deception.[6]

Focusing on the *how* is what Kierkegaard means when he says that "truth is subjectivity." He does not mean that it is relative, or that the *what* is some kind of "working lie," as it is for Becker. He says,

> *When the question about truth is asked objectively* [the *what*], *truth is reflected upon objectively as an object to which the knower relates himself. What is reflected upon is not the relation* [the *how*] *but that what he relates himself to is the truth, the true. If only that to which he relates himself is the truth, the true, then the subject is in the truth. When the question about truth is asked subjectively, the individual's*

5 Soren Kierkegaard, *Concluding Unscientific Postscript to* Philosophical Fragments, trans. Howard V. and Edna H. Hong (Princeton: Princeton UP, 1992), 129. (emphasis added). Henceforth cited as *CUP*.

6 This is a somewhat difficult and abstract analysis we will be undertaking for the next several pages. However, it is important to struggle through it, because the significance of the distinction between deception and self-deception is especially significant for understanding the dangers of modern cynicism. Modern cynicism is focused on the issue of deception, though it is immersed in self-deception. What is especially insidious for modern cynicism is that its focus on deception is the very means used for self-deception. Although the analyses in the remainder of this chapter will appear abstract to the reader, the content will be filled in as we begin to analyze the means of self-deception within modern cynicism, and *how* the cynical therapeutic keeps us within the self-deception—that is, the rationalizations it creates.

> *relation is reflected upon subjectively. If only the how of this relation is in truth, the individual is in truth, even if he in this way were to relate himself to untruth.*[7]

Kierkegaard is saying that it is not only the object to which one relates that determines if one is in the truth (that to which one *says* one commits or invests one's life), but the way—the mode in which—one relates to the object is also essential for being in truth (for having a right or true relation to the object).[8] This is because one can deceive oneself about the commitment. We saw this earlier in the example of the woman who believed love is the right passion to be related to in life (love was her passionate or infinite ideal): while this was objectively true for her, we saw that subjectively she was in self-deception about her object (she could "love" humanity, but not individual people).

Think back to the example of my friend's marriage. What made me so uncomfortable during the ceremony was the untruth of the *how*. The *what* followed all the legal and cultural protocols for the marriage to be objectively true and binding, and yet the *how* made a mockery of the whole thing. Better to have just skipped the vows, in order to make the *how* more in line with the true *what*. It was the deceptive nature of it that made it all seem so bizarre, even crazy. Yet this was a self-deception, one that took place in the *how*, not the *what*. For Kierkegaard, this distinction between the *what* and the *relation to* the what is a central aspect of self-deception, which explains why there is more going on than simply relating to the incorrect object; there is also the entire misrelation to the object, which we have been calling self-deception. This self-deception is related to the risk inherent in freedom or possibility.

When it comes to modern cynicism, it may be the enlightened consciousness of its skepticism is objectively true, but we will come to see that it is subjectively false due to the self-deception of its false consciousness, and the way it is relating to its ability to *see through* everything.

---

7 *CUP*, 199.

8 We have all met someone who seems to relish hurting others with words, and when confronted, says something along the lines that she is only speaking the truth, and she can't help it if people don't want to hear the truth. We understand, however, that the cruelty is not in *what* is said (assuming it is even factual), but in *how* it is said. Objectively she speaks the truth, but subjectively it is not at all about the truth, and so is untruth. This is what Kierkegaard means by truth is subjectivity. It is also in line with what we saw in relation to the ancient cynics' *parrhesia*: it was the *how* that made their relation to the truth *parrhesiatic*. Their relation to the truth was so earnest that they were willing to risk loss and embrace their exile.

1.5 Freedom and Disposition

Let us bring this back to the issue of freedom in order to explain the *how* of freedom. Possibility, as we have seen, is connected to freedom, and so moves into the unknown. A choice is always risky, because we have no idea where the *krisis* will lead us. My friend tamed the risk by believing he could "undo" his decision at any time; indeed, this ability to "undo" his choice most likely seemed to him like freedom itself—he was free even from the constraint of his own vows. However, a true *krisis* or decision does not end with the initial choice, because in the choice we become responsible for preserving it. After all, if we do not preserve it, we did not choose, but followed a momentary whim. As Karl Rahner has said, "Freedom ... does not consist in always being able to do the opposite of what has been done up to now, but it consists in being able to effect oneself once and for all into finality."[9]

For Kierkegaard, this means the *krisis* demands a *repetition*, which is the test of the true earnestness of the choice—that is, *how* serious one really is in the choice. This is what brings integrity to life. Earnestness is the "maturity" Kierkegaard believes takes us from childish self-deception to authenticity. He says that

> earnestness ... is the *acquired* originality of disposition, its originality preserved in *the responsibility of freedom* and its originality in the enjoyment of blessedness. In its historical development, the originality of disposition marks precisely the eternal in earnestness, for which reason earnestness can never become habit.[10]

In the *krisis* we are responsible for preserving the "originality of disposition."[11] The originality of disposition is acquired, and in this very historical development (this acquiring in the process of self-becoming), the infinite and eternal make themselves felt in earnestness (*the choice matters*). Thus, to be earnest is to feel the responsibility of acquiring the originality of disposition; it is to feel the responsibility of the development of the self (the task of self-becoming).

Although this analysis may seem to have become overly complex and abstract, Kierkegaard is explaining a concrete situation that every addict

---

9 Karl Rahner, *Theological Investigations: Volume II* (*Man In the Church*), trans. Karl-H. Kruger (Baltimore: Helcion Press, 1967), 248.

10 *CA*, 149. (emphasis added).

11 By "originality of disposition" Kierkegaard means the initial, passionate choice that will take one's life in a particular direction, and directly impact who one will become (one's disposition). Since we exist as temporal or time-bound creatures, this original choice must be repeated over and over with the same passion.

who has ever tried to be *free* from his or her addiction understands (or anyone who has ever made a New Year's Resolution and failed to remain resolved for more than a month or two). Whether one overcomes the addiction or not—that is, becomes *free*—is all about *repetition*. Making the true choice (the right *how* of freedom) is not simply a whim due to a momentary feeling of resolve (a self-deceptive view of freedom), but making the choice over and over again with an originality of disposition (with the same resolve or passion).

Kierkegaard says, "The earnest person is earnest precisely through the *originality* with which he returns in repetition."[12] The originality is the initial passion in one's choice, the uniquely infinite passion about which we wrote earlier. "Repetition" means we must continually make this choice, continually be on that path, and in this we will find the earnestness in life—that life has meaning. If one loses the originality, one is back to a passionless, disinterested routine—in which one may be related to the right *what*, but in the wrong way (*how*).

What Kierkegaard was trying to show us in his writings is that we run from these *krisis*-decisions. Because of this, and our need to feel that our lives matter, we move into self-deception: we continue to believe that we are free, that we are making choices, when we are simply following the path laid out for us.

This brings us back to our self-deception about freedom, and how we are able to maintain the sense that we are free—in control of our own lives, self-sufficient and self-grounding. We do this through "probability." Probability is not possibility, because probability is not a *krisis*-decision, but a calculation. Probability attempts to take the risk out of making choices, and does so by deceptively making a choice obvious and safe (i.e., as if it is the only reasonable alternative). It is less a choice, than a technique. For instance, in choosing one's career, one can go to a career counselor, take personality tests, etc., which will narrow down the choice to whatever tops the list in the calculations. This is all well and good, but the set of options are often connected to alternatives that fit with the particular cultural path—what will get me the American Dream. One ignores one's own passion, and instead follows the calculation, coming to believe the calculation is better able to get at one's true passions. I can pretty much guarantee that "Philosophy Professor" would *never* have come up on such a test in relation to me in high school, as I was trying to figure out what career path to take. It was not on the radar

12 *CA*, 149. (emphasis added).

because it didn't fit the heroic of that time. However, it is a career I am passionate about, and love to wake up to.[13]

No doubt, probability feels like a choice between a couple of alternatives, but the *how* of the choice has gotten rid of the risk and what is at stake—one can "choose" without anxiety because the calculation makes the choice seem obvious and safe. In a sense, it puts one on a path that has been approved by the established order. No doubt, there are many smaller choices or opportunities on the path, but they are all ruled and governed by the same calculative probabilities. A personality test replaces the self-reflection inherent in a *krisis*-decision. One does not have to make a choice, one simply answers some questions, plugs in the data, and follows whatever the calculations spit out. It is a "choice" without alternatives, and so feels like a choice without risk. The most common approach to probability in our culture is to thoughtlessly follow what the "experts" tell us to do. We are seeking to make the future appear controllable, running from the inherent Excess of possibility. Experts and their calculations are there to tell us what our futures hold for us.

The important distinction between probability and possibility is that while probability calculates what we know, possibility is a movement into the unknown. Probability is connected to the narrowing of life that Becker defined as a central characteristic of neurosis. Karl Rahner points to this all too common reductionism in relation to the Excess:

> In the ultimate depths of his being man knows nothing more surely than that his knowledge, that is, what is called knowledge in everyday parlance, is only a small island in a vast sea that has not been traveled. It is a floating island, and it might be more familiar to us than the sea, but ultimately it is borne by the sea and only because it is can we be borne by it. Hence the existentiell question for the knower is this: Which does he love more, the small island of his so-called knowledge or the sea of infinite mystery? Is the little light with which he illumines this island—we call it science and scholarship—to be an eternal light which will shine forever for him? That would surely be hell.[14]

---

13 If memory serves me right, at the top of the list of my career test in high school was "truck driver." I do love to drive (and especially did in high school), and can see how it would be a life of flourishing for others, but I know life would have "ebbed away" for me if I had taken the test seriously.

14 Karl Rahner, *Foundations of the Christian Faith: An Introduction to the Idea of Christianity*, trans. William V. Dych (New York: Seabury Press, 1978), 22.

The issue of probability will become important in the analysis of modern cynicism and the therapeutic. We will find that within the cynical therapeutic probability becomes translated into various techniques for living in a world no longer guided by positive communities. Cynics believe that freedom from traditional metanarratives and their constraints (laws, commands, ideals) means that they have found a new level of freedom, but we will find that this is not the case: they still run from the risk of freedom, and so must surrender themselves to cultural values and constraints, as well as to technical ways of making "choices."

2 The Cost of the Illusion of Risk-Free Living

2.1 Controlled by What We Do Not Trust

Due to the loss of positive communities that connect people through a shared, transformative and redemptive community, we find ourselves alone and insecure. This isolation becomes more intense as people relate to others as either useful and beneficial for their lives, or as obstacles in the face of the contingencies of life. As the insecurity grows (as it has within modern cynicism), we no longer trust in the "good intentions" of those around us. Further, we are no longer motivated by the same communal purpose, and so expect others' motives to be self-serving. Kierkegaard describes this cynical relation to others: "People therefore seriously think about preserving and safeguarding what they possess; *they therefore distrust each other and life; this mistrust is therefore so common among people that no one finds it offensive*, not even one's best friend. Ah, anyone who has just come of age, as it is called, in the world understands very well what I mean."[15]

Though we live within this general mistrust, we remain bound to what culture has given us to pursue. With cynicism we have reached a point where the alternatives have so disappeared that we give our lives to the very things we know to be illusions. For example, we elect and reelect politicians we know are lying to us, we pay much more for clothes because of the brand, knowing full well branding is simply a way of manipulating us out of our money.

We turn to the world, to things, to calculations, and the scripts of our culture in order to gain a sense of security and comfort. What brings us comfort

15 *EUD*, 182. (emphasis added).

and security is not only the illusion that we are in control, but also that our world of choices is narrowed, and we can take it in "bite-size pieces," as Becker puts it. Kierkegaard wants to show us not only that we are not in control, but we are neither comfortable nor secure in our artificially narrowed world. The reason for this is that ultimately we cannot control all the contingencies in the world.

Kierkegaard argues that in possessing the world (in possessing the material things, the lifestyles, and the self-images that make us feel secure and at home in life, and by which we gain self-identity), one is actually possessed by the world. We gain security and comfort at a superficial and temporary level, but we end up feeling less secure and comfortable at a deeper, psychological level. In our need to possess the world, the world is more powerful than us, due to its contingent character. As we surrender ourselves to these contingent items, our lives become more insecure (we have more that can go wrong, and need to protect from loss). Kierkegaard says, "The imperfect cannot be possessed by a person as his sole possession [his fetish or idol] without his coming to be possessed by it, for when a person only wants to be external, secular, temporal, then are the world and temporality unconditionally more powerful than he?"[16] One's possessions in the world can be lost and diminished, along with one's sense of security, comfort, and worth. It is the contingent nature that makes these things more powerful, since one is forced to "bow to" whatever factors are necessary for keeping all these possessions at hand.

This will become clearer as we look at the cynical therapeutic's continual need for adjustment and adaptation for the sake of self-preservation, and the cost one pays for this type of life. We will see that the modern cynic is forced to lose herself within this situation, and invest in things, people, and institutions she knows are deceptive and manipulative. As I have put it before, the modern cynic is able to deface the cultural currency, but will not move into exile.

2.2 The Loss of One's Self

To say that our character is a lie is to point out that we come to know and define ourselves not in relation to ourselves, but to what is not the self: commodities, possessions, positions, etc. We define ourselves, and so our significance, based on material possessions, which have been given an artificial symbolic meaning

16 *EUD*, 165.

by our culture (through advertising and the media). As Kierkegaard might put the cynic in relation to his possessions:

> What would the sagacious self-knowledge be other than this—that he knew himself in relation to something else but did not know himself in relation to himself; in other words, despite its apparent reliability, all this self-knowledge is altogether vague, since *it involved only the relation between a dubious self and a dubious something.* This something else could be changed, so that someone else became the stronger, the more handsome, the richer; and this self could be changed, so that he himself became poor, ugly, powerless; and this change can come at any moment.[17]

This is the state of enlightened false consciousness, which has contracted and pressed us into a narrow and reductionistic life without alternatives. This, our normal behavior, is an accepted neurosis. It is qualitatively like the abnormal neurotic behavior, though it is able to keep the self-deception intact—while abnormal neurosis is not. Abnormal neurosis has lost the support of culture to maintain the illusion. In order for the ego to feel in control, the narrowing must become more intense (individuated, more self-consumed and self-focused), though the qualitative process remains the same.[18]

For instance, think of the agoraphobic individual, locked away in her house, afraid to venture outside the confines of her four walls, due to anxiety of the "unknown" outside. Most of us can readily see the price she is paying for the neurotic symptom, of how the narrowing of life to only that little island of her house or bedroom is impoverishing her life. We can also readily see that the "security" the neurosis buys is not only not worth the sacrifice (the world outside), but is driven by a strong sense of insecurity and anxiety. For Kierkegaard, we are qualitatively no different from the agoraphobic in how we seek to run from anxiety to find a false security; it is only that the quantitative distance of our four "walls" is relatively broader. We are not held by the four walls of our house, but are held in by our cultural constrictions, by probability and facts, by the experts who tell us how to eat, sleep, with whom to have relationships, etc.

Moreover, the narrowing that is supposed to bring significance to our lives, actually makes them more trivial and insignificant. As we saw with Becker,

---

17 *EUD*, 313. (emphasis added).

18 From what we have seen examining Kierkegaard, having self-concern and individuation is not the essence of neurosis, and is even the means of overcoming neurosis. The issue is not self-concern *per se*, but the *how* of this concern about the self. Neurosis is self-concern gone awry.

we seek significance and meaning through the symbolics of culture, through which our character or self becomes a lie. We fear the future because we fear that the path we take may lead to insignificance, and so we turn to probability or the "certitude" outlined by the cultural script, which has provided us with symbols of value. What is important to see is that approaching life through probability means that we run from the "ventures" of possibility that could lead us to a truly meaningful and significant life, living out of those infinite passions about which we genuinely care, and would fulfill our deepest need for meaning. In relation to this fear of venturing, Kierkegaard says,

> The world considers it dangerous to venture ...—and why? Because it is possible to lose. Not to venture is prudent. And yet, precisely by not venturing it is so terribly easy to lose what would be so hard to lose, however much one lost by risking, and in any case never this way, so easily, so completely as if it were nothing at all—namely, oneself. If I have ventured wrongly, well then, life helps me by punishing me. But if I have not ventured at all, who helps me then?[19]

This narrowing of life gives with one hand only to take with the other: in finding a sense of significance in the established order, we move into a life of mediocrity, triviality, and insignificance. We see this triviality and insignificance in the incredible amount of time we spend consuming entertainment or mindlessly surfing the web, the excessive attention we give to our social media accounts, and our fixation on celebrities, sports, and brands. In the end, comfort and security become simply the path of least resistance. The triviality is covered over by the constant noise and busyness that takes place in our culture, as we try to assure ourselves that something important is going on. All this busyness is a mere diversion used to hide the reality that one has abandoned the real significance of human life (becoming a self); instead, we become the living dead, zombies busily wandering around in *tuphos*, seeking to feed our insatiable hunger. As Kierkegaard says of this character lie:

> But this self does not exist; his innermost being has been consumed and depithed in the service of nothing; slave of futility, with no control over himself, in the power of giddy worldliness, godforsaken, he ceases to be a human being; in his innermost being he is dead, but his loftiness walks ghostlike among us—it lives. When you speak with him, you do not speak with a human being; in his hankering after loftiness, he has himself become what was covered: a title

19 *SUD*, 24.

> regarded as a human being. Within there is sheer emptiness and trumpery—indeed, there is nothing. But the appearance is there, the vain appearance that bears the marks of worldly loftiness that command the deference of the passerby—while he bears all this loftiness somewhat like the cushions that bear his medals at the funeral.[20]

As much as we seek meaning and significance, the tragedy Kierkegaard recognized is that *we never even come to the point of asking about it*; we give ourselves up before the question even arises, and so we give up the *quest*, because it is always accompanied with anxiety.

3 Conclusion

There is no neutral position for humans in life, and we are always choosing how we will relate to our selves, whether we are conscious of it or remain in self-deception. The risk of being human is always being played out—there is always something at stake. As we have seen, the more important question is *how* it is being played out. Most are doing so in a restless and aimless busyness:

> The busy ones neither toil nor are oppressed but are just busy, think that they have escaped when they have contrived to avoid sufferings in life; hence they do not wish to be disturbed either by hearing or thinking of that which is terrible. Yes, it is true that they have escaped. They have also escaped having any insight into life and have escaped into meaninglessness.[21]

Kierkegaard's message is that as we seek to escape risk and anxiety we do so by escaping into meaninglessness. We impoverish our lives, abandoning paths of flourishing for those of routine and languishing. Many, if not most, people are living lives that consist of grim coping. We do not have a reason to live, but at most a reason not to die.

We are busier and more restless than previous generations, and yet we rarely ask what all this activity is for the sake of. We do not have to ask when our lives are planned for us. What has become truly remarkable in the past half century or so is that, in our enlightened consciousness we have seen how meaningless and empty are the things our culture offers, and yet, in our false consciousness,

---

20 *CD*, 58.

21 Soren Kierkegaard, *Purity of the Heart is to Will One Thing*, trans. Douglas V. Steere (New York: Harper, 1948), 58. Henceforth cited as *PH*.

we have "decided" to surrender our lives entirely to this meaninglessness. This has become our "established order," which I have characterized as the "cynical therapeutic" (two terms we must still bring together).

As we have seen in this analysis, Kierkegaard *sees through* the deceptions of others, and defaces the currency of culture in a way that is at least on par with Freud. So why do I point to Freud as influential in our modern cynical culture, and not Kierkegaard? It is in addressing this question that we now turn. Generally, we find that the difference is not merely in *what* they view we repress (a difference I have already analyzed), but more importantly *how* they approach the issue of self-deception.

CHAPTER 11

Kierkegaard and Ideology Critique

We will examine self-deception or false consciousness in light of the analyses of the preceding chapters, and in relation to Sloterdijk's analysis of modern cynicism. We will see that modern cynicism is the result of an enlightened consciousness' unwillingness to move in the direction the enlightenment should lead. It stops short because it is unwilling to abandon the *causa sui* project, an abandonment that would cause it to face the full force of its creature anxiety.

In this chapter, we will examine Kierkegaard's approach to an enlightened consciousness. We will see that Kierkegaard differs from Freud due to his (Kierkegaard's) view that we should despair of the *causa sui* project, and so give up on it. Kierkegaard believed that we must meet and embrace the anxiety and despair of an enlightened consciousness (what he called "essential self-knowledge") in order to find true freedom. He believed that such a journey through anxiety and despair was a necessary "cleansing," which would allow us to come out on the other side into what he called a "second immediacy" (a new relation to the world, one in which the world no longer possesses us, so we remain free in relation to it). After analyzing Kierkegaard's defacing of the currency, we will contrast Kierkegaard with the defacing that took place during the various ideology critiques that arose toward the middle and end of the Nineteenth Century, a general approach I argue led to our modern cynical therapeutic. The cynical therapeutic is unwilling to face the *krisis* that arises with an enlightened consciousness, because it is unwilling to give up its *causa sui* project.[1]

1 Kierkegaard's Defacing the Currency and Exile

The characteristic of modern cynics is not merely that they presume the worst, but that they think this puts them a step ahead of the manipulation they

1 In Chapters 14 and 15 I will focus specifically on Freud's ideology critique, and show that our cynical culture is a direct result of Freud's social theories and his theory of the structure of the psyche. This will eventually set up a contrast between Freud's answer to the *krisis* of nihilism, and Kierkegaard's. Freud's answer has won out over all others, and influenced American culture by guiding it not only into an ideological cynicism, but also the triumph of the therapeutic.

 | HTTPS://DOI.ORG/10.1163/9789004758148-013

know is going on all around them. It is not simply that cynics are suspicious when the evidence points to deception, but that they are *always* suspicious. When another person or an institution makes a decision that impacts the cynic's life, the cynic believes the expressed motive for the decision is hiding the real motive underneath, which is *always* self-interested.[2] This "presuming the worst" comes out of a certain kind of knowledge we can call "cynical knowledge." Cynical knowledge is not about transforming anything (oneself or something external to oneself), but is a type of knowledge that gives a false sense of superiority over the manipulation one believes is going on. It is not simply a sense of superiority over individuals and institutions, but also over entire systems or ideologies (political, social, cultural, religious, etc.). It is a *false* sense of superiority, not only because it over-generalizes its suspiciousness, but because after having seen through the systems and ideologies, the cynic remains invested in them for the sake of self-preservation.

A traditional view of false consciousness is in line with Marx's definition of ideology. As Zizek says, the most elementary definition of false consciousness is in Marx's *Capital*: "They do not know it, but they are doing it." Hence, enlightened false consciousness would be "they know very well what they are doing, but still, they are doing it."[3] We modern cynics reject the manipulation and deception at the level of knowledge, but do not reject it in our actions. In other words, although there is an enlightened consciousness concerning these systems, the cynic remains narrowed or fetishized toward the system. This is the modern neurosis, and a sign that the cynic is repressing something—namely, her true self.

Both Kierkegaard's and the various ideology critiques' defacing of the currency are reactions to the enlightened consciousness that arose out of the Enlightenment, though they differ in important ways, differences that will give us an understanding of how and why modern cynicism (which arose out of ideology critique) remains in a false consciousness.

1.1 Losing Ourselves

We have already looked at the issue of the cultural heroics and character lie by which we deceive ourselves, and the repression of our creatureliness this entails. We hide from ourselves in the crowd and established order, which

2 Liyan Gao, "Ideological Cynicism in the Modern Information Age with Sloterdijk and Zizek," *Eras Journal*, 18, no. 1, (August 2016): 51–65, 55.

3 Slavoj Zizek, *The Sublime Object of Ideology* (New York: Verso, 2008), 25.

means we allow the established order to think or decide for us. We do not know what it means to be a self, let alone to be oneself. As Kierkegaard says,

> Surrounded by the hordes of men, absorbed in all sorts of secular matters, more and more shrewd about the ways of the world—such a person forgets himself ..., does not dare to believe in himself, finds it too hazardous to be himself and far easier and safer to be like the others, to become a copy, a number, a mass man.[4]

We are like the Stormtroopers in *Star Wars*: numbers hidden behind masks. When Stormtrooper 55321 dies, they simply replace him with 55322. We are reducible to a component in the cultural machine, spending our lives keeping the mechanism going. However, if Luke Skywalker dies in the first half hour of *Star Wars*, the trajectory of the entire movie changes. The most valuable thing each person possesses is herself, her irreplaceability. If my car is totaled, it is not a big deal, because they have made thousands exactly like it; however, if one of my children dies, something irreplaceable has left my life, and I will never be the same. This irreplaceability is, according to Kierkegaard, an important aspect of our value and meaning, and yet it is one of the first things we throw away, seeking first to be like our parents, and then like everyone else, for the sake of acceptance. It is tragic that we throw away our inherent value by seeking to become something valuable to someone else.

We can get along quite well doing this. We measure our success by how well we do at *not* being ourselves, at hiding from ourselves, deceiving ourselves—that is, passively living by the cultural heroics or scripts. Kierkegaard views this as despair, and says that we are in this despair without knowing it, much as the normal neurotic believes herself to be healthy because her neurosis functions well for her. This ignorance of despair means we are further from deliverance, and our whole culture is actually constructed in order to keep this despair from rising to awareness.

In response to this situation, Kierkegaard says that, "in order to begin to be oneself, a human being first of all must be finished with what the others are and by that find out then what he himself is—in order to be that."[5] This is what Becker meant when he said that Kierkegaard was attempting to ferret people out of the lie in which they have their lives, a lie they do not know is a lie. Challenging this lie is no easy task, because we love our lie, and have built up internal and external resistances to its discovery.

---

4 *SUD*, 33–34.

5 *CD*, 39–40.

1.2 Anxiety

We seek to keep anxiety suppressed, though just because we succeed at this does not mean the anxiety is not there. It is the energy of the hidden anxiety out of which neurotic symptoms arise. Most can sublimate these symptoms, turn this energy toward accepted cultural activities; however, this is becoming more and more difficult: the tension often comes to the surface as our creatureliness and helplessness become apparent, and we begin to feel that we are in over our heads in life. While experiences of death (whether that of others, or "close calls" we ourselves experience) are the epitome of our creatureliness, we also feel it when busyness subsides, because we must be with ourselves, without anything to distract or divert our attention.

As I said, we have found all sorts of ways to keep this from happening; however, Kierkegaard believes the very beginning of coming to ourselves is learning to be anxious in the right way:

> I must say that this is an adventure that every human being must go through—to learn to be anxious in order that he may not perish either by never having been in anxiety or by succumbing to anxiety. Whoever has learned to be anxious in the right way has learned the ultimate.[6]

To struggle with the unknown that is within possibility—with that which exceeds us and our culture—is to allow the expansive aspect of the self to disclose our despair to us, and bring us before a *krisis*. Anxiety accompanies an unknown we face and cannot wrap our minds around. But the unknown is a nothing, and this realization helps one understand where the real power of anxiety resides: we think it comes from the world, but it resides in us.

Kierkegaard speaks of this in terms of the anxiety we have concerning the "the next day": it is about "the next day" (the future) that we become anxious. It is the anxiety associated with *tukhe*, which the ancient cynics understood as "fortune," and Kierkegaard calls fate: it is the capricious nature of life. And yet, the next day (this fate) is a powerless nothing to which *we, in our self-deception, give strength*. As we saw earlier, with our attempts to possess the world, we are possessed by it, and the mood associated with that possession is anxiety. We need things in the world in order to feel secure and comfortable, and yet we do not ultimately control them; tomorrow ("the next day") can change everything, and at some level we understand this.

---

6 *CA*, 155.

Kierkegaard says anxiety arises because of,

> A craving to become more and more—for nothing, since the whole thing is indeed a nothing; a craving to rise higher and higher in loftiness—that is, to sink lower and lower in the care of the abyss—for what else is the care of worldly loftiness than the care of the abyss! What is the care? It is the care lest someone by slyness, by force, by lies, or by truth will take away his delusion. Therefore he secures himself in every way, since he sees danger everywhere, everywhere covetousness, everywhere envy, everywhere ghosts—as is natural, because for an anxious person not even in the darkest night is there as much to horrify the delusion as there are horrors in a delusion.[7]

The anxious care to become more and more is the power behind modern cynicism, and we will see that Kierkegaard's description above fits quite well with what is going on in the cynical consciousness, as it is driven by a need for security, seeing dangers everywhere—behind every person, every situation, every institution. This is the result of the *causa sui* project, the attempt to be the ground of ourselves. This is our despair, for we are not up to it, and do not have it in us; however, we also do not have it in us to face the anxiety of not being the ground of our own existence. Something has to give.

Freud, in the face of this dilemma, sided with the *causa sui* project, though one with diminished expectations. I will show in the chapters to come that it is his understanding of both the psyche and reality which has led to the triumph of cynicism and the therapeutic in our culture.

Kierkegaard, however, sets forth a different direction, opting for facing the anxiety, and letting it "consume all finite ends and [discover] all their deceptiveness."[8] To consume these finite ends is to turn our world upside-down, and face an identity crisis. It is then that we face the *krisis* (choice) between radically different alternatives or paths. Kierkegaard wants to bring us into the anxiety of this uncanniness in order to awaken our spirits, and awaken us to the *krisis* through which we may become ourselves.

We do not want to be ourselves, and so this *krisis* is the very thing from which we run. We would rather stick with the heroics or scripts that are in line with the *causa sui* project: first, because they provide a ready-made path for us to follow, and second because they allow us to stay in the illusion that we are in control of our lives. Kierkegaard is not without his "heroics," but his heroics are on the other side of the *causa sui* project.

---

7 *CD*, 57.
8 *CA*, 155.

1.3 Throwing Away the Cultural Script

One of the ways Kierkegaard refers to the exile that is a response to the defaced currency is by the phrase "dying to" What he means by this is dying to the cultural heroic or script (what he sometimes simply calls the "world") and the character lie. It is to die to what he calls "selfishness." This is not to die to an appropriate concern for oneself, but to the self concern that has gone awry. As Kierkegaard puts it:

> Therefore, death first; you must die to every merely human hope, to every merely human confidence; you must die to your selfishness, or to the world, because it is only through your selfishness that the world has power over you; if you are dead to your selfishness, you are also dead to the world. But naturally there is nothing a human being hangs on to so firmly—indeed, with the whole self!—as to his selfishness! Ah, the separation of soul and body in the hour of death is not as painful as being forced to be separated from one's soul when one is alive! And a human being does not hang on to his physical life as firmly as one's selfishness hangs onto its selfishness.[9]

Kierkegaard has no illusions about what it means to deface the currency after the end of positive communities and the traditional cultural heroics. It is to come before an abyss; it also means coming into collision with the heroics of the established order, which consists of a willingness to experience the painful side of exile for a time. Exile, in religious language, is a "desert experience," a journey through the wilderness that cleanses one of the old in order to become open to, and prepared for, what is new. Or it is the withdrawal every addict must go through in order to gain the freedom of sobriety.

An important category for Kierkegaard associated with this exile is "the single individual." He often dedicated his books to "The Single Individual," understanding that it is only when a person is alone (singled out) that real upbuilding can begin to take place. Kierkegaard is often criticized for his individualism and anti-social leanings; however, his individualism is not a way of life (though one is never to stop being uniquely oneself), but a place to begin so that one can relate to people in a new way—on the other side of exile. While in exile, one does not abide within or by the cultural script, and so from the

---

9 Soren Kierkegaard, *For Self-Examination*, in *For Self-Examination/Judge for Yourself!*, trans. and ed. Howard V. and Edna H. Hong, 1–87 (Princeton: Princeton UP, 1983), 76–77. Henceforth cited as *FS-E*.

perspective of this script one may appear anti-social; however, the Kierkegaardian individual is not anti-social, but is seeking to take responsibility for herself by no longer hiding in the crowd and established order.[10]

As we saw with the ancient cynics, exile came upon them before they defaced the currency. They were almost all outcasts or exiles, and only then could they see the currency from outside, as artificial and arbitrary. The problem Kierkegaard has set for himself is how to bring people into exile when they are not outcasts in the world, and feel they are doing quite well in it—that is, while their repression and neurosis are helping them function without any felt anxiety or despair. He has hope in this task, because there is always a part of us in exile, always a part of the self that transcends its situation. Even while immersed in the finite and concrete world, the self remains separate from it due to the expansive pole of the self, its infinitude, possibility, and the ideal. We are not simply conscious, but self-conscious; this means we are able to get outside our situation and evaluate our place within it. As he says of the person lost in the world:

> [I]n the same moment [of his lostness] he is different from the world, and he senses a resistance that does not follow the movements of the world's life. If he now wants to gain the world, he must overcome the disquiet until once again, like the undulations of the waves, he vanishes in the life of the world—then he has won the world. However, if he wants to gain his soul, he must let this resistance become more and more pronounced and in doing so gain his soul, for his soul was the very difference: it was the infinity in the life of the world in its difference from itself.[11]

Kierkegaard is hoping to draw out the part of the self that is *not* caught up in the world, to speak to it in a way that brings it forward to consciousness. This aspect of the self is what Kierkegaard views as the "conscience," though it is very different from the typical way of understanding conscience—that is, as the moral "voice" or superego.

---

10 "Wanting to hide in the mass or the crowd, to be a little fraction of the crowd, instead of being an individual, is the most corrupt of all escapes. Even if this makes life easier by making it more thoughtless in the din—this is not the question. The question is that of the responsibility of the individual—that every individual human being ought to be a single individual, ought to make up his mind about his conviction." Soren Kierkegaard, *Soren Kierkegaard's Journals and Papers, Volume II*, trans. and ed. Howard V. and Edna H. Hong (Bloomington: Indiana University Press, 1970), #1996.

11 *EUD*, 165.

1.4 Kierkegaard and Conscience

This "resistance in himself" is his "conscience." Conscience, for Kierkegaard, is neither a moral voice in the traditional sense nor the voice of the superego. Conscience conceived in these ways are more often than not merely the voice of the established order, or an internalization of our parents' superegos. For Kierkegaard, conscience is our own voice, the voice that is free from the established order—in fact, it is the voice that calls us back from that order. He thinks of it as the infinite aspect of the self, which calls us back from the finite.[12] It is our ability to transcend our circumstances and think of our place within them. This entails our continual need to make sense of our place in a situation—the meaning the situation has for us. We are never merely "in" something, but we are in it *for* something.

Kierkegaard speaks about the content of conscience in one of his upbuilding discourses.[13] He distinguishes between the "first self" and the "deeper self." The first self is the immediate or empirical self, the self in touch with the world, the face we put to the world. It is the Freudian ego, and Becker's character lie. It identifies or defines itself by its relation to the world, and the accidental qualities it possesses, such as its talents and appearance. It is the self-centered self, seeking to protect and defend its self-perception, and derive comfort from the world. The world is a means for it: the world exists for *its* projects, *its* agendas, to serve *its* needs, and to bring *it* well-being. The first self's sense of worth and happiness are thus intimately connected to how things go "out there" in the world for it. Its focus is the cultural heroics, by which it maintains the *causa sui* project.

The first self, however, is caught in a contradiction in this relationship with the world: it wants the world both to be flexible and stable. It wants the world to be flexible so that it can mold and manipulate the world to its satisfaction; it wants the world to be stable so that it can remain secure, and not have to feel the anxiety that comes with not being in control—the unknown possible changes.

The deeper self is the voice of conscience, and is involved in turning the self's focus inward, in order to understand what it means to be a self—to become a self. The first self views the deeper self as an "interruption" or disruption to its consciousness of the world. It is that reflective voice that arises when the busyness of life is halted, and one begins to ask questions about the

---

12 *PH*, 189.

13 "To Need God Is A Human Being's Highest Perfection," in *EUD*: 298–326.

meaning of what one is doing. It is the "Why?" that arises for every human being in regards to life, if only one will stop long enough to hear the question.

The deeper self summons the focus of the self back from the purely external. It does not change the world, but leaves it as it is: contingent, changing, fickle, and dangerous. We live in a world where it takes years to build order around one's life, but the world can shatter this order in the blink of an eye. Becker's analysis is the voice of the deeper self, in that he did not change the world, but looked at it from a "raw" perspective (what he would call a more honest and realistic perspective); it is the perspective free from the self-deception of the *causa sui* project. Like Becker's analyses, the deeper self seeks to shape the deceitful flexibility of the surrounding world in a way that is no longer attractive to the first self and its character lie.

The deeper self does not try to annihilate the first self (as say, Buddhism does), or completely destroy its relation to the world, because the first self is necessary for our relation to reality; it is the aspect of the self that relates to the world. Instead, the deeper self seeks to make the world's general character appear different in the eyes of the first self, as it tries to help it to overcome the lie upon which it builds its character. It wants to help the first self admit that the contingency of the world is something that, more often than not, works against the first self's interests, not for them. In this, it shows the self's helplessness in the world, how the world does not fulfill the deepest longings of the self, but is only offering superficial compensations.

The deeper self also seeks to unseat the self-centeredness of the first self, keeping this self-centeredness from the prominent position as the sole "interpreter" of the external world. To do this it must help the first self see through the lies (the repressions) it continually tells itself in order to keep the *causa sui* project going, with its sense of self-sufficiency.

The first self must either stop listening to the deeper self or admit that the world is the way the deeper self presents it. Such an admission is difficult for the first self, for "the surrounding world can actually be so favorable, so tangibly trustworthy, so apparently undeviating, and everyone will vouch for the splendid progress if one just begins."[14] This is a "hard sell" for the deeper self: "The first self sits and looks at the beckoning fruits, and it is indeed so clear that if one just makes the move everything will succeed, as everyone will admit."[15]

Kierkegaard is aware of how alien the deeper self's voice sounds to those immersed in the established order or cultural heroics, but he also knows there is a familiarity to it. We hear the voice of conscience when we have had to

14 *EUD*, 314.

15 *EUD*, 315.

come to a "stop," and are forced to be alone with ourselves. Or when the world has not turned out the way we had planned, and left us in the depths of disappointment. We may even hear the voice when our plans have been victorious, and the deeper self asks, "Really? This is all there is? This is what we worked so hard, and sacrificed so much, to achieve? This is how we are going to spend our life?"

Ultimately, this coming back to oneself in one's creatureliness is, in Kierkegaard's terminology, the recognition of being "capable of nothing." The highest form of self-knowledge is the humbling realization that one is capable of nothing essential in the world: that, as we have said earlier, one may make small ripples in the ocean of the cosmos, but they will eventually go flat. Kierkegaard seeks to direct us to a different focus: "instead of gaining the whole world, to gain himself; instead of becoming master, to become one in need; instead of being capable of all things, to be capable of nothing at all."[16]

To be capable of nothing is Kierkegaard's way of expressing the end of our *causa sui* project: we are not self-grounding, we are not as in control as we believe ourselves to be; rather, we are always giving up control to something else. We maintain our illusion through the narrowing of the world in fetishization, focusing on a relatively small, particular task or goal, in order to feel in control of the whole, like the obsessive-compulsive who must keep washing her hands in order to feel in control of life—but at what cost?

Kierkegaard calls the surrender of the *causa sui* project "infinite resignation," and it means no longer to relate absolutely to what is relative[17]—relating absolutely to what is relative is a good definition of "fetishism." It is to abandon our neurotic fetishism and defense mechanisms, to release the narrowing into which these lead, and so become open to something new, something both unknown and yet familiar. For we do not become someone else in this but become ourselves. As John Elrod has put it, "Resignation is a step in the reconstruction of the self. It is not the abandonment or cancellation of oneself and existence, but a new way of understanding oneself in existence. And this new understanding constitutes a new way of being in existence."[18]

Kierkegaard's type of exile is an alternative to the cynical way we currently process the world, and how we relate to the situations, things, and people in it. Cynicism grasps the friction it experiences in the world, but refuses to move into exile, and will not yield to the deeper self's expression of existential

---

16 *EUD*, 313–314.

17 *CUP*, 400–411.

18 John W. Elrod, *Being and Existence in Kierkegaard's Pseudonymous Works* (Princeton: Princeton UP, 1975), 151n.

guilt. We will see why this is the case by examining how the modern cynical approach arose out of ideology critique.

2 Ideology Critique

Sloterdijk's analysis of how cynical reason and cynical knowledge arose historically in modern culture will allow us to distinguish Kierkegaard's approach to defacing the currency and exile from that of modern cynicism, as well as allow us to draw some insights into the contradictory consciousness within modern cynicism.

The original view of the Enlightenment—out of which modern cynicism arose—is very much in line with the Socratic maxim that knowing the good will lead to virtue and progress in human life: if we allow reason to rule, this will free us from the illusions of the past (its superstitions and currency), and bring us to the truth; truth will bring us progress (human and cultural flourishing). Sloterdijk says the Enlightenment philosophers initially saw this as a peaceful process, rather than one consisting of coercion or force: rational dialogue brings free consent to the truth, without the old traditional and religious methods of power, force, and threats.[19]

There are, for those being enlightened, two aspects in this approach: the acceptance of a better position, and the discarding of a previous one. These two aspects bring an ambivalence of feelings: both gain and pain.[20] The enlighteners were aware of this difficulty, but believed the pain is bearable in consciousness because of the compensation: the losers in the rational argument come to see themselves as actually winning, for they have gained knowledge and been set free from their ignorance.[21]

2.1 The War of Consciousness and Ideology Critique

There is more at stake in this acceptance and loss than first perceived by the enlighteners, a loss we have already noted throughout the preceding chapters. The Enlightenment project was more than a simple exchange of ignorance for truth; it was the dismantling and disillusionment of the beliefs that had informed people's lives for centuries. The Enlightenment consisted of a

19 Sloterdijk, 12.
20 Sloterdijk, 13.
21 Sloterdijk, 13.

defacing of the traditional cultural heroics through which people had gained meaning and significance in their lives, and by which they were able to suppress their anxiety. Thus, the enlighteners were not asking those who are to be enlightened merely to give up their false beliefs, but to surrender their sense of security, their comfort, and a sense of mattering in the universe—the beliefs that helped them defend their fragile self-identity against the terrors of the world and death.

As Sloterdijk puts it, there is far more at stake than truth in this issue: there are "hegemonic positions, class interests, established doctrines, desires, passions, and the defense of 'identities.'"[22] According to Sloterdijk, this changes the entire framework of enlightenment: "these impediments so strongly remold the dialogue of enlightenment that it would be more appropriate to talk of a war of consciousness than a dialogue of peace."[23] It is about annihilating those beliefs by which others have defended themselves against the terrors of life.

The question becomes, then, what is the enlightenment giving in return? Sloterdijk says it "enters the dialogue virtually empty-handed; it has only the fragile offer of free consent to the better argument."[24] The problem is that, while it is a better argument from the enlighteners' side, the traditional beliefs have their own reasons for being accepted, an inner logic founded upon their presuppositions. Thus, for the sake of enlightening others, the enlighteners must address and expose these hidden presuppositions, as well as the entire system that protects them. This change takes place in the nineteenth century, as the Enlightenment project becomes "ideology critique."

Generally speaking, ideology critique is an attempt to expose the realities behind the power structures that resist the enlighteners' insights—that is, not just exposing the hidden hegemony, but also the structures that keep the power hidden (the basis of repression). Marx, Freud, and Nietzsche (the "masters of suspicion," as Paul Ricoeur called them) are all prime examples: they take nothing at face value, but see deeper mechanisms and motives behind the ideals people profess to value.[25] This becomes a war on consciousness: "Strictly speaking, ideology critique wants not merely to 'hit,' but to operate with precision, in the surgical and military sense: to outflank and expose opponents, to

22 Sloterdijk, 13.
23 Sloterdijk, 13.
24 Sloterdijk, 14.
25 Dean Dettloff, "From Cynical Reason to Spiritual Creativity: An Exercise in Religious Anthropology" (Master's Thesis, Institute for Christian Studies, 2015), 44–45. http://hdl.handle.Net/10756/605953.

reveal the opponents' intentions. Exposing implies laying out the mechanism of false and unfree consciousness."[26]

The enlighteners' strategy is no longer to win over the opponent, but to deconstruct their position entirely: for Marx, the bourgeoisie cannot be won over by argument (they have too much to lose), but only by the force of revolution; Freud believed the masses of people would remain in their neuroses; Nietzsche did not expect the weak to become strong. Thus, the point is not to win the opponents over to one's position, but to annihilate their position, leaving them with no ground on which to stand.[27] The drive for knowledge becomes more about gaining power for oneself and the group with whom one identifies, than the good of the whole: it is aggressive, wanting to put opponents in a position where they are forced to respond apologetically for the suffering their ignorance has caused others.[28]

Here we see a sharp distinction between Kierkegaard's attempt to deface the currency and the ideology critique's attempt: in the former it is oneself who is humbled by defacing the currency; in the latter, one is emboldened in one's position and knowledge, seeking to come out on top. Kierkegaard seeks to undercut the *causa sui* project; ideology critique seeks not only to affirm this project, but to show that its particular critique is the only real way of gaining self-grounding. Kierkegaard seeks to encourage the individual toward the task of self-becoming, to humanize each person in such a way that she desires to fulfill her own infinite passion. In ideology critique, those who oppose enlightenment, and fight the destruction of their ideology, become objectified in the process, which further alienates them, and entrenches them in their ideologies. The enlighteners objectify them because the enlighteners no longer see them as persons: they see them as mechanisms of repression and oppression, driven by a false consciousness that refuses to engage in dialogue.

Both Kierkegaard and ideology critique make resistance itself a topic for change,[29] but while Kierkegaard seeks to overcome these resistances through drawing the single individual back to herself, opening her to her conscience, ideology critique sees the "opponents" as "cases of resistance, and their consciousness (or unconscious) becomes an object of study."[30] In other words, while Kierkegaard is interested in the universal processes of resistance in order

26 Sloterdijk, 15.

27 Sloterdijk, 16–17. The point is to annihilate their position for the sake of future generations; the current opponents are viewed as "lost causes".

28 Sloterdijk, 17.

29 Sloterdijk, 15.

30 Sloterdijk, 15.

to help the single individual, ideology critique objectifies individuals in order to understand particular processes of resistance.

At this point, the nature of the Enlightenment project has changed, by becoming more aggressive than caring. At the same time, it becomes apparent to those who are viewed as unenlightened and ignorant, that the enlightener is not their friend, and does not really have their best interests at heart.[31] As Sloterdijk says,

> In the end, the critic of ideology stands before the opposing consciousness like one of those modern, highly specialized pathologists who can, of course, say precisely what kind of pathological disturbance the patient is suffering from but knows nothing about the appropriate therapies because that is not his specialty. Such critics, like the medicos corrupted by their profession, are interested in diseases, not patients.[32]

Knowledge itself takes on a different meaning in ideology critique: it is viewed no longer as transformative (as directed at further self-knowledge), but knowledge becomes power, and is a "weaponized epistemology."[33] The opponents come to sense this, as they become suspicious of self-interest in the enlighteners' positions—that is, the enlighteners have something at stake in the whole project, something to do with power and control, rather than *parrhesia*.[34] The enlighteners eventually come to be seen as driven by the same motive of will to power with which they had been accusing the unenlightened. And this is indeed the case, because as long as the *causa sui* project is in play, and allowed to drive human action without being questioned, will to power, self-interest, and the attempt to defend one's position of security and strength are left in place.

Ideology critique goes from knowledge as a value for inner transformation, to knowledge or critique for the sake of power. By "power" is meant the ability to change the world in terms of how the enlighteners see things, to strengthen their heroics and their place within the cultural heroics—that is, to define and direct (to create, not discover) the heroics or scripts of the culture. This is something Kierkegaard would not seek to do, because it simply plays right

31 Dettloff, 31.

32 Sloterdijk, 19.

33 Dettloff calls it a "militarized epistemology" (p. 21), while Sloterdijk calls it an "espionage epistemology" (p. 332).

34 The characteristics of *parrhesia*, such as, risk and challenges from weakness, are absent from the ideology critique, and so the sense that the critic has nothing individually to gain from what she says is missing.

back into the hands of self-deception and false consciousness (as happens within modern cynicism).

Sloterdijk says ideology critique implies an attempt to construct a hierarchy between masking and unmasking theory: "in the war of consciousness, getting on top, that is, achieving a synthesis claim to power and better insights, is crucial."[35] In his Preface, Sloterdijk implies that his entire book on cynicism is about the statement "knowledge is power."[36] Cynical reason and cynical knowledge change how we see the world, and so change the nature and purpose of our knowledge of it.

2.2 Cynical Knowledge: an Ideological Mistrust

The enlightener expects deceptions, and expects them to be artful and creative, though knows they can be seen through. Sloterdijk says that the enlightenment project as ideology critique declares war on appearances: only naked truths, naked facts, are regarded as valid. What is self-evident about the world to this enlightenment mentality is that the world is full of fraud, threats, and dangers, not openness and generosity.[37] We are not to expect truth straight off, but only through the second effort of seeing through appearances.[38] At this point,

> The world bursts at the seams with problems, dangers, deceptions, and abysses as soon as the gaze of mistrusting investigation penetrates it. In the universe of modern knowledge, the backdrops, trapdoors, panoramas, deceptive images, dissembling gestures, hidden feelings, concealed motives, enveloped bodies predominate.[39]

This is to view ourselves as living in an impoverished world, which withholds what is necessary for a good life. In an impoverished world, knowledge is about seeing through others' deceptions, seeing down into the self-interested motives they hide beneath the spoken justifications. This relates to Kierkegaard's quote above, where craving more and more, and wanting to become higher

35 Sloterdijk, 18.
36 Sloterdijk, xxxvi.
37 Sloterdijk, 330.
38 Sloterdijk, 330. For modern cynicism, the Excess is always an enemy, holding some kind of power that must be seen through, not for personal transformation, but for the sake of power. For the cynic, the Excess is, due to its hiddenness, understood as deceptive, whether as that which hides what we need, or is a mere illusion of the ignorant.
39 Sloterdijk, 330.

and higher creates "danger everywhere, everywhere covetousness, everywhere envy, everywhere ghosts—as is natural, because for an anxious person not even in the darkest night is there as much to horrify the delusion as there are horrors in a delusion." This is why cynical knowledge becomes a "weaponized epistemology," or as Sloterdijk might call it, an espionage epistemology:

> Enlightenment espionage is research on the enemy—the accumulation of knowledge about an object to which I am bound not through well-wishing, or disinterested neutrality, but through a direct, hostile tension with a threatening effect. It nourishes a special kind of wanting-to-know and necessitates a series of peculiarly "indirect" methods of research: dissimulation, secrecy, infiltration of positions of trust, misuse of friendships.[40]

In terms of cynicism, this cynical knowledge is suspicious of ulterior motives behind all actions, all professed ideals, all moral pronouncements. Cynical knowledge approaches the world (others, institutions, even nature) as suspicious and mistrustful. Thus, Sloterdijk says there is a paranoia to cynicism:

> The enemy is everywhere: *powers of nature* that are too powerful, too dangerous for us to rely on; *rivals* who, when it comes to the crunch, will show no mercy and now already envision us as corpses over whom they, determined to "survive," will walk if necessary; *traditions* that fog up our minds and cause us to "believe," but forbid us to know what "the case really is."[41]

This cynicism even extends to knowledge itself, as "Nietzsche had begun to undermine every will to know through the suspicion of will to power."[42]

When all knowledge and critique is seen as a manifestation of will to power, the ideology critique is easily turned against the enlighteners themselves. The enlighteners readily admit that ideologies, which seem false from an external point of view, are, as seen from the inside, precisely the right consciousness. How, then, can the enlighteners not suspect themselves of being in false consciousness as well? What agendas and identities are the enlighteners seeking to protect? Could not the enlighteners be living in false consciousness? The supposed "ignorant" who are to be enlightened have now become cynics; they wonder what makes the enlighteners think they are somehow free from false consciousness, or from a fiction of their place in the power structure.

---

40 Sloterdijk, 332.
41 Sloterdijk, 335.
42 Sloterdijk, 334.

The modern cynic uses the awareness gained from the process of enlightenment and "turns it against the aims of the enlightenment itself."[43] Indeed, the one being critiqued is cynically aware and suspicious of the motives of those critiquing.[44] What grows out of this is a change of focus from the *content* of communication, to a suspicion about the *motive*.[45]

3 Conclusion

The main difference between Kierkegaard's defacing of the currency and that of ideology critique is how they relate to existential guilt and the *causa sui* project. For Kierkegaard, we deface the currency in order to uncover our own vulnerability, to expose whatever we are using to repress our creatureliness, in hopes of ending our own *causa sui* project. He is ultimately interested in addressing existential guilt. Ideology critique seeks not simply to keep the *causa sui* project in play, but to make clear that self-sufficiency and autonomy are the only game left to play. No doubt, the ideology critique hopes to dismantle and abolish traditional approaches to the *causa sui* project, but it keeps faithful to the view that when these are finally demolished, we will then truly be able to stand on our own, free from the authorities and superstitions that have controlled us for millennia.

Eventually, ideology critique gives way to an ideological cynicism. It then brings its own cynical reason to bear on how the world, others, and oneself will be interpreted. We now turn to look at modern cynicism in order more clearly to see its false consciousness, as it self-deceptively seeks to keep its illusion of self-sufficiency. To grasp the false consciousness more thoroughly, we will take a more detailed look at what is at play in the modern cynic's unwillingness to move into exile.

---

43 Robert Halsall, "Sloterdijk's Theory of Cynicism, Ressentiment and 'Horizontal Communication,'" *International Journal of Media and Cultural Politics*, 1, no. 2 (2005): 163–179, 165. https://doi.org/10.1386/macp.1.2.163/1.

44 Halsall, 173.

45 We find, then, the cynic also differentiates between the *what* and the *how*, though the *how* is related to deception, rather than self-deception.

CHAPTER 12

Failure to Launch

1 Cynicism as Ideology

Through the ideological critique's process of seeing through the mechanisms of resistance, and the resulting suspicion of everything, the credibility of the traditional morals and cultural heroics have been shaken. The cynic may still give them plenty of lip-service, but they are not what guides the cynic's action. Several scholars on modern cynicism speak of this in terms of nihilism. As Navia puts it,

> Cynicism, as presented by Sloterdijk, is, not unlike the cynicism described by Tardieu, the final conquest of an all-embracing nihilism that announces and welcomes the bankruptcy of meaningful human existence. For both authors, the modern cynic recognizes no authority or higher standards than himself, and views his accomplishments, most if not all of them provided for him by technology, as the highest point in human evolution, for which reason does not even envision the need or ever the possibility of aspiring to a higher level of intellectual or moral development.[1]

Sloterdijk rightly points to the nihilistic loss of alternatives, whether moral or not, that leads to a deeper entrenchment in cynicism and the lack of will to oppose hegemonic power or the established order.[2] However, the cynic is not a nihilist in the sense of actively being against morality—even traditional morality. As Schreier puts it, "the cynic accepts the validity of ethical principles but is no longer convinced of their viability."[3]

This gives a very different picture of defacing the currency than we saw with Kierkegaard. In a sense, ideology critique defaces the traditional currency, not in order to bring the individual out of the narrowing fetishization of the cultural heroics, but to be in control of the cultural heroics—that is, to

1 Navia, 2.

2 "The more modern society appears to be without alternatives, the more it will allow itself to be cynical" (Sloterdijk, 112).

3 Benjamin J. Schreier, "America and Its Discontents: Cynicism in the American Modernist Imagination" (PhD diss., Brandeis University, 2003), 10. ProQuest Dissertations Publishing (3081827).

HTTPS://DOI.ORG/10.1163/9789004758148-014

destroy the heroics, and to write scripts in line with their agendas and interests. Ironically, this is the very process ideology critique was critical of in the first place: the creation of fictions for the sake of power. This contradiction is at the basis of the contradiction of cynicism as enlightened false consciousness. In order to understand this contradiction more thoroughly, we will look at the most general characteristics of the cynicism that arises from ideology critique, and then examine how the cynic *rationally* justifies the contradiction of enlightened false consciousness. We will start by differentiating three forms of cynicism.

2 Master-Cynics, Insider-Cynics and Outsider-Cynics

It is important to draw a somewhat subtle distinction between three types of modern cynics:[4] master-cynics, insider-cynics, and outsider-cynics. These three types of cynics differ in how consciously they participate in cynical actions, the purpose of their cynicism, and their relation to the cultural ideals and conventions.

Master-cynics are the most conscious of both the cynicism within culture and their own cynical approach to life. The primary goal of master-cynics is to gain power for the sake of their self-interests. Their pursuit of power is both hypocritical and blatant. They approach the world through manipulation, often by adopting an allegiance to particular ideals and morals within society that are useful to their self-interested goals. Morality is, for them, a useful fiction, a tool to be picked up or rejected depending upon the necessity of the moment.

Master-cynics are those with power in society: the politicians, business leaders, and policymakers. They know perfectly well that what the "people" want is not leaders who embody the character ideals put forward by culture, but someone who is watching out for their (the people's) self-interest—who can make their lives more comfortable and secure. And so the master-cynics make promises to fulfill these goals, not with the intent of fulfilling these promises (though they will fulfill them if it is in their interests), but strictly for the power such promises bring.

This type of cynicism is also related to people who are willing to break the rules of competition (whether sports, politics, academics, etc.) for the sake of

4 Sloterdijk 1987. Alan Keenan, "The Twilight of the Political? A Contribution to the Democratic Critique of Cynicism", *Theory & Event*, 2, no. 1. *Project Muse*, muse.jhu.edu.medford.usclancaster.sc.edu/article/32493.

winning or getting ahead. A soccer player who flagrantly fouls another player to save or score a goal is often called "cynical" in this sense: the rules of the game, which they appear to uphold, are optional in the end, because the only reason we play the game is to win.

Insider-cynics are the disempowered who are hanging onto the coat-tails of the powerful, and spend their days propping up the master-cynics in whatever way has been given to them to do so. They are bureaucrats and spin-doctors. As bureaucrats they follow the plans and methods put forward by the master-cynics; as spin-doctors, they re-describe reality in a way to uphold the power of the master-cynics. Together they are the apologists for the powerful, and give legitimacy to the words and actions of the master-cynics, not because they trust in what the master-cynics say and do, but in order to maintain their positions, and to protect their own interests and ideals.

Most insider-cynics do not seek to take over as master-cynics, but to protect the power they have in relation to the master-cynic. The fear of losing their position motivates them, and this is why they uphold the master-cynic's policies. They are relatively conscious of the game, but there is also, with many of them, a projection of idealism to their positions—a sense that they are upholding something essential and significant, beyond merely the master-cynic's position (that is, the master-cynic still stands for something beyond raw self-interest).

Outsider-cynics are without power and are cynical for defensive reasons. Their cynical adaptation to a given situation is not so much for manipulation (an active or offensive stance), but is an adjustment to the situation (a passive or defensive stance). Their cynicism is born of disappointment: the failure of promises that have been made and broken by the master-cynics, by the idealized life portrayed in the media that did not come true, and the knowledge that their own ethical and moral behavior has gone unrewarded in life.

While they distrust the motivation and words of those in power, they tend to align themselves with certain master-cynics, institutions, or policies, in hopes that the interests of these powerful entities align with their own self-interests. They rationalize when the master-cynic they back does not act according to her expressed ideals, and so they will defend the master-cynic's breaking of such ideals simply because of the alignment of particular interests. Thus, outsider-cynics will defend politicians or institutions for egregious moral failures, simply because the former expect the latter to uphold other ideals for the sake of self-interest (they have little problem making a "deal with the devil" for the sake of self-preservation). It is only when it becomes apparent that their self-interest is different from the master-cynic's, that the former will lose faith in the latter.

This shows how little the outsider-cynics actually believe in their ideals, though they remain relatively unconscious of this fact. They do not really believe traditional moral ideals will lead to flourishing, though they have a difficult time admitting this to themselves because of the self-perception or identity that is attached to these ideals—they want to see themselves as good people.

When the issue is less about economics (self-*preservation*), and more about the ideological (symbolic) direction culture is taking (*self*-preservation), outsider-cynics will align themselves with whomever is in control, or whichever side seems to be winning, believing that it is in their interest to be on the side that is determining the cultural "ideals" (they believe there is power in numbers, and so for the sake of a sense of significance, they will follow the crowd). As Dean Dettloff says, outsider-cynics "are opportunists, ready to join the side of whoever appears to be winning. … They know that whatever ideology is calling the shots, the mobilizing ideas are irrelevant provided one ends up on the right side of the line."[5] Thus, outsider-cynics tend to follow the established order. This means they must sometimes split their allegiances (often in contradictory ways) along the lines of both nature (self-*preservation*) and cultural power (*self*-preservation), because they continue to believe in their ideals at some level.

We can say, then, that the outsider-cynic does not always trust the spoken or manifest motivation of the master-cynic, but relies on the hope that the master-cynic's self-interest (the latent motivation) is aligned with their own. They are bound to become disappointed, however, because there always comes a time when the master-cynic's personal self-interest will come in conflict with the outsider-cynics'. This disappointment takes the form of hostility, apathy, and a growing indifference toward how those in power are running things. They begin to lack faith in any positive change, or that anything they do can make any difference—they acquiesce to the situation. Their compensation is in maintaining a fragile sense of control, which they base upon having *seen through* the game—they are enlightened. Anticipating deception is a crucial aspect of their cynicism, and the more cynical they become, the more they see deception everywhere, until they come to distrust anyone with power, simply because that person has power (they believe power can only be attained through lies, deceit, and manipulation).

We will mainly be focusing on the cynicism of the outsider-cynics in this book, because they are living in the deepest self-deception, barely aware of

5 Dettloff, 23.

their cynicism and the effect it is having on their lives. They do not even see themselves as cynical, but as merely maintaining a realistic common sense attitude.

Although the outsider-cynics live in self-deception, we have seen that all three types of cynicism are invested in a system they know to be manipulative, deceptive, and full of illusions. It is due to their knowledge of the deceptions and manipulations that we can say that the modern cynic is enlightened; it is because of their investment in this system that we say they are in a false consciousness. As Sloterdijk puts it, cynicism "is the universally widespread way in which enlightened people see to it that they are not taken for suckers. There even seems to be something healthy in this attitude, which, after all, the will to self-preservation generally supports. It is the stance of people who realize that the times of naivete are gone."[6]

As mentioned in the Preface, my interest in cynicism arose due to my own cynical response to my students, though I have also come to recognize my cynical attitude in politics, marketing, health-care, and various other institutions. I was, and in some ways still am, an outsider-cynic. I do not like to be "conned," or taken as a sucker, so I would tend to interpret the words and actions of others cynically.

I have come to see how negatively this impacted my relationship with students, how apathetic it made me toward politics, and how indifferent I felt toward all attempts to change institutions for the better. I came to see that modern cynicism is no longer about defacing the currency to attain *atuphos*, but is much more a defense mechanism, and has now become a means of entrenching the cultural *tuphos*—in many ways, it is the *tuphos*.

3 Cynicism: Narrowing the *Causa Sui* Project

3.1 Defacing the Currency without Being Exiled

In Chapter 8 we saw that competition becomes central for a sense of significance, as people seek to be more virtuous, more successful, and have "it" more together than others as proof of their value. We also saw that this competitiveness relates to how well we are doing in life, in line with what our cultural heroics has provided us. This competitiveness becomes intensified within a cynical society, since the ideology critique has shown us that

6 Sloterdijk, 5.

self-interest is driving us all, and so we are in competition with everyone. The general suspiciousness that settles over existence means that life becomes a kind of risk-management against the various forms of deception and manipulation within society. This creates a general mistrust and defensiveness in our relationships with institutions, corporations, the media, political bodies, and other individuals.

Most of the competitiveness and mistrust would no longer arise, Kierkegaard argues, if we would overcome the *causa sui* project. It is our need to possess the world, and to become higher and higher in it that necessitates that we play the game culture has created for us. In order to keep from falling into anxiety, we feel we must lean on the world, possess the rewards it provides for significance and self-preservation—we must hang onto our fetishes and idols. The illusion of our *causa sui* project is sustained by the *tuphos* of culture. As Kierkegaard argued, the fragility of one's possession of the world means that one ends up being possessed by the established order, because one must bend to the contingencies necessary for obtaining and keeping the possessions. If we surrendered the *causa sui* project, not only would we be free from this particular kind of self-interest, but also free from the manipulation of the established order (really free, not just free because we know that the manipulation is taking place).

The ideology critique does not overcome the *causa sui* project but narrows it to the individual. With the loss of traditional heroics, which provided general significance to individuals, the individual is now on her own, and this makes her more defensive and self-centered. Add to this the sense of danger everywhere that comes from ideology critique, and one has created a consciousness that is utterly suspicious of all the manifest content of others' actions and words. All true motivation is viewed as hidden and latent, so that we interpret every situation as deceptive and manipulative in some way: "they" are always trying to get a leg up, to take advantage of others in order to maintain their positions. Thus, there is a need always to be one step ahead of others, in order not to be taken advantage of.

This leads us to view all ideals and morals as smoke screens (*tuphos*) for self-interest; they are merely tools one uses to manipulate others, and to make it seem that one is for things like justice, truth, fairness (ideals that consider everyone's interest). There is, as often happens in modern cynicism, a contradiction in this: on the one hand, one tends to uphold the ideals of honesty, justice, and fairness as good things; on the other hand, one who appears to trust in these ideals is seen as either naïve (the outsider-cynic) or as manipulative (the master-cynic). This contradiction, like all the others associated with modern cynicism, is ultimately a result of having defaced the currency without becoming exiled from it. It is the general contradiction of an enlightened (seeing through the currency) false (still pursuing the currency) consciousness.

The contradiction has led to a general loss of *parrhesia* within this environment. This core value of the ancient cynics almost wholly disappears in modern cynicism, no matter how much the ideal of honesty is held up as necessary. The power of *parrhesia* in ancient cynicism was due to the cynic's exile: she had nothing to gain by manipulation in terms of what was said, because she was not after the rewards culture was providing; thus, what she said could be trusted. Since the modern cynic is not exiled, there is a sense of a continual disparity between word and deed. Think of the CEO who refers to employees as a "community" and "family," and then a month later lays off many of them to strengthen company earnings (often receiving a huge bonus for having done so).[7] We could give numerous examples of this in terms of political spin doctors, the speeches of politicians, advertisements, social media, etc. In modern cynicism, rhetoric replaces *parrhesia* as the ideal form of speech.

3.2 Example of Consumer Cynicism

We will look at a particular example (consumer cynicism) in order to bring out these characteristics more concretely; this will lead us into an examination of the ways in which the cynics rationalize their contradictions.[8]

John Bertilsson, in his article "The Cynicism of Consumer Morality," says that for modern cynical consumers "it appears as quite reasonable, even natural, to consciously act against better knowledge and enlightenment."[9] This is simply another way of saying that modern cynics have an enlightened false consciousness. In establishing this argument, he looks at the moral ambiguity of young consumers in Sweden; he does this by examining a study of a fashion forum called "Hamsterpaj." What he finds is a moral stance against the fixation on brand names. Consumers know that they will pay two to four times more for an item of clothing (similar in quality and workmanship to lower-priced brands) simply because of a logo stitched into it.

Bertilsson points to three objects of consumer cynicism: cynicism toward the market, cynicism toward other consumers, and cynicism toward oneself.

---

7 Ronald C. Arnett and Pat Arneson, *Dialogic Civility in a Cynical Age: Community, Hope, and Interpersonal Relationships* (Albany: SUNY Press, 1999), 18.

8 We will come to see that these three rationalizations are related to three illusions of the *causa sui* project: freedom, significance, and self-mastery.

9 Jon Bertilsson, "The Cynicism of Consumer Morality," *Consumption Markets and Culture*, 18, no. 5 (September 2015): 447–467, 450. https://doi.org/10.10253866.2015.1038255.

The cynicism toward the market is a disbelief in the morality of brands: the wrongfulness of marketing techniques that get consumers to pay so much more for the same quality of lower-priced clothing.[10] The cynicism toward others is disbelief in the morality of other consumers. While others say they are buying expensive brand name clothing because they are better fitting and of higher quality, the cynic says the real reason others purchase them is due to their superficiality, ridiculous pursuit of status, and in order to boost their weak self-confidence. Finally, the cynicism toward oneself (the most important in relation to self-deception) is disbelief in one's own moral enlightenment. One knows it is "ridiculous" to buy name brand clothes, because of the reasons given in one's cynicism toward marketers and other consumers, and yet this does not stop one from buying these clothes. One person on the forum, who is more a rule than an exception, sums up this contradiction in discussing his view of buying brand names:

> To claim that a pair of stone washed Nudie or ACNE jeans is better quality than a pair of Crocker is just pathetic, likewise that a Tiger of Sweden sweatshirt is more durable than an H&M sweatshirt.
>
> The question is though how you as a consumer "buy" that a piece of clothing may cost about 200–400% more just because it is made by a certain company. … So what do I buy myself? Almost exclusively name brands, I think they are the nicest, but *I can't actually pretend* that I most certainly wouldn't have been able to find almost as nice clothes at Dressman, JC, or H&M.[11]

As Zizek says, "They know very well what they are doing, but still, they are doing it." Modern consumer cynics can see through the marketing techniques, the manipulation, and the illusion, and yet the foundational beliefs that guide their actions (those related to the symbolics of significance) remain committed to the overall consumer ideology. As Gao puts it, "The exposure of the mechanism behind the fantasy does not undermine the ideological effect as these images still inform beauty standards."[12] Intellectually, they know how ridiculous the whole system is; however, in relation to the fetishized symbolic objects they are committed to, they are invested in what the system provides. They have defaced the currency, but cannot move into exile from it, because it is the only thing to provide them with *self*-preservation. They are in conflict with themselves, split or schizoid.

10 Bertilsson, 454–455. In addition to this type of wrongfulness, there is the knowledge of the exploitation of workers in poor countries for the sake of profits.

11 Bertilsson, 460. (emphasis added).

12 Gao, 55–56.

4 Cynical Reason: the Rationalizations of the Modern Cynic

We will look at three ways in which the cynic rationalizes the contradictions of modern cynicism, and so maintains the false consciousness. We will examine two of these rationalizations in this chapter, and the third in the next.

First, there is a detached, ironic stance that causes the cynic to believe that she has risen above the manipulation, and is in some way superior to it, even while she spends her life possessed by, and immersed within, it. Second, the contradictory approach of the cynic appears reasonable because she is living within a contradictory system with conflicting ideals.[13] In the next chapter we will examine how cynics rationalize their contradictoriness based on the importance of adaptation for the sake of self-preservation.

4.1 Rationalization #1: Ironic Detachment Which Transcends the Deception through Thought

Modern cynics believe that a detached, ironic stance toward situations means that they are not really being controlled or conned by them. Can one be conned if one knows one is being conned? In their book *Escape Attempts: The Theory and Practice of Resistance to Everyday Life*, Cohen and Taylor give an example of this detached stance. In describing a suburban couple, whose lives conform to the social and business expectations they face throughout the day, they write,

> But when the door is shut against the night, and the two children are safely in bed, husband and wife turn to each other and laugh. They are subscribers to the new self-consciousness, apostles of awareness. *Cynically* they deride those who share bourgeois arrangements with them, but *who do not see the joke*. Looking around the room they declare their awareness of their apparent suburbanity, and then with the delicious sense of their own distinctive identities, record their distance from such artifacts. ... For them it is only others who are truly suburban, who play their roles with a routine orientation while they "*see through*" the relativity of the setting, they live against it as much as within it, and thereby preserve their individuality within a conformist world.[14]

They are caught up in dual, and conflicting scripts, between the ability to transcend the situation (and so keep a sense of freedom and worth in relation to

---

13 This rationalization was adapted from Bertilsson, 462–464.

14 Stanley Cohen and Laurie Taylor, *Escape Attempts: The Theory and Practice of Resistance to Everyday Life*, 2nd ed. (London: Routledge, 1998), 53–54. (emphasis added). Citation originally found in Keyes.

their uniqueness), and the need to be a part of the situation (and so maintain their significance in relation to others—that is, socially).

This is the same contradiction that arises from every *causa sui* project: they base their worth on self-mastery, self-sufficiency, and independence (in cynicism, by defacing the currency through their ironic detachment), but also gain a sense of security in following the well-worn path (they must lean on something because they have neither the strength nor courage for exile). They do not truly deface the currency, because they refuse to face the anxiety and exile a true defacing entails. As Kierkegaard would put it, *how* they deface the currency is in untruth, and so their defacing of the currency is a means of self-deception. Their "exile" is an illusion, taking place only in thought (the detached irony that sees it as a joke), while the established order continually controls their lives.

In their thought-life they live in the infinite pole of the self, and so feel secure in their uniqueness (their *self*-preservation); in their actions they live in the finite pole of the self, and so feel secure in their decisions about the future, and the path their lives are on (their self-*preservation*). They hold onto their false consciousness by their ability to transcend, through thought and ironic detachment, the way they actually live. The modern cynic believes that knowing that the situation is deceptive and manipulative frees them from the manipulation of the situation, even while being engaged and invested in it. Further, the contradiction between what they believe and what they do, along with so many others around them, reinforces the cynical suspicion that everyone is hiding their true motivations: they think one way and act and talk another.

I mentioned earlier that modern cynicism has created a more intense or more profound self-deceptiveness, and now we have an idea of what this is. Since the cynics believe they have already reached an enlightened consciousness, any attempt to ferret out their self-deception is met with what I call "a nod and a shrug." I can point out to my students that they are being manipulated and deceived in various ways by society, but I have found that this has no impact on most of their lives: they will nod and agree with what I have shown them, but because they are already enlightened to such a world, and feel there is no other alternative, they merely shrug.

Cynics expect dissimulations and manipulations in society, and so pointing them out, as well as their complicity in them, changes nothing essential in how they act. An ideological critique becomes useless because it has already inoculated cynics against a critical assessment of their cynical consciousness; such a critique is what brought them to their cynicism in the first place, and so adding more critique *further confirms them in their cynical stance* toward the world.

As pointed out in the last chapter, modern cynics have been turned outward due to the ideology critique, and so they resist self-reflection. As the suburban couple show, they cynically deride others who are not in on the joke or deception but do not at all reflect on the nature of their own complicity in the situation, and what it means for their lives. Self-reflection seems useless to them, because they already know they are giving into the manipulative system. They give into it because they feel they have no other alternative. Here the narrowing of their lives begins to show its ugly side, as it keeps the cynic locked into the contradiction and internal conflict, and further reinforces the need to look outward (keeping a watch out for all deception), rather than turning inward.[15]

Add to this the fact that the ruling ideologies are themselves cynical about their manipulations—that is, they do not try to hide their manipulations, but even point them out—and the cynic feels even more secure in the face of these manipulations. For instance, in the movie *Deadpool*, there is the constant (at times, tiring) admission to the audience that the filmmakers know the superhero genre is overdone and contrived, that they are also spouting old, tired clichés that are in every other superhero movie, and that *Deadpool* is a part of this mindlessness. It is this very admission that gives the movie its more comical, cynical, and ironic edge: "We know you know and you know we know, and all this knowing is so much more clever and entertaining, isn't it." Thus, what good would it do to point out the clichés when the movie has already done so? What good is seeing through the manipulation of a commercial, when the commercial has already confessed to it, and even mocked itself? It is thought that being in on the con inoculates one from being conned, and also from living in self-deception.[16] Can one be deceived when one is being told one is being deceived?

It should be clear that the cynic's ironic detachment does not truly bring freedom from manipulation, but entrenches her even more within her self-deception. With the loss of self-reflection, cynics are living almost completely by externals. They see through everyone else's repression, but not their own, because they remain within the *causa sui* project that is the basis of their false consciousness. Thus, they move back into a "heroism" they know is not at all heroic. The anti-hero in entertainment becomes the new hero, of which Deadpool is a perfect example.

---

15 The impact of this narrowing and its contradictions upon the psyche is significant. As the ego attempts to maintain this contradiction through repression, the energy or tension of this process leads to anxiety; as the emptiness of one's investment gets more narrowed, it begins to be felt in symptoms of depression.

16 It reminds me very much of David Mamet's film *House of Games*, where being in on the con, and playing a part of the con, was the very con.

4.2 Rationalization #2: Living in Self-Contradiction Appears Reasonable because the System in Which One Has One's Life Is Itself Contradictory

We saw in terms of consumer cynicism that culture gives us contradictory aims: we are to stand out by what we wear and how we look, but are also told it is superficial to purchase clothes for this reason. As we saw with the suburban couple, they are caught in the conflicting scripts of individual uniqueness and social significance. It seems reasonable for consumers to act in contradiction to their morality (for example, the imperative not to be superficial, or not to be the typical suburbanite), since their consumer culture requires them to live in conflicting roles. As Bertilsson says, "Cynicism thus becomes a reasonable moral position in contemporary consumer culture, because the consumer culture itself is largely cynical."[17]

Consumer cynicism is simply one aspect of this contradiction, but ultimately this contradiction arises as a *conflict of ideals*. For instance, many are still told to live by traditional moral ideals, and yet also told that living by such ideals is naïve, and does not pay off in the end. An example from a student's papers in my ethics class is typical of what I run across as I challenge students to think through these contradictory ideals. In the first paper the student handed in for class, which was on Greek and Roman Ethics, the student wrote on Augustine's ethics. In the paper he wrote,

> we as people of the world today, we cannot understand many of the things that we see or experience. I feel like we have to "trust the process" and be confident that one day God's plan will be brought into the light for us. I have been brought up to believe in God and have strong Christian values. I have maintained these values as I've grown up, even after being exposed to new thoughts and ideas. One of the main reasons I have is because the alternative isn't a very heartwarming thought.

In the next paper for the class the student wrote on Machiavelli, within which he used an example from his experience as a high school football player. During his senior homecoming game, he (an offensive lineman) was up against an all-state defensive lineman that was bigger and stronger than him. In the

17 Bertilsson, 462. My argument is that it is not simply that culture is cynical, but that cynicism is a new means of sublimation in cultures where internalization of cultural ideals is no longer possible.

first three plays against him, my student was no match for his opponent. He recounts what he did to change this:

> The next possession I dug my cleats in and gave him my all and blocked him decent, but it still wasn't enough. After another punt, I went to the sideline and formulated a new plan. While I was on the field I noticed a flaw in this guys [*sic*] game. He came off the ball too hard and aggressive for his own good. I was going to block this guy by any means necessary. The first play of the next possession, *I did something against my teaching and my nature, but had to be done.* At the snap of the ball I took two steps back to draw him in, and I chopped his legs from under him. He fell to the ground and immediately clenched his knee, and didn't return the rest of the game. While some people look at this as dirty play or compromising the integrity of the game. I look at it as doing *what had to be done* to come out on top.[18]

His low block was as cynical an act as there is, in that it not only went against the rules of good sportsmanship (physically injuring another player on purpose) but also flew in the face of his own professed beliefs. However, cynics justify this contradiction on the basis of competing ideals (fair play versus winning, in this situation), and so my student did what he felt *had to be done* in order to come out *on top*. His actions showed that his beliefs in the moral ideals he professed in the first paper were not truly convincing to him—they are ineffective in the real world, and he was not truly able to "trust the process," as he put it in his paper. He seeks, however, to hold onto the identity of being a good person, and so rationalizes his cynical action as against his true "nature," a kind of one-off, and so not evidence of who he truly is. For outsider-cynics, much of this contradictory thinking is taking place unconsciously—that is, self-deceptively.

This contradiction is connected to how the *causa sui* project relates to the established order. On the one hand, there are the old traditional heroics, which taught that obedience to moral ideals would bring some sort of blessing or flourishing. Such a belief may be given lip-service, but it is no longer truly convincing, and so not internalized. On the other hand, there is the issue of what "had to be done" to come out on top in the situation—that is, to remain in control of it. As Schreier put this phenomenon, there is an acceptance of the validity of ethical principles, while no longer being convinced of their viability.

---

18 (emphasis added). These two papers are so contradictory that one would think one were reading the work of two different students. This is the schizoid nature inherent in how modern cynics live.

This internal struggle is what Freud was running into in his practice, which he understood as the basis of the neurotic symptoms with which his patients were coming to him: sublimation was no longer working because his patients were no longer able fully to internalize their moral ideals. This inner conflict becomes more and more difficult to hide and navigate when one's culture is ruled by the conflict as well.

We will see in Chapter 17 that Freud did not at all mitigate this problem, but actually intensified it due to his attempt to hang onto the *causa sui* project. We will come to see that, like so much else in modern cynicism, my student's contradiction is a carry-over from Freudianism: my student's contradiction is a relatively unaware form of the Freudian ambivalence toward culture. Freud saw through culture and yet knew it was necessary for self-preservation. The same ambivalence is continually taking place in the modern cynic, though without the Freudian self-awareness. My student's superego was still in place, though the cultural heroics that allows for sublimation no longer exists for him (the authority and internalization are failing), and it comes out in his contradictory beliefs, actions, and words.

5 Conclusion

For Kierkegaard, the conflict or contradictions we are looking at are those between the expansive and limiting senses of self-identity. For my student, the expansive sense of identity was found in the ideals of the Judeo-Christian worldview, as set forth in Augustine, which consists of a trust in God's plan (God's "process") to make everything turn out. The limiting sense of identity was the audible and concrete cheer of the "crowd" in the stands, which was not going to happen if he continued to be pushed around by his opponent.

Kierkegaard believes that the task of self-becoming is to bring these poles together through an infinite passion, but this requires freedom from the established order.[19] Without this freedom, there is a contradictory movement back and forth between the poles, never fully infinite nor fully finite; one is always dissimulating between the poles, depending on what the situation requires at the moment in order to keep one's self-perception, and feel in control.

19 While it requires a freedom from the established order, once the infinite passion has been accepted and chosen, there is a return to the established order, but in a new, free, and loving manner. This "return" is, in an important sense, what Kierkegaard means by the concept of "repetition." It is also not unlike the ancient cynics, who lived within society even while in exile from it.

Kierkegaard termed this self-deception "despair," because it is a hopeless means of coping in the world, leaving one in a continual internal sense of conflict and frustration. Andreas Huyssen, in the Forward to the English translation of *Critique of Cynical Reason* says, "Psychologically he [Sloterdijk] defines him [the cynic] as a borderline melancholic able to *channel the flow* of depressive symptoms and to continue functioning in society despite the nagging doubts about his pursuits."[20] This is the type of self-preservation that is at stake in modern cynicism: to continue functioning within a world that has lost meaning, and somehow to continue to take part in the activities one knows to be manipulative, illusory, deceptive, contradictory, and ultimately meaningless.[21] Kierkegaard's advice is to surrender to this realization, though few are willing to face the anxiety that accompanies this surrender.

20 Andreas Huyssen, Forward to *Critique of Cynical Reason* (Minneapolis: University of Minnesota Press, 1987), xii. (emphasis added).

21 How do we wake up every morning in order to keep rolling the rock up the mountain knowing all the sacrifice comes to nothing? We must find ways to repress and sublimate this awareness.

CHAPTER 13

Freedom and the Loss of Alternatives

1 Rationalization #3

We saw in the first rationalization that while the cynic can see through the various forms of deception and manipulation, as well as the illusion of significance and meaning in many situations, they are unwilling to break free and move into exile. She feels free in each situation due to her ironic detachment, but refuses to follow the movement into exile. In this chapter we will come to see that the movement is aborted due to a lack of alternative forms of life. The negative therapeutic provides no new heroic, no new alternative that could be appropriated and internalized. The third rationalization, then, is that one has no other alternative than to adapt to, and immerse oneself in, a fallen and empty world for the sake of self-preservation.

This rationalization works because the cynic does not see how fully she is invested in the established order. She views her immersion in the established order (as well as her relationships with others) as her way of living her own particular script. Thus, she believes she is not really invested in the established order, since everything she does within it is for her own self-interest—she is coming out on top. However, *this remains self-deception, since her very "self-interest" is what is being manipulated by the established order*. She does not possess herself but is possessed by the order. She is fully immersed in the illusion of her *causa sui* project, blind to the fact that she is not free, not in control, and not truly pursuing her passionate interest. She seeks the rewards the established order provides, and so she must play by the established order's rules, no matter how corrupt or empty she believes them to be.

In order to fully understand this situation, we must see how deeply the roots of the system or established order go, and the loss of the self that takes place due to the belief that there is no other alternative in life. In this chapter, we turn to Richard Stiver's analysis of "technological morality" in his book *The Culture of Cynicism: American Morality In Decline*. This will provide a more concrete picture of the narrowing of our lives and alternatives within cynical culture, and how it is creating a life that continually languishes. It will also provide an understanding of why abandoning traditional morality does not lead to less constraint and more self-actualization, but more constraint and a loss of the self.

 | HTTPS://DOI.ORG/10.1163/9789004758148-015

2 The Technological Morality

One of the results of the end of traditional cultural norms and morals, and the lack of anything to take their place (anything conceived as "moral," or of higher value), is that the entire symbolics of culture becomes groundless and fluid. Nihilism is the belief that there is no basis for value or meaning, and there is nothing under all the social constructions. Looking at the way the universe is driven by cold and impersonal laws, it seems ridiculous to the nihilist to believe we live in a moral universe. Without a basis for morality, the symbolics that are accepted are viewed as the result of having won a power struggle: the winner in the so-called "culture wars" has won for themselves the ability to determine (at least for a time) what and who matters in life, what meaning to make out of things, what is "morally" right and wrong, etc. This means that the cultural symbolics come to be seen as arbitrary and artificial, just as the cynics (in all historical eras) believe them to be.

We have moved from living a symbolic *heroic*, to choosing a particular symbolic *script* by which to live. It is important to understand the distinction between the creation and sustenance of the traditional heroics, and that of the new symbolic scripts. We will do this by looking at Becker's and Rieff's analyses of this change. While Becker provides an anthropological analysis and Rieff a sociological one, they both give the same general picture of this change from the traditional to the current symbolics.

2.1 The Change in Techniques in the Service of the *Causa Sui* Project

2.1.1 The Cultural Elites

Becker argues that the symbolics gain cultural authority through the "elites" within a culture, whose main task is to manipulate the sacred order for human benefit. These elites are experts of ritual, which are the techniques by which the sacred order can be brought to bear on human life. Following A. M. Hocart, Becker speaks of these rituals as a type of technology, in the service of the universal human ambition of achieving prosperity—the good life of secure self-preservation. Becker says, "[R]itual is *a technique for giving life*. The thing is momentous: throughout vast ages of prehistory mankind imagined that he could *control life!*"[1]

1 *EE*, 6.

This is connected to the *causa sui* project, in that in each culture there are elites who are in control of, and responsible for, making sure its members flourish and secure prosperous self-preservation—that the members of the culture can gain life and power from the sacred order, and are protected from misfortune and suffering. Through these techniques of ritual, people believed they took control of the material world through access to the invisible sacred ground of this world. They believed this control could raise them over and above material decay and death, and was an important aspect of the traditional immortality striving.[2] This is also how they related to the Excess.

Becker points to two significant historical periods in which rituals are understood and administered differently.[3] The first period is from time immemorial until roughly the Renaissance or the Enlightenment. This is a time characterized by a ritualistic view of nature. The second period began with the modern machine age, and the domination of the scientific method and world view. In both periods humans want to control life and death, and they do this in terms of how they relate to the Excess—that out of which all things come into being and return, and so defines what happens in-between.

In the first period they had to rely on nonmachine technology to do so.[4] This type of ritual does not create new power, but transfers the power of life and renovates nature, through various ritualistic and priestly techniques: "Man controls nature by whatever he can invent, and primitive man invented the ritual altar and the magical paraphernalia to make it work. And as the modern mechanic carries around his tools, so did the primitive scrupulously transport his charms and rebuild his altars."[5] The second period uses the scientific method to create machine technology, or social techniques devised by the social sciences. Both are a means of control, one of the world, the other of human beings.

2.1.2 Rieff on World Cultures: First, Second and Third Worlds

Rieff explains this same historical situation in terms of what he calls "world cultures." For Rieff, as for the other thinkers we have been looking at, culture gives people the means of controlling the panic and emptiness to which they are inclined.[6] Prior to the past hundred years or so, this control over anxiety

2 *EE*, 7.
3 *EE*, 8. These are two different ways of relating to the Excess.
4 *EE*, 8.
5 *EE*, 8.
6 *TT*, 3.

and emptiness took place through what Rieff calls "commitment therapies," by which he means that individuals are devoted to (committed to) some sacred ideal or metanarrative, which answers the questions they have about their existence.[7] Each culture has its own therapy: a system of moralizing demands, norms of action, and ideals to strive for, which give meaning and direction to individuals' lives.

Rieff agrees with Freud and Becker that humans create culture; however, unlike Freud and Becker, Rieff does not believe it is grounded only in human striving. For Rieff, the creation of culture is a transliterating of the invisible sacred order into visible modalities, or the social order.[8] Cultures are symbolics of meaning, creations of meaningful "worlds." Rieff believes these symbolics are an interpretation of the sacred order, which is invisible.[9] This invisible sacred order provides what Rieff calls a "vertical in authority" for the cultural symbolics: there is something authoritative, vertically or hierarchically determinative for life, which validates the symbolics. While the sacred order validates the symbolics, the symbolics never fully capture this order, and so they remain fluid and malleable—though in no way groundless. The elites are the earthly authorities who mediate the "vertical in authority"—that is, mediate the sacred and social orders through the rituals Becker discusses.

Rieff writes about three historical world cultures that have taken place in Western Civilization, which he analyzes in terms of how humans have related to the vertical in authority: first world (pagan) culture, second world (monotheistic) culture, and third world culture (in which we live). Generally, these are three different views of, and ways of relating to, the sacred order or Excess.[10]

For first world culture, by which Rieff generally means the ancient cultures of Greece and the early Roman Empire, the Excess or sacred ground is a primordial, irrational, chaotic power over which humans have no power, but are by and large its tragic victims. This ground or Excess is fate, what the ancient cynics called *tukhe*. We are subjected to something greater than ourselves, something that controls human destiny. To conceive of this fate as chaotic means that it is viewed as indifferent to human rationality and plans. The elites of this culture are those who deal with magical powers, various ways of contacting and manipulating the gods, in hopes of altering the individual fate of people or society.

7 These commitment therapies are directly related to the "positive communities" discussed earlier.

8 *DW*, 2.

9 What I have called the Excess.

10 *DW*, 4–7.

Second world cultures begin with the influential rise of the three monotheistic religions in the West: Judaism, Christianity, and Islam.[11] The ground for second world cultures is ordered rather than chaotic, but is still something over which humans have no control: everything is subject to the order of the divine. Though they cannot change God's general will, by relating correctly to it, their lives will become blessed: they will achieve prosperous self-preservation and flourishing. The heart of the sacred in second world cultures is the self-revealed creator of the universe, from whom everything derives its significance and meaning. Truth is grounded in revelation and creed. The dominant motif is *faith*, rather than *fate*. The elites are the rabbis, priests, pastors, caliphates, etc., who render the sacraments or rituals, as well as protecting the decrees and creeds that are important for the imputation of life-giving techniques.

Third world cultures recycle the first world culture's ground, in that it views the ground as ultimately chaotic; however, in third world cultures this chaotic ground is open to rational manipulation and control that was not conceived of in first world cultures. Humans no longer view themselves as the ground's tragic victims, but its master. Francis Bacon is an excellent example of this understanding of the human relation to this ground, which in third world cultures is simply nature, divested of its sacred Excess. Bacon wanted a new system of investigation, in which nature would be forced to divulge her secrets. The new mechanical arts "'do not, like the old, merely exert a gentle guidance over nature's course; they have the power to conquer and subdue her, to shake her to her foundations.' 'Under the mechanical arts, nature betrays her secrets more fully … than when in enjoyment of her natural liberty.'"[12] He believed that "'by art and the hand of man,' nature can be 'forced out of her natural state and squeezed and molded.' In this way, 'human knowledge and power meet as one.'"[13]

This is related to the attempt at self-grounding we have been looking at, and is in line with the espionage epistemology. Third world cultures posit no authority beyond themselves, and are radically skeptical of authority arising from a "sacred order"; like the cynical attitude, they "stick to the facts."[14]

11 The philosophies of Plato and Aristotle provide a transition between these two world cultures, as they view the ground of existence as rational and ordered. Our ability to create an ordered and just society for them is related to the connection between human thought and this ground, both of which partake in *logos*.

12 Quoted in Carolyn Merchant, *The Death of Nature: Women, Ecology, and the Scientific Revolution* (San Francisco: Harper, 1980), 172.

13 Merchant, 171.

14 *DW*, 6–7.

Third world cultures are primarily negations and destructions of second world culture authorities. They read nothing behind the cultural symbolics (as we saw in relation to Freud and Becker). The Excess is to them a "nothing," a *nihil*. It is because of this that Rieff views third world cultures as anti-cultures: they "translate no sacred order into the social" order, something which is needed in order to sustain all cultures.[15] We have already seen that the self-grounding of third world cultures remains in a self-deception in relation to its freedom: it thinks it is free from authority, though it continues to lean on others (the elites) for its security.

The elites of third world cultures deal almost exclusively in the work of negation, which they view as setting people free from the oppressive traditional cultural norms and morality. They are, then, the defacers of cultural currency. If there is anything "positive" that comes from these elites, it is a kind of busyness in building more and more "stage sets" (scripts) behind which they know there is nothing—it is about power for these elites, not values, no matter how much value-language (e.g., "justice," "right," etc.) is being used in their rhetoric. Rieff distinguishes between two kinds of elites in the third world culture: technological elites and psychological elites. We will be dealing with the former in this chapter, and the latter when we examine the triumph of the therapeutic. Together they form the cynical therapeutic. The technological elites are the experts on nature (including human nature), and are in control of running the established order by the ideals of efficiency, redundancy, quality control, bureaucratic administration, etc.—all ideals of power.

2.2 The Morality of Power

The third world culture is controlled through what Stivers calls a "technological morality." It arises out of the realization that we can create reality. This understanding of culture reinforces cynicism. When the distinction between reality and truth disappears, and reality can be manipulated into and out of existence, a cynical, mocking attitude toward life is enlivened.[16] Modern cynicism allows everyone to be in on the con that we create our own reality and truth, and so believe that we remain in control: "The audience is receiving a trade-off: let us con you, but we will admit it so that you can demonstrate your superiority at the same moment you become the spectator-consumer."[17]

15 *DW*, 6.

16 Richard Stivers, *The Culture of Cynicism: American Morality In Decline* (Cambridge: Blackwell, 1994), 152.

17 Stivers, 153.

We have cynically seen through traditional morality, which the first two cultural worlds connect to the sacred order (a "vertical in authority"), and are now left with a morality without traditional meaning; it is now a morality of power.[18] Technological morality and its elites create an efficient order in the form of technical rules and organization. One's personal morality within this situation becomes subjective and assumes the form of instinctual power and pleasure.[19]

While it will become more important as we examine the triumph of the therapeutic, we should understand at this point that with the technological morality the "crowd" socializes its members in the art of consumption, allowing for a therapeutic compensation for a morality without a heroics—a morality whose essence is strictly concerned with power and control.[20] When meaning is destroyed, all norms become norms of power. Thus, all political and social judgments are about power-structures and power-relationships. We often see this concretely in movements toward the centralization of power within institutions, corporations, government, and the like.[21] Centralization comes out in education through the imposition upon instructors of universal means of curriculum and assessment, such as "no child left behind," the redundancy of syllabi and textbooks by administration upon university and college faculty (justified by the ideals of efficiency and the needs of accreditation), etc. While justifications may at first be connected to the ideals and goals related to learning, they become cynical as they turn to the idea of efficiency: the least amount of investment possible for a mediocre and standard(ized) outcome.

The outcomes become mediocre and standardized because there are no longer ideals (apart from efficiency) to guide individuals beyond what is often both the least common denominator, and the path of least resistance. As Stivers says, "This morality replaces the dualism of the real and the ideal with that of the real and the possible. Reality and possibility exist in the space that technology, public opinion, and visual images create."[22] What Stivers means by "possibility," is more in line with what Kierkegaard means by "probability." Rather than striving for an ideal in line with one's infinite passion and unique possibilities—which would require commitment, sacrifice, risk, and

---

18 Stivers, 160.

19 Stivers, 163.

20 This includes not only consumption of material objects, but is the consumption of lifestyles, personalities, images, personal journeys, etc.

21 Stivers, 167.

22 Stivers, 166.

a significant personal investment—we find our strength to push on in life through probability.

To say that the dualism of the real and the possible (probable) replaces the real and the ideal is to say that we define flourishing by, and put off happiness until, the future. Thus, we live by the motto "I'll be happy when.": I'll be happy when the new iPhone comes out, when I graduate from college, when I get my career started, when I get the corner office, when I get to retire. This is a path planned out for us that seems to require little risk, in that one merely follows the well-calculated movement of society (or of one's financial advisor).[23]

It gives the illusion of hope, but provides only a modicum of compensation—enough for us to endure this plodding, redundant, meaningless life. It is maintained by a kind of technological utopianism, which promises happiness through the invention of ever new and exciting technological devices. There is a sense that the promise for happiness is so assured and unquestionable, that to admit to oneself that one is unhappy is tantamount to admitting that there is something wrong with one—since there is nothing wrong with the established order.[24]

With the defacing of traditional ideals, a vacuum for a sense of control over our lives was created. This vacuum has been filled with the value of power itself. As we saw above, values and ideals still exist at the level of discourse or rhetoric, but they only conceal that the disappearance has taken place.[25] These values are of little use in self-preservation—except as tools used for manipulation by the master cynics. This is seen through by all, and so they are no longer fully internalized or convincing.

In place of the guidance traditional morality provided, we are now given technical and bureaucratic rules, which is what Stivers means by technological morality, and Kierkegaard means by probability. This morality, like all things technological, is nothing other than an expression of power,[26] and is now viewed as the only possible way of acting, because the most efficient way of acting.

The point I want to stress here is that we believe that by overcoming traditional morality we have moved into freedom of self-expression and self-actualization; however, this is far from accurate, and we are blind to the intense narrowing constraint that takes place in a technological morality. Technique

23 It reminds me of the Fidelity Investment commercials, where the person, after leaving her Fidelity advisor's office, is given a green arrow to follow through life.

24 Stivers, 171.

25 Stivers, 175.

26 Stivers, ix.

becomes the single most crucial factor in the organization of modern society.[27] Its constraint is as strong and oppressive as the constraints of traditional morality (if not more so).

With the defacing of the cultural currency, technology plays the organizing role for the modern cynic that nature played for the ancient cynic. The surrender to technology partially explains why the modern cynic does not become exiled from culture, since technology is a cultural phenomenon. While it is closely connected to nature, in that our technological devices arise from our understanding of the forces and laws at work within nature, it is also contrived and arbitrary, in that the technology we create, and the techniques we use, are built around human agendas related to the *causa sui* project. Ultimately, the difference between the ancient and the modern cynics' relation to nature is found in the quotes above by Francis Bacon: nature is no longer a friend to humans, nor the means to a happy life, but is that which hides from us the secrets to a happy life. Nature becomes an enemy to conquer.

Our will to act has been co-opted because in technological civilization every possibility is a technical one. We think we are making choices, when we are only following the experts, the calculations, the power structures that appear unquestionable simply because of their efficiency. To say that power is the only value is to recognize that everything is judged by their efficiency to get things done, to give us control over nature, things, and people. Efficiency judges all "choices" according to necessity, which is to say, destroys true possibility and freedom.[28] Efficiency displaces all other forms of measure and value. Such control is an illusion of personal freedom because a technological possibility is not *my* possibility.[29]

---

27 Stivers, 72.

28 In the era that Freud lived, as intellectuals were recognizing and experiencing the nihilism within Western culture, Karl Jaspers wrote about necessity's *annihilation* of possibility, and so what makes us human: "The new world which has arisen as an apparatus for the supply of the necessaries of life compels everything and every one to serve it. It annihilates whatever it has no place for. Man seems to be undergoing absorption into that which is nothing more than a means to an end, into that which is devoid of purpose or significance. But therein he can find no satisfaction. It does not provide him with the things which give him value and dignity. That which, amid the needs and stresses of the past, had persisted as an unquestioned background of his being, is now in course of disappearance. While he is expanding his life, he would seem to be sacrificing the being in which he realises his own selfhood." Karl Japers, *Man in the Modern Age*, trans. Eden Paul and Cedar Paul (New York: Doubleday, 1951), 83.

29 "[F]or technology does not depend upon my subjective experience. Nor can I control its growth and consequences in any decisive way. I am merely along for the ride. More importantly, technology has become the *universal* means of acting. There is no domain of

The surrender to technology is an echo of Kierkegaard's analysis, but in the context of the cynical and nihilistic society in which we live—the "negative community." It points to the narrowing of personal and individual alternatives in terms of technology, efficiency, and functionality. As for where this technology is leading us (what we are striving to be efficient for, what our purpose is, or what is at stake—what we lose—in this surrender to technology), this is a question seldom asked. This lack of questioning closes off all sense of *krisis*, and closes the door to the ability even to imagine what making a free choice would consist of.

Objectified manipulation in the form of technique means that most of us, most of the time, merely adjust to the movement of technology: we are not guiding our lives anywhere, but simply adjusting to where technology is taking us.[30] While it is true that we are beginning to discover that technology's future is looking more and more like a dystopia, this does not break us free from its hold.

2.3 Organizational Techniques and Psychological Techniques

As mentioned above, Stivers speaks of two categories of techniques that are related to a technological morality: organizational techniques and psychological techniques.[31] Generally, organizational techniques refer to bureaucratic rules, and related techniques of administration and human resources (self-*preservation*); psychological techniques refer to advertising, propaganda, public relations, therapeutic techniques, and the "how to" manuals for effective living (*self*-preservation). Both organizational and psychological (symbolic) techniques have as their goal the manipulation and control of human beings.[32] I relate organizational techniques to cynicism, and psychological techniques to the therapeutic. Together they form the cynical therapeutic.

A technique is a procedure whose sole purpose is efficiency, and so contains a set of "effective procedures"—rules that guarantee a successful outcome.[33] These effective procedures arise from calculating the probabilities of various

life not mediated by technique. Every possibility is technical. An exclusive possibility is a necessity. When possibility becomes necessity [when it becomes 'probability'], freedom disappears." Stivers, 176.

30 Stivers, 178.

31 This relates to Rieff's analysis of the technological and psychological elites mentioned above.

32 Stivers, 72.

33 Stivers, 74.

outcomes. As we saw in our analysis of Kierkegaard, because of this "guarantee" of a successful outcome, these techniques diminish the sense of anxiety about the future, offering a way of securing the future for oneself—though it does this by taking away the individual's freedom and real possibilities. They differ from traditional moral norms by not being linked to a larger cultural narrative; technical rules are abstract and take place without a closed logical system, such as a metanarrative.[34]

The "bureaucratic mind," who is the administrator of organizational techniques, is the insider-cynic discussed in the last chapter, as well as the technical elites of Rieff's third world culture. For these insider-cynics, the world is made up of facts that are to be administered in accordance with firm rules, whose aim is to maintain the power and control of the master-cynics. These techniques aim to control nature, individuals, groups, economies, etc. The bureaucratic mind is cynical because it reduces everything to power: a manipulation and adjustment not only *to* reality, but more importantly *of* reality. The most telling result of the bureaucratic mind is its technological fatalism: this fatalism is built on a supreme confidence in our ability to direct the future, and so is central to our current *causa sui* project. The bureaucratic mind is not offering to heal the contradictory struggles in which we continually find ourselves, but is a means of coping with them.

3 Conclusion

As we have seen in this chapter, we are in a time of transition between the traditional cultural heroics, with the ideals and norms connected to the Excess as something sacred or divine, and the new technological culture. We have seen how cynicism is at work in this transition, and the means it uses to rationalize the contradictions inherent in this transition. The overarching belief of the new cultural elites is that the movement out of the traditional cultural heroics will allow us to be more free, gain more personal significance, and become more self-sufficient. In the analysis of the technological morality, we begin to see that the reality is not as the elites would have us believe. We are becoming more constrained by culture, living lives of diminished meaning, and becoming more dependent on the techniques created by culture. Because our ego is so fragile and vulnerable, we must surrender to some order, lean on some form of guidance for our lives. This will become even more clear when we take up

34 Stivers, 74.

the triumph of the therapeutic. With the loss of traditional morality, a technological morality of power and efficiency has taken over.

The technological morality relates very closely to Freud's psychoanalytic approach, both in terms of the latter's cynicism and its therapeutic aspects. We will now return to Freud, in order to connect both modern cynicism and the triumph of the therapeutic to his view of the psyche and his psychoanalytic approach. It is no accident that cynicism and the therapeutic have reigned in our culture: they are the result of following a Freudian understanding of the psyche, and the process of coping with our inner conflicts and neurosis that he provides.

In the next several chapters we turn to Freud in order to re-examine his theories in light of the intervening analyses. We will come to see how and why his theories are the basis of the new cynical sublimation, and how cynicism and the triumph of the therapeutic creates a new ideology I call the *cynical therapeutic*.

PART 2

The Cynical Therapeutic

CHAPTER 14

Freud and Cynicism

1 Freud: the Social Theorist

Although Freud is known for his theories on the psyche and the developmental stages linked to sexuality—most of which have been critiqued and shown to lack the scientific rigor Freud believed they had—Freud's long-term impact has been as a social theorist. His impact on culture remains extremely strong, even though many of his theories on the psyche have been shown not to hold water. It often appears in reading Freud, and seeing the continual fluidity of his views, that his theories on the *psyche* arose more from social concerns than the other way around: it is his ideology critique that informed his view of the structure and workings of the psyche. This critique has had an incredible influence on our culture, in relation both to cynicism and the triumph of the therapeutic.

As we saw in Chapters 3 and 4, his social critique is very much along the lines of a cynic's defacing of the cultural currency, in that Freud viewed morality, and the repression it necessitates, as the source of our mental illness. Freud saw that the price people were paying for living a moral life was beginning to cost too much: the sacrifices expected were not worth the damage they were doing to the psyche. The cynicism arising out of the Enlightenment influenced Freud's answer to this problem, and in turn, his answer became influential in the rise and reign of the modern cynical consciousness as enlightened false consciousness. He models his conception of the psyche (most likely unconsciously) around a cynical consciousness; the acceptance of this cynical view of the psyche turns cynicism into an ideological approach to life. Freud internalized the cynical views arising from the Enlightenment, modeled the psyche upon this cynicism, which then became a new form of cultural sublimation. Freud did not invent the modern cynical approach to life, but in making it a model for the nature of the human self, as well as the process toward health, he formed the basis for its hegemony within our culture.

2 The Enlightenment: *Rameau's Nephew*

We have already seen how ideology critique arose out of the Enlightenment project, and although it is essential to understand how the seeds of cynicism

HTTPS://DOI.ORG/10.1163/9789004758148-016

were already present in the Enlightenment, there are many good books that make this general argument.[1] There is, however, one work from the Enlightenment I would like to focus on, which was written by one of its preeminent intellectual leaders: Denis Diderot's *Rameau's Nephew*. I choose this book because it is clear that Freud himself had read this work (he refers to it in his writings), and that it influenced his thinking. Further, the nephew in the novel is a good representation of how cynicism was already at work during the Enlightenment period, and is a precursor to modern cynicism. We will take several pages to focus on this work in order to bring out central themes that arise, and even guide, Freud's social theories and critiques.

The book is a conversation between an intellectual (*Moi* or "Me") and the nephew of the famous composer Rameau (*Lui* or "Him"). The former is in line with the general views of the Enlightenment philosophers, who were optimistic about human progress, and held to the traditional views of human goodness, even though they had rejected the religions upon which many of these views rested. The Nephew is a cynic, who sees through the cultural currency, and believes that the old morality is as groundless as the religious mindset the intellectuals had already rejected. The message that comes out most strongly from the Nephew, whose life has fallen on some difficult times, is that living a moral life is no longer worth the sacrifice: more harm will come to oneself by trying to live virtuously, than living by one's natural self-interest. In a statement of pure cynicism, the Nephew says,

> And since I can find happiness through vices natural to me, which I've acquired without working, which I maintain without effort, which are compatible with the customs of my country, which suit the taste of those who protect me and are closer to their small particular needs than virtues which would embarrass them, by criticizing them morning and night, it would be really odd if I were to go on tormenting myself like some soul in hell in order to cut myself up and make myself other than I am, to give myself a character foreign to my own, very worthy qualities—I will concede, to avoid an argument—but which would cost me a great deal to acquire and to practise, and which would lead to nothing, perhaps worse than nothing, because all the time I'd have to satirize the rich people among beggars like me to have to find a living. People praise virtue, but they hate

1 For instance, see Sharon Adele Stanley (*The French Enlightenment and the Emergence of Modern Cynicism* [Cambridge: Cambridge UP, 2012]); Ian Cutler (*Cynicism from Diogenes to Dilbert*); R. Bracht Branham and Marie-Odile Goulet-Cazé (*The Cynical Movement in Antiquity and Its Legacy*).

> it. They turn away from it, because it makes them freezing cold, and in this world one has to have warm feet.[2]

Here we find the wisdom of modern cynicism: personal fulfillment is found not in virtues, but in vices, which are natural to us, easily come by, require little sacrifice, can be made to look socially acceptable, and focus on self-preservation. Seeking to be virtuous will only bring judgment and shame upon the self (not only from others, but even worse, from one's own superego), tormenting the self and demanding one be other than who one is, creating falseness that requires great sacrifice and provides practically no reward. Here is the truth, according to the Nephew: people praise virtue, but they hate it. When the choice is between having warm feet or virtue, they will turn from virtue, because it only leaves them cold.

The very basis of the neurosis that Freud's patients were suffering from came, he thought, from the continued "belief" in morals that they had already seen through—not with the clarity and awareness of the Nephew's sight, but at a more unconscious level. Freud's views are in line with the Nephew's, when the latter says, "they've imposed on themselves a task which isn't natural to them. … Virtue makes itself respected, and respected is uncomfortable. Virtue makes itself admired, and admiration is not amusing."[3]

The Nephew and Freud agree with the ancient cynics, in that they seek to deface the currency of moral virtues by turning to what comes easily to humans, and by which they justify their view that morality leads to falseness. However, unlike the ancient cynics, the Nephew does not advise turning to the natural world: nature is not a place of comfort for the Nephew, but impoverishment. While the ancient cynics, the Nephew, and Freud all agree that the conventions of civilization are causing unnecessary suffering—because of their artificial or unnatural demands—the Nephew and Freud do not see nature as a "friend" to humanity. I already mentioned the disingenuousness of the ancient cynics around this issue, in that the comfort they found in "nature" relied on the various things culture provided for them. In a sense, the Nephew is more authentic than the ancient cynics in this regard, admitting that humans need cultural comforts in order to be happy.[4]

---

2 Denis Diderot, *Rameau's Nephew*, trans. Ian C. Johnston (Gutenberg Australia eBook, eBook No.: 0700101.txt), First posted January 2007, 27.

3 Diderot, 27.

4 There is an obvious quantitative difference between the ancient cynics' need for culture, and the Nephew's. The virtue of asceticism allowed the ancient cynics to put up with less comfort than the Nephew. However, the cultural comforts available in ancient Greece and those in Eighteenth Century France are quite far apart. One wonders how much Diogenes would

There is an ambivalence toward culture for the Nephew. This is an aspect of the Nephew's cynicism that Freud also holds to, and which we have seen to be a central characteristic of modern cynicism. The Nephew understands that there are competing and conflicting demands between his natural self-interests and his need for others (culture). On the one hand, he sees through the artificial and arbitrary demands of culture, which require much more sacrifice than they are worth. On the other hand, in order to be comfortable, he knows he must act a false part ("pantomime," as Diderot puts it in his book), and so "prostitute" himself to those who are providing for his comfort. He knew full well that the reason he was suffering (why he was in his current impoverished position) was because of a moment of "common sense" and *parrhesia*, in which he dropped the pantomime, and risked telling his benefactors what he really thought.[5] This *parrhesiastic* act of defacing the currency got him kicked out of the house of luxury, and back into a life of poverty.

Moi's answer to him is in keeping with ancient cynicism: embrace the poverty and exile, just as Diogenes did, and stop prostituting yourself by using the very currency you know to be counterfeit and worthless. That is, stick to the enlightened consciousness alone, not succumbing to the false consciousness of returning to that which he has seen through. However, the Nephew, as a modern cynic, cannot do this, because he loves too much the comfort the counterfeit provides. When *Moi* tells the Nephew to be like Diogenes, and embrace life in a barrel, the Nephew says, "But I need a good bed, a fine table, warm clothing in winter, and cool clothing in summer, spare time, and lots of other things which I prefer to owe to charity than acquire by work".[6] The Nephew is well aware of his dependence on culture for his comfort, and this awareness becomes the source of his ambivalence toward cultured living, in which he both mocks culture and yet lives upon it.[7]

What is so compelling about *Rameau's Nephew* in relation to Freud, is how their answers (their therapeutic process) to this conflict coincide. Both point to a type of education that will lead one toward the more self-conscious

---

have found contentment in a barrel with the availability of cultural comforts in the Nephew's era. While this is all relative, it is clear that the ancient cynics still lived off the goods culture provided.

5 "I lost everything because once—the only time in my life—I have common sense. May that never happen to me again!" (Diderot, 11).

6 Diderot, 63.

7 We will find this ambivalence to be a central aspect of Freud's cultural theory, and one of the main influences on modern cynicism as enlightened *false* consciousness.

master-cynic. In talking about educating or socializing children, the Nephew says, concerning his son,

> The important thing, the difficult point which a father has to attend to above all is not so much to give his child vices that will make him wealthy, or foolish behaviour that will make him valuable to great people—everyone does that, if not systematically, as I do, at least by example and in lessons—but to give him a sense of proportion, the art of dodging shame, dishonor, and the law. Those are dissonances in the social harmony which he must know how to set up, prepare, and resolve. Nothing is so insipid as a sequence of perfect chords. There has to be something which acts as a spur, which breaks up the light and scatters its rays.[8]

The Nephew knows that socialization is necessary in order to overcome shame, but that it is a matter of proportion or balance. Socialization is not about bringing us to a "higher point" in life (i.e., progress, the "salvation" proposed by the Enlightenment); rather, it is an education that is in line with our actual lives, here and now—in Freud's terminology, in line with the reality principle, not the superego. As the Nephew puts it:

> Everything living, including human beings, seeks benefits for itself at the expense of whoever they belong to. And I'm sure that if I left the little savage to his own way, without speaking to him about anything, he'd want to be richly clothed, splendidly fed, liked by men, and adored by women, and would like to gather around him all the fine things in life.[9]

Our natural aim in life is happiness and to live comfortably; our truest desires are not for the virtues or "higher" capacities of life, but to be well-clothed, well-fed, and accepted by others.

Moi's response to this view of the primitive or savage self is *a statement upon which Freud's entire theory of socialization is an echo*:

> If the little savage were left to himself so that he retained all his imbecility, uniting the little reason possessed by a child in the cradle with the passionate

8 Diderot, 55. As we will see, this "sense of proportion" is a central aspect of the Freudian therapeutic process, which he viewed as a balance within the ambivalent relationship to culture.

9 Diderot, 56.

> violence in a man of thirty years old, *he'd wring his father's neck and sleep with his mother.*[10]

Freud himself says of this very quote:

> Yet more than a century before the birth of psycho-analysis the French philosopher Diderot gave evidence of the importance of the Oedipus complex by expressing the difference between the primitive and the civilized. … I venture to assert that if psycho-analysis could boast of no other achievement than the discovery of the repressed Oedipus complex, that alone would give it a claim to be counted among the precious new acquisitions of mankind.[11]

The Oedipus complex is about the conflict between the primitive or savage (the natural) self and the civilized (symbolic) self. It is the conflict, contradiction, and paradox that has continually shown up in this analysis. This conflict is our most earnest struggle, something we face every day of our lives, as we attempt to make our way through both the world of nature and the world of culture.

It is Freud's answer to this conflict that we will be looking at in the next several chapters. This answer is his social theory, and it is what has had a significant influence on our culture (perhaps greater than any other Nineteenth or Twentieth Century thinker). We have already examined Freud's general theories in Chapters 3 and 4, as well as the nature of modern cynicism; in the next several chapters, I will bring these together in order to show how cynicism impacted Freud's theories, and how his theories, in turn, led our culture into the modern cynicism I have described. We will see that the acceptance of Freud's answer to this conflict resulted in both our cynical ideology and the triumph of the therapeutic.

Freud's answer, which comes out in his therapeutic process, is the same answer the cynical Nephew gives to *Moi*'s criticism of the primitive or savage child just above: "That proves the need for a good education. Who'll argue about that? And *what's a fine education if not one which leads to all sorts of pleasures, without danger and without inconvenience*?"[12] Freud's therapeutic answer is for "re-education" through psychoanalytic therapy: a new type of socialization, with a new focus of internalization or identification, not one based on authority, but on a strengthening of the ego through mistrust and an

10 Diderot, 56. (emphasis added).
11 *OP*, 61.
12 Diderot, 56. (emphasis added).

espionage epistemology. This new internalization, he believed, would lead to a new and healthier type of sublimation and individual. In terms of how I conceived the process in the preceding chapters, we will find that Freud critiques and abandons the traditional *causa sui* project (the cultural heroics) in order to create a new *causa sui* project.

3 The Freudian Diagnosis of Human Neurosis

3.1 Ideology Critique

The Enlightenment had an instrumental or functionalist view of religion (i.e., people were religious as a means to some other, self-interested, end), which Sloterdijk saw as leading to "the future dynamite of ideology critique, the seeds of the crystallization of modern, self-reflective cynicism."[13] Sloterdijk argues that "In this climate, enlightenment leads to a training in mistrust that strives to outdo deceptions through suspicion."[14] As we saw in Chapter 11, this is what led to ideology critique.[15] Sloterdijk sees Freud as a prime example of this, and likens his ideology critique to the ancient cynics:

> The miracle of psychoanalysis is how it so respectably conjures all its objects—oral, anal, and genital. It is as if in refined society someone had burped at the dinner table and nobody found anything exceptional in it. Freud managed what would leave Diogenes green with envy: He erected a theory that makes us all, whether we like it or not, into kynics (if not even into cynics).[16]

Freud's ideology critique and cynicism, is much more complicated than the original hope of the Enlightenment. Freud is not as optimistic as the Enlightenment philosophers, because he does not believe the conflict within the human self is resolvable. The "healthy" among us are simply those who are

---

13 Sloterdijk, 29.

14 Sloterdijk, 30.

15 "The opponent is cut open in front of everyone, until the mechanism of his error is laid bare. The outer skin of delusion and the nerve endings of 'actual' motives are hygienically separated and prepared. From then on, enlightenment is not satisfied, of course, but is better armed in its insistence on its own claims for the distant future. Ideology critique is now interested not in winning over the vivisected opponent but in focusing on the 'corpse,' the critical extract of its ideas, which lie in the libraries of enlighteners and in which one can easily read about their grave falsity." Sloterdijk, 16–17.

16 Sloterdijk, 295.

most unconscious about their neurosis, because it has the backing of culture. We can see how the ideology critique of Freud deconstructs the normal as inherently neurotic by examining how neurosis relates to something as ordinary as religious belief.

3.2 Religion: Normal or Mass Neurosis

As we saw in Chapter 4, Rieff says that pathological neurosis is the price one pays for the failure of normative authority. When sublimation takes place through culture, our neurosis is "normal" and "healthy," by which we mean functional. Sublimation no longer "works" when culture is no longer internalized or convincing to us. When this happens, our repressed contents come out in "abnormal" ways—one succumbs to individual or singular "sublimations" of repressed desires. This is what we *call* "neurotic."[17] Thus, "healthy" means we have socially usual forms of neurosis. This allows healthy neurotics (most people) to deceive themselves about their *causa sui* project, convincing themselves that they are free, significant, and self-sufficient, when in reality they are controlled and repressed by various cultural authorities.

Religion is a prime example of this for Freud, which he views as "mass neurosis." As Freud puts it in *The Future of An Illusion*, the "true [religious] believer is in a high degree protected against the danger of certain neurotic afflictions; *by accepting the universal neurosis he is spared the task of forming a personal neurosis*."[18] As religion loses its authority, however, it ceases to help humanity and becomes a detriment. In writing about religion, Freud says,

> For many thousands of years it has ruled human society; it has had time to show what it can achieve. If it had succeeded in making happy the greater part of mankind, in consoling them, in reconciling them to life, and in making them into supporters of civilization, then no one would dream of striving to alter existing conditions.[19]

Further on he says, "now we may say that the time has probably come to replace the consequences of repression by the results of rational effort, as in the analytic treatment of neurotics."[20] In other words, religion and its moral rules have failed us, and it is time to stop leaning on its authority as a means

---

17 Brown, 6.
18 *FI*, 777. (emphasis added).
19 *FI*, 653.
20 *FI*, 777.

of dealing with our inner conflict. Freud argues that it is time to grow up, and lean upon our own rational efforts. He sought a new basis for the *causa sui* project—a new, and more real means of becoming self-grounding.

This critique is not merely about religious dogma, but about all morality that constrains and represses the instincts—which includes all notions of value and heightened worth in civilization, as well as its continued progress. Here Freud's ideology critique moves beyond what he took from the Enlightenment, in which he views its ideas of human progress as misplaced optimism. No one socialized into Western culture is healthy, in terms of being free from neurotic suffering.

When Freud studies the nature of neurosis within the psyche, he is not merely interested in understanding those whose neurotic symptoms are causing them obvious suffering, but is interested in how the normal are also sick. As Freud puts it, in the spirit of ideology critique, "neuroses do not differ in any essential aspect from the normal, their study promises to afford us useful contributions to our knowledge of the normal. It may be that we shall thus discover the 'weak points' in a normal organization" of the psyche.[21]

We are all sick. Everyone is trying to keep it together, to keep a lid on the irrational forces just below our cultural masks (our character lies). We are all one or two traumatic events, or an existential crisis, away from slipping into abnormal neurosis. What moves one from healthy to unhealthy neurosis is that the conflicts of life become too difficult to bury. When the ego has become overly weakened by the struggle of both internal and external conflicts, the repression and self-deception it tries to maintain overwhelm the fragile ego (that is, its anxiety intensifies), as it attempts to remain in some form of balance. Freud says that the neurotic has "won an unmistakable, though in the end too costly, advantage through illness."[22]

Neurotic symptoms are a type of "unconscious exile," in which the person chooses individual sublimations or neuroses over the unconvincing culturally acceptable ones. Rieff likens the neurotic to a rebel out of weakness rather than strength. The neurotic cannot find the strength or self-mastery for a healthy exile due to her intense anxiety. To be a rebel in weakness is to have so defaced the currency that one can no longer lean on it, and yet is unable to stand by one's own strength. The *causa sui* project becomes psychologically crushing.

The rebel of strength (which Freud hopes to create in the psychoanalytic process) can accept an abstract exile—though often not a concrete one.

---

21 *OP*, 50.

22 *PP*, 194.

These are people who are successful in their revolt, who, through the Freudian re-education into the analytic attitude, can lead an active and achievement-oriented life in the outer world of culture. This is what Rieff calls the "managerial ego" of the normal personality who devotes herself to aggression against the environment through the practical use of objects, rather than the fixation on them.[23] This Freudian managerial ego, which is modeled after cynicism, abandons traditional sublimation in favor of cynical sublimation—the old *causa sui* project, for a new one.

4 Conclusion

The Freudian view of traditional sublimation is of an internalization of cultural and ethical ideals, which allows for these ideals to become the desexualized "outlet" for the instincts of the id. The internalization begins when the child identifies with the parents (the parents' superegos), and continues into adulthood in the internalization of cultural ideals or the cultural heroics. Identification and internalization are central for socialization and the initial "education" of the primitive or savage child.

Sublimation is,

> shifting the instinctual aims in such a way that they cannot come up against frustration from the external world. In this sublimation of the instinct lends its assistance. One gains the most if one can sufficiently heighten the yield of pleasure from the sources of psychical and intellectual world.[24]

This is the desexualization of our desires, which Freud considers the essence of sublimation, and so our cultural content.[25] Civilization, and the "higher" products of culture (what the Enlightenment thinkers thought of as "progress") are merely the fruits of sublimation, the desexualization of the id's desires: taking the instinctual energy, desexualizing it, and cathexing it in culturally acceptable actions. All the higher products of culture and the human psyche

---

23 *MM*, 353. What Rieff calls "fixation," I have been calling, following Becker, fetishizing. It is, then, a new attempt to ground oneself, to attain *true* self-mastery and freedom.

24 *CID*, 26.

25 Freud says, "the question arises, and deserves careful consideration, whether that it is not the universal road to sublimation, whether sublimation does not take place tough [*sic*] the mediation of the ego, which begins by changing sexual object-libido into narcissistic libido [the ideal ego]" (*EI*, 14).

are ultimately sexual and irrational.[26] The fundamental sexual nature of culture is the great Freudian social critique, a humiliation of the human pride of progress and nobility: all products of culture are grounded in the unconscious sexual drives of the id, so that the ground of culture, of everything we value in ourselves, and by which we attempt to matter, is sex. This is Freud's powerful act of defacing the currency, showing it to be a kind of counterfeit purpose (a secondary process rather than primary).

The critique that began with the Enlightenment and on into the various ideology critiques of traditional morality, brought an end to the effortless and efficient internalization of cultural morals and ideals by the individual. The end of internalization means that sublimation no longer works for gratifying the instinctual drives with socially constructive ideals. Since sublimation is what compensated the id for sacrificing its true desires, the sacrifice of these sublimations (e.g., the restraints upon the id that come with moral rules) were no longer worth it, no longer satisfying to the id. The lack of compensation created a tension within the psyche that required some sort of release or resolution.

This tension abides in a "gap" that arises between what we do and what we want to do. This gap must be filled with something. Earlier I likened the tension of this gap to holding one's breath: a tension grows and grows until the need to breath will be greater than the danger such a breath will entail (as in drowning). If cultural means of sublimation do not fill the gap, it will be filled by personal, neurotic symptoms which hamper the functioning of life for the individual. This situation brings to an end, in Freud's mind, the traditional *causa sui* projects, which consisted of cultural heroics that allowed for the internalization of morals and ideals.

We will now turn to the re-education that is the essence of the analytic attitude in order to see how Freud proposes to deal with the failure of traditional sublimation. In the final chapters, we will see that his hope for an exile and strengthening of the ego through a new (I argue, cynical) sublimation does not become a reality, but leads instead to a new level of self-deception. The re-education through reason turns out not to be a path to freedom and self-mastery, but a way of rationalizing the modern cynical contradictions.

---

26 "Sublimation of instinct is an especially conspicuous feature of cultural development; it is what makes possible for higher psychical activities, scientific, artistic or ideological, to play such an important part in civilized life" (*CID*, 44).

CHAPTER 15

Resistance, Therapy and Cynicism

1 The Cynical Rationalizations and Freud

We will be analyzing Freud's relation to our cynical culture by drawing a close connection between the three rationalizations for false consciousness and Freud's psychoanalytic process. These three rationalizations we looked at above closely connect to three central and necessary aspects of Freud's view of a "healthy" psyche. Our acceptance of the structure of the self Freud erected is, in part, why we view cynicism as a good, rational approach to life. It is through looking at these three aspects of Freud in relation to the three rationalizations for cynical false consciousness that we will come to see the intimate relationship between Freudian social theory and the cynical ideology within our culture.[1]

The three rationalizations already analyzed are: (1) seeing through deceptions by a detached irony toward situations, and the sense that this ironic stance raises one above the deceptions, even though one still takes part in them; (2) society creates competing and contradictory goals and purposes that require its members to act in contradictory ways; (3) The focus and purpose of life becomes self-preservation, which requires investing in the defaced cultural currency, since there are no other alternatives for individuals.

In terms of Freud's psychoanalytic theories, these three rationalizations are related to (1) the psychoanalytic process of breaking down resistance, and the focus on the mechanics of repression; (2) Freud's ambivalent attitude toward culture, in which he argues that culture remains necessary for a healthy psyche, even though it is also the cause of mental illness; (3) Freud's view that health consists of learning to cope with life as it is rather than trying to change it—that is, that the conflict is irredeemable, and so there are no other alternatives open to us. As is the case with the three rationalizations in cynicism, the three aspects of Freud we will analyze are not strictly delimited, but intertwine and flow into one another, being built upon the same presuppositions about life.

1 We will look at one of these aspects in this chapter, and the other two in the next two chapters.

 | HTTPS://DOI.ORG/10.1163/9789004758148-017

2 The Analytic Process: Overcoming Resistance through Ideology Critique

Freud presents a definition of neurosis and the process of overcoming it in a short statement in his book, *The Future Prospect of Psychoanalytic Theory*:

> You know, of course, that the psychoneuroses are substitutive gratifications of instincts the existence of which one is forced to deny to oneself and others. Their capacity to exist *depends on this distortion and disguise. When the riddle they hold is solved* and the solution accepted by the sufferers, these diseases will no longer exist.[2]

This quote points to the central aspect of the need to *see through* the distortions and disguises, as well as the issue of mistrust toward the inner workings of the psyche. We must admit that we do not *want* to know the truth.

Freudian social theory is very concerned with the issue of deception, and how overcoming this deception is the road to a healthier way of living. He is critical of traditional *causa sui* projects as self-deceptive, and so ultimately harmful. Ideology critique arose to understand the mechanisms of resistance, which keeps people from accepting the truth. A presupposition of ideology critique is that even when the solution to the riddle is solved, it is often not accepted. Ideology critique attacks the mechanisms that allow for this non-acceptance, in order to break down the naïve individual's resistance to the truth.[3] For Freud, this is the basis of developing a healthier psyche.

2.1 The Goal of Therapy: from Outsider-Cynic to Master-Cynic

Freud's ingenious move was to attempt to lessen the internal conflict between nature and society by internalizing the ideology critique and growing cynicism.[4] He did this by both modeling the self *and* his therapeutic process around this cynicism. In terms of the self, the id is "nature" within the psyche, focused on individual self-interest and instinctual satisfaction; the superego is

---

2 *FP*, 292. (emphasis added).

3 We will see that this acceptance is not simply the acceptance of a stronger rational argument, as the Enlightenment had hoped. Rather, this breaking down of resistance requires transference, which is a cynical "move" within Freudian psychoanalysis.

4 Again, this connection to cynicism was not the way Freud viewed his work; he viewed himself as a scientist, not a cynic.

the social or cultural aspect, focusing on the ideals through which one gains acceptance and a sense of significance; the ego is the detached mediator between the two, which focuses on the situation (the reality principle), and on moving the organism on the basis of rational thinking. In terms of therapy (the process of wellness), the ego is to pick up and internalize the Freudian ideology critique, as it weaves its way through the deceptions and illusions of its traditional means of seeking freedom, significance, and self-mastery. Freud's therapeutic process becomes the new picture of freedom and self-sufficiency: *seeing through* all manifest content into the "riddle." In this, one becomes free from the "con" of the social structure in which one lives.

I view the psychoanalytic approach to therapy as *an attempt to move the ego from an outsider-cynic to a master-cynic* within the psyche. The patient comes to the analyst as a kind of outsider-cynic, who has seen through the cultural heroics, but in a weak, passive, and relatively unconscious manner. As we saw in Chapter 12, the outsider-cynic is a powerless individual, whose adjustment to life is passive and defensive, and whose unconscious cynicism is born in the disappointment of no longer being convinced of the language of higher ideals. What distinguishes the outsider-cynic from the master-cynic is that the former is not as conscious as the latter in having given up on the higher ideals of culture. This lack of consciousness keeps the outsider-cynic attached to the ideals, even sacrificing for them, though she is no longer truly convinced the sacrifice will pay.

Freud's patients were also unconscious that they were no longer convinced of the ideals in which they claimed to believe, and were unconscious of why they turned to neurotic symptoms to relieve the tension of this situation. This unconsciousness of the neurotic is grounded in the ego's lack of transparency—the ego is not entirely conscious to itself—and so there remain unconscious aspects of the ego, which it uses in its resistances and defenses.[5]

The unconsciousness residing within the ego is the basis of the resistance, and the analogue to the outsider-cynic. The ego must move from outsider-cynic to the more conscious master-cynic (an enlightened deceiver), in order to overcome the neurotic symptoms. This is done through the therapeutic process, as the analyst takes on a cynical consciousness in regards to the patient, in order to break down resistances. The patient is eventually to take over the analyst's cynical consciousness, allowing the ego to be a master-cynic. We will take a

---

5 "[I]t is indeed the case that large portions of the ego and super-ego can remain unconscious and are normally unconscious. That is to say, the individual knows nothing of their contents and it requires an expenditure of effort to make them conscious. It is a fact that ego and conscious, repressed and unconscious do not coincide." *ILP*, 62.

look at this therapeutic process by first examining the analyst's cynicism, and then the patient's movement from outsider-cynic to master-cynic.

2.2 The Process of Therapy: Breaking Down Resistance through Cynical Interpretation

Resistance is a central issue for Freudian psychoanalysis, and has a strong influence on its cynical approach, in keeping with the ideology critique out of which it grows. For instance, the analyst expects dissimulations and deceptions from the patient, as she fights to keep her mechanisms of resistance and denial intact. The analyst believes the patient is *always* hiding something, and the analyst should never trust what the patient says. This mistrust of the patient is why, for Freud, therapy is the art of interpretation, and he believes that the analyst, being an objectively detached observer, is in a better position to know what is truly happening within the patient than the patient herself.[6]

While the analyst does not believe what the patient is saying, she does believe clues to the patient's "riddle" are found within what the patient says, whether these clues are in the interpretation of dreams, slips of the tongue, jokes, or the like. This is why free association is important for the analytic process: not only does it allow for a more unconscious and non-defensive communication, but it also provides more material and clues for the analyst to draw upon for her interpretations.

What stands out in this process is the completely cynical mistrust the analyst has for the patient: because the patient is trying to hide from the anxiety and shame induced by things she has repressed, she is unable to communicate what she really feels and thinks; she is being deceptive, dissimulating in order to conceal the truth about what it is she fears about herself. In a sense, she is trying to con the analyst (as well as herself) into believing the manifest content of what she says, in order to hide the anxiety-producing latent content. Neurosis, or mental illness, is due to this inability by patients to "be honest, own up to the instincts that are at work in them, face the conflict."[7] Thus, it is in making the patient aware of the content, by her becoming her own detached observer (master-cynic), that healing will take place.

There is also an analogue between psychoanalysis and cynicism in that one views this *seeing through* as an act of freedom: one sees through the false and irrational surrender to authority in order to gain a more self-sufficient approach to life. This freedom is to allow the patient to be self-grounding, and

6 "Psycho-analysis was then first and foremost an art of interpretation." *PP*, 18.

7 *FP*, 194. This is very much in line with the false consciousness of the outsider-cynic.

continue the *causa sui* project in a healthier manner—with a strengthened ego. The old, faulty beliefs upon which the patient leaned and propped up the *causa sui* project are dismantled, and a new basis is created through the therapeutic process. At least this is what Freud imagined to be the case.

2.3 A Critical Problem with the Analytic Process: the Need for Transference

There is a critical problem that arises in the analytic process: within the process, the patient's ego does not get stronger, but merely exchanges one authority for another. It is this exchange that maintains the illusions of self-grounding for the new *causa sui* project. Although Freud does not see the extent of this problem, it comes out in a section in which he addresses transference:

> Since this did not solve the therapeutic problem, a further aim quickly came into view: *to oblige the patient to confirm the analyst's construction* from his own memory. In that endeavour the chief emphasis lay upon the patient's resistance: the art consisted now in uncovering [seeing through] these as quickly as possible, in pointing them out to the patient and in *inducing him to human influence*—this was where suggestion operating as "transference" played its part—to abandon his resistances.[8]

Freud himself points out that what breaks down the resistance, and allows the patient to accept the analyst's interpretations, is not the rational argument of the analyst,[9] but the *transference* that takes place between patient and analyst. The patient is "obliged" to confirm (internalize) the therapist's interpretation by the same irrational mechanism that was used to confirm the parent's ideals. It is, as Freud himself says, something accepted due to "human influence," rather than rational thinking.

As we saw earlier in Becker's analysis, transference is treating the analyst with the same authority with which the child treated her parents. Transference means that the patient seeks the acceptance of the analyst so profoundly, that she will eventually accept whatever interpretation the analyst gives in order to receive acceptance, whether it makes rational sense to her or not. Thus, although it appears the patient moves from authority to reason, this move is

8 *PP*, 18. (emphasis added).

9 Such an approach would be more in line with the Enlightenment, which thought a good, rational argument was enough to enlighten the ignorant and naïve.

actually made for what Freud himself views as the irrational need of gaining acceptance by another authority.

While it is true that, once the analyst breaks through the resistance, the patient is to overcome the transference, and, through re-education, come to rely on her own rational ego, the fact remains that the initial acceptance of the interpretation (i.e., what puts the patient on a particular path) takes place out of the irrational need of the patient for the analyst's acceptance. All reasoning of the ego after this acceptance is simply a rationalization for what one accepted on the basis of the therapist's authority. This is precisely what happens in the initial education with the parents: the acceptance of a particular *causa sui* project, which is later rationalized by its own presuppositions and inner logic. Thus, in exchanging one *causa sui* project for another on the basis of authority, one remains within the self-deception that one has made one's own choice, and so is self-grounding.

Like modern cynicism, the act of seeing through is neither an act of freedom nor self-grounding based on reason, but the exchange of one authority for another. This is the basis of modern cynicism as enlightened *false* consciousness: *a seeing through that does not see through the irrational basis of its seeing through*, and the exchange of one interpretation of life for another, not arrived at through rational critique, but due to the need of being accepted. This is critical to our understanding of how we have *internalized* our cynicism based on the Freudian model of the psyche.

What is important to recognize is that, even though much of Freud's analyses of the *primary processes* of the psyche have been called into question and shown to be false, we still hold onto his (social) analysis for its social impact. This process is not unlike the transference we experienced with our parents, in which the initial acceptance starts us down a path that we continue to walk, even though we have seen through the irrational basis of this path (we have seen that our parents are as fallible, imperfect, and weak as everyone else).

3 The Analytic Process as a Training in Mistrust

3.1 The Ego as Deceived: a Weakening through Mistrust

In accepting Freud's view of the psyche, and the ideology critique and cynicism inherent in the analytic process toward a healthy psyche, we have also accepted the view that a generalized mistrust within our social relations is the wise approach to life. As we have seen, resistance relates to cynicism through their shared relation to ideology critique. Ideology critique views resistance everywhere, and believes that what is driving each individual is self-interest and the desire to cover this up. Further, ideology critique believes cultural manifestations are attempts to hide this self-interest and the shame associated with it. Rieff points to this cynicism in Freud's ideology critique: "But to charge that all aversions betray their opposite is as misleading as to accept all aversions at face value. Rejection is a proper activity of the super-ego. To uncover an acceptance beneath every rejection is to be incredulous of human goodness. It *encourages too easy a cynicism*, this principle suspicion of our dislikes."[10]

Cynicism is not knowledge, but is an interpretive act, for when we cynically mistrust what a person says, it is not because we actually know she is lying, but we have come (that is, chosen) to interpret everything and everyone uncharitably, from the point of view of a mistrust of motives, and a resistance to truthfulness. Just like the Freudian analyst, the cynic sees resistance everywhere due to the conflict between self-interest and the communal expectation of selflessness (sacrificing for the greater good). Thus, the cynic believes that the person who espouses moral ideals is not to be trusted. When such a person makes proclamations about the greater good of the community, the cynic immediately asks, "Yeah, but what's in it for you?" If our deepest motive is self-interest, and yet we are talking about sacrificing for the good of all, the reasonable question to ask, according to the cynic, is how this person is hiding his or her self-interest.

Freud recognized that this mistrust was already happening within his culture, and realized that it was having an impact on the ability to internalize the ideals by which people sacrifice their personal interests for the good of all. He knew this was connected to the failure of authority that arose out of the Enlightenment, and that the neurotic symptoms of his patients were directly related to this failure. With this growing lack of trust in traditional authorities, individuals were no longer able to internalize the ideals of society, and to believe that adhering to them would lead to a life of flourishing. The growing cynicism within society was having an impact on the way individuals were able to give themselves to the cultural heroics, as they wondered whether such a way of life was genuinely heroic—or just naïve.

Freud's answer to this problem was not to overcome the cynicism and mistrust that was the very cause of neurotic symptoms, but *his therapeutic process consists in going all the way with this cynicism*, by moving the patient from the passive and weak outsider-cynic, to that of the master-cynic. Having broken down resistances in psychoanalytic sessions, which, as we have seen, are

10 *MM*, 81. (emphasis added).

modeled on the more cynical aspects of ideology critique, the patient's ego can now take the place as a master-cynic in order to guide the organism as a whole.

3.2 The Ego as Deceiver: the Master-Cynic

We can view Freud's road to health as a movement from being the relatively unconscious and weak outsider-cynic to the more self-aware and strong master-cynic, who has consciously abandoned the traditional commitment therapies (the old *causa sui* projects) for a type of therapy in line with the analytic attitude. Freud says, "Psycho-analysis is an instrument to enable the ego to achieve a progressive conquest of the id."[11] This "conquest" is not something that changes the nature of the id—that is, it is not an attempt to change the primary process, as is the approach of traditional "commitment" therapies of the positive communities—rather, the "conquest" consists in the ego's *manipulation* of the id into believing that what the ego is after is in line with what the id desires (this is the nature of sublimation). This conquest consists, as we saw earlier, of the ego making itself the object of the id's desire or love. This is in line with how the master-cynic works: manipulating others' self-interest by making them think that the master-cynic's self-interest is in their own interest.

Just as the master-cynic must convince those she desires to manipulate that she is on their side, so the ego must convince the id that it is on its side, and that it is trying to help it get what it desires. As Freud puts it,

> Whenever possible it [the ego] tries to remain on good terms with the id; it clothes the id's Usc. commands with its Pcs. *rationalizations*; it *pretends* that the id is showing obedience to the admonitions of reality, even when in fact it is remaining obstinate and unyielding; *it disguises the id's conflicts with reality* and, if possible, it conflicts with the super-ego too. In its position midway between id and reality it only too often yields to the temptation to become sycophantic, *opportunist and lying, like a politician who sees the truth but wants to keep his place in popular favor.*[12]

The ego pretends to be trying to fulfill the id's self-interest when in reality it is all a ruse in order to gain control over the id for the sake of self-preservation. The ego uses deception in order to get the id to surrender its self-interest to the interest of the ego. The ego must do this because it needs the energies and

11 *EI*, 32.
12 *EI*, 32. (emphasis added).

resources of the id to accomplish its tasks, having no strength of its own. Its methods of extracting energy consist of what Freud calls "dodges."[13]

This is very much in line with what the master-cynic does, as she views the masses of people as resources for her own agendas and interests, manipulating them by making them think she works for their interests. Within the psychoanalytic therapeutic process, the ego is trained or re-educated to act like the master-cynic in order to gain control over more of the psyche for its own purposes (this is what Freud means when he speaks of strengthening the ego), convincing the id and superego to trust it, because it is merely trying to fulfill their desires. The more the ego succeeds in this task, the more healthy the individual is, so that master-cynicism is an analogue of health within psychoanalysis.

The reason Freud believes manipulation rather than reason is necessary for health is because the id and superego are both irrational and "self-serving" in their goals, goals that are not good for the organism as a whole. Further, manipulation is necessary because no reconciliation (rational or otherwise) can be brought about between the various aspects of the psyche. It is because traditional commitment therapies believed reconciliation was possible that they viewed reason and knowledge as the means to transform the appetites in line with the "greater good." No such view is held by Freud, which is why reason and knowledge are seen in terms of the power to subdue—often through shrewd manipulation. The only way to a healthier psyche is for the ego to learn how to manipulate the id and superego.

4 Implications and Results of the Connection between Cynicism and Psychoanalysis

There are a couple of things to take away from how Freud's psychoanalytic theory relates to cynicism. First, reason and knowledge are cynical for Freud, in that they are tools for gaining power: they are used to solve the "riddle" of dissimulation, which is accomplished through an uncharitable and suspicious interpretive act, in which one sees through the manifest content. In this, one gains freedom from deceptions (whether one's own or others'), in the sense of no longer being conned. *Not being conned is the image of health even when*, as we will see in the next couple chapters, *one still must invest in the very cultural ideals one has seen through.*

---

13 "From a dynamic point of view it [the ego] is weak, it has borrowed its energies from the id, and we are not entirely without insight into the methods—we might call them dodges—by which it extracts further amounts of energy from the id" (*ILP*, 68).

This re-investment in what one has seen through appears rational and even enlightened because one is investing in these ideals in a merely *functional manner*—that is, to achieve one's own self-interest. However, this cynical rationalization makes *rational* sense only because we have been provided presuppositions by Freud about the self, the world, and a healthy relationship between them—presuppositions we no longer question.

The second take away from this analysis is that, in Freud's ideology critique, the mechanisms of resistance are not socially grounded, but grounded in the individual psyche. Because a theorist like Marx views the mechanisms of resistance as built into economic structures (specifically, capitalism), he views resistance as a social phenomenon: a means one group uses to hold onto hegemonic power at the cost of another group. Freud, however, argues that the mechanisms of resistance are built into the psyche, so that it is only secondarily a social phenomenon. This distinction is important because, for Freud, even if we were to change the economic structure (for instance, by creating a "utopian" Marxist communist world), we would still be sick, and the actual conflict and struggle that causes us to suffer would remain untouched.[14]

If I am correct in viewing the structure of the Freudian psyche as cynical, and that our acceptance of this view of the self has a significant impact on our being cynical as a culture, then our cynicism has become rooted in our character. Cynicism is the basis of our new character lie, as Becker would put it. This means that cynicism is only secondarily a social problem. Making changes in the structures and institutions of society would not bring more trust among us at this point—that is, when we are already so entrenched in a cynical ideology. Instead, it is a problem of the self, so that we (each individual person) must change who we are, and only then will social changes begin to take shape. The focus of the problem of cynicism is not to be addressed *en masse*, so to speak (which is how most research on cynicism addresses it), but individually. To put this in a single statement, which is as obvious as it is difficult: I must decide (*krisis*) no longer to be cynical.

All social answers to cynicism will be viewed by the cynic as simply new means of manipulation. A social answer will make the cynic think only of the cost of giving up her cynicism, of how she will be taken advantage of by others, be dispossessed of what she desires, and how she will be walked on by others. There is no doubt that one must face and resolve this fear, but one resolves it

14 As a social theorist, Freud was not blind to the impact the social structure can have on neurosis. Indeed, this has been a major focus of the analysis up to this point. The impact, however, is more quantitative than qualitative: neurosis comes with being a socialized person, but it can be made more intense by the failure of culture to sublimate the id, or by creating too strict of a superego.

through *krisis*. The way of overcoming cynicism is to decide to abandon the *causa sui* project.

5 Conclusion

Freud did not set out to be a social critic or to deface the currency, but his work moved in that direction out of the recognition that the currency was already defaced, and the impact this was having on individuals: the patients coming to Freud were those for whom the currency was defaced, but who were unable to exile themselves from the content of sublimation (the moral rules). Freud's answer to this struggle was not to "prop up" the old authorities, and try to make them appear more trustworthy. Those days are gone.[15] What we need, according to Freud, is further liberation from authority, in order to give power back to the ego through "re-education." This re-education will develop a new means of sublimation.

In the face of the ineffectiveness of the traditional *causa sui* project, Freud did not abandon the *causa sui* project, but proposed a new, radically different one. As we saw concerning the demands of the id, Freud said, "Where there is id, there shall be ego." Freudian re-education is an attempt to help the ego gain more control over the conflict, by gaining more and more "territory" from both the id and the superego (having consciousness rule more and more), thus negotiating the conflict between them.

In these attempts, the ego tries to expand its power and control. In this chapter, we have begun to see that this expansion is modeled after cynicism, and that many of the characteristics of cynicism are found within the structure of the psyche as conceived by Freud. Using cynicism as the very model of the self further intensifies and entrenches the cynicism within culture, which is what I mean by the "new means of sublimation" that arise out of Freud's re-education: it is an internalization of cynicism, which is replacing the sublimation of traditional morality.[16] Cynicism and the therapeutic are the new *causa sui* project.

---

15 This is where Freud is clearly a social theorist and critic, as he proposes a social response to the growing inner conflict within the psyche, and in many ways patterns the psyche in terms of this response (a cynical response).

16 One should note that I differ from Freud as to the nature of the repression that leads to the necessity of sublimation. As I have shown above, I do not believe the repression is due to the sexual instincts, but the need for meaning and to matter. It is this repression that is being sublimated in new ways by cynicism, now that the traditional ways of mattering have been defaced and seen through. This will be examined in more detail in relation to the triumph of the therapeutic.

As we move into the next relationship between the rationalizations of cynicism and the Freudian re-education, we should remember that the ambivalence of leaning on the culture one has seen through has not gone according to Freud's prediction: the new sublimation has led to a more strict and efficient authority. Thus, rather than having surrendered to the authority of its own ego, as Freud hoped, the ego has surrendered to a technological morality and the authority of the new elites. As we saw in an earlier chapter, this morality is closely connected to cynical consciousness, and is not a surprising outcome of this process—especially since most people cannot accept the pessimistic and nihilistic views implicit in Freud's social theories. We will now look at this in terms of the second rationalization: Freud does not overcome the traditional *causa sui* project in order to give control to the id, but in order to again relate to culture in terms of a new *causa sui* project.

CHAPTER 16

Freudian Ambivalence and the Irreconcilable Conflict

1 Coping in the Moment

The analytic attitude does not see a natural harmony among human goals: there is no hierarchy of values inscribed upon the universe or the human psyche. Freud does not focus on ideals that have value across all situations, and to which the individual is to remain committed no matter the sacrifice. Instead, for Freud, it is the needs of the specific and contingent situation that rules and decides what is the best course of action. Freud says the ego, as related to the reality principle, is to be focused on the moment, the here and now.

The id is ultimately focused on the past, with its desire to re-experience the paradise of its earlier life, where it was free to fulfill its desires at whim and without shame; the superego focuses on the future, in hopes of progress and salvation that consist in the ego's and id's complete surrender to its view of perfection (the ego ideal). For Freud, there is no going back to an earlier paradise or innocence, and there are no new alternatives for progress and salvation that one should strive for in the future; there is only coping in the moment, finding the best solution in any given situation, and adapting to the contingencies of life, even if that means acting in contradiction to how one acted before. The ego's purpose is self-preservation, and that is defined not by our instincts or by our ideals, but by the present moment, and the reality within which we find ourselves.

2 Unending Conflict

2.1 Belief in the Green Light

There is, in both cynicism and Freud, an ambivalence toward the cultural currency. We saw this in *Rameau's Nephew*, for whom there is an unwillingness to move into exile in response to the enlightenment of the arbitrary nature of the cultural currency. Even when we come to see that the cultural currency is deceiving us or making us mentally ill, there is still a hesitancy to move away from it. The ambivalence in both cynicism and Freud is due to the lack

 | HTTPS://DOI.ORG/10.1163/9789004758148-018

of alternatives: both cynicism and psychoanalysis are negative ideologies that offer no new heroics to replace what they have seen through. There is no higher human purpose; there is only the reality against which one is continually struggling, and the various—often contradictory—ways of coping with it. Freud is especially aware of the conflict and contradictions that arise from this ambivalence, but since he sees no way out of these conflicts, the solution he provides is one that *accepts the contradictory nature of this state of affairs*, rather than trying to resolve it or provide new ideals to replace the old.

Rieff believes that the most important ideas in Freud surround his ambivalence, which leads to his acceptance of the conflict as perennial and without resolution.[1] This is the basis of Freud's pessimism: he sees no higher ideals or purpose for which to strive, and no alternative to unhealthy neurosis than for humans to learn to cope with the conflict between nature and culture. Rieff thinks that Freud came up with a strange compromise for the conflict, a compromise I believe is essential in understanding the contradictory enlightened false consciousness of cynicism: Freud believes that people need to accept themselves as they are, and yet also place their "hopes" in the very human capacity that is the cause of their suffering—the capacity *not* to be who they are—and run with that as well. This peculiar advice is in line with the second rationalization discussed in terms of cynicism: the situations of our lives are fraught with contradictory expectations and necessities, and so it is reasonable that we should continue to live in ways that contradict our enlightened consciousness.

Freud recognizes the different expectations within society, and how it is affecting the fragile ego; in response, he internalizes the conflict into the very structure of the psyche, which allows for a conscious sublimation. He does this in order to maintain the *causa sui* project (which is ultimately the basis of this contradictory situation), but on a new basis; he overcomes the traditional cultural heroics upon which the traditional *causa sui* project is grounded, in order to provide a new *causa sui* project (which we will examine under the third Freudian characteristic).

As Richard Rorty says in his pragmatist analysis of Freud, the Freudian theory of the unconscious allows for a "counter-purpose" self—a self whose purpose is in contradiction to the purposes of the conscious self.[2] The id has its

---

1 Philip Rieff, *The Feeling Intellect: Selected Writings*, ed. Jonathan B. Imber (Chicago: University of Chicago Press, 1990), 6. Henceforth cited as *TFI*.

2 Richard Rorty, "The Mechanical Mind: Hume and Freud," in *Pragmatism's Freud: The Moral Disposition of Psychoanalysis*, ed. Joseph H. Smith and William Kerrigan, 1–27 (Baltimore: John Hopkins Press, 1986), 5–6.

own purposes, driven by self-interest alone, which is a counter-purpose for the need of self-preservation. This view of the self provides a rational ground for acting in ways that contradict one's own better knowledge.

Thus, the point for Freud is not to learn to live without contradiction, but to learn to live with it. As we saw earlier, the modern cynic must continue to "channel the flow of depressive symptoms and to continue functioning in society despite our nagging doubts about his pursuits."[3] Modern cynics must channel the flow of their meaninglessness, and continue to function by staying busy, even if it is meaningless; if they do not do this, they will succumb to a paralyzing depression and anxiety. As Rieff puts this same point in relation to Freud, "The 'end' or 'goal' is to keep going. Americans, as F. Scott Fitzgerald concluded, believe in the green light."[4]

It does not matter that the cynic has seen the impoverishment and bankruptcy of the current cultural currency; in the absence of alternatives she has no other option (aside from emotional paralysis) than to continue to live for this same currency, to roll the rock (the only one she has been given) back up the mountain, knowing full well nothing lasting will come of it. Life within the cynical therapeutic becomes a matter of putting up with the madness of *tuphos* as best one can, and find a way to sublimate the dissatisfaction into cultural activities. In terms of the danger of neurosis that this situation creates, Freud's analytic attitude espouses, in the words of Rieff, a "trained capacity to keep the negotiations from breaking down."[5] If the negotiations break down, we are no longer able to channel the flow of depressive symptoms, and we will hit the yellow light of neurosis, or the red light of psychosis. Life is not progressing toward any higher consciousness that will lead to flourishing; this impossibility of progress is the Freudian pessimism that causes him to rationalize his ambivalent attitude toward what he knows is making us sick.

2.2 The Pessimism of Freud

If culture is making us neurotic, the obvious answer for overcoming this neurosis would seem to be abandoning the cultural ideals and conventions that are making us sick, and to live according to the id. Indeed, this is an answer given by many, such as Brown, Ernest Reich, and is a general theme of the modern therapeutic approach to health (the source of Carl Rogers' and Abraham Maslow's negative views of socialization and culture). Freud, however, did not

3 Huyssen, xii.
4 *TT*, 21.
5 *TT*, 24.

believe we could achieve happiness by the panaceas of social permissiveness or sexual plentitude. Giving into the instincts of the id will not bring the happiness for which one hopes, and will make self-preservation more difficult.

In contrast to the popular view of Freud, he did not believe the aim of life is a form of happiness in line with the pleasure principle. Freud believed that the pleasure principle's

> programme is at loggerheads with the whole world, with the macrocosm as much as the microcosm. *There is no possibility at all of its being carried through*: all regulations of the universe run counter to it. One feels inclined to say that the intention that man should be 'happy' is not included in the plan of creation.[6]

In terms of the external world, the universe is full of dangers and situations that make the experience of pleasure difficult and episodic; in terms of the internal world, our very constitution works against our ability to experience pleasure for very long. As Freud argues, pleasure is the satisfaction of needs that have been dammed up; pleasure is the experience of a release of the tension caused by an excitement of energy, which we feel as displeasure.[7] Given this, the happiness that comes from pleasure "is from its nature only possible as an episodic phenomenon. When any situation that is desired by the pleasure principle is prolonged, it only produces a feeling of mild contentment."[8] In other words, what at first brings pleasure, eventually feels normal, so that we no longer feel it as pleasure. In modern language, we build up a tolerance in regards to pleasure; thus, our constitution already restricts the possibility of continued happiness.[9] Pleasure is an impermanent state that we cannot sustain, and is much more ephemeral than people believe—they would see this if they would pay attention to how they really experience life at any given moment. As Rieff says, "Happiness, for Freud, is not the proper end of living, but a transitory feeling; it is a relief between extremes."[10]

Further, Freud understands that the pleasure principle, and the desires of the id, are no friends of the self. As Rieff says, "Freud is, surprisingly, the architect of a great revolt against pleasure, not for it. He made no briefs for the pleasure principle but rather exhibited its futility. It is toward the reality principle

6 *CID*, 23. (emphasis added).
7 *CID*, 23.
8 *CID*, 23.
9 *CID*, 23–24.
10 Rieff, "Freudian Ethics," (1957), 179.

that Freud turns us, toward the sober business of living and no-nonsense about its goodness or ease."[11]

For these reasons and others, Freud believes that giving into the pleasure principle is not the answer to our unhappiness. Freud's ambivalence toward culture is due to the recognition that, although it is making us sick, we need it for the sake of self-preservation. If giving into culture is our sickness, and not giving into culture is a zero-sum game (or even a loss in terms of self-preservation), then we are left with an irresolvable conflict. In Brown's view, Freud himself continually vacillates between two opposite answers when dealing with the perpetual question of unhappy humanity: sometimes he counsels instinctual renunciation, and sometimes he counsels instinctual liberation.[12] Instinctual renunciation comes out as: grow up and give up your infantile dreams of pleasure; recognize reality for what it is. Instinctual liberation comes out as: change this harsh reality so that you may recover lost sources of pleasure. Brown believes that it is this dilemma or ambivalence that explains Freud's drift into pessimism.

Rieff argues that, while Freud criticizes culture for being burdensome, in the end, he respects it as necessary.[13] Freud can see and accept the social value of repression, and the complex nature of satisfaction. For the most part, it is in the therapeutic context (the patient on the analyst's couch, which is, after all, not life) that Freud rejects repression.[14] Freud believed that we must accept culture as a despotic and inescapable god. We must accept some of the limits culture puts on the id because the instincts are in no way benign.[15]

3 The Analytic Attitude

3.1 No Hierarchy of Values

Freud's pessimism and ambivalence are summed up in what Rieff calls his "analytic attitude," which is in contrast to the attitudes of the "commitment therapies" of positive communities. We live in a time when the commitment therapies and their cultural heroics are no longer authoritative. Freud's analytic

11 Rieff, "Freudian Ethics," (1957), 178.

12 Brown, 57. It has been my argument that this vacillation is due to what the given situation requires. It is the context of the situation in which one finds oneself that dictates whether the focus is to be instinctual renunciation or instinctual liberation.

13 *MM*, 110.

14 *MM*, 343–344.

15 *TT*, 37.

attitude is the method of learning how to endure the loneliness produced by the negative community in which we now live. Psychoanalysis is the representative therapy of this negative community.[16]

Commitment therapies conceive the hierarchy of goals and ideals as the means for structuring personality into character—the integrity of the personality. For instance, with Plato's view of the soul, one is willingly to surrender the appetites to the leadership of the rational part of the soul, through the passion provided by the spirited part of the soul. If the appetitive aspect of the soul ruled, then the soul would succumb to irrationality and conflict, torn apart by various competing goals, and ultimately succumbing to an enslavement to the passions, resulting in a lack of well-being. The rational part of the soul, however, can understand what is truly valuable and real in life, and so rule the soul and the individual's life according to this understanding of what is higher and lower—aligning or transforming one's desires with what is of value. The ancient cynics also developed a hierarchy, viewing the natural as higher than artificial culture, and they developed virtues of character in line with this hierarchy. Within a Christian context, one is to surrender the "lusts of the flesh" and the workings of the "old self" to the life of the Spirit, and live by a new creation through the death of the old. In this way, sanctification brings redemption to the soul by putting all things under the law of God or love.

An important result of Freud's abandonment of a hierarchy of values is that one is to be willing to shift perspectives and allegiances according to the needs of the present situation. This conscious fluidity of commitment is not easy to attain (due to the demands of both the id and the superego), but it is what the process of re-education is to help bring about.[17] We are not to be unconditionally committed to any ideal, whether it be "justice," "loyalty," or even "love." As Rieff puts it, "The best one can say for oneself in life is that one has not *been taken in* even by that 'normal psychosis' of love."[18] It is no accident that the way Rieff puts this analytic attitude has affinities with the way a cynic would talk: for both the analytic attitude and cynicism, the main goal (that which will bring the most health and success) is not to *be taken in*, not to become the sucker of any ideology or doctrine, but to remain fluid, adapting to the situation, and adjusting as necessary.

We saw this at work in my student's contradictions in Chapter 12. In his desire to be accepted or to matter (*self*-preservation), he is continually caught in a struggle between conflicting expectations: he is told to hold onto the ideals

16 *TT*, 25.
17 *TT*, 42.
18 *TT*, 42. (emphasis added).

he accepted from his parents and stay true to them across all situations, and yet he is also told that his significance comes down to how he performs on the gridiron. Since he is no longer entirely convinced about the ideals, they become important for significance only in certain situations, and for a specific kind of self-perception. On the one hand, traditional authority figures within culture have taught him that what makes him matter (and so what really matters) is how he abides by the traditional ideals his parents passed down to him. These ideals, he believes (at least in part), are what will gain him acceptance. On the other hand, he is no longer convinced of this (convinced of the "process," as he put it), since much of society has called into question the cultural authorities that gave backing to these ideals.

The traditional ideals become difficult to internalize, which means that in many situations where he is called on to sacrifice his desires and stay true to these ideals, he is no longer able to do so (though he wants to maintain the self-perception that he is willing to do so). He knows, at a certain level, that they will not pay, so he chooses what the situation calls for (what "had to be done"). Although he is not completely conscious of this fact, his ideals are not the only way in which he measures himself, because they are no longer the way he is being measured by most people with whom he comes in contact. They have become for him, without his even knowing it, artificial and contrived. He knows the crowd in the stands does not really care about ideals like sportsmanship and fair play; they care about winning, about coming out on top and defeating the opponent. These are the *real* ways we define success, and gain our sense of value and esteem.

All of us modern cynics are torn between the significance we are told we gain through measuring up to the cultural ideals (a cultural heroics we have seen through), and the significance we gain through projecting our individual skills and strengths (a personal script in line with the therapeutic). We are not presented with any resolution to this conflict, and so the approach we take is to do whatever seems most appropriate for the sense of *self*-preservation at any given moment. We have, for a long time, been abandoning the idea that there is a universal, absolute, an unconditional hierarchy of values that is to guide our actions. When these old securities and reassurances of our value have been sufficiently impoverished due to our enlightenment, the best we can say for ourselves is that we are no longer taken in by them—i.e., we can no longer be taken as a naïve sucker. Not being conned is the negative "ideal" of the analytic attitude and cynicism.

The movement from commitment therapy to analytic therapy is also a change in focus from the analysis of ideals, to self-analysis. Commitment therapy consists in building personal character by learning self-discipline in line with moral ideals and constraints; this leads to a transformation in our character, because our deepest motivating desires are not merely controlled, but transformed.[19] This type of healing takes place within (that is, provides courage for) the communal purposes of the positive community.[20]

In the analytic attitude, where the traditional guiding "symbolics" are absent, therapy takes the form of a cynical self-analysis. As stated before, knowledge is no longer transformative, but informative.[21] The knowledge of the analytic attitude is an espionage epistemology, which helps us make our way through the minefield of deceptions all around us and within.[22] The analytic attitude is the creation of an enlightened consciousness that sees through all the ideals of the traditional positive communities. Thus, the analytic attitude is Freud's new *causa sui* project.

3.2 No New Doctrines

Freud understood the dangers of this situation, and the vulnerability the individual faces when life has become meaningless, but he refused to provide any new doctrines that would appear to decrease this vulnerability. To give new doctrines would only be giving the neurotic a new self to pursue (implying that one is to be ashamed of the self one is), which is what caused the neurosis in the first place.[23] It would be to strengthen the superego rather than the ego. The neurotic would need to repress those aspects of the self that do not measure up to this new self. Rather than providing new doctrines, the analytic attitude seeks to limit the power of culture upon the individual. In other words, Freud's approach to health was not to create new cultural ideals by which to rescue people from their misery, but to change the way people relate to any culture, helping them to cope with their misery. This way of relating is in line with a weaponized epistemology of distrust or cynicism. When Freud contemplates changes to culture, it is with an eye to lightening the load of culture so that we do not have to be continually working to become something we are not—something conceived as "higher" or "better."

Rieff says that the best an analyst can do is teach the patient how to become her own therapist (what I interpreted above as becoming a master-cynic), being strengthened in the knowledge of her particular weaknesses, and their

---

19 Elisabeth Lasch-Quinn, Introduction to *The Triumph of the Therapeutic* (Wilmington: ISI Books, 2006), xv.

20 Lasch-Quinn, xv.

21 Lasch-Quinn, xv.

22 *TT*, 63.

23 *TT*, 24.

causes. This is the modest and conservative purpose of psychoanalytic therapy in a culture no longer capable of inventing doctrines of salvation (at least none that could be internalized by anyone): "Freud proposed a therapy that did not try to charm the suffering out of humanity, but only restored the capacity to endure living."[24] For those no longer childlike and naïve enough to be charmed by the old illusions, a restoration of ego-capacity is the one gift to be given. Greater ego-capacity is Freud's rendition of the ancient cynic's value of self-mastery and self-sufficiency.

Freud replaces the sacred authority of the "vertical" with the therapeutic ideal of adjustment by becoming a cynic toward all ideals. Rieff points out, "Freud's greatness seldom elevates. This was not his purpose. He was a digger, not a builder, an archeologist of the psyche."[25] He digs at the foundations, wiping away the facades, the layers of dissimulation, knowing he has reached bottom when he hits self-interest—specifically, sexual desire.

Digging itself is not what makes one a cynic; most academic work is busy with this (from science to philosophy), trying to see through the obvious to the less obvious. It is what I am doing in this book. It is what Kierkegaard, Becker, Rieff and every other author I have drawn from are doing. So why do I view Freud's digging as something detrimental to human flourishing, viewing it not merely as inherently cynical, but as an important element and justification for our cynicism? It is because of the abandonment of hope, the loss of alternatives, the completely uncharitable interpretation that expects nothing of real value to be found in digging, and nothing new we can build. Freud does not dig hoping to find treasure, but in order to show that there is no treasure; Freud does not dig in order to build something new, but in order to show that we can build nothing higher upon our foundation of self-interest. As Rieff implies, Freud does not seek to make people more heroic, but to make the unheroic healthier.[26] Or, as he puts it elsewhere, Freud's therapeutic approach "promises not more happiness but less misery."[27]

4 Conclusion

If Freud does not seek to implement new moral ideals or doctrines, why does Rieff argue that he has "the mind of the moralist?" Rieff calls Freud's psychology

24 *TFI*, 14.
25 *MM*, 322.
26 *MM*, 329–330.
27 *TT*, 30.

a "moral psychology because Freud not only studies the conduct of life, but also seeks to affect it; he is not simply descriptive, but has an imperative element to it in the sense that he wants to affect culture."[28] My argument is that this imperative element is basically cynical: *he has called on us to internalize the ideology critique, which has resulted in a cynical consciousness and mode of life*. Freud's analytic attitude, along with the ambivalence toward the defaced currency of culture, has had an impact on the way we perceive the world, others, and ourselves. In terms of the analysis of this section, it has enabled us to justify the contradictory ways we live, in the sense of *rationalizing to ourselves an investment in the very things we have come to see as unworthy of investment*.

Psychoanalysis justifies this through the ego's prime goal of self-preservation, and the abandonment of any alternative approaches to the contradictory modes in which we live. Freudianism wants us to accept this state of affairs, rather than turning to fantasies that claim to resolve or transcend the conflict—fantasies that only add more pressure upon the ego, and cause it to repress more and more of itself, rather than gaining control over more and more of itself.

Most modern cynics have not *consciously* accepted Freud's analytic attitude, which is why their views have not taken on the self-aware aspects of his social theory—those aspects that lead to his pessimism. It has been picked up or received through various authorities, such as the cultural "elites" described in an earlier chapter. This internalization of Freudian views of the human psyche has turned therapists and psychologists into the new cultural priests, who are the only ones to be trusted for our psychological health; they are the ones who can guide us in the best means of self-preservation.

This leads us to the third rationalization for the cynical false consciousness. While the first rationalization dealt with the need to see through culture, and the second dealt with our continued need for culture, this third rationalization shows how internalization takes place, and of what the new internalization should consist.

---

28 *TT*, 31.

CHAPTER 17

Re-education as Coping

1 An Answer to Nihilism

The problem Freud examined in his analytical studies was how the social order is able to be internalized (i.e., what grounds sublimation), since this is what had become problematic for his patients. As we have seen, traditional processes of internalization were built around authority arising out of the Oedipus complex. In sociological terms, commitment therapies are authoritarian, which ground and provide backing for the internalization of values, mainly related to a symbolic action system or cultural heroics. With the end of commitment therapies, due to the failure of authority, we have moved into a time of "nihilism," where *nothing* is providing a ground for our ideals, purposes, or meanings—symbolics as a whole have become trivial. Nihilism is an impoverishment of interpretation concerning the individual's relation to culture, others, and herself—basically, to the whole of life.

Freud knew there was no returning to traditional authority once it has been so thoroughly defaced, and thought the only alternative was that the ego becomes its own *rational* authority, which is, as Rieff says, the "final step in resolving the corporate identity that no longer serves to integrate the self."[1] In the face of this nihilistic situation, Freud proposed a re-education in which the individual breaks from all authority in order to become her own authority. This re-education (the analytic attitude) is the new *causa sui* project, one which Freud conceived in line with our impoverished world and weakened ego. Freud's project (and so our project) is not the attempt to progress to some higher individual or social structure (which would be an attempt to overcome nihilism), but he provides a process to help us cope with the fact that there *is nothing higher* (an attempt to live within nihilism, to find a way to live nihilistically).

This answer is in line with the attempt to hold onto the *causa sui* project in the face of the humiliation of a meaningless and insignificant life. This nihilism or impoverishment of interpretations is the historical *krisis* that took place at the end of the nineteenth century, and for which Freud became the most accepted answer in the twentieth century, as a re-education of the ego. We

1 *TT*, 64.

now turn to an analysis of the Freudian re-education, in which we learn to live with what Freud called the "common unhappiness" of self-preservation. This is making peace with a life of languishing. Freud is not leading us anywhere, and is assuring us of nothing; rather, he is attempting to make the burden of our misery somewhat lighter. He is not providing a new symbolic, but a technique; he promises not transformation, but helpful information.

Since the time of Plato, Western Civilization has viewed reason (*logos*) as a means of transforming the self in line with the order (*Logos*) of the cosmos, a transformation that leads to greater flourishing and thriving. Since we no longer believe there is a meaningful order to the universe, this can no longer be the task of reason; instead, reason is now a tool for mitigating the cruelty of living, and is to help us cope with the conflicts with which we struggle.[2] Knowledge and reason are about gaining more power and control for the ego.

2 The Approach

2.1 Learning How Not to Be Good

In re-education, Freud does not ask what the good life is. As we have already seen, he does not want to replace the old traditional heroics with something positive. Instead, psychoanalysis says, "Let's see if we can better understand what hinders you from leading a life that you consider to be good."[3] In other words, let's see what is deceiving you. What are the forces at work that are trying to get you to do what you do not really want to do? In terms of how it was put in relation to the ancient cynics—what are the false judgments of value? For Freud, the false judgment is that society still has us looking for some kind of hierarchical value in life. There is only the strictly negative undertaking of seeing through this "deception." Freud conceives of health as a negating move—i.e., the continual removal of hindrances. To be healthy, the ego needs to stop being the "sucker" of culture and the superego.

An important aspect of what hinders us is, according to Freud, our attempt to be more than what we are or can be. Freud understood that the ego has too

2 *MM*, xii.

3 Joseph H. Smith, "The Analytic Attitude," in *Pragmatism's Freud: The Moral Disposition of Psychoanalysis*, ed. Joseph H. Smith and William Kerrigan, 52–78 (Baltimore: John Hopkins Press, 1986), 54–55.

much pride, thinks too highly of itself due to its narcissism.[4] People need to learn to deal with their insignificance in the universe: we must go from a heroic and delusional *causa sui* project to a more modest one, which Freud proposes as a re-education of the ego.[5]

In order to humiliate the old *causa sui* project, which seeks to take the psyche higher than it can actually go, we must personally destroy our old symbolics (that which turns one's eyes to such heights). In his analysis of Freudian re-education, Rieff likens the analyst to another well-known cynic: Machiavelli. Rieff says,

> The analyst plays a Machiavelli to the overdignified sovereign ego, proscribing all moralizing and advising merely a close attention to the demands and opportunities of the external world [the reality principle]. The ignorant ego could not censure itself, except badly. Self-criticism presupposes self-knowledge; and by destroying what he thought was the illusion of self-knowledge, Freud's theory also proscribes the use of self-criticism. This is Freud's powerful psychological revision of the Socratic injunction, Know thyself, and the form in which Freud intended his science to be the most final of techniques of disenchantment since Copernicus and Darwin.[6]

We have here what D. S. Mayfield calls the "artful immorality" of the cynic, in line with Machiavelli.[7] We must, as Machiavelli put it, learn how not to be good (not be over-dignified).[8] For Freud, this is not for the purpose of gaining power for external political gains, as it is for Machiavelli's cynicism, but for the

---

4 "You conduct your life as an absolute sovereign who is content with the information supplied by the highest officials, and never goes among the people to hear their voices. Look into the depths of your soul and learn first to know yourself, then you will understand why this illness is bound to come upon you and perhaps will thenceforth avoid falling ill." Sigmund Freud, "A Difficulty in the Path of Psycho-analysis," in *Freud: Complete Works*, trans. Ivan Smith, (2010): 3626–3615, 3614.

5 As we will see, this is in distinction to Kierkegaard's approach, where the lack of significance is to divest us completely of the *causa sui* project, by which we repress the true nature of our significance.

6 Rieff, "Freudian Ethics," (1957), 177.

7 See D. S. Mayfield, *Artful Immorality—Variants of Cynicism: Machiavelli, Gracian, Diderot, Nietzsche* (Berlin: De Gruyter, 2015).

8 "[A] man who wishes to act entirely up to his professions of virtue soon meets with what destroys him among so much that is evil. Hence it is necessary for a prince wishing to hold his own to know how to do wrong, and to make use of it or not according to necessity." Nicolo Machiavelli, *The Prince* (Australia: Planet eBook.com). https://www.planetebook.com/free-ebooks/the-prince.pdf, 91–92.

internal "political" gains of the ego. A weakened ego is like a weakened prince, and where Machiavelli presents knowledge for the sake of gaining and maintaining power over political reality, Freud presents knowledge for the sake of gaining and maintaining power over intrapsychic reality.

To say that a person must learn how to do wrong is to point to the work we must do in regards to the moral conscience. What relates cultural deception to internal deception is conscience, and so Freud believes conscience must be undercut in order to gain accurate self-awareness. Conscience, being related to the traditional morality, is too stringent, expects too much of the ego—expects too much sacrifice. Re-education, then, consists of an individual's personal ideology critique of the traditional morality, which is also a training in becoming a cynic. The enlightened, healthy, self-mastered person is the one who sees through traditional symbolics of meaning as arbitrary and contrived sublimations of hidden desires (our true nature), just as all good cynics, from the time of Antisthenes until the present, have done. The therapist must teach the patient, who is the product of an overly ascetic culture and overly stringent and cruel superego, to see through traditional morality to its groundlessness; it is *tuphos*, clouding the mind, based entirely on an irrational desire for acceptance by those who hold authority in one's life. In place of the rigid moralizing of the superego and conscience, Freud proposes a more flexible administration of the ego, as we saw earlier.[9]

2.2 Reason as a Technical Instrument

Reason is a technical instrument used for the ego's self-awareness by the breaking down of that which keeps it in false consciousness. This is a purely negative undertaking of the analytic attitude. As Rieff says, in Freud's eyes, there is something more therapeutic than belief: a therapeutic unbelief.[10] Rieff likens this to a more democratic understanding of the ego, in line with the individualism of our time. Rather than a hierarchy of values to order the various purposes within the ego, there is a jostling democracy of contending purposes.[11]

In traditional moral education, therapy consisted of the attempt to re-order and transform the contradictory purposes and directions within the soul through a hierarchy of values; Freud's re-education turns away from this idealistic demand of the superego. Re-education is a pedagogy in line with the reality principle, which means overcoming the naivete of the superego.

---

9 *MM*, 71–72.
10 *MM*, 96.
11 *TT*, 45.

3 The Freudian *Causa Sui* Project

3.1 Adaptation and Narrowing

The re-education does not seek to weaken the superego for the sake of more pleasure, but for the purpose of self-preservation.[12] Freud seeks a strengthening of the ego over both the id and the superego, not choosing one over the other, for neither are genuine friends of self-preservation, having purposes at variance from this. This changes the nature of the *causa sui* project, because we have come to recognize the ego as weak and untrustworthy. It must be freed from ideals, improve its knowledge and control of reality, and seek a modest well-being by gaining satisfaction through control over more portions of the id. Freud envisions the ego as maintaining a better balance between the forces of the civil war within it. As Freud puts it,

> Our plan of cure is based on these views. The ego has been weakened by the internal conflict; we must come to its aid. The position is like a civil war which can only be decided by the help from an ally from without. The analytic physician and the weakened ego of the patient, basing themselves upon the real external world, are to combine against the enemies, the instinctual demands of the id and the moral demands of the superego.[13]

In the face of a weakened ego, Freud does not go the direction of Kierkegaard in relinquishing the *causa sui* project in order to become open to new possibilities; Freud sees no other alternative than for the ego to grow up, face the world, and admit its weak position within it, as best it can. We can trust nothing else for self-preservation except the facts and their rational organization. Freud says, "At first we are inclined greatly to reduce the value of the criterion of being conscious since it has shown itself so untrustworthy. But we should be doing it an injustice. As may be said of our life, it is not worth much, but it is all we have."[14]

What is essential to keep in mind is that having no alternatives means we must narrow and reduce our lives and the world to what we know we can accomplish, without a thought of an Excess or transcendence (what Kierkegaard called the infinite and possibility). We have already seen that unhealthy neurosis is the process of a personal narrowing of reality. Freud's answer to

12 *MM*, 325.
13 *MM*, 36.
14 *ILP*, 62.

nihilism is not to expand the self, as Kierkegaard and Nietzsche argue,[15] but to make this narrowing approach normal—that is, move it in the direction of a kind of mediocre functionality, which Kierkegaard calls "spiritlessness" and Nietzsche calls the "last man." In both Freud and modern cynicism, hopelessness is the way we rationalize our return to what we have seen through.

Without Excess there is no flourishing, and the more narrowed our world becomes (must become, in Freud's view), the more languishing and neurotic each of our lives will become. When this narrowing becomes a cultural affair, it may feel like we are becoming healthy, free, and autonomous, though it is only a grim acquiescence to our being sick. Indeed, in this dialectic of a sickening culture, it is now those with "unhealthy" symptoms who are showing themselves to be sane, as they are no longer able to live effectively in this normalization of despair. It is the standard way of life that has become crazy: irrational, contradictory, false, delusional, frenzied, contracting.

3.2 The Illusion of Openness

3.2.1 Lack of Commitment

Freud maintains an *illusion* of freedom and expansion, in that he writes about the need for openness to opportunities for the sake of health. This illusion of freedom will become the theme of the triumph of the therapeutic, and will be critiqued in the final chapters. We will see that the illusion is maintained by what Rieff calls the "primacy of possibility." While it will be critiqued more thoroughly and concretely in the final chapters, we will take a brief look at this issue now in order to understand the narrowing of Freud's approach (what is often called his conservatism), which is the justification used in the cynical therapeutic.

When the Excess is no longer in play, we should understand the term "possibility" by the Kierkegaardian concept of "probability," for one is dealing with what is *calculatively available*, rather than with ontological possibility—an unseen and unknowable im/possibility beyond one's control (as Derrida would put it). Freud views the openness of opportunities as the ability to adjust according to the facts within a given situation, where movements and

15 Although Freud sees no other alternative because he cannot imagine one, this does not mean that Kierkegaard can see or imagine specific alternatives. The difference is not in what they hope for, but what they hope upon: Freud has no hope upon anything beyond the facts, whereas Kierkegaard, maintaining a relationship to the Excess, has a "hope against hope".

changes are never completely certain. This is what Rieff calls "a trained capacity for entertaining multiple perspectives upon oneself."[16]

Basically, there is a tolerance for ambiguity and contradiction within the given perspectives available to one, both in reference to one's own inner motives, and the social world. This tolerance is the Freudian key to a genuinely stable character, suitable for living in an uncertain time, when directions for action and choices are fluid, and no longer clear.[17]

Living in contradiction is a rational act in a world that is itself full of contradictory demands. In such a world all options are to be kept alive for the sake of adaptation.[18] Keeping all options alive means, of course, that one cannot commit to any single option, and must be willing to give up a particular direction if a new, better option presents itself. As my friend put this idea: "I can always get a divorce." Such a statement is simply the knowledge that all options are always open to him, and nothing is set in stone. There is no grand moral order in the universe (no hier*archy*) that organizes life, but a chaos (an*archy*), a sea awash in contradictions, in which one never knows what a particular situation will call for.

3.2.2 Maintaining a Balance

The strengthening of the ego is toward the ability to maintain a truce in the civil war within the psyche (to keep the negotiations going, as we put it earlier). This truce is about maintaining a balance among the warring aspects of the self. Freud's theory is one of equilibrium toward which the emotional life tends after every disturbance (pleasure as the release of tension). We are to grow equable, keeping the tension to a minimum.[19] When the inner life is not easily disturbed—for instance by the high ideals of the superego—it will have achieved what to Freud is as nearly an ideal condition as he could imagine.[20]

When one is no longer convinced the ideals will bring greater rewards than the sacrifice of the pleasure, the inner tension rises as one seeks to maintain the ideals. What the neurotic needs is less enthusiasm; thus, well-being for Freud is a lack of excitement and drama within the self. Even this well-being is viewed by him as an ephemeral and transient state, because the conflict between the

16 Rieff, "The Analytic Attitude," 22. I would say it is multiple *given* perspectives.

17 Rieff, "Analytic Attitude," 22.

18 *TT*, 41.

19 One finds within both ancient cynicism and Freud an association with stoic approaches to life.

20 *MM*, 342.

competing instincts and culture (not to mention those between the various instinctual desires themselves) will continue to arise.[21]

This lowering of the tension is accomplished, as we saw earlier, in the ego's ability to take over more and more "territory" (in the name of reason and reality) from the id and superego. This necessity for balance relates to Freud's ambivalence about culture: he is not unsympathetic to the old moralities, and could admire the repressions of the id through sublimation; however, he understood that the cultural ideals had become too much for the ego to bear, and would need to be lightened (balanced).

4 Health as Languishing: a Critique of Freudian Re-education

Freud's therapeutic answer leads to general human languishing.[22] Since there is nothing to hope in that will make humans higher and more noble, Freud argues that it is rational to do away with such striving. No doubt, immortality striving continues, but it is no longer related to a heroic, but to scripts within culture. As we will see in the next couple chapters, this is when cynicism becomes a therapeutic process. It becomes locked within the cultural expectations of the technological morality. Our expectations are connected to probability within our culture, and not to true possibility. As Freud says, "Thus by withdrawing his expectations from the other world and concentrating all his liberated energies on earthly life he will probably attain a state of things *in which life will be tolerable* for all and no one will be oppressed by culture anymore."[23] This is Freud's (and I argue, cynicism's) highest aspiration: a tolerable life. And even this tolerable life seems to be walked back in Freud's later writings, where the best we can hope for is a resolve to continue the discontented "detour" toward the real aim of life: death.[24] For Freud, problems begin when we aspire to something more than this tolerable and meaningless self-preservation. The moment we want to

---

21 *MM*, 342–343.

22 In Chapter 20 we will take a close look at this languishing in terms of Kierkegaard's critique of the esthetic stage of existence (into which Freud's re-education and therapeutic processes fall). This languishing, as a lowering or levelling of the ideals leading to self-becoming, is what Kierkegaard calls "despair".

23 *FI*, 872. (emphasis added).

24 "For a long time, perhaps, living substance was thus being constantly created afresh and easily dying, till decisive external influences altered in such a way as to oblige still surviving substance to diverge ever more widely from its original course of life and make ever more complicated *detours* before reaching its aim of death" (*PP*, 46). For Freud, life is not

be something higher, which requires of us too much sacrifice to our personal well-being, we fall into neurosis.

In a letter to Marie Bonaparte, Freud says, "The moment a man questions the meaning and value of life … he is sick, since *objectively* neither has any existence."[25] Freud views the meaninglessness of life as if it were some sort of scientifically objective certainty. He would have us believe that in his supposed scientific stance, he has stepped out of existence and the universe in order to grasp it as a whole and make the judgment about what it all means—namely, nothing. However, this is not a view he came to from his scientific studies of the world or humanity, but is an interpretation, as is all Freudian analysis.[26] No one can *know* such a thing, because we are too deeply and thoroughly immersed within existence itself, and cannot grasp life *sub species aeternitas*, as Kierkegaard put it. We choose our interpretations, often based on how we would like life to be, and then later justify them through experience and "evidence."

That life is meaningless and without alternatives is Freud's interpretation, his succumbing to the nihilistic presuppositions that were gaining intellectual traction during his own time. There is nothing intellectually wrong with making such interpretations, as long as one has the humility to admit what they are, and not stamp them with some sort of *authority*, such as "science" (something that far too often happens). Without this admission, one falls into false consciousness. Such views (whether life is meaningless or meaningful) are a *krisis*, a judgment and decision that we must make in the face of insufficient evidence (that is, in the face of Excess). This *krisis* is a decision about our *causa sui* project, and whether we are willing to give it up in the face of our creatureliness.[27]

Freud's false consciousness around the issue of a lack of alternatives in the face of nihilism was picked up by modern cynicism, which has become a rationalization for its own false consciousness. One of the most significant

---

the aim of the organism, but death; life is a "detour" on the way to the true aim of the organism.

25 Quoted in *TT*, 27. (emphasis added).

26 The most unrelenting attack by critics upon Freud's psychoanalytic practice itself (that is, the case studies he presents about his patients), is that his interpretations were wildly inaccurate, and yet were claimed to have the certainty and rigor of scientific observation.

27 I am pushing this point because an important aspect of false consciousness is the many ways we seek to ignore the *krisis* we face in life. This "objective" attitude about life's meaninglessness is a way in which people create an illusion around choices or decisions they make about life—and guide their interpretations about life. This helps them keep the anxiety that comes from such choices from coming to consciousness.

distinctions between ancient and modern cynicism is that the latter remains solidly connected to the culture it sees through, and it does this because it cannot imagine any other alternative; in order to keep moving, it grabs on to what is available, no matter how empty and meaningless it has become. Further, to even ask about the meaning of what one is giving one's life to is, according to Freud, to become sick.

The world is a lonely and competitive place for Freud, and one that is absurd when searching for some kind of meaning in it. His analytic attitude and therapeutic re-education move the patient toward a gentle acceptance of this interpretation. My presupposition has been that no human being can *truly* surrender to this absurdity and at the same time continue to function in life. It is easy to wax eloquently about it in abstraction, and I have myself felt the energy that comes from these dark and uncanny thoughts, but we cannot live such a life, because humans are never neutral—never not seeking meaning. The ground of human life, its deepest motive, is this need for meaning and significance, and whenever people deny this ground and are able to keep moving (get out of bed), one will find that they have some sort of transcendental meaning that they remain blind to, and so deceive themselves about—or they have numbed themselves through palliative means.

Even Freud needed a meaning that he hoped would transcend his individual life and give it durability. His was the self-image as a scientist (much like we saw earlier with Carl Sagan), which gave him a personal cosmic heroic, a meaning tied to a hope of durability and immortality. Becker analyzes Freud's *causa sui* project in *The Denial of Death*,[28] and, pointing to Paul Roazen's interpretation of Freud, says, "the psychoanalytic movement as a whole was Freud's distinctive *causa-sui* project; it was his personal vehicle for heroism, for transcendence of his vulnerability and human limitations."[29] As Rieff says about Freud,

> Work was the one way out of his tiredness. Thus Freud turned necessity into therapy; there was no other way out, before death, for the community was no longer therapeutic but had become an environment—the arena of conflict. In a sense we can now better understand, there is something to the gross charge that psychoanalysis is the best profession for neurotics—but only for extremely intelligent neurotics, those who can *learn to inhibit successfully their religious impulses*.[30]

---

28 See *DD*, 98–128 for the full analysis.

29 *DD*, 109.

30 Rieff, "Analytic Attitude," 23. (emphasis added).

What Rieff here calls "inhibit," we can just as easily call "repress"; and what he calls "religious impulse" we can call "desire for meaning." Freud was able successfully to sublimate his desire for meaning into his immortal child (or so he hoped) of psychoanalysis. Further, Rieff says that it is the "intelligent neurotics" who can "learn to" do this; this "learning" is, I would argue, the very re-education of psychoanalytic therapy: an attempt to repress our longing for meaning, which, like all repression, needs to be sublimated.

Freud was not unaware of the importance of this need for meaning and significance, but as we saw in his letter to Bonaparte, he viewed it as the cause of mental illness, not because it is being repressed (as I argue), but because it is for him a sublimation of what we are repressing: sexuality. Our desire to matter, our yearning for meaning, is, like everything else for Freud, about sex. Our desire to matter is a desexualization of the instincts of the id. As we have already seen, repression proceeds from the ego, and in the specific relation to the desire for meaning and significance, it proceeds from the "self-respect of the ego."[31] The ego does not want to see itself as the nasty sexual creature that it is, and thinks of itself as better than merely a copulating organism—that is, it thinks it matters for more than this need for sex.[32]

The target of this self-love is the ideal ego, which was enjoyed in infancy as the actual ego: the omnipotence experienced in primary narcissism, in which the infant felt itself to be the world. As the infant inevitably learns that it is not the world, it needs to rescue some sense of self, and so the primary narcissism gives way to a secondary narcissism: the ideal ego. Like the infant ego, the ideal ego finds itself possessed by every perfection that is of value (that will gain it acceptance).

In other words, having ideals is a form of narcissism, a blowing oneself up, a form of self-love as a way to prove to oneself and others that one is worthy of love—that one matters. It was just this target that Freud sought to humiliate, as we have already seen. Thus, according to Freud, our desire for meaning and significance is simply a second form of narcissism, which, like all things in a Freudian psyche, seeks to return to the happiest and most satisfying time of its life: the time of infant omnipotence and instant gratification.

There is truth in this analysis, though I am not at all convinced that Freud has undercut our value and worth through it. What he has accomplished is to show how the *causa sui* project corrupts our significance, making it into

31 Sigmund Freud, *On Narcissism: An Introduction* (New York: Routledge, 2018). http://ebookcentral.proquest.com/lib/usclancaster/detail.action?docID=879954, 23. Henceforth cited as *ON*.

32 *ON*, 23–24.

something neurotic, and that our self-concern can go awry. This does not show that the need for meaning and significance is necessarily sick, but that it is dialectical.

5 Conclusion

As we have seen, psychoanalysis sees itself not as a theory of belief, but as a theory that instructs us how to live without belief. We must learn how to live in an untrustworthy and deceptive world. We must learn how to be cynics. Freud's analysis and cynical reaction to nihilism won out in the twentieth century, and became the strongest influence in our culture's means of dealing with nihilism. Our modern cynical culture, and the triumph of the therapeutic, are the fruits of Freud's powerful social theories, and the direction he provided for dealing with the loss of meaning, value, and purpose.

What is so intriguing about this victory is that Freud offered so little in the way of hope, promised so little in the way of alleviating human suffering under the impoverished symbolics, and yet he gained such a vast and powerful acceptance. In *Studies on Hysteria* Freud himself writes on the modest accomplishment psychoanalytic treatment can bring:

> When I have promised my patients help or improvement by means of a cathartic treatment I have often been faced with this objection: "Why, you tell me yourself that my illness is probably connected with my circumstances and the events in my life. You cannot alter these in any way. How do you propose to help me, then?" And I have been able to make this reply: "No doubt fate would find it easier than I do to relieve you of your illness. But you will be able to convince yourself that much will be gained if we succeed in *transforming your hysterical misery into common unhappiness. With a mental life that has been restored to health you will be better armed against that unhappiness.*"[33]

There is no promise in Freud for happiness in life, but only that we can better learn to cope with the common unhappiness. We again run into the despair of the analytic attitude, something I believe modern cynics have picked up from Freud as well (though unconsciously): without hope for anything better than coping with life, we should spend our lives seeing through the manipulative deceptions that make life more difficult for us, and by doing what is necessary

33 *SH*, 269.

in any given situation to keep things going in the easiest and most secure way possible.

This is a life of languishing, without passion or enthusiasm. Who enthusiastically struggles toward a "common unhappiness"? However, to Freud's credit, he is honest enough to admit the weakness of the ego, and that his patients are not to become enthusiastic for anything; it is about conserving one's energies for everyday life and survival, rather than having them leak away in neurosis.[34] As we have seen throughout this analysis, this is the most we can expect from the Freudian *causa sui* project. We are weak and fractured, and Freud says that we must first admit this. Once we make the admission that we have only an impoverished ego with which to work, we must determine our goals in life in line with this impoverishment: a tolerable life, a common unhappiness.

The cynical ideology arising out of Freud easily accepted his critique of the traditional therapeutics, as well as his blanket distrust of institutions and others, but it does not abide by his pessimistic reality. Not even the best and brightest of Freud's inner circle would abide by the pessimism of his analytic attitude.[35] This inability of most people to follow Freud's pessimism leads us to what Rieff calls the "Triumph of the Therapeutic." In the next two chapters, we will analyze this triumph, and see how intimately it is related to cynicism, and is even necessary in order for modern cynics to maintain their false consciousness.

---

34 *MM*, 327.

35 Freud himself admits that in the Clark Lectures, which brought psychoanalysis to America, he had to tone down his pessimism, in order to gain an audience from the more optimistic American academics.

CHAPTER 18

Freud and the Therapeutic

1 Freudian Influence on American Society

Several years ago I happened to mention Freud in an Introduction to Philosophy class, and a girl in the front row, whom I knew to be a psychology major, blurted out, "He's crazy!" I assumed she had learned this from her studies at the university. I can understand where this comes from: Freud's specific theories seem not only out of line with current psychological theories, but strangely idiosyncratic and arbitrary. His fixation on sex, and aspects of his views on childhood development, appear to have arisen out of his own personal fetishes. Because of this, it can be easy to forget the tremendous impact Freud has had on our culture and society.

There is hardly any part of our society that is not touched by psychological theories, and seemingly every problem and situation is now diagnosed according to psychological maladies or needs. We can see psychology's influence in education, politics, magazines, newspapers, television shows, talk shows, advertising, and much more. This "triumph of the therapeutic" was in great part due to Freud's ability to provide a new interpretive framework to fill the void left by the failure of religion.[1] As Illouz points out, "Freud almost singlehandedly created a new language to describe, discuss, and manage the psyche, but in doing so he addressed what had become one of the most dominant and problematic features of modern life, namely the private sphere, thereby transforming it."[2]

Freud sought not merely to see through the structures of culture, but also the mechanisms of resistance within the human psyche. Freudianism is the uncovering of a person's inner life, an approach to the problems of life from within, rather than without. The rejection of his specific psychoanalytic theories has not at all caused our faith in this approach to waver: psychological investigation continues to be toward the hidden or latent motives and mechanisms, as well as focusing on problems that stem from the traumas of childhood and cultural development.

---

1 I will be dealing with only the most general themes and characteristics of the therapeutic, and will not be analyzing specific therapeutic theories or schools of thought.

2 Eva Illouz, *Saving the Modern Soul: Therapy, Emotions, and the Culture of Self-Help* (Berkeley, CA: University of California Press, 2008), 35.

 | HTTPS://DOI.ORG/10.1163/9789004758148-020

Freud's influence was especially strong in America. As Rieff says,

> Freud is America's great teacher, despite his ardent wish to avoid that fate. … Freud taught lessons which Americans, prepared by their own national experience, learn easily: survive, resign yourself to live within your moral means, suffer no gratuitous failures in a futile search for ethical heights that no longer exist—if they ever did.[3]

Philip Cushman noted that Freud's successor was not Jung or Ferenczi, was not an individual at all, but a country: the United States.[4] Cushman points out that the Freudian inner self—the unconscious—was used by industry and advertisement in order to bring about American economic and political success.[5] We will be taking a more in-depth look at consumerism and the therapeutic later in this chapter, but suffice it to say at this point that Freud's influential theories had a significant impact on the direction of American consumer culture through his impact on the therapeutic consciousness.

Freud's influence in America could only have taken place if his pessimism was toned down and tamed. Freud himself had a hand in this. Jan Goldstein notes that Freud's

> Ideas spread out from their Viennese place of origin quite rapidly in the first two decades of the twentieth century. The Americans greeted them with notable enthusiasm, which the ever-pessimistic Freud could only see as a bad sign: given their well-known superficiality, Freud surmised, the Americans must be watering down his theories in order to accept them. Nonetheless, Freud deliberately aided the popularization effort by tailoring his 1909 lecture at Clark University in Worcester, Massachusetts, to what he perceived as the prejudices and intellectual limitations of his American audience; and in the wake of World War I, according to one historian, an ambient Freudianism meshed perfectly with the new Fordist consumer economy of the United States.[6]

The pessimistic aspects of Freud were left behind by American Freudians, as well as by some of his most prominent disciples (such as Jung, Adler, and Reich). Specifically, they abandoned his pessimistic views of the human

3 *TT*, 48.
4 Cushman, 142.
5 Cushman, 143.
6 Jan Goldstein, "Neutralizing Freud: The Lycée Philosophy Class and the Problem of the Reception of Psychoanalysis in France," *Critical Inquiry*, 40, (Autumn 2013): 40–82, 40.

psyche and its prospects for healing, for a more optimistic—and I would add, self-deceptive—view. Rieff notes in *The Feeling Intellect* that Freud's disciples could not tolerate the ambiguity of Freud's vision, his understanding of the ego as weak and pathetic, that natural desires are dangerous, or his nihilistic death instinct.[7]

While they did not hold to his pessimism of human nature, they retained Freud's cynical understanding of culture. Without his pessimism, however, they would not accept his ambivalent attitude toward traditional culture—at least not in theory. Thus, his successors were cynical toward culture, and abandoned his ambivalence toward it, due to their optimistic view of the unconscious instincts. They did not see any need for the Freudian friendliness toward traditional culture. Rieff says,

> But with the decline of the superego, in a parental culture without enough moral earnestness to hand to its children, Freud's shard of traditional moralism, which he put over the emptiness he found in the very center and bottom of our lives, cannot appeal to his successors—in particular his American successors. Their recourse has been to the strange fiction of the ego as really a very powerful and independent person, who can by conforming to reality master it.[8]

While Freud saw the instincts as cruel, sadistic, lascivious, predatory, envious, and generally not to be trusted (hence, his cynicism toward the psyche), the post-Freudians saw them as good, pure, and beautiful.[9] This optimism led to an even stronger emphasis on the internal aspects of the psyche, as these become a trustworthy basis for living a psychologically healthy life, while culture alone, as a face for repression, becomes the basis for psychological illness and suffering.

Again, while Freud's specific theories were tamed and many were ultimately abandoned, his influence remains strong due to his cynical mistrust and social critique. His understanding of morality and culture as ultimately based on irrationality and authority has become an unquestioned presupposition. The therapeutic retains the cynical stance toward culture and turns its focus toward the healing of the individual, which it finds in the fulfillment of individual personal needs and desires. In this chapter, we will come to see that this self-centered focus (self-concern gone awry) undergirds and allows for the

---

7 *TFI*, 14.
8 *TFI*, 9.
9 *TT*, 126.

false consciousness of modern cynicism, and so is closely related to the three rationalizations analyzed in Chapters 12 and 13.

2 The Therapeutic: Self-Interest and Personal Well-Being

2.1 Becoming an Egoist

Freud's cynicism toward traditional morality and ideals, and his focus on the hidden and latent motivations of the unconscious make the "higher" (superego) aspects of the psyche appear hypocritical, and the "lower" aspects fascinating. The higher, civilized aspects of both the individual psyche and culture appear pretentious in Freud's analysis, while the lower becomes an endlessly fascinating area for exploration.[10] Such an understanding leads to a deconstruction of deeply held moral demands, so they come to be not only invalid but detrimental for a healthy psyche and life.

Thus, reason becomes cynical: traditionally reason was used to serve culture (to lead us out of the Platonic cave to the ideals necessary for a good society and life), but due to the Freudian ideology critique, it is now used to subvert culture.[11] This subversion of cultural authority is seen as a means for greater empowerment, so that the unconditional commitments and obligations of traditional morals no longer deceive us.[12] The subversion of traditional cultural ideals legitimizes the cynical approach toward others and leads to a life filled with continual mistrust.

This mistrust arises from the lessons we learned from Freud, especially the cynical view that communal "commitments" are in reality personal commitments. Politics and social justice are merely smokescreens (*tuphos*) for the attainment of more personal power and fulfillment.[13] The social and communal movements we see in politics, religion, education, etc., are attempts by the individuals within these movements to put themselves in a better position for gaining their self-interests, and taking power away from those who now possess it. The point is not so much the ideals of justice, but of coming out on top, and getting as big a piece of the pie as possible.

10 *TT*, 24.

11 *TT*, 24.

12 Alan Woolfolk, "The Therapeutic Ideology of Moral Freedom," *Journal of Classical Sociology*, 3, no. 3 (2003): 247–262, 254–255. Stage Publications: 1468–79X (200311) 3:3; 247–262; 038151.

13 John B. Imber, Introduction to *The Feeling Intellect*, xi–xxiv (Chicago: University of Chicago Press, 1990), xxiii.

This mistrust and cynicism are justified within the therapeutic through such things as psychological experiments and textbooks. Michael A. Wallach and Lise Wallach have shown that most psychological experiments contain cynicism, or the espionage epistemology discussed earlier: there is an expectation of hidden, self-interested motives built into most experiments.[14] Wallach has argued that it is probably unavoidable for psychology not to foster cynicism because it views the grounding motivations as self-centered, and health in line with freedom of expression and gratification of the self.[15]

These presuppositions mean that, with the therapeutic mindset, personality is not organized around classical concepts of the morally "good life."[16] We are to relax social constraints and obligations, allowing our desires to have more freedom for fulfillment, for the sake of happiness. "Better living" replaces the "good life" as the standard for social existence. We become "healthier" without being made "good." This is the lesson Freud's analytic attitude taught us: being comfortable with becoming "morally worse."[17]

Personality, then, is to be organized around personal fulfillment of those desires and needs that will bring happiness. With the loss of objective criteria for making right and wrong choices, the self and its feelings become the "moral" and trustworthy guide.[18] Thus, self-centered concern takes precedence over social concern. Any concern we have for the social aspects of life contains an ironic insight on the part of the self toward all that is not the self,[19] in order to maintain freedom from any manipulation and constraints the social attempts to put upon the individual. This freedom becomes viewed as the process of self-actualization. The theorists of self-actualization, such as Maslow and Rogers, argue that action governed by social convention, rather than individual preference, is tantamount to self-violation. To conform to social expectations is to be psychologically sick, and is to close off the path to attaining one's full potential.[20]

---

14 Michael A. Wallach and Lise Wallach, *Psychology's Sanction for Selfishness: The Error of Egoism in Theory and Therapy* (San Francisco: Freeman and Company, 1983), 25–26.

15 Wallach, 29.

16 Peter Paik, "A Kindly Apocalypse: Philip Rieff and the Endgame of the Therapeutic," *English Language and Literature*, 61, no. 3 (2015): 433–458, 441.

17 Paik, 441–442.

18 Robert N. Bellah, Richard Madsen, et al, *Habits of the Heart: Individualism and Commitment in American Life* (Berkeley: University of California Press, 1985), 76.

19 *MM*, 330.

20 Alan Woolfolk, "The Dubious Triumph of the Therapeutic: The Denial of Character," in *Therapeutic Culture: Triumph and Defeat*, ed. Jonathan B. Imber, 69–88 (New Brunswick: Transaction Publishers, 2004), 72.

We will come to see a false consciousness in this approach to self-actualization, as well as a stronger social control over the individual. because it does not lead to greater uniqueness, but to the pursuit of standardization. The phenomenon reminds me of the contradiction I noticed while watching some shows on the Disney Channel when my children were young. Every show seemed to contain the self-actualizing message of the importance of being a unique and independent human being, of being true to oneself and accepting oneself as one is. What became evident, however, is that what the shows meant by "unique" and "independent" was always in line with Disney's "style" or model. The continual implicit message was: "To be unique, you need to think and act exactly like us." This is in line with the false consciousness of modern cynicism and the therapeutic: a self-deceptive surrender to current cultural manipulation.

2.2 More Is Better

With Freud, the emphasis on ego strength for creating a tolerable life was focused on the reality principle; within the therapeutic this gets narrowed down to a focus on one's own personal well-being. When the idea of social or communal well-being is no longer viable, personal well-being becomes the default alternative. As Rieff points out, with the loss of communal purposes, there is nothing more at stake than a personal manipulable sense of well-being.[21] This well-being is not only connected to material well-being (self-*preservation*), but also psychological well-being (*self*-preservation). Within the therapeutic, personal well-being becomes the proof of one's mental health.

What is important to note is that the therapeutic does not focus on qualitative values for the sake of well-being, but on quantitative values: more is better. Cynicism has called into question the qualitative values of culture ("higher" and "lower," "good" and "bad"), and so the focus becomes a continued flow of new commodities and experiences. This is why Rieff thought that without the affluence that allows for a steady flow of new things by which to feel well, we could not maintain the therapeutic focus on personal well-being. As he says, people live for nothing more within the therapeutic than the "sweetening of time."[22] As Peter Paik puts it,

> The therapeutic emerges as a collective form of wishful thinking that is sustained by the vast material abundance and enormous productivity of the capitalist

21 *TT*, 10.
22 *TT*, 17.

> market. So long as the capitalist system is able to deliver rising standards of living … psychological men and women may not only persist in their delusions but also insist that others adopt their particular forms of solipsism.[23]

As we will see, this therapeutic self is an empty self, and the way it seeks to cover this emptiness, and so maintain a sense of well-being, is by continually bringing new things into its life—not just material things, but also lifestyles, roles, and personas. We consume material items not merely for the sake of self-*preservation*, but commodities become symbolic for the sake of *self*-preservation.

2.3 "Psychological Man"

Much like Becker, Rieff views culture as an order that had traditionally created the motives that directed the individual toward outward, communal purposes (a cultural heroics), through which alone the self could be realized and satisfied.[24] We create a world through which we learn what it means to be human; it provides the symbols that guide us, the institutions through which we fulfill this guidance, and explanations of our suffering. We come to understand ourselves, the meaning of our lives, the significance of our actions, and the ultimate value of life through culture. Culture makes it easier for us to make it through life, guiding, consoling, and protecting us. The problem we now face is whether we are making life more difficult (a toilsome languishing) by the way in which we are addressing the fact that traditional culture has failed. Has the ideal of personal well-being brought more peace, fulfillment, and thriving to our lives, or has it become self-concern gone awry?

Rieff points to four different character ideals of culture, related to four periods of Western history: political, religious, economic, and psychological. Each of these ideals answers the question: "How are we to be consoled for the misery of living?"[25] The political ideal reflects the time of ancient Greece and Rome; the religious ideal arrives with Christianity; the economic ideal is a quick transitional period between the Enlightenment and the beginning of the twentieth century; the psychological ideal begins with Freud.

The ideal of political men and women is the good, the beautiful, the true; the religious ideal focuses on how and by whom we are saved; the economic ideal points to the historical development toward which economic and material justice find their fruition; the psychological ideal is, as we have already

---

23 Paik, 454.
24 *TT*, 3.
25 *TT*, 23.

seen, personal well-being through adaptation. The political is about might, the religious about right, and the psychological about insight—a practical and experimental insight leading to the mastery of one's personality. As Rieff puts the distinction between the religious and psychological ideals: "Religious man was born to be saved; psychological man is born to be pleased."[26]

With the psychological ideal we are called to withdraw from culture into the inner world that is always in some way involved in a civil war.[27] Past cultural ideals lose their authority for psychological man, and adaptation and self-preservation become the focus, guided by a sense of inner well-being. "Psychological man" is a trained egoist, a private person, turning away from the arenas of the public realm (which have failed us) in order to re-educate the ego. When he is involved in the public arena, it is not for the good of the community, but for personal well-being.

Self-concern, and even self-absorption, are now legitimate paths to well-being and better psychological health. The focus is no longer the traditional heroics necessary to cover over the helplessness and creatureliness of the human organism; psychological man is unheroic. Indeed, Rieff says "he is anti-heroic, shrewd, carefully counting his satisfactions and dissatisfactions, studying unprofitable commitments as the sins most to be avoided."[28] He learned the lessons of profit from economic man and turned them inward to the economy of the psyche.

Psychological man is left to fend for himself, forced to create himself in some way. It is because of this that he relates to culture as a consumer or user of cultural commodities and institutions. He can work efficiently in all kinds of institutions, but without feeling trapped by institutional service: he has learned the cynical lesson of not being taken advantage of by any institution. He consumes what the institution provides for self-interest, being ever diligent not to be taken advantage of. However, this does not mean that he has attained freedom from being socialized, only that the socialization becomes superficial and fluid—that is, not fully internalized, and never committed to.

He has moved from high culture into pop culture, where his life is scripted by the continual movement and changes in style. As Rieff sees it, we are now acting out the latest script (a supposed personal narrative) written by pop culture.[29] This script is sustained by the entertainment industry, social media,

---

26 *TT*, 19.

27 *MM*, 356–357.

28 *MM*, 356.

29 *TT*, 228.

and advertising, which create a continual, arbitrary, and irrational motion to which the individual surrenders.[30]

Although the cynical therapeutic maintains a critical stance toward culture, there remains the tension between individual and culture, in that psychological man feels himself to be separate and independent of culture, but is, at the same time, wholly defined by it. He maintains this false consciousness by the lack of attachment to social institutions, which is due to his ironic detachment from everything external to himself. Although conformism is rampant, there is a unique and peculiar kind of instability within it, where the old and passé is continually being broken down to make room for the new, in order to maintain a quantitative excess. One never feels oneself to be committed to any new form or script that culture gives the self, and this provides a sense that one is choosing one's style of life independently and freely. Such non-commitment is a negative relation to culture, but a relation nonetheless. Again, the best way to understand this is that one breaks all connections with a qualitative sense of value within culture, and instead relates to culture quantitatively.

Ultimately, this leads to what Philip Cushman calls the "empty self," which is not unlike the self Becker understands apart from culture—the natural, non-symbolic self. It is that self we seek to repress, the consciousness of which creates anxiety and despair. As we saw with Kierkegaard, we must either allow this anxiety to educate us into the task of self-becoming, or find new ways to hide from it—a new means of self-deception. The cynical therapeutic has chosen the latter option.

2.4 The Empty Self

As we have already seen, Freud did not treat the gnawing meaninglessness of life in any systematic way, because he did not view it as something we could overcome. Life is meaningless, in the traditional sense, and so his therapeutic process was focused on people learning to live without meaning—"unheroically." While he focuses on the creatureliness of the psyche, even taking pride in his having humiliated the self-sufficient ego, he refuses to surrender the *causa sui* project: he maintains the project by seeking to strengthen the ego through re-education into cynical reason and knowledge.

The therapeutic rejects the pessimism of Freud, though accepts the inward direction of his *causa sui* project, believing that the inner drives are friendly toward human flourishing, or can at least be brought into alignment with it.

30 *MM*, 330.

The cynical therapeutic does not move toward a positive community in the traditional sense, but remains a negative community—that is, it does not provide any new moral ideals, or a sense of shared purpose to unify us. Its main intellectual work, in line with Freud, is to remain cynical about all qualitative ideals raised in culture. There are no metanarratives or communal heroics for the therapeutic, at least none that could become convincing enough to ground ideals within culture. With the loss of hope in ideals that would raise us above our creatureliness, we begin to experience the human self, and our lives, in a new way: as empty.

A void is left when the currency of culture has been defaced, a kind of exile from what has given humans meaning; we feel this exile and meaninglessness as emptiness. Cushman explains: "through the empty self concept I mean to convey the prevalence of the subjective experience of interior lack, absence, emptiness and despair; the desperate yearning to be loved, soothed, and made whole by filling up the emptiness."[31] Cushman points out that part of this emptiness is due to a lack of conviction and worth that lead to a chronic, undifferentiated emotional hunger.[32] As social ideals are impoverished, one finds nothing to which to be committed.

This lack of anything but highly conditional "commitments" is in line with Freud's analytic process, in that he believed the pressure commitments put on the ego become too much for it to handle in a healthy manner. Thus, we are to remain uncommitted, always keeping our options open.

One of the effects of this is that the sense of worth we gain through commitments is no longer provided, and we are left with our own particularity—our individual ego—by which to find significance. While there is a sense of significance that comes with one's uniqueness, we have already seen that apart from a metanarrative through which to heroically manifest one's uniqueness, one cannot help but admit that one is a minor and insignificant player in a vast universe—the unique ripples of one's life barely register in existence.

The loss of a qualitative and symbolic means of significance and worth leads to a yearning to acquire and consume material things and identities as an attempt to compensate for this symbolic emptiness. The need for this type of compensation is because the empty self of the therapeutic does not move in the direction of embracing its impoverished ego, but continues to repress it due to the *causa sui* project—that is, continues the attempt to master its life (its self-*preservation* and *self*-preservation). As Homans describes the triumph

31 Cushman, 245.

32 Philip Cushman, "Why the Self is Empty: Toward a Historically Situated Psychology," *American Psychologist*, 45, no. 5 (1990): 599–611, 600.

of the therapeutic, it "does not lead to a new or better organized symbolic but to a virtually permanent … state of inner emptiness and despair brought about by the new conviction that what was formerly always assumed to be a solution for despair (namely, commitment to an organizing symbolic) has in fact become the problem."[33] Our sense of well-being goes from a qualitative symbolic sense of fulfillment, to a quantitative compensatory fulfillment. The result of this, Homans argues, is a "hideous and bottomless spiral inward in which each new 'insight' produces a deeper sense of alienation."[34]

2.5 The Empty Self as a Perfect Consumer

One of the reasons we do not feel the need to embrace the exile is because the empty self fits very well within a capitalistic consumer economic system. Cushman says, "the insatiable, gnawing sense of internal emptiness drives the individuals to yearn to be filled up; to feel whole, solid, self-confident, in contact with others. Advertising preys on this yearning by linking it with images and slogans from liberationist ideology."[35] We consume mass amounts of commodities to escape the horrible feelings of emptiness and anxiety associated with the empty self: consumerism in all its forms becomes the means of overcoming the sense of emptiness. Again, we abandon the idea of qualitative excess (what exceeds our understanding, our control, and yet has an impact on our lives), for that of quantitative excess.

The empty self's insatiable yearning feeds business and the capitalistic economic machine. Satisfied people tend not to purchase items they do not need, or spend their time watching huge amounts of television. Thus, there are good economic reasons not simply to keep the empty self in its emptiness, but even to exacerbate it. There are many ways of tapping into the emptiness of the self and exploiting it:

> [L]ow self-esteem (the absence of a sense of personal worth), values confusion (the absence of a sense of personal conviction), eating disorders (the compulsion to fill the emptiness with food, or to embody the emptiness by refusing food), drug abuse (the compulsion to use drugs to produce chemically induced

33 Peter Homans, *The Ability to Mourn: Disillusionment and the Social Origins of Psychoanalysis* (Chicago: Chicago University Press, 1989), 300.

34 Homans, 300. We will examine this more closely in Chapter 20 in terms of what Kierkegaard called the esthetic stage of existence. We will see that this "spiral" is an important aspect of coming to an existential *krisis*.

35 Cushman (1995), 245–246.

> sensory or emotional experiences, or to attempt to deaden all feeling including emptiness), and chronic consumerism (the compulsion to fill the void by acquiring consumer items and the need to experience "receiving" something from the world).[36]

These manifestations of the empty self are not unrelated to the therapeutic, which includes an intensely self-focused and private sense of well-being. This sense of well-being becomes an end in itself, rather than a result of a greater communal or higher life, and consumerism (often with the help of credit cards) allows the self to believe it is fulfilling this end.

The self becomes narrowed even more as consumerism becomes connected to the therapeutic (which we will see in more detail in the next chapter). As has been pointed to throughout this book, it is one's narrowing reductionism, or one's fetishization, which gives one a sense of control and releases the tension of anxiety. This fetishizing process is at the heart of the *causa sui* project, as well as the nature of neurosis. Cynicism and the therapeutic intensify this contracting of the self inward. Indeed, in practice the cynical therapeutic is this intensified contraction around the ego.

3 Conclusion

Because of the rejection of Freud's pessimism, therapeutic schools that focus on self-actualization no longer think in terms of diseases to be cured, but of constraints to our self-actualization to be overcome. If we do have a personal problem to be overcome, the argument goes, it is because we do not believe enough in ourselves, and that we have allowed external forces to oppress us and keep us from personal fulfillment. For this reason, the various therapies of the therapeutic (and there are many, varied, and often contradictory, therapeutic "treatments") tend only to treat the symptoms, but not the disease.

The cynical therapeutic is like treating cancer with pain medicine. While this approach allows one to feel comfortable, it does not address the real problem, which will only get worse with time. There is a reluctance to treat the problem because the cure is painful and uncomfortable, and this goes against the overriding ideal of the cynical therapeutic: a sense of personal well-being. Health will come by relinquishing the very ideas that have soothed

---

36 Cushman (1995), 80.

one's anxiety: that one is independent and free, one has significance that is durable, and that one has attained self-mastery.

To maintain this deception of the *causa sui* project, the therapeutic must find ways to prop up a self-perception of ourselves as free, significant, and self-sufficient—the characteristics of one who is self-grounding. It is by looking at these three characteristics, and how they relate to the rationalizations for false consciousness already analyzed, that we will come to see the close relationship between modern cynicism and the therapeutic, and how together, as the cynical therapeutic, they keep us in a state of self-deception.

CHAPTER 19

The Therapeutic False Consciousness: the Illusions of Freedom and Significance

1 The Three Rationalizations in Reference to Cynicism, Freud and the Therapeutic

The *causa sui* project of the therapeutic has three main characteristics of health: the self is to be free, significant (have good self-esteem), and possess self-mastery or self-sufficiency (be independent, or free from needing others). The therapeutic envisions the healthy self as independent and worthy of regard. However, we will see that psychological men and women do not truly maintain these characteristics, and it is the "stage-sets" of the cynical therapeutic culture that allow the self to deceive itself about its freedom and strength. In Chapters 12 and 13, we saw how the false consciousness was internalized in terms of cynicism, and we will now look at how we can understand these same rationalizations in relation to the therapeutic. That these rationalizations are closely connected should come as no surprise, since as we saw in the last several chapters, these rationalizations are related to Freud's therapeutic process. We will take a moment to review these rationalizations and connect them to the present analysis.

The first rationalization, which I connect to the characteristic of freedom, is the ironic detachment of the cynic. The cynic believes she is *free* from the manipulative institutions and situations of which she is a part because she is aware of the manipulation. This approach, I have argued, arose out of Freud's ideology critique, in which one gains detachment from manipulation (including one's manipulation of oneself) through discovering the mechanisms at work in resistance. The therapeutic maintains this illusion of freedom by embracing abstract possibility. This is related to Kierkegaard's analysis of "possibility's despair." Rieff conceptualizes the same phenomenon as the "primacy of possibility" and "order-hopping," which characterize the cynical therapeutic relation to culture. We will see that the primacy of possibility does not lead to freedom, but a greater dependence on experts, technicians, and the organizing techniques of a technological morality.

The second rationalization is connected to the issue of significance, and relates to the contradictory and conflicting ideals of significance we find in cynical consciousness. Culture presents us with contradictory means of

HTTPS://DOI.ORG/10.1163/9789004758148-021

significance, one in terms of our individual uniqueness and the other in terms of cultural acceptance. Since we are given these contradictory forms of significance, we feel justified in pursuing them both, even though they are often in conflict and opposition. As we saw in regards to Freud, this arose due to his general ambivalence toward culture, and the inability to overcome this conflict. Coping with the conflict means accepting culture as both sick and necessary. This comes out in the therapeutic in terms of consumerism, and what Cushman calls the "lifestyle solution," through which we are to find significance both in our individuality and our cultural acumen. We must create a personal script, whose uniqueness and acceptance by culture bring about a sense of individual significance. We will see, however, that this does not bring greater significance, but greater irrelevance, as we lose ourselves to the "crowd," and surrender our autonomy to the psychological techniques of the technological morality.

Finally, the sense of self-mastery is related to the cynical emphasis on self-preservation, adaptation to each situation, and especially the loss of all alternatives (hopelessness or despair), which causes us to return to the empty and manipulative situations we have seen through. This arose through Freud's view that there is no alternative than to strengthen the ego for the sake of the reality principle, and so learn to cope in line with the analytic attitude, focusing on what the situation calls for or demands. In terms of how this relates to the therapeutic (which will be taken up in the next chapter), we will return to Kierkegaard to examine his analysis of consciousness within the esthetic stage of existence.[1] This will allow us to see the repression that takes place within the esthetic stage, and its lack of self-mastery. We will find here a deeper movement into the consciousness of despair due to the empty self or creatureliness.

In our analysis so far I have not distinguished between the various levels of deception or false consciousness that takes place within cynicism and the therapeutic, except in relation to the varying degrees of consciousness of cynicism between the master-, insider-, and outsider-cynics. Kierkegaard will allow us to analyze this distinction in more detail. This is important, because it is the rise in transparency or consciousness that shows us the despair of the esthetic (cynical therapeutic) stage, and leads to the *krisis* at the end of it. This *krisis* offers an opportunity to abandon the *causa sui* project, as we self-consciously face the hopelessness of the self-mastery of the esthetic stage.

---

1 Kierkegaard presents three stages of existence: the esthetic, ethical, and religious. The therapeutic and cynicism remain within the esthetic stage.

2 Rationalization #1: Freedom

2.1 Primacy of Possibility and the Hypothetical Self

The loss of traditional moralities led to a sense of freedom from external constraints. This freedom from moral constraints leads to what Rieff calls the "primacy of possibility": "Where it is forbidden to forbid, there is the primacy of possibility."[2] With the loss of firm cultural paths and heroism, life and the self become an experiment which consists of the ability to become whomever one wishes. This is therapeutic freedom: the freedom from absolute values and rigid moral obligations, allowing one to alter one's behavior and social roles at will, to be anyone that one chooses. We will see, however, that this freedom is not actual, but an abstract, hypothetical freedom; it is like the freedom of a child to play dress up, pretending to be a doctor or teacher. The pretense may be fun, but it is a role without depth and reality, because without commitment, and so it is untrustworthy.

As we saw earlier, Kierkegaard views the self as made up of limiting and expanding poles. The self is to relate to both poles, actualizing them in a way in which the individual becomes an actual self—indeed, the task of the self is to become a self. Such a task demands decisive and consistent choices—the risk of moving in a committed direction toward concrete goals. If we are not willing to do this, we will deceive ourselves, and this deception takes place by relating to only one pole of the self. This misrelation of the self to itself is what happens within the therapeutic in relation to freedom: the therapeutic individual wants the self-perception of freedom, but without the risk that free choice entails. By only relating to the possible, the individual runs from the risks of the actual (as we saw concerning my friend's wedding "vows").

Every possibility, every choice, is an act that limits, that takes us in a particular direction. To be a self, we must combine the choice (possibility) with the *specific* direction of the choice (necessity); "possibility's despair" is to neglect the necessary (limiting) aspect of the self. Kierkegaard writes that in possibility's despair, "possibility seems greater and greater to the self; more and more becomes possible because nothing becomes actual. Eventually, everything seems possible, but this is exactly the point at which the abyss swallows up the self."[3]

In abandoning limits, we lose sight of our necessity—the demand that steps be taken to actualize the possibilities. Relating only to the possibilities

---

2 *DW*, 113.

3 *SUD*, 36.

feels like freedom, but it is an aimless and meaningless abstract freedom, a detachment from all situations, as we saw with cynicism's ironic detachment. As Kierkegaard puts it,

> [N]o matter how long one idea is pursued, the entire action is within a hypothesis. The self is so far from successfully becoming more and more itself that the fact merely becomes increasingly obvious that it is a hypothetical self. The self is its own master, absolutely its own master, so-called; and precisely this is the despair. … [I]t is easy to see that this absolute ruler is a king without a country, actually ruling over nothing; his position, his sovereignty, is subordinate to the dialectic that rebellion is legitimate at any moment. Ultimately, this is arbitrarily based upon the self itself.[4]

This "hypothetical self" is a self-deceptive aspect of the empty self. It is a lack of commitment, which gives an illusion of freedom, but instead *causes the self to be controlled by every whim and fad that arises within culture*. The hypothetical nature of the self hides its emptiness by continually focusing on abstract possibility, by which it projects some image of fullness into the future.

There is a close relation between emptiness and this false freedom, as both are related to a lack of any earnest conviction. Freud's ambivalence toward culture is associated with this empty and abstract freedom, in that he viewed the attempt to strengthen the ego as a movement of freedom (freedom from authority), while also understanding that no one could live entirely in this freedom (this emptiness). This conflict is also where our ambivalence toward culture arises: humans need some form of guidance, other than the raw instincts of the id; we need some way of narrowing, and so navigating, the reality principle. Freud was conscious of this relationship between the individual self and culture, and so he stayed true to this awareness; however, we have deceived ourselves as to our dependence on culture.

2.2 The Hypothetical Self and Culture

2.2.1 Superficial Consumption of the Available Symbolics

While the therapeutic denies the constraints of cultural limits, it moves into false consciousness by taking up new, groundless, and superficial symbolics from culture, by which it seeks meaning and significance. The problem is that,

4 *SUD*, 69.

at various levels of consciousness, psychological men and women have seen through these symbolics, and so find it foolish to invest in them, or commit themselves to them (be limited by them). Thus, in order to deal with the qualitative emptiness of these symbolics, they focus on the quantity.

This is the nature of the primacy of possibility, which allows for ever new array and variety of symbolics to choose from, none of which are genuinely committed to (that is, they are only hypothetically actualized). This allows one to maintain a sense that one is neither manipulated nor controlled by these symbols. For both the therapeutic and modern cynicism, this perceived freedom from this cultural control is paramount, and is a necessary aspect of pursuing one's personal well-being.

The illusion of this freedom is seen, however, in terms of the groundlessness of these superficial symbolics, a groundlessness *through which consumers are controlled*. For instance, there is nothing written into the universe about what colors are to be fashionable this spring. Such fashions are arbitrary, completely contrived. The only reason this spring's colors are not the same as last spring is that the fashion industry needs people to buy new clothes, which means they need to make our current, perfectly fine, clothing appear out of style (old). As we will see, in the therapeutic, to be *out of style*—to have no style—is to be nothing.

While the primacy of possibility allows for an infinite variety of styles, and so a seemingly infinite variety to "choose" from, this continual revolving door of colors and shapes are a means of control, not freedom.[5] One loses oneself in this approach to the self, as one must continually guess who one is to be, what type of self will find acceptance, and what one must buy for this acceptance. One becomes a soulless and characterless person, a chameleon, in a continual holding pattern, assessing who one is to be next, and what pose to adopt. The illusion of freedom is maintained by the variety and quantity of different lifestyles, though everything comes with a judgment of worth and value upon it.

2.2.2 Lifestyle Solution

Primacy of symbolic possibility is related to what Cushman calls the "lifestyle solution," which is one of the ways the therapeutic seeks to fill the empty hypothetical self, and gain significance. Lifestyle solutions are driven by advertising (as well as social media), as the ad offers the fantasy that it can transform

---

5 The point to grasp is that, simply because one has more choices does not mean one is more free—more choices does not correlate to more freedom. Freedom is grounded in the self, not in external variety.

the consumer's unremarkable and irrelevant life into a glorious, problem-free life. To be healed of one's emptiness (or more precisely, to minimize the symptoms), one need only purchase and digest the product being sold.[6]

The traditional therapy of positive communities used a web of meaning to bring a sense of significance: stories, songs, beliefs, folk wisdom, rituals, ceremonial objects, costumes, etc. In contrast to this, advertising and media hold up a model of "lifestyle," which serves as a substitute for traditional webs of communal meaning.[7] Although the old symbolics are seen through as arbitrary and unconvincing, the new symbolics are not any less arbitrary, and are also not convincing. Businesses use this lack of convincing symbols to their advantage: it allows for a fluid movement of styles, the ability (and need) to continually reinvent oneself. As the current symbolics become empty—old, passé—businesses make promises that their products will finally bring that lifestyle solution for which one has been looking. These symbolic lifestyles are a transient form of life, adopted for as long as they continue to bring well-being—which turns out not to be for long, since they are often so superficial and blatantly artificial. We buy these new lifestyles in a vain attempt to transform our lives, which have become dissatisfying under the older lifestyle.

This consumption of lifestyles is simply an entrenched false consciousness grounded in self-centered and self-indulgent fetishes, which focus the individual away from dealing with the actual problem she faces: her helpless, fragile, empty self. It is, as I said before, focusing on relieving symptoms, rather than curing the disease. The freedom one feels, and through which one rationalizes this false consciousness, is an illusion: we do not possess these lifestyle solutions, but they possess us.

The supposed strength and confidence (attributes of freedom that relate to significance) that comes from the lifestyle symbolics are a lie; in reality, they destroy our confidence. Through the media and advertising, we are continually having our inadequacies (our unattractive, incomplete, and insignificant lives) pointed out to us. We become controlled and oppressed, as the media and advertisers provide the ways by which we can prove to ourselves and others that we are worthy of acceptance. They are an attempt at self-justification in the face of existential guilt. Cushman does not view advertisements as benign types of guidance, but they condemn the average consumer to strive for beauty and control that is not possible (the bar is set to impossible levels).[8]

---

6 Cushman (1995), 81.
7 Cushman (1995), 81.
8 Cushman (1990), 605.

Our cynicism may free us from traditional ways of seeking significance through commitment to ideals, but only to become enslaved to the impossible ideals of the lifestyle cure. There is at least as much, if not more, pressure upon the ego to measure up to cultural demands in this situation, which is made even more difficult due to the continual fluidity, contradictory nature, and the expense of maintaining the correct lifestyle. As Cushman has argued, culture no longer controls people by restricting their impulses, "but by creating and manipulating their wish to be soothed, organized, and made cohesive by momentarily filling them up."[9] Setting our desires free does not set us free: *the more our desires are set free, the more power gained by those we trust to fulfill those desires.*

3 Rationalization #2: Significance

To matter, to be significant, means that we must be unique in some way, and that we make a difference or have an impact that carries on: we are not the next of them, not replaceable like an anonymous stormtrooper, not a cog in a machine. However, uniqueness and particularity can get lost, and become irrelevant within an enormous context. For the uniqueness of our small particularity to matter, it must be an essential part of something bigger and significant, though without being swallowed up by it (that is, while maintaining its particularity). The traditional heroics provided just such a picture of existence: one was able personally and uniquely to shine within a larger cosmic context. One's uniqueness meant that one played an essential part in the heroic, and that the heroic would be in some way impoverished if one did not play one's part. The traditional heroics provided a sense of significance and durability within some type of cosmic metanarrative. With the defacing of these metanarratives, the symbolics connected to them no longer convince us of our worth.

As Becker says, this leaves us in a bind. It alienates the single individual from the larger and enduring cultural world. Freud's patients were coming to him more out of the pain of this lost significance (nihilism) than due to the repression of their sexual drives. However, even with this mistake, Freud was able to interpret for us a new way of conceiving our lives, and offer a direction for coping. This reinterpretation of ourselves and our relation to the world is his enduring legacy. Freud left us with a way of talking about our relationship to

9 Cushman (1990), 600.

the impoverished symbolics of culture, even if the pessimism that came with his enlightened consciousness would be rejected.

As I have argued, no one can endure this pessimism, because the need for meaning is a primary value for humans. Even Freud needed a sense that his life was meaningful, finding it in terms of his psychoanalytic school, which he hoped would guarantee that the impact of his life and work would not fade away into obscurity.[10] This was his personal contradiction and false consciousness, but we have already seen that each of us is living this contradiction between individual significance and cultural significance: we move back and forth between our individuality and the culture, rationalizing it based on the human conflict itself. If we hope to function within this continued struggle, we must find a means of pulling off this contradiction without being conscious of it. In other words, we must rationalize the contradiction, so it makes sense to us. If we cannot *make sense* of it … well, that's the very nature of meaninglessness. We have already seen how this takes place in a general way in terms of cynicism, and now we will examine it more specifically in terms of the therapeutic.

3.1 Consumerism

The cynical therapeutic "ideal" is of an individual who can be the source of her own standards, who can love herself, rely on her judgment without deferring to others, and gain significance by merely telling herself that she is significant. These are the needs that arise after defacing the traditional *causa sui* projects. We can see in this description all three characteristics of this *causa sui* project: the need for freedom, the need for self-sufficiency, and the need for significance.

Although we have gained the enlightened consciousness of modern cynicism, we will find that we keep this deception going in the same way humans always have: by surrendering to culture. However, the combination of the enlightened consciousness toward culture, and the false consciousness that continues to surrender to it, creates a more uncanny paradox than any traditional cultural surrender had created. The paradox results in the illogical, though now common, behavior we saw from the "Hamsterpaj" example, as well as from the two papers my student in Ethics wrote. It is the common ordinariness of these irrational behaviors that make them seem sane. If one

---

10 I wonder if part of Freud's ambivalence toward culture was due to the knowledge that he needed culture in order for his psychoanalytic child to survive, and so to gain durability and significance for himself.

person were unique in expressing the contradictoriness present in the Hamsterpaj blog, we would see it as a form of irrationalism bordering on insanity. But when insanity becomes a cultural affair, and such contradictoriness is not at all uncommon, we fail to recognize it.[11]

Freud always argued that culture is neurotic, but in our culture, it has hit a whole new level of insanity, due to the further narrowing of the therapeutic, and the cultural irrationality of fetishism within consumerism. We are not, in the face of symbolic impoverishment, following Freud by strengthening our ego, but follow him by learning better how to live and act pathologically. Culture itself has become so paradoxical, that we can no longer strengthen our ego in relation to it, but merely go along with the conflict it already rationalizes. Ole Jacob Madsen, who recognizes the therapeutic as having taken over all aspects of our life and culture, including our media and entertainment, writes in reference to *The Sopranos*: "*The Sopranos* functions … as a good illustration of psychology's paradox in a pathological culture. Therapy can offer individual adaptation strategies, but provides no tools to change society. Tony learns how to become an improved psychopath in an unchanged psychopathic culture."[12]

3.2 Character and Personality

What we need in order to pull this off (that is, in order for the self to buy into the cultural contradictions and irrationality) is a new understanding of the self. Cushman says that Freud provided such a new view of the self, which Cushman understands as a change from the "self" interpreted in terms of *character* or integrity, to a "self" interpreted as *personality*. In the Victorian era (and really, since the time of Plato and Aristotle), the idea of character was put forward as defining the essence of the self. No doubt, as we saw concerning

---

11 The writer in the blog calls buying brand names, simply because they are brand names, "pathetic." He wonders why someone would pay so much more for a piece of clothing just because of the brand; then, just a little lower, he admits that he buys almost exclusively name brand clothes, even though he "can't actually pretend" there are cheaper clothes that are equal in quality. This is clearly irrational, even bizarre, though upon reading this, few would be surprised by this statement (it might even reflect one's own struggle with how one determines to buy clothes, accessories, cars, etc.). If it does not seem irrational to us (at least not to the level I am presenting it here—as pathological), this is only because we are familiar with its inner "logic." Most forms of insanity have just this type of internal thought process taking place: an inner logic, which from the inside appears justified, but from the outside appears to have lost touch with reality. The inner logic uses rationalizations in order to resist the contradictions.

12 Ole Jacob Madsen, *The Therapeutic Turn: How Psychology Altered Western Culture* (New York: Routledge, 2014), 40.

the four *character*-ideals outlined by Rieff (political, religious, economic, and psychological), each age had their own content or ideal of what makes up character, but the goal was always to consistently align one's thoughts, actions, and words with the ideal. Within the Victorian age in which Freud lived, the ideals of character were of moral toughness, integrity, discipline, self-sacrifice, and strict adherence to moral laws.[13] Freud's new idea of the self cynically deconstructed this view of character, describing the self in a new way; this new description was taken up by the therapeutic, and formulated as personality (in line with the term *persona*—a mask spoken through).

Personality is the ability to be attractive to others, to stand out in a crowd, the quality of being "somebody."[14] While character was related to an extensive and comprehensive cultural heroics in which one was to find one's significance, personality is related to one's own ability to project the qualities others find attractive and appealing. This idea epitomizes the very pathological contradiction we have been looking at: it is one's individual attractiveness and ability to stand out (one's uniqueness and independence) that gives one significance; and yet, to convince others of one's attractiveness, one must surrender to whatever standard of attraction (beauty, intelligence, physical acumen, etc.) happens to be esteemed within a culture at any given time (and as we have seen, this is fluid and arbitrary, and often connected to specific consumer brands—not just in relation to clothes, but also smartphones, cars, houses, accessories, and the like).

This view of the self arises out of Freud's ideology critique, and the cynicism that results from it, which comes to see character as a façade or *persona*. It sees through this façade into the latent content of chaotic desires and instincts, which makes up one's self-interest. The latent content remains hidden, chaotic, and insubstantial, and so what matters is the attractiveness on the surface—"curb appeal," so to speak. We know it is not wise to judge a book by its cover (it is "pathetic," as it was put in the Hamsterpaj blog), but since the pages of the book are empty, the only substance we have is the cover.

Cynicism changes the basis of why we matter, and personality is that fluid way of conceiving the self, as that which can appropriate and live through a variety of *personas*. Thus, we have the strange phenomenon, grounded in the existential contradiction described above, that a family like the Kardashians can be almost unanimously mocked as superficial, and yet still be the object of cultural obsession and fanaticism—they can still be a "thing."

---

13 Cushman (1995), 64.
14 Cushman (1995), 64.

What is being sold as the *persona* are lifestyles, which, as we saw above, relates to consumerism: particular lifestyles are particular ways of consuming goods, choosing some goods and services over others. For instance, what makes someone a "hipster" is living the lifestyle of a hipster; living the lifestyle of a hipster is consuming certain products and experiences while demonizing others. We could say the same for an eco-friendly lifestyle, a vegan or vegetarian lifestyle, a Christian lifestyle, a survivalist lifestyle, etc. We cannot disconnect lifestyles from consumption, for consumable goods are the very things that provide the empty self with its external (hopefully attractive) symbolics. As Kierkegaard argues, there is no solid consistent self under this approach to being a self (a self defined by externals), but only a constant experimental or hypothetical self. We do, in a sense, internalize lifestyles, but always as "working lies," by which we create hypothetical selves whose supposed freedom consists in the ability to be given up at any moment—to be constrained by no particular lifestyle.

Although the therapeutic and consumerism are not a direction Freud would have agreed with, they align with an essential aspect of his therapy of coping: personality makes life easier than character.[15] With character, the challenging tasks in life take precedence, things that require commitment and sacrifice—things which the fragile ego, on its own, can no longer bear. With personality, it is about developing a unique style or lifestyle, one that will attract others. One merely needs to make enough money (or have enough credit), to develop a particular style. Personality is shaped by the attempt to gain recognition from others; this is done not by following moral codes or adhering to religious ideals, but by presenting oneself in a particular way—a way others envy. Cushman says that charm and nicety take precedence over adherence to any moral ideals; grooming and health become more important than hard work and sacrifice.[16] Further, if a particular lifestyle becomes too difficult, or is not providing enough personal well-being, then the primacy of possibility allows one to switch one's style of life, one's *persona*.

In this situation, significance is not about internalizing a metanarrative, but gaining immediate recognition. Selfies are a symptom of this external performance; social media and its "influencers" become an outlet needed to prove that one's lifestyle is attractive (a life others wish they could live). We seek "karma" on Reddit, "likes" on Facebook, and "followers" on X/Twitter and Instagram. Cushman points out that we have replaced the "heroes" of character

---

15 Cushman (1995), 64.
16 Cushman (1995), 64.

with the "celebrities" of personality.[17] Celebrities become famous by performing, being attractive, doing things that cause them to stand out—and sometimes the more bizarre and immoral, the better. Celebrities are not admired for their moral character, but their personal skills, wealth, and good luck.

3.2.1 Lifestyle Enclave

According to Robert Bellah, this therapeutic approach to significance does not create a community in the way a cultural heroic does—namely, by binding people together through a shared purpose. Instead, the new social glue is personal self-esteem, and the new community is what Bellah calls a "lifestyle enclave."[18] Lifestyle enclaves are ways we associate with others primarily based on individual choice, rather than a shared purpose. This frees the group from traditional ethical and religious boundaries. They are defined not by a common purpose, but by shared personal interests of the various individuals in the enclave, such as recreation, dress, and taste in things like music, food, hobbies, or "issues" (both personal and political).[19]

Lifestyle enclaves fulfill a critical need: since the significance of one's individuation has always been linked to the ability to find others who reflect and affirm (recognize) one's selfhood, lifestyle enclaves are necessary social forms of private life in a society such as ours.[20] In lifestyle enclaves, the individual gains significance by being a part of a group where everyone pats each other on the back, affirming their lifestyle as attractive and important. As Bellah says, "In a period when work is seldom a calling and few of us find a sense of who we are in public participation as citizens, lifestyle enclave, fragile and shallow though it often is, fulfills that function for us all."[21] The uniqueness one finds in the enclave, then, is not by standing out within the enclave (it is "sameness" that defines the group), but by the distinction from others (that is, other lifestyles) that the enclave affords.

Thus, we see that being a consumer is not merely about the consumption of goods and services, but more importantly about consuming symbolics, personalities, and lifestyles, through which we can continue to believe that we have significance, and are living an interesting (if not meaningful) life. Recognition and significance mean being "better" (more attractive and shining brighter)

---

17 Cushman (1995), 65.
18 Bellah, 72.
19 Bellah, 73.
20 Bellah, 73.
21 Bellah, 75.

than others. It is an attempt to maintain the *causa sui* project through a further narrowing of one's fetishes. The modern cynic continues to need significance because the exile (the empty self) is too much to handle alone. Thus, in the move of false consciousness, she returns to find significance in the very things she knows to be insignificant. On the one hand, the cynic disdains the symbolics that would gain her acceptance (that she must play this kind of game); on the other hand, there are no other alternatives, and so she must give herself to these, rationalizing this irrationality through the contradictory expectations of society, and the illusion of her freedom.

3.2.2 Obligation and Significance

The view of human purpose changes with the therapeutic, as it goes from the fulfillment of a corporate purpose, which entails personal sacrifices for the good of the whole, to human purpose as individual and self-regarding. The former view believes that the fulfillment of the corporate purpose will ultimately lead to personal well-being and flourishing; the latter believes that fulfilling personal well-being will lead to corporate progress. This emphasis on personal well-being reinforces the cynical opinion that one cannot trust the ideals espoused by institutions, organizations, and individuals within society, because they are all focused on self-interest (some kind of "profit"). One must protect oneself against being used as a mere human resource, to be used (up) by an organization, and thrown out. Thus, we remain ever defensive and diligent in each situation, so as not to be used or manipulated by the system.[22]

What this means, therapeutically, is that we are ultimately responsible *for* ourselves, and only *to* ourselves. We are on our own, and so responsible for our sense of well-being, which we attain through freedom and self-mastery. Others are also responsible for themselves, and so we are not to view our obligations to others as a requirement or duty. If we, for whatever reason, become overly responsible for others (what the therapeutic mindset would view as not creating sufficient "boundaries" between oneself and others), we will become irresponsible toward ourselves (we will be taken advantage of). Thus, our first, and perhaps only, responsibility is to the well-being of "me and mine."

22 It should be noted that many (if not most) companies, institutions, and organizations have also become cynical and self-serving. They will "use up" their employees for greater profits. Their purpose is narrowed to profit. Drug companies are not in the business of making drugs for greater overall health; they are in the business of making money, and drugs are the means of this—not the end.

This view of responsibility defines our relationship to institutions and organizations, in which our obligation to them extends only to the point where they continue to help us fulfill our responsibility to ourselves (as they continue to bring us personal well-being). Thus, our social relationships are no longer held together by a bond of moral obligation or duty, but by utility. This change of bond means two things. First, one's ultimate goal or purpose is to discover one's personal fulfillment or self-actualization (that which leads to the greatest personal well-being), which will then define how one relates socially. This self-actualization defines one's "obligations" to the company one works for, the clubs one is a part of, and even one's marriage. Second, it means that every institution or organization is related to in an instrumental manner: it is a useful tool for one's individual fulfillment, or an obstacle to it. In an important sense, we have all become *mercenaries* socially.

This is how we gain our sense of freedom: we feel free *from* social obligations and constraints. We see this with cynicism in terms of our ironic detachment, and in terms of the primacy of possibility in the therapeutic: both point to the ability to abandon any current situation for a better situation ("better," meaning more personally fulfilling). We also saw this in the contradictory ways we seek significance, which is determined by the need of the situation. In terms of a Kierkegaardian understanding of the situation, we seek freedom in the expanding pole, and significance in the limiting pole. We have already seen how this works in terms of consumerism in relation to the lifestyle cure, and will now see how it works in terms of the psychological techniques of the technological morality.

4 Technological Morality: Psychological Technique

As I explained in Chapter 13, organizational techniques of the technological morality relates to cynical reason: the organization of individuals in terms of technical rules and methods, for the sake of efficiency and greater power. The psychological techniques of the technological morality are in line with the therapeutic view of how we gain significance, and its constraining effects. Technological morality largely supplants traditional manners and morality, which had guided individual purposes, the means of fulfilling these purposes, and ways we relate to others given these purposes.[23] Psychological techniques provide the means for attaining the success that will bring about personal

23 Stivers, 94.

well-being. These techniques are related to advertising (as we saw above), propaganda, public relations, therapeutic methodologies, and the "how to" manuals for effective living. *The Oprah Winfrey Show* was a cultural phenomenon that included all these various psychological techniques. We are given the techniques in order to help us effectively live in a world where one is responsible only to and for oneself, and in which one cannot truly trust others to have one's back.

Psychological technique is about becoming socialized into the type of consumption analyzed above in relation to the empty therapeutic self. Consumption is a technique by which we attempt to deal with the impoverishment of our traditional symbolics. The well-being attained through consumption is a compensation for the empty self. We have already seen that we not only consume material goods for the sake of comfort, or simply to fill the emptiness, but also for the sake of identity—that is, as a means to stand out through the attainment of a particular lifestyle, one that consists in the consumption of the "right" kinds of goods or objects.

Both first and second world cultures viewed well-being and significance *as a result of* fulfilling communal purposes—well-being is the result of living a good life, not the content of a good life itself. These cultures believed that if one did the right thing, then things would go right for one, because the "right thing" was in line with the order and purpose of the universe. It is this very belief that became unconvincing in the third world culture, and why my Ethics student chose cynically to injure his opponent rather than play by the rules: he no longer believed that playing in the right way would bring about the recognition and happiness he desired. Or better, he no longer viewed well-being and significance in the same way: as the fulfillment of a cosmic purpose.

In third world culture the value of well-being is connected to personal self-actualization, in line with whatever one's fellow citizens specifically esteem at any given time and in any given situation (winning football games, wearing brand name clothes, or one of several and ever-changing views of the American Dream). This is where the primacy of possibility and consumerism come together to form one's identity: consumption becomes a psychological technique connected to the definition of the self as infinite in its consuming possibilities, so that one can prove to oneself in multiple and fluid ways one's significance, through being attractive to others (or gaining their recognition). The self, or one's lifestyle, is built through this consumption, which is driven and defined by advertising, social media, and entertainment.

And yet, this lifestyle is, in an important sense, only another commodity one is consuming, in that there is no actual grounding or commitment to it, other than how it happens to make one feel (or how it makes others feel about one). In a society where consumption becomes an end in itself (the meaning of life), the human being is persuaded to become an object (an image, persona, personality). What it means to be human is to become a mere role player who puts himself or herself on display, sometimes for the consumption of others. We become a self by what we put on, what we drive, where we live, etc. As long as society remains affluent, and the credit card applications keep coming, one can maintain this illusion of self-mastery through the fetishization of consumer goods.

Through the psychological technique of advertisement (what Stivers calls secular sermons[24]), consumer products seem to hold a kind of magic, through which we become identified symbolically. As Stivers points out, it does not matter that we see through this illusion, or that we know that the consumable object will let us down; the deception is maintained through our primacy of possibility (the illusion of being free from the manipulation), because there is always another magical, consumable object that contains some hope or promise for happiness. Stivers says, "The emptiness of present consumption is compensated for by the fulness of the future promise."[25] I believe Stivers puts his finger on the neurotic nature of this enterprise in pointing out that "when life-style is reduced to consumption, the consumption of life-style becomes the consumption of consumption. This represents consumption taken to its *logical and absurd conclusion*."[26] With the loss of a sense of durability in life, which in the past gave a sense of significance, the realization that all things are consumed takes over, and consumption becomes an ideal.

This absurd conclusion, where we exist to be consumed with consumption, leads neither to well-being nor significance; it is a despondent life of merely waking up each day to go to work, in order to make money to buy more stuff. As Tyler Durden says in the movie *Fight Club*:

> Advertising has us chasing cars and clothes, working jobs we hate so we can buy shit we don't need. We're the middle children of history, man. No purpose or place. We have no Great War. No Great Depression. Our Great War's a spiritual war. ... Our Great Depression is our lives. We've all been raised on television to believe that one day we'd be millionaires, and movie gods, and rock stars. But we won't. And we're slowly learning that fact.[27]

---

24 Stivers, 59.

25 Stivers, 55.

26 Stivers, 45. (emphasis added).

27 *Fight Club*, directed by David Fincher (1995, Los Angeles: 20th Century Fox, Home Video, 2002). DVD.

Our Great Depression is that we spend our lives toiling and laboring for what we know is empty and meaningless. We are both aware of this and unaware, and so "learning that fact" has no impact on how we live. The very enlightenment of modern cynicism has inoculated us from our ability to respond to this false consciousness with anything other than a shrug.

5 Conclusion

As we have seen in this chapter, the therapeutic fails in its promise of both freedom and significance. It hides its failure through cynical reason, specifically by an ironic detachment and the desperate attempt to fulfill the contradictory approaches we use to gain personal worth provided by society. These rationalizations lead to the false consciousness inherent in the cynical therapeutic.

The main difficulty with addressing the cynical therapeutic in a critical manner that will lead to a *krisis*, as thinkers like Becker and Kierkegaard see it, is that this false consciousness seems to "work": we are able, as Ivan Ilych puts it, to think we are going uphill when in reality our life is ebbing away. All the thinkers we have looked at thus far have, as their purpose, an unmasking of this apparent "success" at living. They all realize that people are living in varying degrees of self-deception, and that those who are most deceived are succeeding the best at keeping at bay the anxiety necessary for an awakening or *krisis*. Those who have not been successful in this are the neurotic—that is, those suffering from various psychological maladies.

As we turn to the issue of self-mastery, we will take a closer look at this rise in consciousness, and see that it is a matter of moving from an almost completely external focus, to a more inward focus, in which one discovers that the self is more than what it owns and identifies with externally. This is difficult, for such a movement entails the recognition and acceptance of the empty self of creatureliness.

CHAPTER 20

Self-Mastery and the Despair of the Esthetic Stage of Existence

1 Rationalization #3: Self-Mastery

The main argument throughout this book has been that our supposed self-mastery, arising from our *causa sui* project, is an illusion, a form of false consciousness currently kept in place by the cynical and therapeutic ways we relate and surrender to culture. Because it is an illusion and false consciousness, it is hopeless, a journey into despair. Freud, Becker, Kierkegaard, and Cushman have shown that we can keep the deception of self-mastery going because of fetishization: a narrowing of reality that allows us to put all of our sense of mastery onto an object or fetish (product, lifestyle, position, artifact, ritual, etc.) we can control.

Further, because of this fetishization, we are all neurotic to some degree, but we vary in our recognition of this based on how unconsciously or consciously we surrender to culture—that is, the degree to which we repress our creatureliness and infinite passion. It is easy for most of us to recognize the neurotic symptom of washing one's hands until they bleed. We can see this as an attempt to symbolically place all we cannot control onto that thing we can control. This fetishization helps the individual overcome the anxious feelings in her lack of substantial control over life—the lack of self-mastery. However, when we all share the same narrow fetishes and neurotic symptoms, the ability to discern this becomes much more difficult. Thus, we have found ways of rationalizing our neurotic behavior through the cynical therapeutic.

2 The Kierkegaardian Stages of Life: Esthetic, Ethical, Religious

We will approach the issue of therapeutic self-mastery by examining Kierkegaard's view of the esthetic way of life. Kierkegaard developed the idea that there are three existential stages to life: the esthetic, ethical, and religious. Although we will be focusing only on the esthetic stage, I will give a very brief overview of Kierkegaard's understanding of these stages.

 HTTPS://DOI.ORG/10.1163/9789004758148-022

Each stage is a different life-view or way of approaching life, and so relates to life with a different sense of what purpose, freedom, significance, and self-mastery consists. For the esthetic existence, the purpose of life is well-being, pleasure, and comfort. It lives by immediacy, or from situation to situation, focusing on the well-being present in each individual situation. It is focused almost completely outward, and views the self in relation to the external—that is, in terms of what is not the self. In terms of its understanding of freedom, it views freedom as freedom *from* constraints upon one's pursuits of pleasure, in line with the primacy of possibility examined earlier. Its significance is found in terms of the pleasure one receives from the recognition of others. The esthetic stage is the least self-aware of the stages, and is caught in significant self-deception. The esthetic stage is in line with the cynical therapeutic. We will be examining it in order to show its potential movement into the consciousness of the despair of this approach to life.

The purpose of the ethical stage is to fulfill the unconditional requirement, which requires transcending immediacy in order to bring coherence and integrity to one's life. This unconditional requirement is in some way connected to a moral order of the universe, as well as to *how* humans relate to this moral order. This is in line with the traditional cultural heroics. Freedom for the ethical stage is self-determination. Self-determination means that one makes one's way through life out of one's own center, though it is related to the moral order established in one's culture. Significance is found in fulfilling one's unique *telos* or purpose within the cosmic heroics. One becomes oneself in relation to this heroic.

The ethical stage has greater consciousness of the self than the esthetic, but it remains deceived about the relationship between its creatureliness and the cosmic heroic. In other words, an ethical individual is more aware of her infinite passion, but remains deceived about her helplessness in relation to it. This means that, like the esthetic stage, the ethical stage also ends in despair.

Freud and Kierkegaard agree about the despair of the ethical stage, but disagree about what should be done once this despair is accepted. Freud seeks to lead us back to the esthetic stage in a more self-aware manner; Kierkegaard believes the *krisis* of the ethical should lead us into the religious stage.

The purpose of the religious stage is an unconditional relationship to what I have been calling the Excess (the sacred, divine, transcendence, the infinite, the abyss etc.). This stage transcends the ethical in the sense of having an absolute and individual relationship to the sacred, rather than one mediated by the cultural heroics or the superego. Freedom in the religious stage consists in embracing one's creatureliness (that is, that one is capable of nothing) and overcoming the *causa sui* project, while remaining infinitely and unconditionally engaged with the absolute. As Kierkegaard puts this relation: "*to come to oneself in self-knowledge and before God as nothing before him, yet infinitely, unconditionally engaged*."[1] This is what Kierkegaard means by earnestness: to engage with what exceeds us, and so brings us to a place of hope, freedom, and trust.

This engagement brings us into a new relationship with the world, potentially through the second ethics of love. The esthetic and ethical stages are not abandoned in the religious stage, but given new meaning, and related to in a new way due to the rise in consciousness of the self. The religious stage does not seek self-justification, but finds personal significance in relation to the Excess—it leaves the issue of significance undecided in terms of its *what*. This is the least repressed stage, aware both of its creatureliness and its infinite passion.

Kierkegaard believed that an individual immersed in a particular stage was not able to grasp the self-deception and defenses that are used within the stage due to the desire to maintain the repression of the self. It is those who have moved out of the stage that have the best understanding of it. Thus, we will be looking at the esthetic stage through a representative of the ethical stage: Judge Wilhelm, whose analysis of the esthetic stage takes place in part two of Kierkegaard's book *Either/Or*.[2] We will see that the esthetic stage of existence is unconscious of its despair or neurosis, and defends itself against becoming conscious of its creatureliness by remaining in a narrowed and superficial state of existence. We will also see that its view of self-mastery is an illusion, due to its living at the level of necessity. The analysis of the esthetic stage will show that there can be incremental "growth" in terms of consciousness, and that this growth impacts the esthetic person's relation to the world and to her self. The growth in consciousness will lead to a recognition of the despair of this stage, and so bring one to a *krisis*.

3 The Esthetic

3.1 Spiritlessness

The most unconscious level of human existence is what Kierkegaard calls "spiritlessness." The purpose of life at this level of existence is simply to enjoy life.[3]

1 *JFY*, 104.

2 For those unfamiliar with Kierkegaard's writings, many of his books (indeed, the most famous of his books) were written as pseudonyms. These pseudonyms approach the topic of the book from the viewpoint of a particular existential stage. The first part of *Either/Or* is a series of writings from an esthete, known only as "A." The second part is a series of letters (or lectures) written to "A" by Judge Wilhelm, imploring him to abandon the esthetic stage in order to move into the ethical stage.

3 Since this purpose sounds not only reasonable to us, but obvious, we can be fairly certain that we live in a spiritless culture.

This life-view has as many variations as there are definitions of enjoyment, though all variations have in common the belief that certain conditions in life must be met in order for life to be enjoyable, conditions which are "*not there by virtue of the individual himself*."[4] For most spiritless individuals, the conditions are completely external to the self, such as, wealth, honor, status, recognition, and those things necessary for immediate pleasure. One will enjoy one's life, it is thought, if one can become wealthy, or be revered by others.

Thus, the focus of life for the esthete is found in the attainment of the conditions necessary for enjoyment, because only then does one gain a sense of well-being. In American culture, this is very much in line with the consumerism discussed earlier, in which one is ruled by the conditions necessary for attaining the external items through which one gains a particular lifestyle. The variety in our consumer culture gives the illusion of being free, since there is so much to *choose* from; however, one is constrained not only by the external conditions necessary for attaining what is necessary for enjoyment, but also by the judgments of the established order about issues of mattering (e.g., attractiveness, influence, power, and so forth).

Some esthetes find enjoyment in relation to certain traits or talents they possess. While this has a relation to aspects of one's personality, they remain unchosen, and so are more a matter of fate, which relates to the distinction between character and personality analyzed in the previous chapter. The Judge points specifically to talents:

> It is a talent for practical affairs, a talent for business, a talent for mathematics, a talent for writing, a talent for art, a talent for philosophy. Satisfaction in life, enjoyment, is sought in the unfolding of this talent. Perhaps one does not stop with the talent in its immediacy, but refines it in every way, but the condition for satisfaction in life is the talent itself, a condition that is not posited by the individual.[5]

This remains immediacy because at this level the self remains a conglomeration of disorganized forces in which there is nothing higher than the immediate moment (what the situation is calling for). The esthete does not have control over these forces, and in this sense lacks a self that has taken hold of itself—it does not possess itself, but is possessed by the world. As the Judge says,

4 Soren Kierkegaard, *Either/Or, Part II*, trans. Howard V. and Edna H. Hong (Princeton: Princeton UP, 1987), 180. Henceforth cited as *E/O II*.

5 *E/O II*, 183.

> When an individual considers himself esthetically, he becomes conscious of this self as a complex concretion intrinsically qualified in many ways; but despite all the internal variety, all these together are nevertheless his nature, have equal right to emerge, equal right to demand satisfaction. His soul is like soil out of which grows all sorts of herbs, all with the claim to flourish; his self consists of multiplicity, and he has no self that is higher than this.[6]

This is what we saw in our analysis of Freud's view of the self: there is no hierarchy by which to organize the various talents and desires within the person, no purpose they are to serve, and so they find value only within the immediate moment.

For Kierkegaard, this is a chaotic approach to life, because there is nothing that organizes the various moments in one's life. This is in line with the analogy of the movie that does not make sense: it is a random series of scenes, with nothing that transcends the scenes in order to give them meaning (nothing to make sense of them individually). When this is one's life, the individual is tossed around by the randomness of her own chaotic desires in relation to the random situations in which she finds herself: she is like a leaf blown by the wind of cultural influences. In practice, it becomes an aimless life, which always takes the path of least resistance, so that it is the external world that controls and directs one's life, rather than oneself.

The spiritless person is unconscious of the despair of this approach to life—that is, of the depth of her repression, the hopelessness within her *causa sui* project, and her lack of freedom. If life is enjoyable and pleasant, such a person finds it ridiculous to view herself as being in despair. She judges her life by her sensate experience, which allows her to repress her despair and neurosis in the fetishism of objects that bring enjoyment. The people around her can often see the despair and emptiness of her life, the triviality of her pursuits, and the falseness of the self she projects, but she remains oblivious to all this.

Kierkegaard says the person maintains this self-deception by holding a low conception of what the self is, and what it means to be a self (what I have been calling a narrowed sense of the self). Kierkegaard says in relation to this,

> However vain and conceited men may be, they usually have a very meager conception of themselves nevertheless, that is, they have no conception of being spirit, the absolute that a human being can be. … Imagine a house with a basement, first floor, and second floor planned so that there is or is supposed to be a

---

6 *E/O II*, 225.

> social distinction between the occupants according to the floor. Now, if what it means to be a human being is compared with such a house, then all too regrettably the sad and ludicrous truth about the majority of people is that in their house they prefer to live in the basement. Every human being is a psychical-physical synthesis intended to be spirit; this is the building, but he prefers to live in the basement, that is, in sensate categories.[7]

We have already seen that this low view of the self is in line with the Freudian conception of the self, of Freud's lowering and narrowing of what a human life should be—i.e., a pursuit of a tolerable, common unhappiness in line with the sensate, with culture providing the safety and relative organization necessary to pull off even this modest goal. We saw that this is a critical aspect of the analytic process, because the lower the conception of what it means to be a self, the less pressure on the fragile ego. One must keep from reflecting on what meaning one's life may have, or whether what one does has any significance; the focus is to be on obtaining a superficial happiness. This *superficial* happiness is a modicum of relief from the discontent they normally feel. What they dread is being bored (feeling their emptiness and the insignificance of what they are doing), uncomfortable, or facing a strenuous ideal. They choose comfort over freedom.

We can think of it this way: What does it mean for a human being to move from a state of "I want" to "I can"? A child lives in the state of "I want," driven by the desires it feels in the moment, without thought of what value such desires may have for her life, or the dangers they may bring. The "I can" means that one has a choice in what one will pursue, in what or whom one will become—it is setting a value to the desires, a value conceived beyond the enjoyment of the immediate situation. The "I want" has no genuine will, is prey to the id or appetites of the moment, and runs from all opposition to these desires. As we saw earlier, the id does not understand the word "No." The "I can," however, arrives with the world's resistance, the challenges one overcomes and dominates, and the costs to be paid in our choices that move us in the direction of a particular self. Once we understand that there are costs in choices and that something is at stake in the way we choose to live, the question of worth, and the meaning of what we pursue, awakens in us. It is only at this point that our will truly becomes engaged.

We have already seen the problem that arises in this spiritless approach to life: culture becomes the exclusive means by which we determine the "I want," replacing our own will (or own *krisis* or decision of what is worth pursing) with

7 *SUD*, 43.

culture's various scripts. For Kierkegaard, the spiritless person has not *chosen* to live by the established order, but is completely socialized into it. The only way spiritlessness can maintain its illusion is if one's culture remains affluent enough to provide a vast quantity and variety of goods to consume, as well as a constant availability of entertainment to enjoy.

At this level of the esthetic stage we are dealing with "frat boys," or the cast of *The Jersey Shore*, whose parents are footing the bill, carrying life for them, so that they do not have to move from the "I want" to the "I can." The fear for Kierkegaard, is that Western Civilization is becoming populated with spiritless individuals. No culture or civilization can last long in such a state—which is another reason it is in despair.

3.2 Pure Immediacy

The next level of consciousness within the esthetic stage is what Kierkegaard calls "pure immediacy." Some reflection is developed at this stage, though not enough to create a space between the person and the immediate moment to become self-conscious, or be wrenched from the finite. Reflection is locked down in the moment: what the moment has to offer, and how to make the most of what it is offering. One is moved by desires, but is more reflective than the spiritless person. One has begun to deal with some of the struggles in life, but these struggles are always for the sake of enjoyment. To put it concretely, the person living in pure immediacy believes life is about the weekends. When it comes to their despair, they believe "Mondays" are the problem with life: despair is connected with circumstances, rather than having to do with the lack of self.

In pure immediacy, one is passive in relation to the world, and one remains possessed by the world, believing that it is the world that determines whether one flourishes in enjoyment or languishes in boredom. Thus, one senses one's despair only when some misfortune happens in the world. Kierkegaard is pointing out that the despair is always there: the person has not become a self, his life is insignificant, and it is just this (this despair) that he covers over with the help of culture and the therapeutic. Kierkegaard says, when the world deals this person a blow, and he feels his despair, he points at the wrong object of the despair: "he stands and points to what he calls despair but is not despair, and in the meantime, sure enough, despair is right there behind him without his realizing it."[8]

8 *SUD*, 52.

Though there is a consciousness of despair when the world does not go his way, there is no consciousness of what despair is. When life becomes "better," then he believes he is no longer in despair; however, genuine despair is rooted in the loss of the self (the neurotic repression of who he is), something which does not change when external circumstances change. The problem of life is not Mondays, but that one is being the kind of person, and so living the kind of life, where Mondays are a problem.

All passive forms of despair, of which pure immediacy is an example, are an unwillingness to be oneself. One seeks to be rid of the self one is, refuses to start with the first step of facing one's creatureliness, and runs from the anxiety of this awareness. Kierkegaard's description of such a life is very much in line with the lifestyle solution Cushman wrote about: "This form of despair: in despair not to will to be oneself. Or even lower, in despair not to will to be a self. Or lowest of all: in despair to will to be someone else, to wish for a new self."[9] One despairs by wishing to have been someone else: "If only I had been born wealthy (beautiful, intelligent, powerful), I would be a happy self." This is what the lifestyle solution is supposed to address, by the attempt to become someone who embodies a lifestyle in line with what receives recognition. Such a life is prey to advertisements, who push the goods (symbolics) by which one can "put on" such a lifestyle or "self," so that one can change selves simply by changing one's clothes (or accessories, car, house, relationships).

3.3 Reflective Immediacy

Reflective immediacy is the next step in consciousness for the esthete. While there is a rise in consciousness, a person in reflective immediacy still does not see the true source of despair, and remains in self-deception about the emptiness of her self. Still, there is an increase in the understanding of what the self is (namely, that it is in some way separate from externals—that the self is more than what it wears), and so also a rise in the true nature of despair—though despair is still suffered passively as a blow from circumstances.

Kierkegaard says this is a movement from enjoying life to enjoying oneself, which means there is a more active role in enjoyment, and a higher form of self-possession. There is not yet enough reflection to become transparent to oneself (that is, to see the amount of self that is being repressed), but there is enough reflection to become more separate from the world. Here we are

9 *SUD*, 52–53.

reaching the point of the enlightened consciousness of the relatively more self-aware cynic, and the variation of the therapeutic that seeks "self-actualization."

The Judge says of this view of life that

> in enjoyment you are to enjoy yourself. ... Here, too, the condition of enjoyment is still an external condition, that is not within the individual's power; for although he, as he says, enjoys himself only in the enjoyment, but the enjoyment itself is linked to an external condition. Thus, the entire difference is that *he enjoys reflectively, not immediately*.[10]

The movement from enjoying life to enjoying oneself becomes necessary because one has become more aware that life is not predisposed to one's enjoyment, and so one must be more "creative."[11] This is in line with Freud's more conservative approach to life, as one understands that the external world is not conducive to a life of enjoyment, and so one must add something to find enjoyment. Freud, as an academic, enjoyed himself in the process of his thoughts, his analyses, his "scientific" approach to the problem of human life, and the recognition he attained.

This is an important point of growth in consciousness because there is a separation, however small, between the external and the internal, and so a recognition that the self is somewhat disconnected from the external. With this growth in consciousness, the person is no longer able to lose herself in what is merely external—is no longer easily amused by "bread and circuses." For instance, such a person does not simply enjoy a movie, but enjoys analyzing the movie afterward, developing insights about the movie, and sharing these insights with others.[12] Such a life becomes more refined in its tastes, having

---

10 *E/O II*, 190–191. (emphasis added).

11 In recognizing that one cannot simply enjoy life, one is becoming more conscious of one's creatureliness or helplessness; in moving from enjoying life to enjoying oneself, one is attempting to maintain the *causa sui* project in relation to this growing consciousness.

12 I think this difference can be seen in relation to social media platforms; for instance the difference between Facebook and Reddit users. Facebook shares content that is much more along the lines of the first two views of life, portraying how one is enjoying life, without any irony. Reddit, on the other hand, is full of irony and cynicism, and finds great joy in analyzing the superficiality or ignorance of Facebook, X/Twitter, and Instagram posts—as well as practically everything else in life. In Facebook one sees people portraying their enjoyment of life (what they are doing, eating, accomplishing); in Reddit one finds people enjoying themselves by their ironic and sarcastic analyses of life. One imagines the Facebook person spending her free time doing things out in the world that bring enjoyment (and taking a lot of pictures of it); one imagines the Reddit user spending her free time at her computer, writing about life, and how pathetic most people's enjoyment is.

seen through the superficiality culture provides for enjoyment. A person in reflective immediacy needs higher forms of amusement. Thus, in reflective immediacy, a person can no longer simply take the moment in all its nakedness, because she has gained insight into its superficiality, and knows that this will eventually leave her bored; instead, she dresses it up with her own reflection (whether viewed as profound, humorous, cynical, or nihilistic), enjoying herself reflectively (her profundity, wit, sarcastic bite, or the depth of her "darkness").

In terms of the therapeutic, this life-view is often packaged as a kind of "spiritual quest" or process of self-actualization. When people in pure immediacy go on a trip overseas, they are going on a tour; when people in reflective immediacy go overseas, they are on a pilgrimage.[13] In other words, while the former is to take in the sights, the latter is to be changed in some way by the experience, becoming more sophisticated and cosmopolitan. They feel a sense of superiority (significance) over those who have not travelled to exotic locations.

This also relates to Stiver's analysis of psychological techniques. The first two life-views of the esthetic are in line with the psychological techniques of advertising and propaganda (which we saw in the analysis above); reflective immediacy is related to the techniques of public relations, therapeutic methodologies, and how-to manuals on effective living. Such a life is still connected to outward performance—since this is how one gains recognition for oneself—but is more reflective, in that it internalizes the techniques for enjoyment and gaining recognition. These techniques and insights allow one to manipulate situations and people in one's favor (that is, try to have more control over the situation).

Stivers uses as a prime example of this Dale Carnegie's book *How to Win Friends and Influence People*. One seeks to be attractive to others through one's reflective ability, but it is still intimately connected to externals, and so one is not attaining self-mastery in this internalization: one is surrendering both to what the established order finds attractive in people, as well as how the "experts" determine what is important. Indeed, Stivers says that in this technique, we surrender to a "dependency on experts."[14]

For instance, psychotherapists are the new "seers" or wise sages, our new healing priests, in that they offer us the *hidden truths* behind virtually every act and situation of our waking hours, from choosing a career to disciplining our children. This knowledge is often dispensed through the ever-present

13 They want exotic, out-of-the-way destinations.

14 Stivers, 103.

new "psychological finding," which comes from scientific studies published in professional journals, and then dispensed daily in popular media. Whether "earth-shaking" or trivial, they are meant to show us that our lives must be interpreted for us by the new expert and seer.[15] Our ability to enjoy ourselves, and our sense of self, are enhanced by all this information, which we can then spout to others in order to show our wisdom. For instance, we no longer simply enjoy something like eating, but enjoy showing how much we understand about the right way to eat, about our knowledge of exotic or healthy foods and spices, and our ability to prepare them.

Despair is still suffered passively as a blow in reflective immediacy, though despair can now arise through reflection on the possibility of the world's blows. Reflective immediacy realizes that the self is "essentially different from the environment and external events and from their influence upon it."[16] In this, one is becoming more aware of one's creatureliness (the lack of one's control and one's vulnerability). However, because the esthetic *causa sui* project is still in place, this reflection remains within immediacy.

While the weekend is the cure for the person in pure immediacy, the primacy of possibility is the cure for the despair of reflective immediacy. If imagining negative possibilities can bring one to despair through reflection, then grabbing hold of the variety of positive possibilities will serve as a "cure" for this despair (the therapeutic approach of "positive thinking" is an example of this). While the person in reflective immediacy still seeks "nourishment" from the world, she may realize this connection is in some way artificial (as any good cynic will know due to enlightened consciousness); still, she loves the world too much to give it up. Like Rameau's nephew, the modern cynic has enough enlightenment or reflection to be separate from the world, but enough of a therapeutic false consciousness to still be immersed in the world through immediacy.

As the despair of this situation increases (as the person in reflective immediacy is forced to face the creatureliness she represses, and the hopelessness of her *causa sui* project), there can be two different reactions, moving in opposite directions: a movement backwards into pure immediacy, or a movement forward in a rising consciousness of despair. In the former, one thinks of the questions about the self as a kind of false door with nothing behind it.[17] One

15 Martin L. Gross, *The Psychological Society: A Critical Analysis of Psychiatry, Psychotherapy, Psychoanalysis, and the Psychological Revolution* (New York: Random House, 1978), 56–57.

16 *SUD*, 54.

17 *SUD*, 63.

will say to oneself, "I must grow out of this youthful despair. I must grow up; I can't spend my entire life in this concern for the self, because I have things I must take care of in the world." One now has a family to worry about, a career to take care of. Besides, it can become obvious to one that all this worry about the weakness of the self and its imperfections is ridiculous, because one can look at all one's accomplishments in the world as evidence that one is a successful person.

However, one may also move into a deeper, more conscious, form of estheticism: the final stage, which the Judge calls "despair itself." This is where the knowledge of human failings and weakness (creatureliness) becomes itself a source of enjoyment. One develops enough reflection so that the enjoyment one seeks is gained through one's own thought-life. Further, the self is no longer at stake in the fortunes and misfortunes of external circumstances, because one sees that all of existence ends in misfortune. Yet even with this realization, the esthete is still not able to give up the view that the purpose of life is enjoyment, and continues to hang onto the esthetic *causa sui* project.

4 Despair Itself

By "despair itself" the Judge does not mean that the esthete has reached a consciousness of what despair truly is; "despair itself" is a disappointment with the world, rather than consciousness of a loss of the self. As the Judge says, despair itself "is an esthetic life-view because the personality remains in its immediacy; it is the final esthetic life-view, for up to a point it has absorbed the consciousness of nothingness of such a life-view. But there is a difference between despair and despair."[18] At this point the esthete has recognized the despair of finding life in one's external conditions,[19] and yet this recognition is not grasped in a way in which the esthetic existence (that is, the *causa sui* project of the esthetic existence) itself is despaired of, nor is it a concern for the self. Instead, true to the esthetic stage, the esthete has found this knowledge of despair interesting.

This is the later Freud, the Freud of *Civilization and Its Discontents*, who embraces (and even finds interest and enjoyment in) thinking through the nihilistic process of moving toward death. Or this is the poet, who finds in the sufferings of life and love a source of inspiration and pleasure.

18 *E/O II*, 194.

19 What Homans called the "hideous and bottomless spiral inward".

In the Forward to Becker's *The Denial of Death*, Sam Keen writes about his meeting with Becker, who was by then in the hospital dying of cancer. Keen opens the Forward with this reflection:

> The first words Ernest Becker said to me when I walked into his hospital room were: "You are catching me in extremis. This is a test of everything I've written about death. And I've got a chance to show how one dies, the attitude one takes. Whether one does it in a dignified, manly way; what kinds of thoughts one surrounds it with; how one accepts his death."[20]

Becker is reflecting on whether all his work was done as an esthete (speculatively, for the personal enjoyment and recognition of it), or from a person beyond the esthetic, from a dignified (what Kierkegaard would call "ethical") existence.

At this level of the esthetic stage, we move into that aspect of neurosis that becomes pathological or abnormal, having become exiled from an immediate relation to the cultural heroics. Freud had a keen understanding of how such an exile is sublimated in works of art, philosophical works of speculation, philanthropic endeavors, and the like. Kierkegaard understood as well that the esthete at this level becomes a "deep" thinker, for she is lost in her thoughts, and finds well-being, or release from anxiety and boredom, in thought. He understood, as well, that this reflection on the meaninglessness of life was a defense against existentially having to face it (which is what the Judge meant when he said there is a difference between despair and despair). The issue is not the amount of reflection attained, but the aim of the reflection: is the reflection aimed at transparency or further self-evasion? Is it owning up to one's despair and so one's creatureliness, or a deeper continuation of the *causa sui* project?[21]

This is the despair that "A," the esthete who authored the first part of *Either/Or,* is in; he has become absorbed in the consciousness of the emptiness and futility of the esthetic stage, though he also finds a sense of well-being within this consciousness. The well-being comes from the sense of significance and ironic detachment "A" gets from having *seen through* culture, and all it provides to make life more palatable. He feels unique and significant in this cynical stance. "A" is no longer an outsider-cynic, but has become a master-cynic,

20 Sam Keen, Forward to *The Denial of Death,* xi–xxii (New York: Free Press Paperbacks, 1971), xi.

21 It is not the *what* of meaninglessness and emptiness that is decisive, but the *how.*

the culmination of which is found in the last chapter of his writings: "The Diary of a Seducer."

The nothingness "A" sees is always in regards to the desire of living a pleasant life, or enjoying oneself in life. "A" has come to recognize the ultimate emptiness of such a formulation of enjoyment. He expresses his disappointment with these approaches to life by stating,

> Marry, and you will regret it. Do not marry, and you will regret it. Marry or do not marry, you will regret it either way. ... Laugh at the stupidities of the world, and you will regret it; weep over them, and you will regret it. Laugh at the stupidities of the world or weep over them, you will regret it either way. ... Trust a girl, and you will regret it. Do not trust her, and you will regret it. Trust a girl or do not trust her, and you will regret it either way. ... Hang yourself, and you will regret it. Do not hang yourself and you will regret it. Hang yourself or do not hang yourself, you will regret it either way.[22]

"A" has experienced the various levels of esthetic existence long and deeply enough to know that, no matter what one does, eventually it will become boring and empty, and one will wish one had done otherwise, since the other direction now looks much more interesting and enjoyable.

"A" has reached a level of consciousness to realize that the primacy of possibility is not enough to satisfy the insatiable human desire for enjoyment and pleasure. The esthetic human being is an empty self, and as such is like a vacuum that sucks out all the enjoyment external conditions have to offer, eventually leaving them empty and bland.

For instance, when one buys a new house there is an initial feeling of fullness and meaning that comes with its novelty, with the new possibilities it brings, and with the sense of identity it provides. It will not be long, however, before the new house, which stood out so prominently in one's life, finds its place within the "mundane" and "invisible" of routine languishing. As Freud pointed out, what at first brings one pleasure eventually only brings a mild contentment—or becomes a symbol of what one has given up or does not have.

While "A" has developed enough reflection to recognize the despair inherent in estheticism, and so has seen that it is meaningless to seek enjoyment in life, he is not horrified by this knowledge; he does not grieve for himself, for others, or for the human race in general. "A" has what Rieff calls a tragic

---

22 Soren Kierkegaard, *Either/Or, Part I*, trans. Howard V. and Edna H. Hong (Princeton: Princeton UP, 1987), 38. Henceforth cited as *E/O I*.

sensibility, though without a sense of the tragic.[23] This is because his reflection allows him to gain an ironic detachment from the situation. Ever the cynic, "A" finds this knowledge to be a source of enjoyment:

> When I was young, I forgot in the Trophonean cave how to laugh; when I became an adult, when I opened my eyes and saw actuality, then I started to laugh and have not stopped laughing since that time. I saw that the meaning of life was to make a living, its goal to become a councilor, that the rich delight of love was to acquire a well-to-do-girl, and that the blessedness of friendship was to help each other in financial difficulties, that wisdom was whatever the majority assumed it to be, that enthusiasm was to give a speech, that courage was to risk being fined ten dollars, that cordiality was to say "May it do you good" after a meal, that piety was to go to communion once a year. This I saw, and I laughed.[24]

In his cynicism, "A" has seen through it all, but he is much too cynical to see any higher possibilities (he sees no other alternatives), because he himself is stuck in a stage where existence has no higher destiny than enjoyment. As "A" puts it: "I assume that it is man's destiny to amuse himself."[25] He relishes the ironic detachment, and the wittiness that comes from it, finding his amusement in the same ironic cynicism one finds in Diderot's *Rameau's Nephew*.

Because "A" recognizes the emptiness of life, he is capable of what Kierkegaard calls "finite resignation." Kierkegaard calls it "finite" (in distinction to what earlier we called "infinite resignation") because the esthete does not resign the finite for the sake of something higher—namely, to become himself—but for the sake of enjoying the finite in its absurdity. "A" finds his significance from being in on the con, in having risen above the fools who are controlled by the established order—much like the suburban couple in Chapter 12. This is why his despair is not true despair. The Judge says that "A" is in "thought-despair," which does not appropriate the despair existentially, but remains distant from it through abstraction. He plays with despair for the sake of enjoyment.

Freud himself is an example of this, for in his very musings on the meaninglessness of life, and the proclamation that the aim of life is death, he protected himself from having to existentially appropriate or internalize the

---

23 *DW*, 7.

24 *E/O I*, 34. "A" even understands that this loss of a sense of the tragic is the tragedy. He says, "In a theater, it happened that a fire started offstage. The clown came out to tell the audience. They thought it was a joke and applauded. He told them again, and they became still more hilarious. This is the way, I suppose, that the world will be destroyed—amid the universal hilarity of wits and wags who think it is all a joke" (*E/O I*, 30).

25 *E/O I*, 290.

knowledge—that is, to accept existential guilt. Becker says that on at least two occasions, when Freud was forced to face the reality of his own pessimistic view of life, he fainted. Fainting represents the most massive denial: the refusal or inability to remain conscious in the face of a threat. Freud fainted in the absolute denial of the threatening reality he had himself written about in a non-threatening manner.[26] The two occasions when Freud loses complete control of himself must contain, Becker argues, some vital insight about the very heart of his life-problem, which Becker relates to Freud's specific *causa sui* project. Fortunately, Jung gives first-hand reports of both incidents.

The first incident came during Jung's discussion of preserved peat-bog corpses in Bremen. This talk of corpses got on Freud's nerves, and he asked Jung several times "Why are you so concerned with these corpses?" The situation came to a head during a conversation they were having during dinner, when Freud suddenly fainted. Afterward, Freud told Jung that he was convinced all the chatter about corpses meant that Jung had a death-wish toward him. The other episode happened during a discussion about historical incidents which Freud thought proved the desire of the son to destroy the father by destroying the works of the father. Jung began to offer counter interpretations for these historical happenings, attempting to show that many of the incidents were not in contempt of the father, but in respect of the father's gods. Jung says, "At that moment Freud slid off his chair in a faint."[27]

The psychoanalytic movement was Freud's distinctive *causa sui* project and source of immortality; it was his personal vehicle for heroism, the means by which he attempted to transcend his vulnerability, and defend himself against the knowledge of his own creatureliness (though he had been writing about such things for decades). Freud was particularly sensitive to the idea of father-murder, being a complex symbol for him. An attack on his identity as father (i.e., father of the psychoanalytic movement as his *causa sui* vehicle) was an attack on his immortality. As Becker puts it, "Father-murder would mean his own insignificance as a creature. It is just such an interpretation that the fainting episodes point to."[28]

Freud's pursuit of the *causa sui* project was the attempt to use the psychoanalytic school he had created as a mirror to reflect power back upon himself.[29] Jung's conversation about corpses was interpreted by Freud as Jung's desire to take over his immortality vehicle. As much as Freud wrote about the

26 *DD*, 107.
27 *DD*, 109.
28 *DD*, 110.
29 *DD*, 116–117.

meaningless of life, the insignificance of all we do, it is clear from his reaction when actually faced by such a reality, that earlier talk was abstract, all in the service of the enjoyment received for recognition (an enjoyment he expected to be eternal).

5 Conclusion

This is the path of the esthetic life, and the path we have accepted due to our reception of Freud's interpretation of life. In our esthetic cynicism, we now find enjoyment in seeing through everything, and yet refuse to move into the exile this seeing through should lead us. We find a sense of personal power and a sense of significance from seeing through everything, and yet refuse to fully internalize what this means; instead, we repress it or sublimate it in some way. As the Judge says to "A": "you are in despair. It is not a despair involving something actual but a despair in thought. Your thought has rushed ahead; you have *seen through* the vanity of everything, but you have *not gone further*."[30]

The judge's admonition to go further is the encouragement to come to a point of *krisis*, where one has come to the end of one's defenses and rationalizations, and must make a choice about one's life. The Judge's advice to the esthete is to *choose despair*. To choose despair is to choose oneself in one's absolute validity—in one's eternal validity, as the Judge puts it. It is a choice for becoming oneself, and abandoning the attempts to overcome despair through the world. Or, in terms we have used throughout this book, to choose no longer to overcome one's neurosis and repression through fetishization. This is to abandon the cynical therapeutic of the esthetic *causa sui* project, and choose to be oneself in this *krisis*.

30 *E/O II*, 194. (emphasis added).

CHAPTER 21

Seeing through the Cynical Therapeutic

1 Courage, Humility and Patience

1.1 Culture

I have been hard on culture throughout this book, mainly because I have been focusing on the modern cynical culture. However, like Freud, I have tremendous respect and love for culture. Culture is an amazing phenomenon, which allows humans to function in ways that we could never do apart from an organized way of living together. It is through culture that we take what is in the world, and modify it in a way that brings beauty, thriving, flourishing, and health. We take a plot of land and turn it into a farm that produces a harvest to feed hundreds; or it becomes a bed of flowers that bring beauty to our everyday lives. We take plants and turn them into medicines that allow us to live pain free, extend our lives by decades, and alter our states of mind (caffeine being one of the most prevalent). The list could go on and on, and includes the sciences, arts, literature, architecture, and so forth. A healthy culture is an amazing gift we give to ourselves, which is able to bring meaning and value to what we do.

But cultures do not do these things automatically. Cultures are also capable of great destruction. These cultures take things in the world and modify them in a way that brings suffering, destruction, and death. Culture can also become a mind numbing and spirit killing phenomenon that takes the joy and meaning out of human existence. It is a tragedy that this happens, and a double tragedy that we surrender to it with such ease and even desire. Culture is capable of stretching us as human beings, strengthening our spirits to move into their full potential, but we have allowed ours to narrow us, and even ground us down flat, making us not only into copies of one another, but causing us to desire to be copies.

The modern cynical therapeutic is a driving ideology within our culture, and it is having the negative impact described above. It is profoundly unfortunate that we do not feel this negative impact or care about it, because it means we will not fight against it. We are reaching a time when, as Nietzsche saw it, the soil of the human heart could become too shallow for anything great to ever grow from it again:

> And thus spoke Zarathustra to the people: "The time has come for man to set himself a goal. The time has come for man to plant the seed of his highest hope.

© 2026 THE AUTHOR(S) | HTTPS://DOI.ORG/10.1163/9789004758148-023

> His soil is still rich enough. But one day this soil will be poor and domesticated, and no tall tree will be able to grow in it. Alas, the time is coming when man will no longer shoot the arrow of his longing beyond man, and the string of his bow will have forgotten how to whir!
>
> Alas, the time of the most despicable man is coming, he that is no longer able to despise himself. Behold, I show you the *last man*.[1]

Nietzsche is here addressing the danger we face from nihilism. It is the same danger Kierkegaard saw, describing it as a fall into a spiritlessness out of which we will not be able to climb. We need a new goal and highest hope, one that will deepen and enrich the soil of our spirits, so that new and great things can grow from our cultures. As we have seen, Freud's answer to nihilism (the one we accepted) offers no new goal or highest hope, but rather the opposite: a lowering of expectations, a narrowing of alternatives, and doing whatever is necessary to make life easier for the fragile ego so that it can wallow in its poverty and spiritlessness.

1.2 *Krisis*

Originally, I had written for this book what I believe to be a strong, though difficult, alternative to the cynical therapeutic, one presented by Kierkegaard. However, it was as long as the critique I have written here, and I could not find publisher that would take on a book of that length. Upon reflection, perhaps offering a single alternative after the critique would not have been wise. It is enough, I now believe, to open the possibility of, and perhaps even create a desire for, an alternative way of living. In other words, it is enough to point to the *krisis*. Only after an openness can be created will alternatives gain a hearing.

It takes courage, humility, and time (patience) to reflect on the effects of a particular way of life, especially when there are no alternative perspectives from which to stand. The cynical therapeutic is the smog we have been breathing in for half a century or more, and we no longer have the perspective to sense that it is choking the life out of us. We need the courage to step out of this *tuphos* in order to understand the cynical therapeutic's impact on our lives. First, however, we must see and admit that the unhappiness we are experiencing in life is not due to strictly external factors that if changed would make our lives happier; rather, we must understand our own responsibility for the lack of contentment we have in life. We have chosen to interpret life and ourselves

1 Friedrich Nietzsche, *The Portable Nietzsche*. Editor and Translator, Walter Kaufmann (Penguin Books: New York), 1982, p. 129.

through the cynical therapeutic to such an extent that it is now a part of us (our character lie), and the cause of a deep discontent with life. We have to understand that being cynical is not the obviously right reaction to the world; we have chosen this reaction, and due to the nature of the cynical therapeutic, all other alternatives appear closed off.

I mentioned in the Preface to this book that there was a particular day my cynicism "broke." This happened at the beginning of one of my Ethics classes, toward which I had an especially cynical view. I never developed a connection with the students in this class, and I saw them as particularly passive and even lazy. This was a class I dreaded walking into.

One morning, when I came into the classroom, only a quarter of the lights were on. It was a new building, and the light switches were not easy to figure out. I spent about fifteen seconds turning the lights off and on until I finally got them all on. I looked at the student next to the door, whom I was especially cynical toward (she sat in the back of the class looking bored); she looked back and smiled at me, sympathizing with my frustration and embarrassment. That seemingly insignificant smile broke through to me, and my cynicism was shattered. She was nothing like how I had been interpreting her. I walked into that class changed, and from that day on the class was never the same.

When my cynicism broke at my student's smile, and the defenses (smog) that the cynical therapeutic had set in place lifted for the first time in years, I was again able to relate to my students as individuals, and with a trust and concern about their welfare and good that I had not had for some time. My classes opened up again to vibrant conversations about life and the wisest way to live. It was humbling to recognize my despair, and to admit it was not so much due to what was outside of myself (it was not my students' fault), but due to how I had *chosen* to interpret others and situations. I remember the shock I experienced as I realized the incredibly negative impact my cynicism had been having on my life. At the same time, the freedom I experienced was exhilarating, as I was again able to breath the fresh air of hope and trust, which allowed me to reach out into the world in a positive, hopeful, and excited manner.[2]

As I think back to the time when I was immersed in the cynical therapeutic, I am able to recognize the despair of those who are still deeply immersed in their cynicism. I have written much about the psychological difficulties that arise when giving into systems and organizations whose meaninglessness one has

2 I have thought much about how a single, momentary smile could have broken through my cynicism. As I have reflected on it, I have found Kierkegaard's alternative to come closest to what I believe happened. This is why I focused on him as providing an alternative to relating to one another through cynicism.

seen through, but there is also the day-to-day anger, impatience, and bitterness that comes with being part of an organization one does not trust. One sees manipulation everywhere (whether it truly exists or not), regards all decisions about the organization as being made in secret in order to hide the self-serving motives of those making the decisions, and one becomes incapable of sharing enjoyable relationships with others. There can be little community with others for the cynic, except during those all too often cynical "complaint sessions."

I have come to see that the most cynical among us are incapable of finding fulfillment in their work, relationships, and even hobbies, as a toxic mistrust poisons their relationships in every aspect of their lives. They come at each situation and each person as if in a battle, carrying a mistrust that every person and organization is ultimately a malevolent force to work against (that is, complain about—since there is seldom any work they find to do to solve all the perceived problems they talk about). They are never working with or for anything, but always against. The cynical therapeutic does not allow for contentment, and is driven by the constant attempt to not be taken advantage of within a system or organization one believes is always taking advantage of one. My hope is that we can let the stage sets of the cynical therapeutic collapse—both the rationalizations and compensations outlined in this book—and move into exile.

Modern cynicism offers a rational and intellectual stage set; the triumph of the therapeutic offers compensation for the emptiness of the stage set, which keeps us numbed just enough to feel no need to reflect on the common unhappiness of our lives. We have settled for a life of relief, languishing, and what might be thought of as a slow death through a spiritual carbon monoxide, which causes our spirits (*pneuma*, "breath") to drift into unconscious despair and suffocate. Many have seemingly lost the capacity to trust others, and interactions between people have become defensive, angry, and rude, viewing others as enemies to their individual well-being.

Ultimately, what we have been working toward in this book is the *krisis* between the dichotomies of openness and closedness, expansion and narrowing, flourishing and languishing. With the cynical therapeutic, we walked through a door that promised expansion and flourishing, but has ended in a languishing within an artificial narrowing. Our hope was for greater freedom, significance, and self-mastery, but it has turned into a state of unconscious oppression, emptiness, and undiscipline. The anxiety that comes with freedom, exile, and the vulnerability of the human condition has been too much for us, just as Freud predicted. Being unable to face the nihilistic pessimism that came with his psychoanalytic approach to coping with living unheroically, we fell into illusion and fetishization, which makes us a perfect subject for a consumer culture. The existential openness Nietzsche expressed (an openness of quality) becomes a superficial openness of variety (an openness of quantity). This is not a life of fulfillment; it is a lonely, suspicious, unhappy existence that needs variety to stay diverted and numbed.

1.3 Choose to Be Anxious

Before the consideration of any new alternative way of life can be envisioned, we must choose to despair of the cynical therapeutic. To do this we must learn to be anxious in the right way. This means confronting anxiety in a way that does not narrow our lives but opens them up to the freedom we are capable of. It is to embrace the responsibility of becoming a self in the midst of the inherent riskiness of existence. What narrows our lives is the attempt to maintain the illusion of the *causa sui* project, since the illusion is maintained through fetishization upon something we feel we can control. To become anxious in the right way is to give up the illusions that maintain the *causa sui* project, and thus move into exile.

We have looked at the intellectual means of rationalizing the impossible task of the *causa sui* project, a rationalization that means we must invest ourselves in the empty pursuits we have seen through. This is the modern cynical aspect of the cynical therapeutic. We have also looked at the triumph of the therapeutic, through which we are provided compensation for the emptiness of our pursuits. In the remainder of this final chapter, I want to examine both the intellectual and compensatory aspects of the cynical therapeutic in terms of the *krisis* we must face in order to choose the despair of the cynical therapeutic, and move forward in life. I want to examine how the choices we make, and are always making, flow from an ideological standpoint we have "fallen" into, and not from a supposed place of intellectual integrity, objectivity, or honesty.

I want to close the book by examining the unconscious choice that takes place in the cynical therapeutic, and show that it is not as objectively certain as it feels to us; it is an ideological means of confronting a world and running from the anxiety that is part of our human creatureliness, vulnerability, and longing for self-justification. I will examine this by looking again at Kierkegaard.

2 Kierkegaard's "Epistemology"

2.1 Awakening from Self-Concern Gone Awry

2.1.1 The Fragile Interpretations

Modern cynicism, growing out of Freud's ideological critique, is a dogmatic mistrust of people, institutions, companies, governments, and all else that is constructed by culture. Freud's mistrust was based on his self-proclaimed scientific authority, which the modern cynic picks up as an ideological (unquestioned) cynical stance of culture. That people are not to be trusted, and that their deepest motivations are selfish, are things that are seldom questioned by the cynics, and so are often viewed as facts. I hope to show, however, that such conclusions are not indisputable facts, but fragile interpretations, based on inferences whose presuppositions are no longer questioned. My contention throughout this book has been that this interpretation is not only far from certain, but arises from an attitude that is self-deceptive—instead of mistrusting ourselves and our illusions, we project the mistrust on to others. It is this dogmatic approach to relationships that I want to address through Kierkegaard's epistemological analysis.

Kierkegaard's authorship is not meant to be strictly theoretical, nor is he working through a purely intellectual problem, but he seeks to awaken a response in the reader—awaken a responsibility. He views disinterested intellectual exercises, more often than not, as a means of not having to respond to the content of the reflection. Kierkegaard does not think we arrive at our conclusions about life (e.g., that people are inherently and intractably deceptive) through a disinterested knowledge that leads to our certainty; rather, we arrive at this "certainty" of our knowledge based on our pre-established way of relating to the world (through our commitments—or lack thereof—through unquestioned and deeply held presuppositions, the acceptance of ideologies, and even due to the limitations of our language).[3]

Kierkegaard's epistemological interests are focused on *how* our self-consciousness and freedom define our nature, and so allow us to be the kind of creatures that can, as Nietzsche put it, "shoot the arrow of longing beyond" our present state of being and potential. We have narrowed this "shooting" to our intellectual abilities—mainly to the technological products we create. But self-conscious freedom should open itself to more than this, in order to put our hope beyond our limitations, and into the excess out of which newness and *dunamis* (potential, "dynamite") come. We must abandon the *causa sui* project and embrace our existential guilt. Self-consciousness and existential guilt are closely related, as both are connected to our deepest passion for meaning and significance. It is out of our existential guilt that self-consciousness arises.[4]

3 See Louis Mackey's "The loss of the world in Kierkegaard's ethics," *The Review of Metaphysics*, 15:4 (June, 1962), pp. 602–620, accessed May 30, 2015, Stable UR: http://www.jstor.org/stable/20123908.

4 One sees this in the Judeo-Christian story of the Fall, which is the moment that Adam and Eve become self-conscious—that is, conscious of themselves as naked, of their need to hide, which becomes the beginning of their need for self-justification as they blame something or someone else for their guilt.

As spirit, we do not simply exist, but we assess and value existence, and make decisions about what is worth paying attention to and what is not. Self-conscious spirit is the greatest of miracles on this planet, yet we have lost all wonder of it, along with all passion and earnestness for what it can become.

2.1.2 Inter-Esse

While it is easy to understand that reflection is necessary for self-consciousness, the type of self-consciousness Kierkegaard is driving toward requires more than the ability to reflect on contrasting views within a situation; it requires *interest* or concern, what Kierkegaard sometimes calls *inter-esse* ("between-being," and so the *interest* that arises between our interaction with the world and our actions). We saw in the last chapter that the spiritless and immediate individual has not yet even raised the question of the meaning of everything she does. That *concern* for meaning, which needs to be answered in order for her to get herself out of bed in the morning, is locked into immediacy with the culture, so her "self" is not really a self, but more an extension of culture.

She does not "possess" her concern for herself, but is given the objects of her concern by the cultural heroics or script. The question has not yet even arisen as to what everything she busies herself with in life means, or whether it has any value—that is, whether it is *worth* pursuing. The concern has not yet announced itself, and to that extent she is not self-conscious—not a self, not involved with her life or her self.

This is partly what I mean by "self-*concern* gone awry." The cynical therapeutic offers no exile from the established order because the nihilistic situation offers no new heroics. One is left with a self-concern that is always narrowed and self-focused on personal well-being. One becomes a mercenary toward all that is not oneself. The world outside oneself becomes a dangerous world that cannot be trusted, so that one believes one can only trust oneself; however, one cannot trust oneself, as one continues to give oneself to the world one claims not to trust, and is unwilling to acknowledge one's true concerns.

Think of it this way: because one's true concern has not yet announced itself, the "analysis" of costs and benefits (the basis or process by which one lives as a mercenary) is the very thing that has gone awry in one's self-concern. Thus, the critical problem we need to address is not that we have become focused selfishly and narrowly around our own "well-being" and "best interest," but that we have not even thought about what our well-being consists of, or what is in our best interest. Is it really in one's best interest to invest oneself in the very things one has seen through as empty and meaningless? It is ironic that our supposed *self*-focus does not have a truly personal self on which it is focused.

The cynic thinks she is looking out for her best interest, but she is blind to the fact that her very sense of "best interest" is what has gone awry. She feels herself to be living by her own particular script as she surrenders to the established order—a kind of pseudo-exile—but since she has not truly moved into her own concern self-consciously, she is unaware that her self-interest (her *inter-esse*) has been coopted by the established order. It is her very "self-interest" that she is allowing to be manipulated by the cynical therapeutic—in her attempt not to be manipulated. She is not free, her life is an insignificant and disposable "resource" in a consumer culture, and she is utterly dependent on the very things she thinks she is free from, always leaning on some fetishized and narrowed object or lifestyle culture provides.

She seeks the rewards of significance given by the established order, and so must play by its rules, no matter how empty or corrupt she views them to be, and no matter how much she distrusts them. She thinks she is fighting against them with her distrust, complaints, and even disdain, but her comfort and sense of self are so connected to them that she is incapable of being free. Both her embrace of, and fight against, the established order have together become an essential part of how she makes sense of herself and finds significance for herself in this meaningless and devaluing situation. She has the potential to think about the meaning of her life, and to direct her life toward her own infinite passion, but relinquishes this power to the established order in which she resides, due to the anxiety she experiences in the face of the question of meaning.

2.1.3 The Anxiety of Having to Make Sense

Animals do not ask about meaning. Such a *concern* never announces itself to them, which is why Kierkegaard does not view animals as "spirit." They do not think about the meaning of what they do, and do not care if it has meaning. They do not have to, because what they do is hardwired into them by their instincts. The "problem" for humans is that they do not have this instinctual hardwiring, and so must *make sense* of what they do. The question of meaning, however, is both important and unclear, which is why anxiety always comes along with it.

It is the anxiety that causes most people to bury the question of meaning, and act as if it has already been answered. It is because of the anxiety that is inherent in the question of meaning that nihilists have viewed the question as the basis of our psychological problems; this is why Freud speaks of our *quest* for meaning as the beginning of our sickness. The two typical responses to this question have been either to denigrate the question as a form of narcissism, or surrender to the meaning supplied by the established order so that the question never arises.

Kierkegaard wants to awaken this question in consciousness. To struggle with this question is what he views as the ethical or earnest task for humans. What it means to be human, then, begins with the concern about what it means to be human: "Not until the moment when there awakens in his soul a concern about what the meaning of the world has for him and he for the world, about what meaning everything within him by which he himself belongs to the world has for him and he therein for the world—only then does the inner being announce its presence in this *concern*."[5]

The concern is always there but our true personal concern is buried by accepting the concern the established order has given us. It is easier to simply fall in line with how the world makes sense of our lives, rather than experience the anxiety of the question. Still, we must always find sense and meaning in our lives, and there is a negative impact on our conscious experience when the order we have allowed to make sense of our lives is the very order we also do not trust.

I want to examine how our conscious concern arises out of a natural and necessary unconscious concern, which provides the basis of both self-consciousness and freedom. We will see how this moves into the more conscious concern that is necessary for there to be a human self or spirit.

2.2 The Structure of Consciousness as a "Positive Third"

2.2.1 Making Sense of the World

There is within consciousness an unconscious process or basis of making sense—an automatic way of making sense of the world that allows us to function at the most basic levels. But there is a moment or point of concern at which we can and should move into a more intentional and free way of making sense; it is at this moment that the human self is engaged and comes to "life."

Consciousness arises because humans have the ability and need to be symbolic. It arises from an initial unconscious process of making sense of the world. This process originally arises as doubt about the validity of that which is immediately experienced, asking the question, "is it what it seems?"[6] This doubt consists of a *collision* between the sensed experience and its relation to

---

5 *EUD*, 86.

6 Kersten Nordentoft, *Kierkegaard's Psychology*, trans. Bruce H. Kirmmse (Pittsburgh: Duquesne University Press), 1978, 82.

other things and oneself. Consciousness is a function that compares, judges, gives meaning to things, and makes sense of what is being experienced.

For instance, when I look at an egg, I do not just see the egg in its raw thereness and thatness, but I bring all sorts of information and relationships to bear on the egg. When I see an egg whose shell is brown or blue, and so unlike eggs I am used to seeing, doubts will arise about what the egg means for me: Is it edible? What kind of animal did this egg come from? What I am doing is taking the particularity of the egg (its *thatness*) and trying to move toward an understanding of its "ideality" or "universal" (its *whatness*). Kierkegaard calls this symbolizing or conceptualizing of a particular existing thing "ideality," "possibility," or the "universal." Basically, we are categorizing the things in order to make sense of them—to understand them. We are removing the "collision" in regards to a category of particulars, and identifying them as the same. However, they are not truly the same; the "sameness" comes from our intellectual action of conceptualization—from our attempt to make sense of them and *what* they are. Much of this is done unconsciously.

We have an automatic and unconscious drive to understand the world and the things of which it is made up. To understand the particular things in the world, we must put them within categories or universals. For instance, if we did not have the universal of say, "elm tree," or "maple tree" (or even simply "tree") by which to categorize and make sense of all the different trees we run into, we would have to give each individual tree its own concept (name), which would make understanding the world impossible. As soon as we need to make sense of the world (its objects and our relation to them), we must become symbolizers by idealizing and universalizing them. It is important to understand that, when we idealize the object, we are adding something to the object that is not there, and it does not give of itself—we are adding the symbolization and its meaning, which in its most basic sense comes out in language.

Thus, consciousness deals with idealities or universals, and a relationship I posit between two or more objects that I regard or identify as the same. I regard them as the same because they share many of the same characteristics. However, they are not the same objects in actuality: the "sameness" is the "work" of the intellect. Thus, in an important sense, I no longer am dealing with the object itself, but have abstracted from the object and am now dealing with ideality. The word "abstract" means, etymologically, to "draw away from." And so, with symbolization our attention moves away from the object itself, and settles in the concept we give it, which is full of meaning in relation to our own *concerns*. The world is what it is for us due to our *concern*. This is why it is important not simply to give this *concern* away to the established order. We are giving our "self" away, its way of relating to everything we confront in the world—how we understand things, feel about them, value or devalue them.

2.2.2 Making Sense of Our Relationship with Others

I have moved into this analysis, not because I am interested in how Kierkegaard's epistemological views relate to things like eggs or trees, but in how they relate to other human beings, whose ambiguities become infinitely more complex due to their freedom—their lack of "hardwiring." As soon as I form a concept of a person, I am putting into that concept something more (as well as less) than is in the experience itself. The question, of course, is whether what I am putting into it comes from some sort of experience that gives me certainty about my concept, or if there is something else at work, as I choose which evidence to regard as significant and which to ignore.

This is where we move into the more self-conscious process of making meaning, which arises when we feel something is at stake, and is often attended by anxiety—an anxiousness over what is at stake, and so the loss of what concerns us. For instance, we run into the problems we saw in the United States during the COVID pandemic as to how we arrive at what a mask or vaccine *mean*. Since, as I said, we are interested in how we relate to and interpret people, including around social arrangements, we are interested in how these relationships are made sense of. Thus, we find that Kierkegaard is not interested so much in the interpretations of, say, *what* a mask means, but in *how* we arrive at what the mask means, and this meaning's impact on how we relate to others (e.g., how we identify them, categorize them, feel about them). Since the meaning of wearing a mask or the safety of the vaccine is connected to the scientific method, and the method is done by humans, we should ask what are the *interests* that go into research on these items in relation to the coronavirus? Others' concerns are focused not on the ideals of scientific knowledge, but on issues of personal freedom and independence. Their concern most likely includes cynicism toward both government decisions and scientific conclusions. There is a deep distrust and cynicism toward others, and this is what is driving their interpretations about the meaning of masks. This gets even more complex when it comes to the vaccines that were initially distributed with an "emergency approval."[7] What is

---

7 The scientific method is a powerful form of gaining knowledge about our world, but it has its limitations, both in terms of the types of phenomena it can address, and the degree of certainty it gives at any given moment. My point in bringing up this issue of "emergency approval" is to admit that the evidence was not all in when the vaccines were first distributed, though many people talked as if the safety of the vaccines was certain, simply because it was arrived at scientifically. This safety was not certain, and so the talk of certainty was added to the meaning of the vaccines to alleviate the anxiety of the uncertainty. This is what both "sides" of the vaccine issue did, and this drive for certainty in order to alleviate anxiety is just

at stake concerns us very much (our health, death, freedom, potential manipulation, etc.), and so anxiety arises in the "collision" of meanings.

This question is not one we can evade: we either take the vaccine or we do not, and since the evidence is not all in, we make the decision to be vaccinated or not based on something beyond what we know—that is, choice is at work, often driven by all sorts of other concerns and anxieties because of the importance of what is at stake. The anxiety arises because we know, at some level, that we are ultimately responsible for this choice. We seek to rid ourselves of this anxiety by ridding ourselves of the responsibility—i.e., our freedom. We want to make the choice feel safe and seem obvious.

This means that something is added to the judgment of meaning: the observer (the conscious person) is personally and critically involved in the observed relationship, and so something personal is at stake in what is being observed.[8] As Nordentoft puts it, "Consciousness is the relationship which arises when comparisons are made between dissimilar things, because what has been given in sensing and experiencing is no longer simply registered, but is made the object of criticism as to its validity and truth value for the person who experiences it."[9] In other words, consciousness is the act (the collision) in which incongruent things are put in relation to one another, and in such a way that the questioner is herself involved (concerned and interested, because something is at stake) in the question.[10]

While the mere registration of the contradiction or collision is a condition for coming-to-consciousness, it is not sufficient for self-consciousness in a Kierkegaardian sense. Self-consciousness is a third factor that is implied in this structure: the registering person herself (What Kierkegaard calls spirit or "self"). This means that human consciousness carries with it what Kierkegaard, in *The Sickness Unto Death*, called the "positive third" element of the relation.[11] The positive third is what Kierkegaard means by *inter-esse*: the relation or incongruence somehow matters to the person, and is a matter of personal *interest* to her.

Human reality and consciousness means to be *between* thinking and being, reflection and action (*inter-esse*: between-being).[12] This points to an important relationship between self-consciousness and freedom: when we recognize something important is at stake, and we confront a *krisis*, we do not perform

---

the epistemological arrogance Kierkegaard wishes to disrupt, in order to recognize and admit how much "choice" goes into these decisions, and how risky these choices are. It is this very vulnerability we seek to hide through our ideologies and fetishes.

8 Nordentoft, 82.

9 Nordentoft, 82.

10 Nordentoft, 83.

11 *SUD*, 13–14.

12 Mackey, 603.

or act automatically, as do animals. We confront ideality or possibility (thinking) prior to choosing our action, and there is a tension in this confrontation, because there is an ambiguity. This *inter-esse* is the basis of both human self-consciousness and freedom.[13]

Kierkegaard, then, does not view the self as a pure and simple substantial thing, but it *is* the function of relating itself to what is not itself in concern.[14] This concern is the self's concern about itself—its preservation, recognition, mattering, durability, justification, etc. In a way, this is what Freud means by the ego arising out of the id due to the "reality principle": it is the collision with reality that creates the need to relate to the world as a separate entity—a relation (the "positive third") that relates to the relation, as Kierkegaard defines spirit. Kierkegaard is looking at the structure of this "arising" of consciousness, and connecting it to the *interest* that is the basis of self-consciousness itself.

As I mentioned above, animals have it easy in regards to consciousness: they do not doubt, but act instinctively. As birds migrate south, they fly the route hardwired into them, without reflecting on whether to turn right or left at the river, or whether they really want to fly south this year. The birds have no alternatives to how the concrete things of the world are given to them, and so are not free. They do not confront the "collision" that leads to *krisis*.

This spiritless inner unity is how most humans desire to live, because it is free from the anxiety of freedom. This desire is behind the view that our need for meaning (our self-consciousness) is what causes our psychological problems and disruptions. It is also how Freud wants to make life easier for the battered ego: the point is adaptation, and to close off (narrow) the possibilities and alternatives to what is being given—the path laid out by the cultural script. This "no alternative" is also the security the cynical therapeutic seeks. And so it hides its existential doubt and self-criticalness behind its cynical doubt and criticalness of others, denying or repressing that it is making a choice in this—that it is responsible for its formulations. It is "choosing" to live by an immediacy without freedom, because it closes off possibility—the most it gets is probability, a calculation of the best odds within a narrow window.

Further, this is what the evasion of the task of self-becoming consists of in the cynical therapeutic. As we saw when analyzing the therapeutic mindset, those within it succumb to the externals and dissimilarities by which they define themselves. The lowest form of human consciousness (spiritlessness) is when a person's concern for herself does not exist, because the established order has told her to focus almost exclusively on what is external to her. She is

13 Mackey, 604.
14 Nordentoft, 84.

concerned about social things: titles, bank accounts, houses, "likes" on Facebook, etc. Her concern is not earnest, because the anxiety that comes with the existential concern of consciousness is buried—it is repressed by simply letting her surroundings make her "choices" in false consciousness.

It is in this sense that we can again speak of her concern as having gone awry: she is not so much concerned with her self, as she is concerned with the externals by which she has come to identify herself, or by the dissimilarities she has from others, which have given her an advantage over them. She asserts herself according to her perceived merits. Her self is like the value of money, and she keeps tabs on how much she is worth; she knows herself as an object of comparison to others; she values herself as an article of trade by applying the norms of her social environment as a measure of he own worth.[15] With the triumph of the therapeutic, she is caught up in relating to herself through dissimilarities and similarities outside of herself (in the mode of self-justification); this is how she maintains the "concern" about who she is.

Thus, no matter how much she sees through the established order on the intellectual level through her cynical interpretation, she remains locked into the order at the level at which she seeks self-justification. It is the enlightened false consciousness we have been examining throughout this book in relation to the cynical therapeutic: she knows very well what she is doing, but still she is doing it.

Kierkegaard calls this the self-concern of the "bourgeois-philistines": it is to abandon a concern for the task of the self, by abandoning one's unique criteria for oneself, and instead uncritically surrendering to the established order.[16] She is not viewing herself in her particularity (as the "single individual"), but makes sense of her self as she makes sense of everyone else: through the categories created by the established order through advertisement and social media. The ethical requirement, as Kierkegaard would call it, is that a person know herself in relation to herself, which begins with facing her existential guilt transparently, as well as the implication of this guilt (her longing for self-justification, her need to matter).[17] When we seek self-identity through the established

15 Nordentoft, 87.

16 "What is bourgeois-philistinism? What is spiritlessness? It is to have changed the criterion by leaving out the ideals, to have changed the criterion in accord with how we human beings who now live here in this place happen to be." *JFY!*, p. 199.

17 By "ethical," Kierkegaard does not only, or even primarily, mean the study of good and evil, the concern about moral actions, and so forth. He is more concerned about the confrontation with the anxiety of self-becoming, especially when confronted with our existential guilt. It is about responsibility in the sense of how we *respond* to the world. To respond is to pledge (*spondere*), and so it is about what we pledge ourselves to. This is one of a most

order (the lifestyle approach in our current culture), our *inter-esse* is no longer our own interest, but the *inter-esse* is taken over by the established order, and one begins to focus primarily on the dissimilarities through which one can find self-justification.[18] The individual is no longer focused on her ideal passions, but has become fixated on such things as promotions, bank accounts, and other forms of prestige. Further, because consciousness is *inter-esse,* all this, and more, is at play when we interpret and make judgments about other people, institutions, and businesses we have to deal with in life.

3 Knowledge and Interpretation

3.1 Choosing How to See the World

As we see, Kierkegaard characterizes thinking as possibility: I am always representing (re-presenting) things in the world to myself through ideality or universals. I cannot, for instance, experience what is going on inside another person as she acts—I do not experience or *know* her actuality. If the *cogito ego* was as Descartes thought (namely, able to reach complete transparency in its representations of things in the world—the so-called "clear and distinct ideas"), I would have more certainty and so security in my knowledge of things (which was the point of Descartes' radical doubt). With this type of certainty, the *causa sui* project seems much more possible, as I could know the world in itself, and overcome the Excess. The problem is that an individual has access to reality *as* reality *only* through her own reality, which is to say, she can relate to others only cognitively or esthetically by translating what she experiences from others into possibilities or universals.[19] On top of this, the ego is, as Freud and others have shown, full of self-deception, repressions, and illusions, which also impact how we experience and interpret reality.

Thus, for instance, what the aggressiveness of another person is (if, indeed, it is even aggressiveness), or even more complicated, the ultimate basis of the aggressiveness (it could be insecurity), is abstracted from the actual experience. In other words, one is interpreting it, not arriving at it with certain

critical points I have sought to make throughout the book, especially when writing about topics like transference objects or fetishizations.

18 This issue of seeking dissimilarities is one of the drives of modern cynicism, as one seeks to remain "on top" by seeing through others' deceptions, rather than one's own self-deceptions. It relates to the earlier analysis of immortality striving.

19 Mackey, 604.

knowledge. One places upon it a category through which one determines (re-presents) the meaning of what one is confronting. This is why projection is such a powerful defense mechanism when on does not want to face what one is experiencing within oneself: it is not me who is being aggressive, but that person is being aggressive ("She started it!"). Kierkegaard is not critiquing this process (it is how we work in and with the world and others), but is pointing out the significance of realizing that I project my reality upon the possibility of another, and so I should not stamp my judgment or interpretation of another with certainty—such as, "scientifically arrived at knowledge." A hundred years removed from Freud's theories, their supposed certainty becomes much more easy to question, and so open to the question of whether these so-called scientific discoveries of his are not really quite arbitrary and idiosyncratic interpretations. Kierkegaard believes that we always relate to the world through some framework (our "software"), and we should remain humble enough to admit this. One of the reasons we cannot be *causa sui* is because we cannot get behind this process to control it.

As I mentioned above, Kierkegaard's reflections on these issues were not, for him, primarily an epistemological issue, but were what he would call "ethical" in nature, because the problem (viewing uncertain knowledge as certain and obvious) becomes a place in which we hide from the task of self-becoming. We ignore our epistemological vulnerability due to our concerns for a sense of safety and security in the world, which we gain when we feel our judgments and thoughts are securely accurate—and so, free from the ambiguity that causes us to become anxious when faced with the unknown consequences of our choices and actions. Kierkegaard wants to awaken us to the vulnerability inherent in the recognition that, because consciousness is *inter-esse*, we do not apprehend the world strictly through thinking, but we grasp the world in passion and decision—that is, we relate to the world through our commitment to it, to others, and ourselves. We are not passive receivers of the raw world, but interpreters of it, givers of meaning to what we confront.[20]

Freud readily sees this in relation to others, but hides it in relation to himself through the supposed authority of his "scientific" knowledge. In *Civilization and Its Discontents*, when analyzing the difficulty in accepting the idea of the death or aggressiveness instinct, he writes,

> I remember my own defensive attitude when the idea of an instinct of destruction first emerged in psycho-analytic literature, and how long it took before I

20 Mackey, 608.

> became receptive to it. That others should have shown, and still show, the attitude of rejection surprises me less. For "little children do not like it" when there is talk of the inborn human inclination to "badness," to aggressiveness and destructiveness, and so to cruelty as well.[21]

Freud, throughout his writings, turns to *ad hominem* arguments against those who *childishly* hold onto their faith in humanity, religion, the power of the ego, etc.

Kierkegaard has no problem with having to live by interpretations, and even less with wholehearted commitments to our interpretative framework; what he decries is turning these interpretations into ironclad knowledge or "facts," and a failure to recognize that ultimately our intellectual judgments have quite a bit of "choice" in them. As he says in *Philosophical Fragments*, "The conclusion of a belief is no conclusion, but a resolution."[22] As Nordentoft puts it: "the knower himself structures his understanding of what is given. He does so by virtue of language, but language contains many possibilities of understanding, and therefore the knower establishes his interpretations by virtue of a subjective use of language—I.e., 'essentially by virtue of belief.'"[23]

3.2 Ethical Considerations

It might appear that Kierkegaard is making our conclusions seem less important, something not worthy of commitment, because uncertain. The opposite is the case: Kierkegaard is trying to draw us into earnestness about our conclusions. Freud, in order to maintain his scientific objectivity (the only epistemological method that now has an authority to bring "certainty"), presents his views of others as a disinterested scientific fact. Kierkegaard would see this type of objectivism as fraught with ethical self-denial. The aggressiveness of others is never a disinterested fact to those whose consciousness is *inter-esse*.

---

21 *CID*, 67.

22 Soren Kierkegaard, *Philosophical Fragments*, Edited and Translated by Howard V. Hong and Edna H. Hong Princeton: Princeton University Press (1985), p. 84. In *Works of Love*, Kierkegaard says, "Knowledge places everything in possibility and to that extent is outside the actuality of existence in possibility. The individual first begins his life with 'ergo,' with *belief.* But most people live so negligently that they do not notice at all that in one way or another, every minute they live, they are by virtue of an 'ergo,' of a belief. There is no decision in knowledge; the decision, the determination, and the firmness of personality are the first in the 'ergo,' in belief." *Works of Love*, trans. and ed. Howard V. and Edna H. Hong (Princeton: Princeton University Press, 1995), pp. 230–231.

23 Nordentoft, 337.

Yes, there is aggressiveness in others and myself, but in the face of this I am still bound in some way to deal with them—and myself. We often do not know the reality that is behind this aggressiveness. If it is not instinct or an inherent principle of human action, then that changes how I will potentially react to someone. If I do not know with certainty the answers to these questions (and nobody does), then Kierkegaard would ask me to reflect on why I choose one possible interpretation over another. Indeed, this has been the central question of this book: Why have we chosen the interpretation given to us by the cynical therapeutic, and what has this meant to our lives?

The desire not to face these types of questions with any sort of ethical earnestness is what fascinates me in relation to the cynical therapeutic. Why have we chosen mistrust in order to feel in control within the world? Obviously, we do not know for each individual cynic, but we have found all sorts of possible reasons, many of which are connected with false consciousness.[24] One of the biggest reasons is that the cynical therapeutic allows us to continue to narrow existence, others, and ourselves in order to feel in control, and so maintain the illusion of being *causa sui*. With the collapse of the traditional therapeutic and heroics that narrowed existence for us, the cynical therapeutic provides a means of narrowing existence within nihilism. Nihilism should open our existence to a radical freedom, but this is too much for us; the cynical therapeutic provides a way to evade this freedom in a manner that makes us believe we are free. Mistrust is simply another way in a long history of ways to narrow existence and reduce others to manageable concepts and categories.

For Kierkegaard, human existence cannot be reduced to a concept, because the individual is not a concept or universal, but a unique particularity. The universal is a symbolic representation of the particular, and in making this representation we abstract from the individual. No doubt, it makes life easier to feel like we understand and have a grasp of another human being, but the *concept* is an ideality, and the person's existence is beyond the concept (beyond

24 I am aware that what I have written, and the *ergos* I have come to, fall under this same critique. I am aware that I am approaching this situation from my own existence and experiences, and that I cannot come close to capturing and grasping the problem as a certainty. But I also realize that Kierkegaard's way of looking at the situation gives the possibility of freedom, significance, and direction, and that there is a strong element of choice in my acceptance of this interpretation. There is no way out of this for humans. It is just this type of epistemological claim that often leads to Kierkegaard's categorization as an "existentialist": we cannot stand outside of existence *sub specie aeternitas*, we cannot gain a "God's-eye" perspective of life, and so the choices we make in the direction we take in life are fraught with uncertainty and risk—and the anxiety that accompanies these.

nailing down and completely capturing it).[25] These idealities and universals are necessary for humans to make their way through the world and relate to others, but we need always keep in mind that every person we interact with transcends the categories we put on her, categories bound up in our own personal concerns and agendas. Universals "make safe," allowing me to think that I am confronting, whether intellectually or practically, the right approach to life—the only rational approach to life. In terms of navigating through life, the universals provide us with the rules for actions, and allow us to feel that our decisions are "safe," stamped with the universal's approval. The universals allow us to maintain our *causa sui* project, feeling in control and self-sufficient. This project is the very thing Kierkegaard believes must be disrupted in order to take on the task of self-becoming.

3.3 The *Krisis*: Accept the Shipwreck

An important part of overcoming the *causa sui* project is the recognition that life is inherently risky. We are not the ground of ourselves, cannot pick ourselves up by our bootstraps, and cannot get life totally under our control. Ideologies, heroics, ethics, etc., make it appear safer, but that is because they ignore the Excess, the unknown, and so much of what is out of our control and our manageability. One of the main reasons the cynical therapeutic seems safe (beyond the narrowing of alternatives it creates) is that we believe we are living according to our own best interests.[26] We feel (through anxiety) that we cannot have all the knowledge we need before making a decision, but believe that if we focus on our own self-interest above all else we can make the safe decision. I can trust that the cost-benefit analysis is in my control, and is being done for my own well-being. This is why the therapeutic puts such an intense emphasis on personal well-being: because culture is manipulative and oppressive, I must carefully make my way through life focusing on my own well-being above all else, having learned from cynicism that my self-concern is the only concern that ultimately matters.

The rationalizations that take place within cynicism and the therapeutic make us think we are in exile, and are not invested in the established order; we believe we are merely using every situation for our own self-interest. While the

25 Maximilian Beck, "Existentialism, Rationalism, and Christian Faith." *The Journal of Religion*, Vol. 26(4); October 1946 (pp. 283–295), accessed on July 24, 2020, Stable URL: http://www.jstor.org/stable/1198987.

26 I touched on this above, but want to point out the connection of this self-concern gone awry to the *causa sui* project.

modern cynic always thinks she is looking out for her best interest, she is blind to the reality that her very sense of what is in her "best" interest has gone awry. She feels she is living by her own particular script within the order, unaware that her self-interest has been coopted by the established order, and so it is not really her script. She has been convinced she is the star of the script, when in reality she is a bit player—an "NPC" or Non-Player Character.

Within the cynical therapeutic, it is one's very self-interest that is being manipulated: one believes it is in one's best-interest to be cynical and skeptical about everything and everyone within culture, but the cynic still needs culture to gain significance, and so her self-interest is closely connected to the very system she does not trust.

My argument is that she must learn to be anxious in the right way, to confront anxiety in a way that does not narrow her life, but opens it up, and allows her to step into her true freedom through a *krisis*. What she dreads is that she will be taken advantage of and conned, and yet this is sure to happen if she runs from anxiety into the comfort of the manipulations. Her anxiety is trying to disclose something about her life to her, something about who she has become. Let the anxiety consume the finite ends by which she is possessed by the established order, so that she can be truly free to discover the brainwashing of the ideology—attain the *atuphos* of exile. She will find courage for the *krisis* when she realizes that no true safety, comfort, and justification are being given up when abandoning the cynical therapeutic.

Another way of saying the same thing is that being anxious in the right way is accepting one's existential guilt. For Kierkegaard, our deepest problem is not that we are lost, but that we do not realize our lostness, or do not care about it. As Jose Ortega y Gasset wrote in *The Revolt of the Masses*,

> The man with a clear head is the man who … looks life in the face, realizes that everything in it is problematic, and feels himself lost. As this is the simple truth—that to live is to feel oneself lost. Whoever accepts this has already begun to find himself, to be on firm ground. Instinctively, as do the shipwrecked, he will look around for something to which to cling, and that tragic, ruthless glance, absolutely sincere, because it is a question of salvation, will cause him to bring order into the chaos of his life. … He who does not really feel himself lost, is lost without remission; that is to say, he never finds himself, never comes up against his own reality.[27]

27 José Ortega y Gasset, *The Revolt of the Masses*, trans. Anonymous (New York: Norton, 1960), 157.

Kierkegaard thought that our only hope for healing was to recognize the shipwreck, and that is what the bulk of his authorship was attempting to do. But he knew that we are unwilling to recognize it because we approach anxiety in a way that causes us to set up resistances to this knowledge.

We must accept the shipwreck of the cynical therapeutic and move into exile; only then can we examine the *parrhesia* or authenticity that will bring individual and corporate flourishing. We must see how the constant uncharitable interpretations of everyone and everything is making us miserable. Then we can begin to formulate ways to look at people and things with a charitable interpretation, and find a hope for how this might lead us to greater fulfillment and even joy.

Bibliography

Abi, Doukhan. "From Exile to Hospitality: A Key to the Philosophy of Levinas." *Philosophy Today* 54, no. 3 (2010): 235–246.

Abramson, Neil Remington. "Kierkegaardian Confessions: The Relationship Between Moral Reasoning and Failure to be Promoted." *Journal of Business Ethics* 98 (2011): 199–216. Accessed May 20, 2014. https://doi.org/10.1007/s10551–010–0542-x.

Andersson, Lynne M. and Thomas S. Bateman. "Cynicism in the Workplace: Some Causes and Effects." *Journal of Organizational Behavior* 18 (1997): 449–469.

Aqueveque, Claudio and Catherine Encina. "Corporate Behavior, Social Cynicism, and Their Effect on Individuals' Perceptions of the Company." *Journal of Business Ethics* 91 (2010): 311–324. Accessed September 29, 2014. https://doi.org/10.1007/s10551–010–0621-z.

Arnett, Ronald C. and Pat Arneson. *Dialogic Civility in a Cynical Age: Community, Hope, and Interpersonal Relationships*. Albany: State University of New York Press, 1999.

Baier, Annette. "Trust and Antitrust." *Ethics* 96, no. 2 (1986): 231–260. Accessed February 12, 2014. http://www.jstor.org/stable/2381376.

Barnett, Clive. "Ways of Relating: Hospitality and the Acknowledgement of Otherness." *Progress in Human Geography* 29, no. 1 (2005): 5–21. Accessed November 19, 2014. https://doi.org/10.1191/0309132505ph535oa.

Beck, Maximilian. "Existentialism, Rationalism, and Christian Faith." *The Journal of Religion*, Vol. 26(4); October 1946 (pp. 283–295). Stable URL: http://www.jstor.org/stable/1198987.

Becker, Ernest, *The Birth and Denial of Meaning: An Interdisciplinary Perspective on the Problems of Man*. 2nd ed. New York: Free Press Paperbacks, 1971.

Becker, Ernest. *The Denial of Death*. New York: Free Press Paperback, 1973.

Becker, Ernest. *Escape from Evil*. New York: Free Press, 1975.

Becker, Lawrence C. "Trust as Noncognitive Security about Motives." *Ethics* 107 (1996): 43–61.

Bellah, Robert N., et al. *Habits of the Heart: Individualism and Commitment in American Life*. Berkeley: University of California Press, 1985.

Bernardo, Allan B. "Hope Grounded in Belief: Influences of Reward for Application and Social Cynicism on Dispositional Hope." *Scandinavian Journal of Psychology* 54 (2013): 522–528. Accessed September 2, 2015. https://doi.org/10.1111/sjop.12081.

Bertilsson, Jon. "The Cynicism of Consumer Morality," *Consumption Markets and Culture*, 18, no. 5 (September 2015): 447–467. https://doi.org/10.10253866.2015.1038255.

Boyers, Robert, ed. *Psychological Man*. New York: Harper & Row, 1975.

Branham, R. Bracht. "Defacing the Currency: Diogenes' Rhetoric and the *Invention* of Cynicism." In *The Cynics: The Cynical Movement in Antiquity and Its Legacy*, edited by Bracht Branham and Marie-Odile Goulet-Cazé, 81–104. Berkeley: University of California Press, 1996.

Brockway, Jennifer Howard, et. al. "Development and Validation of a Scale for Measuring Cynical Attitudes Toward College." *Journal of Educational Psychology* 94, no. 1 (2002): 210–224. Accessed September 30, 2014. https://doi.org/10.1037//0022–0663.94.1.210.

Brown, Norman O. *Life Against Death: The Psychoanalytic Meaning of History*. 2nd ed. Middletown: Wesleyan University Press, 1985.

Buechner, Fredrick. *Listening to Your Life*. Edited by George Connor. San Francisco: Harper-Collins, 1992.

Caldwell, Wilber W. *Cynicism and the Evolution of the American Dream*. Washington, D.C.: Potomac Books, 2006.

Camus, Albert. *The Myth of Sisyphus and Other Essays*. Translated by Justin O'Brien. New York: Random, 1955.

Casey, M. A. *Meaninglessness: The Solutions of Nietzsche, Freud, and Rorty*. Lanham: Lexington Books, 2002.

Chaloupka, William. *Everybody Knows: Cynicism in America*. Minneapolis: University of Minnesota Press, 1999.

Chiaburu, Dan S., et al. "Antecedents and Consequences of Employee Organizational Cynicism: A Meta-Analysis." *Journal of Vocational Behavior* 83 (2013): 181–197. Accessed September 20, 2014. https://doi.org/10.1016/j.jvb.2013.03.007.

Cohen, Stanley and Laurie Taylor, *Escape Attempts: The Theory and Practice of Resistance to Everyday Life*. 2nd ed. London: Routledge, 1998.

Critcher, Clayton R. and David Dunning. "No Good Deed Goes Unquestioned: Cynical Reconstruals Maintain Belief In the Power of Self-Interest." *Journal of Experimental Social Psychology* 47 (2011): 1207–1213. Accessed September 30, 2014. https://doi.org/10.1016/j.jesp.2011.05.001.

Critchley, Simon. "The Split Subject." *Journal of Chinese Philosophy* 35 (2008): 79–87. Accessed September 21, 2015. https://doi.org/10.1111/j.1540–6253.2008.00522.x.

Cushman, Philip. *Constructing the Self, Constructing America: A Cultural History of Psychotherapy*. Boston: Addison-Wesley Publishers, 1995.

Cushman, Philip. "Why the Self is Empty: Toward a Historically Situated Psychology." *The American Psychologist* 45, no. 5 (1990): 599–611.

Cutler, Ian. *Cynicism from Diogenes to Dilbert*. Jefferson: McFarland & Company, 2005.

Cutler, Ian. "A Tale of Two Cynics: The Philosophic Duel Between Jesus and the Woman from Syrophoenicia." *The Philosophical Forum* 41, no. 4 (2010): 365–387. Accessed September 29, 2014. doi. 10.1111/j.1467–9191.2010.00369.x/pdf.

Dancey, Logan. "The Consequences of Political Cynicism: How Cynicism Shapes Citizens' Reactions to Political Scandals." *Political Behavior* 34 (2012): 411–423. Accessed September 29, 2014. https://doi.org/10.1007/s11109–011–9163-z.

Dettloff, Dean. "From Cynical Reason to Spiritual Creativity: An Exercise in Religious Anthropology," (Master's Thesis, Institute for Christian Studies, 2015). http://hdl.handle.Net/10756/605953.

Derrida, Jacques. "Hospitality." Translated by Barry Stocker and Forbes Morlock. *Angelaki: Journal of the Theoretical Humanities* 2, no. 3 (2000): 3–18.

Derrida, Jacques. *Of Hospitality*. Translated by Anne Dufourmantelle. Stanford: Stanford UP, 2000.

Detert, James R. and Linda Klebe Trevino. "Moral Disengagement in Ethical Decision Making: A Study of Antecedents and Outcomes." *Journal of Applied Psychology* 93, no. 2 (2008): 374–391. Accessed November 20, 2014. https://doi.org/10.1037/0021–9010.93.2.374.

Diderot, Denis. *Rameau's Nephew*. Translated by Ian C. Johnston (Gutenberg Australia eBook, eBook No.: 0700101.txt). First posted January 2007.

Eddy, Paul Rhodes. "Jesus As Diogenes?: Reflections on the Cynic Jesus Thesis." *Journal of Biblical Literature* 115, no. 3 (1996): 449–469.

Elliott, Cain. *Fire Backstage: Philip Rieff and the Monastery of Culture*. New York: Peer Lang Edition, 2013.

Elrod, John W. *Being and Existence in Kierkegaard's Pseudonymous Works*. Princeton: Princeton University Press, 1975.

Elrod, John W. *Kierkegaard and Christendom*. Princeton: Princeton UP, 1981.

Eseje, Uvahy. "Ancient Cynicism and Modern Philosophy." *Filozofia* 65 (2010): 571–576.

Eubanks, Cecil and David Gauthier. "The Politics of the Homeless Spirit: Heidegger and Levinas on Dwelling and Hospitality." *History of Political Thought* 32, no. 1 (2011): 125–146.

Ferreira, Jamie M. *Love's Grateful Striving: A Commentary on Kierkegaard's* Works of Love. New York: Oxford UP, 2001.

Fetchenhauer, Detlef and David Dunning. "Do People Trust too Much or too Little?" *Journal of Economic Psychology* 30 (2009): 263–276. Accessed September 30, 2014. https://doi.org/10.1016/j.joep.2008.04.006.

Fincher, David. *Fight Club*, 1995. Los Angeles: 20th Century Fox, Home Video, 2002. DVD.

Foucault, Michel. "Discourse and Truth: The Problematization of Parrhesia (Six Lectures given by Michel Foucault at Berkeley, Oct–Nov. 1983)." Accessed October 22, 2014. https://www.cscd.osaka-u.ac.jp/user/rosaldo/On_Parrehesia_by_Foucault_1983.pdf.

Freud, Sigmund. *Beyond the Pleasure Principle*. Translated by James Strachey. New York: Norton, 1961.

Freud, Sigmund. *Civilization and Its Discontents*. Tranlated by James Strachey. New York: Norton, 1962.

Freud, Sigmund. "A Difficulty in the Path of Psycho-analysis," in *Freud: Complete Works*. Translated by Ivan Smith, (2010): 3626–3615. https://www.valas.fr/IMG/pdf/Freud_Complete_Works.pdf.

Freud, Sigmund. *The Ego and the Id*. From the Standard Edition of the Complete Psychological Works of Sigmund Freud, Volume XIX (1923–1925). Accessed February 10, 2022. https://www.sigmundfreud.net/the-ego-and-the-id-pdf-ebook.jsp.

Freud, Sigmund. *The Future of an Illusion*. Translated by Gregory C. Richter. Blacksburg: Wilder, 2010 (Kindle Version).

Freud, Sigmund. "The Future Prospect of Psychoanalytic Therapy." In *Collected Papers of Sigmund Freud, Volume 2*. Translated by Joan Riviere, 285–296. New York: Basic Books, 1959.

Freud, Sigmund. *New Introductory Lectures of Psychoanalysis*. Translated and edited by James Strachey. New York: Norton, 1964.

Freud, Sigmund. *On Narcissism: An Introduction*. New York: Routledge, 2018. http://ebookcentral.proquest.com/lib/usclancaster/detail.action?docID=879954.

Freud, Sigmund. *An Outline of Psycho-Analysis*. Translated by James Strachey. London: Hogarth Press, 1959.

Freud, Sigmund. *Studies in Hysteria*, in *Freud—Complete Works*. Translated by Ivan Smith, 2010: 1–269. https://www.valas.fr/IMG/pdf/Freud_Complete_Works.pdf.

Gao, Liyan. "Ideological Cynicism in the Modern Information Age with Sloterdijk and Zizek." *Eras Journal*, 18, no. 1, (August 2016): 51–65.

Gardner, Stephen L. "Philip Rieff and the Self-Destruction of Democracy." *Review* of *Charisma: The Gift of Grace, and How It Has Been Taken Away from Us*, by Philip Rieff, *Sociology* 46 (2009): 181–189. Published online February 3, 2009, *Springer Science+Business Media.*

Girard, Renc. *Deceit, Desire, and the Novel: Self and Other in Literary Structure*. Baltimore: John Hopkins Press, 1965.

Giroux, Henry A. "Pedagogy of the Depressed: Beyond the New Politics of Cynicism." *College Literature* 28, no. 3 (2001): 1–32. Accessed September 30, 2014. http://www.jstor.org/stable/25112600.

Goldstein, Jan. "Neutralizing Freud: The Lycée Philosophy Class and the Problem of the Reception of Psychoanalysis in France." *Critical Inquiry*, 40, (Autumn 2013): 40–82.

Goulet-Cazé, Marie-Odile. "Religion and the Early Cynics," in *The Cynics: The Cynical Movement in Antiquity and Its Legacy*. Edited by Bracht Branham and Marie-Odile Goulet-Cazé, 47–80. Berkeley: University of California Press, 1996.

Gross, Martin L. *The Psychological Society: A Critical Analysis of Psychiatry, Psychotherapy, Psychoanalysis, and the Psychological Revolution*. New York: Random House, 1978.

Guastello, Stephen J., et. al. "A Study of Cynicism, Personality, and Work Values." *The Journal of Psychology* 126, no. 1 (1989): 37–48.

Hall, Amy Laura. "Poets, Cynics and Thieves: Vicious Love and Divine Protection in Kierkegaard's *Works of Love* and *Repetition*." *Modern Theology* 16, no. 2 (2000): 215–236.

Hall, Amy Laura. "Self-Deception, Confusion, and Salvation in *Fear and Trembling* with *Works of Love*." *Journal of Religious Ethics* 28, no. 1 (2000): 37–61.

Halsall, Robert. "Sloterdijk's Theory of Cynicism, Ressentiment and 'Horizontal Communication.'" *International Journal of Media and Cultural Politics*, 1, no. 2 (2005): 163–179. https://doi.org/10.1386/macp.1.2.163/1.

Hardin, Russell. "Trustworthiness." *Ethics* 107 (1996): 26–42.

Harding, Matthew. "Responding to Trust." *An International Journal of Jurisprudence and Philosophy of Law* 24, no. 1 (2011): 75–87.

Hasse, Andrew, *Being 97*. *Vimeo*, 275760948. June 19, 2018. https://vimeo.com/275760948.

Haswell, Janis, et al. "Hospitality in College Composition Courses." *College Composition and Communication* 60, no. 4 (2009): 707–727. Accessed November 19, 2014. http://www.jstor.org/stable/40593426.

Heidegger, Martin. *Being and Time*. Translated by John Macquarrie and Edward Robinson. New York: Harper and Row, 1962.

Higgie, Rebecca. "Kynical Dogs and Cynical Masters: Contemporary Satire, Politics, and Truth-Telling." *Humor* 27, no. 2 (2014): 183–201. Accessed September 21, 2015. https://doi.org/10.1515/humor-2014–0016.

Holmes, Ksusha. "What is the Relation Between Conditional and Unconditional Hospitality?" Accessed November 20, 2014. https://www.academia.edu/4840492/What_is_the_relation_between_conditional_and_unconditional_hospitality_in_the_work_of_Derrida_.

Homans, Peter. *The Ability to Mourn: Disillusionment and the Social Origins of Psychoanalysis*. Chicago: Chicago University Press, 1989.

Houston, B. Kent and Christine R. Vavak. "Cynical Hostility: Developmental Factors, Psychosocial Correlates, and Health Behaviors." *Health Psychology* 10, no. 1 (1991): 9–17.

Humbert, David. "Desire and the Politics of Anti-Culture: Rene Girard and Philip Rieff on the Mystique of Transgression." Accessed November 17, 2015. https://transformingviolence.nd.edu/assets/26602/humbert_paper.pdf.

Hung, Ruyu. "Educational Hospitality and Trust in Teacher-Student Relationships: A Derridian Visiting." *Studies in Philosophical Education* 32 (2013): 87–99. Accessed November 19, 2014. https://doi.org/10.1007/s11217–012–9326–3.

Huyssen, Andreas. Forward to *Critique of Cynical Reason*. Minneapolis: University of Minnesota Press, 1987. x–xviii.

Illouz, Eva. *Saving the Modern Soul: Therapy, Emotions, and the Culture of Self-Help*. Berkeley: University of California Press, 2008.

Imber, Jonathan B. Introduction to *The Feeling Intellect*. Chicago: University of Chicago Press, 1990: xi–xxiv.

Imber, Jonathan B. *Therapeutic Culture: Triumph and Defeat*. New Brunswick: Transaction Publishers, 2004.

Inesi, M. Ena, et. al. "How Power Corrupts Relationships: Cynical Attributions for Others' Generous Acts." *Journal of Experimental Social Psychology* 48 (2012): 795–803.

Japers, Karl. *Man in the Modern Age*. Translated by Eden Paul and Cedar Paul. New York: Doubleday, 1951.

Jones, Karen. "Trust As an Affective Attitude." *Ethics* 107 (1996): 4–25.

Kafk, Franz. *The Blue Octavo Notebooks*. Edited by Max Brod. Translated by Ernst Kaiser and Eithne Wilkins. Cambridge: Exact Change, 1991.

Kahneman, Daniel. *Thinking, Fast and Slow*. New York: Farrar, Strous and Giroux, 2011.

Kameniar, Barbara. "Dilemmas in Providing Hospitality to Others in the Classroom: Stories About One Christian Religious Education Teacher." *Transnational Curriculum Inquiry* 4, no. 3 (2007): 1–11. Accessed December 16, 2014. http://nitinat.library.ubc.ca/ojs/index.php/tci.

Kaye, Howard L. "Rieff's Freud and the Tyranny of Psychology." *Journal of Classical Sociology* 3, no. 3 (2003): 263–267.

Keen, Sam. Forward to *The Denial of Death*. New York: Free Press Paperbacks, 1971: xi–xxii.

Keenan, Alan. "The Twilight of the Political?: A Contribution to the Democratic Critique of Cynicism." *Theory and Event* 2, no. 1 (1998): 1–64. Accessed October 21, 2014. http://muse.jhu.edu/journals/theory_and_event/v002/2.1keenan.html.

Kenyon, Tim. "Cynical Assertion: Convention, Pragmatics, and Saying 'Uncle.'" *American Philosophical Quarterly* 40, no. 3 (2003): 241–248. Accessed September 29, 2014. http://www.jstor.org/stable/20010119.

Keyes, Dick. *Seeing Through Cynicism: A Reconsideration of the Power of Suspicion*. Downers Grove: IVP Books, 2006.

Kierkegaard, Soren. *Christian Discourses/The Crisis and a Crisis in the Life of an Actress*. Translated by Howard V. and Edna H. Hong. Princeton: Princeton University Press, 1997.

Kierkegaard, Soren. *The Concept of Anxiety: A Simple Psychologically Orienting Deliberation On the Dogmatic Issue of Hereditary Sin*. Edited and translated by Reidar Thomte and Albert Anderson. Princeton: Princeton UP, 1980.

Kierkegaard, Soren. *Concluding Unscientific Postscript to* Philosophical Fragments. Translated by Howard V. and Edna H. Hong. Princeton: Princeton University Press, 1992.

Kierkegaard, Soren. *Eighteen Upbuilding Discourses*. Edited and translated by Howard V. and Edna H. Hong. Princeton: Princeton University Press, 1990.

Kierkegaard, Soren. *Either/Or, Part I*. Translated by Howard V. and Edna H. Hong. Princeton: Princeton UP, 1987.

Kierkegaard, Soren. *Either/Or, Part II*. Translated by Howard V. and Edna H. Hong. Princeton: Princeton UP, 1987.

Kierkegaard, Soren. *Fear and Trembling/Repetition*. Edited and translated by Howard V. and Edna H. Hong: Princeton: Princeton UP, 1983.

Kierkegaard, Soren. *For Self-Examination*, in *For Self-Examination/Judge for Yourself!* Edited and translated by Howard V. and Edna H. Hong. Princeton: Princeton University Press, 1983: 1–87.

Kierkegaard, Soren. *Judge for Yourself!*, in *For Self-Examination/Judge for Yourself!* Edited and translated by Howard V. and Edna H. Hong. Princeton: Princeton University Press, 1990: 89–215.

Kierkegaard, Soren. *Philosophical Fragments*, Edited and translated by Howard V. Hong and Edna H. Hong. Princeton: Princeton University Press, 1985.

Kierkegaard, Soren. *Purity of the Heart is to Will One Thing*. Translated by Douglas V. Steere. New York: Harper, 1948.

Kierkegaard, Soren. *The Sickness Unto Death: A Christian Psychological Exposition for Upbuilding and Awakening*. Edited and translated by Howard V. and Edna H. Hong. Princeton: Princeton University Press, 1980.

Kierkegaard, Soren. *Soren Kierkegaard's Journals and Papers, Volume II*. Edited and translated by Howard V. and Edna H. Hong. Bloomington: Indiana University Press, 1970.

Kierkegaard, Soren. *Soren Kierkegaard's Journals and Papers, Volume III*. Edited and translated by Howard V. and Edna H. Hong. Bloomington: Indiana University Press, 1975.

Kierkegaard, Soren. *Two Ages: The Age of Revolution and the Present Age, A Literary Review*. Translated by Howard V. and Edna H. Hong. Princeton: Princeton UP, 1978.

Kierkegaard, Soren. *Works of Love*. Translated by Howard V. and Edna H. Hong. Princeton: Princeton University Press, 1995.

Kramer, Peter D. *Freud: Inventor of the Modern Mind*. New York: HarperCollins, 2006.

Kramer, Roderick M. "Trust and Distrust In Organizations: Emerging Perspectives, Enduring Questions." *Annual Review of Psychology* 50 (1999): 569–598.

Krueger, Derek. "The Bawdy and Society: The Shamelessness of Diogenes in Roman Imperial Culture," in *The Cynics: The Cynical Movement in Antiquity and Its Legacy*. Edited by Bracht Branham and Marie-Odile Goulet-Cazé, 222–239. Berkeley: University of California Press, 1996.

Lasch-Quinn, Elisabeth. Introduction to *The Triumph of the Therapeutic*. Wilmington: Intercollegiate Studies Institute, 2006. vii–xvi.

Lerner, Michael. *The Politics of Meaning: Restoring Hope and Possibility in an Age of Cynicism*. Reading: Addison-Wesley, 1996.

Li, Fuli, et. al. "Expecting the Worst: Moderating Effects of Social Cynicism on the Relationships Between Relationship Conflict and Negative Affective Reactions." *Journal of Business Psychology* 26 (2011): 339–345. Accessed September 29, 2014. https://doi.org/10.1007/s10869-101-9192-3.

Litt, Edgar. "Political Cynicism and Political Futility." *The Journal of Politics* 25, no. 2 (1963): 312–323. Accessed September 29, 2014. http//www.jstor.org/stable/2127467.

Long, A. A., "The Socratic Tradition: Diogenes, Crates, and Hellenistic Ethics," in *The Cynics: The Cynical Movement in Antiquity and Its Legacy*. Edited by Bracht Branham and Marie-Odile Goulet-Cazé. Berkley: University of California Press, 1996.

Lowrie, Walter. *A Short Life of Kierkegaard.* Princeton: Princeton University Press, 1970.

Macaskill, Ann. "Exploring Religious Involvement, Forgiveness, Trust, and Cynicism." *Mental Health, Religion & Culture* 10, no. 3 (2007): 203–218. Accessed September 30, 2014. https://doi.org/10.1080/13694670600616092.

Macauley, Robie and Larzer Ziff. *America and its Discontents*. Waltham: Xerox College Pub., 1971.

Machiavelli, Nicolo. *The Prince*, (Australia: Planet eBook.com). https://www.planetebook.com/free-ebooks/the-prince.pdf.

Mackey, Louis. "The Loss of the World in Kierkegaard's Ethics." *The Review of Metaphysics* 15, no. 4 (1962): 602–620. Stable URL: http://www/jstor.org/stable/20123908.

Madsen, Ole Jacob. *The Therapeutic Turn: How Psychology Altered Western Culture*. New York: Routledge, 2014.

Manning, Philip. "Philip Rieff's Moral Vision of Sociology: From Positive to Negative Communities—and Back?" *Journal of Classical Sociology* 3, no. 3 (2003): 235–246.

Mansson, Niclas and Elisabet Langmann. "Facing Ambivalence in Education: A Strange(r's) Hope?" *Ethics and Education* 6, no. 1 (2011): 15–25. Accessed November 19, 2014. https://doi.org/10.1080/17449642.2011.587343.

Matustick, Martin Beck. "Becoming Human, Becoming Sober." *Continental Philosophy Review* 42 (2009): 249–274. Accessed May 31, 2015. https://doi.org/10.1007/s11007-009-9105-1.

Mayfield, D. S. *Artful Immorality—Variants of Cynicism: Machiavelli, Gracian, Diderot, Nietzsche*. Berlin: De Gruyter, 2015.

Mazella, David. *The Making of Modern Cynicism*. Charlottesville: University of Virginia Press, 2007.

Merchant, Carolyn. *The Death of Nature: Women, Ecology, and the Scientific Revolution.* San Francisco: Harper, 1980.

Mills, Candice M. and Frank C. Keil. "The Development of Cynicism." *Psychological Science* 16, no. 5 (2005): 385–390. Accessed November 29, 2014. http://www.jstor.org/stable/40064235.

Milus, Thomas B. "A Systems Model of Cynicism Based on Social Theory." PhD diss., Saybrook Graduate School and Research Center, 2001.

Minister, Stephen. "Derrida's Inhospitable Desert of the Messianic: Religion within the Limits of Justice Alone." *Heythrop Journal* 48 (2007): 227–242.

Moore, Danny Steven. "The Development and Validation of the Scale of Interpersonal Cynicism." PhD diss., University of Tennessee, Knoxville, 1999.

Moses, John L. "Cynic Cosmopolitanism," in *The Cynics: The Cynical Movement in Antiquity and Its Legacy.* Edited by Bracht Branham and Marie-Odile Goulet-Cazé, 105–120. Berkeley: University of California Press, 1996.

Moskowitz, Eva S. *In Therapy We Trust: America's Obsession with Self-Fulfillment.* Baltimore: John Hopkins UP, 2001.

Mullen, John Douglas. *Kierkegaard's Philosophy: Self-Deception and Cowardice in the Present Age.* Lanham: University Press of America, 1995.

Mustain, Megan. *Overcoming Cynicism: William James and the Metaphysics of Engagement.* London: Continuum International Publishing, 2011.

Navia, Luis E. *Classical Cynicism: A Critical Study.* Westport: Greenwood Press, 1996.

Neisser, Ulric. *Cognitive Psychology.* New York: Appleton-Century-Crofts, 1967.

Nietzsche, Friedrich. *The Portable Nietzsche.* Edited and translated by Walter Kaufmann. New York: Penguin Books, 1982.

Nordentoft, Kersten. *Kierkegaard's Psychology.* Translated by Bruce H. Kirmmse. Pittsburgh: Duquesne University Press, 1978.

O'Gorman, Kevin. "Jacques Derrida's Philosophy of Hospitality." *The Hospitality Review* 8 (2006): 50–57.

O'Hara, Daniel T. "Another Avatar of the Circle: Philip Rieff's Counter-Enlightenment." *Boundary* 2 36, no. 2 (2009): 209–215. Accessed May 31, 2015. https://doi.org/10.1215/01903659-2009-012.

Ortega y Gasset, José. *The Revolt of the Masses.* Translated by Anonymous, New York: Norton, 1960.

Paik, Peter. "A Kindly Apocalypse: Philip Rieff and the Endgame of the Therapeutic," *English Language and Literature*, 61, no. 3 (2015): 433–458.

Parkin, Alan J. *Essential Cognitive Psychology.* Philadelphia: Taylor & Francis, 2000.

Pascal, Blaise. *Pensées.* Translated by A. J. Krailsheimer. Baltimore: Penguin Books, 1966.

Pattyn, Sven, et. al. "Stripping the Political Cynic: A Psychological Exploration of the Concept of Political Cynicism." *European Journal of Personality* 26 (2012): 566–579. Accessed September 30, 2014. https://doi.org/10.1002/per.858.

Perkins, Robert L., ed. *International Kierkegaard Commentary:* Two Ages. Macon: Mercer UP, 1984.

Plato, *The Apology*, in *The Trial and Death of Socrates.* Translated by G. M. A. Grube, 21–42. Indianapolis: Hackett, 1975.

Plutarch. *Life of Alexander.* Trans. Bernadotte Perrin. Chapter 14. Accessed February 10, 2022. https://penelope.uchicago.edu/Thayer/E/Roman/Texts/Plutarch/Lives/Alexander*/3.html.

Postman, Neil. *Amusing Ourselves to Death: Public Discourse in the Age of Show Business.* New York: Penguin Books, 1986.

Rahner, Karl. *Foundations of the Christian Faith: An Introduction to the Idea of Christianity*. Translated by William V. Dych. New York: Seabury Press, 1978.

Rahner, Karl. *Theological Investigations: Volume II* (*Man In the Church*). Translated by Karl-H. Kruger. Baltimore: Helcion Press, 1967.

Rakow, Katja. "Therapeutic Culture and Religion in America." *Religion Compass* 7, no. 11 (2013): 485–497. Accessed May 31, 2015. https://doi.org/10.1111/rec3.12074.

Rank, Otto. *Beyond Psychology*. New York: Dover, 1941.

Rice, Suzanne. "The Educational Significance of Trust." *Philosophy of Education Archive* (2006): 71–78. Accessed December 2, 2014. http://ojs.ed.uiuc.edu/index.php/pes/article/view/1516/256.

Ricoeur, Paul. *The Conflict of Interpretations: Essays in Hermeneutics*. Edited by Don Ihde. Evanston: Northwestern University Press, 1974.

Rieff, Philip. "The Analytic Attitude." *Encounter* 17, no. 6 (June, 1962), 22–27.

Rieff, Philip. *The Crisis of the Officer Class: The Decline of the Tragic Sensibility*, Ed., Alan Woolfolk. Charlottesville, University of Virginia Press, 2007.

Rieff, Philip. *The Feeling Intellect: Selected Writings*. Edited by Jonathan B. Imber. Chicago: University of Chicago Press, 1990.

Rieff, Philip. *Fellow Teachers: Of Culture and its Second Death*. Chicago: University of Chicago Press, 1985.

Rieff, Philip. "Freudian Ethics and the Idea of Reason." *Ethics* 67, no. 3, Part 1 (1957): 169–183.

Rieff, Philip. *Freud: The Mind of the Moralist*. New York: Viking Press, 1959.

Rieff, Philip. "History, Psychoanalysis, and the Social Sciences." *Ethics* 63, no. 2 (1953): 107–120.

Rieff, Philip. Introduction to *Collected Papers of Sigmund Freud: With an Introduction*, by Sigmund Freud. New York: Collier Books, 1978.

Rieff, Philip. *The Jew of Culture: Freud, Moses, and Modernity*. Edited by Arnold M. Eisen and Gideon Lewis-Kraus. Charlottesville: University of Virginia Press, 2008.

Rieff, Philip. *My Life Among the Deathworks: Illustrations of the Aesthetics of Authority* (*Sacred Order/Social Order, Volume 1*). Edited by Kenneth S. Piver. Charlottesville: University of Virginia Press, 2006.

Rieff, Philip. "The Newer Noises of War in the Second Culture Camp: Notes on Professor Burt's Legal Fictions." *Yale Journal of Law & the Humanities* 3, no. 2 (1991): 315–388.

Rieff, Philip. "The Origins of Freud's Political Psychology." *Journal of the History of Ideas* 17, no. 2 (April, 1956): 235–249.

Rieff, Philip. *The Triumph of the Therapeutic: Uses of Faith After Freud*. Wilmington: Intercollegiate Studies Institute, 2006.

Roberts, David. "In Defense of Defenselessness: Kierkegaard and an Accepted Narcissism." *The Heythrop Journal*, 55, no. 5 (September 2014): 827–844.

Roberts, Peter. "Happiness, Despair and Education." *Studies in Philosophical Education* 32 (2013): 463–475. Accessed May 20, 2014. https://doi.org/10.1007/s11217-012-9325-4.

Rorty, Richard. "The Mechanical Mind: Hume and Freud," in *Pragmatism's Freud: The Moral Disposition of Psychoanalysis*. Edited by Joseph H. Smith and William Kerrigan. Baltimore: John Hopkins Press, 1986: 1–27.

Sandler, Joseph, Holder, Alex, et al. *Freud's Models of the Mind: An Introduction*. London: Karnac Books, 2005.

Saeverot, Herner. "Educative Deceit: Vladimir Nabokov and the [Im]possibility of Education." *Educational Theory* 60, no. 5 (2010): 601–619.

Sagan, Carl. *Pale Blue Dot: A Vision of the Human Future in Space*. New York: Random House, 1994.

Sayre, Farrand. "Greek Cynicism." *Journal of the History of Ideas* 6, no. 1 (1945): 113–118. Accessed September 29, 2014. http://www.jstor.org/stable/2707062.

Schopenhauer, Arthur, *The Works of Arthur Schopenhauer: The Wisdom of life and Other Essays*. Roslyn: Walter J. Black, 1932.

Schreier, Benjamin J. "America and Its Discontents: Cynicism in the American Modernist Imagination." PhD diss., Brandeis University, 2003.

Schwartz, Barry. *The Paradox of Choice: Why More Is Less*. New York: Ecco, 2004.

Sloterdijk, Peter. *Critique of Cynical Reason*, trans. Adreas Huyssen. Minneapolis: University of Minnesota Press, 1987.

Smith, Joseph H. "The Analytic Attitude," in *Pragmatism's Freud: The Moral Disposition of Psychoanalysis*. Edited by Joseph H. Smith and William Kerrigan. Baltimore: John Hopkins Press, 1986: 52–78.

Stanley, Sharon Adele. *The French Enlightenment and the Emergence of Modern Cynicism*. Cambridge: Cambridge University Press, 2012.

Stivers, Richard. *The Culture of Cynicism: American Morality In Decline*. Cambridge: Blackwell, 1994.

Swift, Jonathan. "The Lady's Dressing Room," Accessed May 28, 2019. https://www.poetryfoundation.org/poems/50579/the-ladys-dressing-room.

Tarc, Aparna Mishra. "Education as Humanism of the Other." *Educational Philosophy and Theory* 37, no. 6 (2005): 833–849.

Tayfur, Ozge, et. al. "The Mediating Effects of Emotional Exhaustion, Cynicism, and Learned Helplessness on Organizational Justice-Turnover Intentions Linkage." *International Journal of Stress Management* 20, no. 3 (2013): 193–221. Accessed September 20, 2014. https://doi.org/10.1037/a0033938.

Tolstoy, Leo. *The Death of Ivan Ilych and Other Stories*. Translated by Aylmer Maude. New York: Signet, 1960.

Turner, James H. and Sean R. Valentine. "Cynicism as a Fundamental Dimension of Moral Decision-Making: A Scale Development." *Journal of Business Ethics* 34 (2001): 123–136.

Van Erp, Stephan and Lea Verstricht, eds. *Longing In a Culture of Cynicism*. Berlin: Lit, 2008.

Vandermeersch, Patrick, "Reducing Faith to Belief: Religion in a Cynical Culture." From *Longing in a Culture of Cynicism*. Edited by Stephan van Erp and Lea Verstricht, 33–48. Piscataway: Transaction Publishers (Rutgers University), 2007.

Vitz, Paul C. *Psychology As Religion: The Cult of Self-Worship*. Grand Rapids: Eerdmans, 1977.

Wallach, Michael A. and Lise Wallach. *Psychology's Sanction for Selfishness: The Error of Egoism in Theory and Therapy*. San Francisco: Freeman and Company, 1983.

Weber, Max. *The Protestant Ethic and the Spirit of Capitalism*. New York: Scribner, 1958.

Wei, Xueyan and Rongrong Wang. "Exploring the Relations Between Student Cynicism and Student Burnout." *Psychological Reports: Employment, Psychology & Marketing* 117, no. 1 (2015): 103–115. Accessed September 2, 2015.

Westphal, Merold. *Kierkegaard's Critique of Reason and Society*. Macon: Mercer UP, 1987.

Woolfolk, Alan. "The Dubious Triumph of the Therapeutic: The Denial of Character," in *Therapeutic Culture: Triumph and Defeat*. Edited by Jonathan B. Imber. New Brunswick: Transaction Publishers, 2004: 69–88.

Woolfolk, Alan. "The Therapeutic Ideology of Moral Freedom." *Journal of Classical Sociology* 3, no. 3 (2003): 247–262. Stage Publications: 1468–79X (200311)3:3;247–262;038151.

Wyschogrod, Edith. "Autochthony and Welcome: Discourses of Exile in Levinas and Derrida." *Journal of Philosophy and Scripture* 1, no. 1 (2003): 36–42.

Zizek, Slavoj. *The Sublime Object of Ideology*. New York: Verso, 2008.

Zondervan, Antonius A. W. *Sociology and the Sacred: An Introduction to Philip Rieff's Theory of Culture*. Toronto: University of Toronto Press, 2005.

Index of Names

Index of Subjects

www.ingramcontent.com/pod-product-compliance
Ingram Content Group UK Ltd.
Pitfield, Milton Keynes, MK11 3LW, UK
UKHW022219051026
15624UKWH00001B/233

9 789004 758131